M000275187

Dreaming with the Ancestors

Race and Culture in the American West
Quintard Taylor, Series Editor

Alice Fay in the doorway of the old adobe house on her ranch, Guadalupe, in Nacimiento, Mexico, at the foothills of the eastern Sierra Madre Oriental mountains. Institute of Texan Cultures, University of Texas at San Antonio. Photo by John Feist.

Dreaming with the Ancestors

Black Seminole Women in Texas and Mexico

Shirley Boteler Mock

University of Oklahoma Press : Norman

Also by Shirley Mock

(ed.) *The Sowing and the Dawning: Termination, Dedication, and Transformation in the Archaeological and Ethnographic Record of Mesoamerica* (Albuquerque, 1998)

Library of Congress Cataloging-in-Publication Data

Mock, Shirley Boteler, 1942–
Dreaming with the ancestors : Black Seminole women in Texas and Mexico / Shirley Boteler Mock.
p. cm. — (Race and culture in the American West ; v. 4)
Includes bibliographical references and index.
ISBN 978-0-8061-4053-7 (hardcover : alk. paper)
1. Black Seminoles—Texas. 2. Black Seminoles—Mexico. 3. Seminole women—Texas. 4. Seminole women—Mexico. 5. Oral tradition—Texas. 6. Oral tradition—Mexico. 7. Sex role—Texas. 8. Sex role—Mexico. I. Title.
E185.93.T4M635 2010
976.4004'973859—dc22

2010010775

Dreaming with the Ancestors is Volume 4 in the Race and Culture in the American West series.

The paper in this book meets the guidelines for permanence and durability of the Committee on Production Guidelines for Book Longevity of the Council on Library Resources, Inc. ∞

Copyright © 2010 by the University of Oklahoma Press, Norman, Publishing Division of the University. Manufactured in the U.S.A.
All rights reserved. No part of this publication may be reproduced, stored in a retrieval system, or transmitted, in any form or by any means, electronic, mechanical, photocopying, recording, or otherwise—except as permitted under Section 107 or 108 of the United States Copyright Act—without the prior written permission of the University of Oklahoma Press.

1 2 3 4 5 6 7 8 9 10

To Alice Fay Lozano,
whose friendship I have cherished over the last fifteen years,
and to Black Seminole women

CONTENTS

Illustrations

FIGURES

MAPS

ACKNOWLEDGMENTS

To the following, I wish to extend many thanks for their important contributions to this book. I thank Dr. Nancy Kenmotsu, former cultural resources director, Texas Department of Transportation (TXDOT), for first bringing the Black Seminole topic to my attention. Dr. Fred Valdez, associate professor and director of the Mesoamerican Archaeological Research Laboratory at the University of Texas at Austin, persuaded me to act as a consultant for his Cultural Resource Management (CRM) Macaw project documenting the Black Seminoles in Brackettville. That work as consultant started me down this long path of inquiry. I extend my appreciation to the Texas Historical Commission, including the late Curtis Tunnell, former executive director; Dr. James Bruseth, director, Archeology Division; and Dr. Pat Mercado-Allinger, Texas state archeologist, for their invaluable in-kind support during my early research endeavors.

Special thanks are due to Dr. Michaele Haynes, cultural anthropologist, and historian Phyllis McKenzie for their critical reading and invaluable comments as the book evolved. Alcione Amos, coeditor of *Black Seminoles, History of a Freedom-Seeking People,* extended her hospitality during my early research in Washington, D.C., and provided assistance at the Schomburg Center for Research in Black Culture, New York, in examining the Kenneth Porter notes.

The book has benefited greatly from my association with the National Park Service and their invitations to participate in the Network to Freedom programs. Included in the joint project was a trip to Brackettville and Nacimiento, which included Iantha Gantt-Wright, Cal Calabrese, Keith Everett, Art Gomez, Jenny Masur, Tara Morrison, and Barbara Tagger. Special thanks go to Diane Miller, national program manager, National Underground Railroad Network to Freedom; Guy Washington, regional manager for the National Park Service's National Underground Railroad Network to Freedom; and Aaron Mahr Yáñez, now superintendent of the National Park Service, National Trails-Intermountain Region System, Santa Fe, New Mexico. I thank Yolanda Elizondo, director of the Casa de Cultura, and Eduardo Enriquez, director of the Instituto Nacional de Antropología e Historia (INAH), Coahuila, for their hospitality during our National Park Service visit to Nacimiento.

My association with the Seminole Indian Scout Cemetery Association and Fort Clark Historical Society played a pivotal role in writing this book. Bill Haenn, author of *Fort Clark and Brackettville: Land of Heroes,* was always willing to share his consummate knowledge of the Seminole Negro Indian Scouts and Fort Clark. Russell Nowell took me on a tour of the ruins of the Black Seminole village, Las Moras, and the late Donald Swanson, curator of the old Guardhouse Museum, Fort Clark Springs, my first contact in Brackettville, provided me hospitality and invaluable historical information. Bennie J. McRae, Jr., researcher and site manager of the "Lest We Forget" website, proved to be a valuable source of information on the Seminole Negro Indian Scouts, their enrollment history, the internees in the Seminole Indian Scouts Cemetery, and histories of individual scouts. I thank Lynn Beliveau for providing the diaries of her ancestor, Lt. Francis Henry French, commander of the Seminole Negro Indian Scouts at Fort Clark from 1882 to 1888 and who later was promoted to general.

The research and writing of this book have been supported by grants from the San Antonio Area Foundation and the Summerlee Foundation and in-kind assistance from Dr. John Davis and Dr. Rex Ball, former executive directors of the University of Texas at San Antonio's Institute of Texan Cultures (ITC).

Fieldwork assistance on the recorded interviews of descendants in Brackettville and Nacimiento was provided by the ITC director of media productions, Leslie Burns; photographer John Feist, whose image of Alice Fay graces the cover of this book; and soundman Charles Cruz, who assisted with Spanish translations. The veteran archaeologist Michael Davis also accompanied Alice Fay and me on some of the Nacimiento trips and provided crucial logistical support on his own and on behalf of the Texas Historical Commission. Archival assistance from Evelyn V. Beliveau, chief curator of Gen. Francis Henry French's archives and the National Archives Regional Archives (NARA) in Fort Worth, was much appreciated. Michael Hironymous of the Rare Books and Manuscripts section of the Benson Latin American Collection of the University of Texas at Austin assisted me in my search through the Latorre Collection. Thanks also to Kristina L. Southwell, manuscript librarian of the Western History Collections at the University of Oklahoma, and her graduate assistant Josh Clough for their assistance in locating and sending me documents.

My sincere appreciation is extended to Ed Johnson and the staff of the ITC library directed by Yu Li. Senior curator Tom Shelton brought his skills into solving the mysteries of dating faces and places in Black Seminole photos. Charles Barksdale was the custodian of the many "Seminole" photos we borrowed from descendants and scanned and put in electronic files; Patrick Lemelle assisted me with permissions and Rebecca Probst was my lifeline to many publications through the UTSA inter-library loan service. ITC designer Jim Cosgrove used his artistic talents in designing a map of the Black Seminole diaspora. I thank Sylvia Reyes for contributing her administrative skills and Sylvia Campos for her unfailing and always cheerful logistical support over the years at ITC.

I thank Alice Barnett, the great-great-granddaughter of Cornelia Perryman, for her recollections and photos, and Genevieve Payne, descendant of runaway slaves and July and Teener Factor's family. Emily Eggleston (Williams), Sandra Gay Kinney, and Joetta Knight, the three descendants of Nadra, a Biloxi Indian woman, provided stories and never-before-seen photos of their ancestors.

I benefited from conversations with Ian F. Hancock, professor of linguistics, University of Texas at Austin; Jane Landers, associate professor of history, Vanderbilt University; Rosalyn Howard, associate professor of anthropology, University of Central Florida; Terrance Weik, associate professor, Department of Anthropology,

University of South Carolina; Dr. Lilith Haynes, assistant dean of Continuing Education, director of the Institute for English Language Programs, Harvard University; and Sheila S. Walker, professor of Afro-American Studies, University of California–Berkeley.

Clay Dillingham, son of Beth Dillingham, who lived off and on with the Mascogos for three years, shared his experiences in Nacimiento with me.

Particular appreciation is extended to Black Seminoles who spent many hours talking about their ancestors and answering my endless questions: Anita Daniels, Izola Warrior Raspberry, Lillie Mae Dimery, Gertrude Vázquez, Genevieve Payne, Steve Warrior, Carmen Vázquez, the two sisters Ophelia Thompson and Nancy Williams, Gracie Lasky, and of course, the remarkable Miss Charles Wilson. The always helpful William "Dub" and Ethel Warrior brought their own experiences and many insights to complement my research. Dub served as my official encyclopedia of information on Black Seminole history. I thank the many officers of the Black Seminole Historical Association, such as Clarence Ward, who have always welcomed me into their group.

I am indebted to Alessandra Jacobi Tamulevich, University of Oklahoma Press acquisitions editor, for believing in my book after reading the initial draft, and to the anonymous reviewers for critical comments that guided my revisions. I thank Alice Stanton, special projects editor for OU Press. My deepest appreciation goes to Emily Jerman, for bringing her enthusiasm and her professionalism to the editing of this book and her patience with my endless changes. I, however, take responsibility for all errors and shortcomings in the book.

I thank my husband, Bill Mock, who has provided unwavering support that has sustained me through the years of research and writing. Without his encouragement I never would have finished this daunting enterprise. I thank my family for their patience through the years as I was tethered to my computer.

Finally, I thank my friend Alice Fay, my enthusiastic traveling companion in south Texas and Mexico, and her family, in particular, her daughter Raphaela (Effie), for welcoming me as an extended member of their household, and teaching me what it means to be Black Seminole.

Dreaming with the Ancestors

Introduction

Black Seminole Women

> It's the women who have led. I just have a feeling, a very strong feeling, that if ever this world is civilized, it would be more the work of women.
>
> Emma Tenayuca

> So, for me, working with an African American woman who wanted me to write the story of her life seemed a natural research project. She wanted to tell me everything. She wanted me to listen and write it all down. I wanted to know all about her. It seemed straightforward. What I didn't expect is that in documenting her life, I would learn so much about myself [blurring] the lines between subject and friend, and causing me to examine some uncomfortable realities, both about myself and the world I come from.
>
> Tracy Bachrach Ehlers

The day was cloudless, and the sun beat down relentlessly on the dusty ancestral arena, an inauspicious stage for drama, surrounded as it was by thorny huisache and clumps of cactus, enclosed by a leaning stick fence. A tall white metal sign greeted arriving visitors with the words "Seminole Indian Scouts Cemetery," the name recorded in an official charter. The occasion was one of my first visits to the cemetery in Brackettville, Texas, on a Sunday morning in

September 1996. More than 125 years had passed since the cemetery was established, the burial ground of Black Seminole descendants whose ancestors were runaway slaves. Beginning in the 1700s, they had been given refuge with the Seminole Indians in Florida. Although they call themselves Black Seminoles or, on more familiar occasions, "those old Seminoles," they are a distinct people—a maroon culture, also called Afro-Seminole, swathed in the traditions of Africa, birthed in conflict and diasporas as they searched for freedom and a home. They still gather at the cemetery today on the third weekend in September to share stories, sing spirituals, eat "Seminole" food, and sing their ancestors into memory.

In addition to the "Seminole Days" celebration, descendants also commemorate Juneteenth in honor of the freeing of enslaved blacks on June 19, the date on which emancipation was announced in Texas in 1865, several years after blacks in the Union had been notified.[1] Although they participate ardently in the holiday, Black Seminoles' perspective on Juneteenth is unique—they consider themselves distinct from other African Americans because they fled from bondage and fought for their independence in Florida with their allies, the Seminole Indians. Black Seminole elder Miss Charles Wilson clarified this distinctness of her community's identity during one of my visits: "We were never slaves," she said, "but we show our sympathy for the people who *were* slaves on Juneteenth." Alice Fay Lozano, another Black Seminole elder, hereafter referred to as Alice Fay, related, "Juneteenth is beautiful. . . . We should celebrate it because we all should feel for one another even if we are not the same."

On this occasion, Alice Fay slowly guided me around the cemetery. The Black Seminoles' pilgrimage to the Seminole Indian Scouts Cemetery is a journey of validation and identity to a place where the past merges with the present, where their history is mapped on the landscape. It is the final resting place of unsung men and women who have vanished into the distant past. They were not all heroes, certainly—but during a turbulent time of slavery, bigotry, and bitter endless conflicts, they forged meaningful lives out of diversity, parts of which we only know about through conversations with their descendants. Seeing no chance to survive the devastation of these

Fig. 1. In 1911, Miss Charles Wilson was the last Black Seminole descendant born at Las Moras on the Fort Clark military reservation near Brackettville, Texas. This photograph was taken at Seminole Days in 1999. Photo by Shirley Boteler Mock. Author's collection.

Fig. 2. Alice Fay sits in a chair outside the ruins of her adobe house on her ranch, Guadalupe, in Nacimiento, Mexico, in 1997. In the background are the Buena Vista foothills of the eastern Sierra Madre Oriental mountains. Behind her is the "stick house," made of intertwined branches chinked with small stones, where she lived as a little girl. Photo by Shirley Boteler Mock. Author's collection.

conflicts, these maroon families were put on steamships in Florida and they traveled up the Mississippi River to homes in Indian Territory. Their new homes were fraught with more problems and again they were pursued by slave hunters. In a little more than a decade one group of Black Seminoles under a young man named John Horse would make the brave choice to flee to Mexico, where slavery was not practiced. It is this group, vested in courage, the ancestors of Alice Fay, who provide the essence of this book.

I had first met Alice Fay the previous day as I attended the Saturday morning festivities, which many of the older Black Seminoles attended, at the former George Washington Carver school grounds in Brackettville. I recall that Saturday fondly. Alice was selling her homemade tamales and *tettapoon* (or *tettapone,* a sweet potato pie) in her family's small shaded booth, surrounded by her grandchildren and great-grandchildren. "Granita," they called her affectionately. I felt rather conspicuous at the time, a white face in a sea of browns, blacks, and coppers. Ethel and William (Dub) Warrior, old-timers in the community, had told me I should talk to Alice, for she knew a lot about those old Seminoles.

Alice Fay received me with her gracious smile and asked me to join her so we could talk. I was struck by the commanding presence of this old woman, her burnished copper skin and high cheekbones of Indian ancestors. Every Black Seminole carries an eclectic gene pool, which may manifest itself in the cheekbones of a descendant like Alice Fay, or in the unexpected blue eyes of her great-grandson. On another visit, Alice graciously invited me to attend the Sunday morning ceremony at the cemetery that provides a finale to the festivities. I arrived early and she took me through the cemetery, her graceful hands lingering at the tombstones of her ancestors, her dark eyes glowing with memories of her people. The clouds played hide-and-seek in the sky as her great-grandchildren played tag around the memorials. Alice admonished them not to walk on the graves of the "old ones," as she called her ancestors. She pointed to a sun-bleached wooden marker that looked like a sculpture with outstretched arms. "My grandmama, Rosa Fay, she's buried right there," she said. "All my people came from Florida—both sides."

Fig. 3. Rosa (Dixon) Fay, daughter of Clara and Joe Dixon, in Brackettville, Texas, circa 1930 to 1940. Prints and Photographs Division, Library of Congress, LC-USZ62-125218, ppmsc 01102.

Fig. 4. Shown here as an elderly woman in Brackettville, Texas, in February 1955, Rebecca July Wilson holds up photos of her ancestors, including her father, Florida-born Sampson July. Institute of Texan Cultures, University of Texas at San Antonio. Courtesy of the Hearst Corporation.

Rosa Dixon Fay is one of the prominent actors in this story.[2] In Mexico, she led the women up into the Santa Rosa foothills of the eastern Sierra Madre Oriental mountains, where, like Black Seminole women before them, they prayed and fasted to have dreams that would provide spiritual sustenance and prophesize the future for their community. Rosa Fay also was a vivacious storyteller who extolled the valor of female heroes and embellished them with superhuman qualities.

Alice Fay paused at one of the graves. "You know, Shirley, Miss Charles's mama, Rebecca July—she's buried here.[3] She started Seminole Days. That's right," Alice added with emphasis and what I came to recognize as a characteristic nod of her head.

Miss Charles Wilson continued Seminole Days in honor of her mother, Rebecca July Wilson. She was determined to empower her people and initiate liberal reforms to bring them into the twentieth century.

It is appropriate that both Miss Charles Wilson and Alice Fay introduce this book—a story of how their female ancestors nourished a culture preserved in historical consciousness and everyday practice as part of their distinct ethnic identity. The histories of the two old women are intertwined in the veils of time.

Alice Fay finished my brief introduction to her ancestors—the Sunday ritual was beginning. She led me to the shade of the green pavilion where participants were gathering for the final ceremony of Seminole Days. It is the day of remembrance. She joined Miss Charles Wilson in front of the assembled group, both old women dressed in their Sunday finest. The recalcitrant sun, still refusing to surrender to autumn, defiantly vibrated in the sky, lending drama to this ceremony that merged past and present.

Alice held hands with Miss Charles and began her testimonial, reminiscent of expressions of devout Christian Evangelicalism, in which her people are steeped. Her voice took on a life of its own, defying with grace the proprieties of the English language. She spoke with an accent tempered by both the Spanish of Mexico and the Afro-Seminole of her ancestors. Alice fought back tears, giving an impassioned plea for those present to remember the old people in Nacimiento, Mexico, where she was born in 1916. Nacimiento, which means "birthplace" in Spanish, is where the Black Seminoles finally found the home they had been desperately seeking, where they could be free. Or so they thought.

Miss Charles Wilson animatedly began her customary spiritual and gestured to the audience to continue the verses. Her voice had a plaintive quality that reached to the depths of your soul. She pointed her white-gloved finger at the gathered participants just as she had as a schoolteacher in Brackettville many years before. Most of the descendants remember Miss Charles fondly as their teacher and mentor.

By and by, I'm so glad that troubles don't pass our way.
Oh glory. Oh my Lord, oh my Lord, what shall I do?

A slender black man standing in the shade of a patch of oaks joined in, lending his soulful a cappella voice to the spiritual "The Lord Is My Shepherd" on the reverential occasion.

With what I would come to know as her typical spontaneity, Alice Fay enthusiastically joined in the singing, waving her hands and swaying to the age-old rhythm. She provided her testimonial to the audience, saying, "My people are here in this cemetery, the others in Mexican cemeteries. Some is here; some is over there. I'm really proud about it. They come from Florida, Oklahoma, and Arkansas."

Miss Charles provided the requisite shout response, another tradition of their Afro-Seminole ancestors: "Amen!"

Alice:	"I don't know too much. When I was growing up, my grandmama would never let us talk to my great-grandmama Rose Kelly."
Miss Charles:	"Right on."
Alice:	"What little I can tell you is that we used to go to the back of the house and listen."
Miss Charles:	"That's right."
Alice:	"That's why I know they traveled so hard, running from slavery. They arrived in Mexico on July 4th [in 1850]."
Miss Charles:	"So a full year."[4]

As the brief ceremony ended, some descendants remained to linger around the graves of their ancestors and say a prayer of remembrance. Others visited relatives they had not seen in a long time, while some made a quick getaway in their hot cars. The reentry into the past had ended on this Sunday morning—the spell was broken. As tradition goes, some of the descendants would meet at the old school grounds—where Miss Charles Wilson taught as a young woman—to eat leftovers from the day before. The older women in the group continue to nourish out-of-town visitors before they start their trips home. It is a matter of pride among the women to do this, despite the fact that some of them are living on fixed incomes. It is part of being a Black Seminole woman.

I recall this occasion during Seminole Days in 1996 vividly because meeting Alice Fay was the beginning of a new journey for me. Fourteen years ago I would never have guessed that I would be writing this book on Black Seminole women. I was trained as an archaeologist within the field of anthropology, and my research was focused on Maya coastal sites in Belize, Central America—a far cry from the Black Seminole hearth lands of Florida, Indian Territory, and the *frontera* of Texas and Mexico. Like Florida, Belize also was colonized by the Spanish in the early sixteenth and seventeenth centuries. Spain's dreams of empire in Belize, as in Florida, vanished in the wake of the determined British Empire. In the 1800s English woodcutters laid down rudimentary camps on top of the graceful Maya ruins and brought black slaves and laborers from the Caribbean to cut down the giant ceibas and mahoganies. In the country of the Seminoles and other southeastern Indians, though, it was not logwood or mahogany that enticed Europeans. It was deerskins and cotton.[5] The children of Africa in the other part of the Americas also formed communities of fugitives, or "maroons," who resisted and fled the yokes of slavery.[6] Today, small enclaves of descendants live in scattered villages in Belize along green serpentine rivers flowing to the Caribbean.

While pursuing my archaeological fieldwork, I was leading a double life, with research also focused on the early African American community in San Antonio, Texas, as part of a Cultural Resource Management (CRM) archaeological project. CRM projects are salvage excavations required when alterations are made to city, state, or federally owned lands. The objective is to insure that cultural resources are not compromised and to produce a written report accessible to the general public. My interviews of African Americans were to correlate with excavations of particular black residences, churches, and businesses, all scheduled for demolition so a large sports facility could be built. Black populations had spread out from this heart of San Antonio and given birth to a vibrant community in the 1800s, later cleaved by political and economic forces promoting "progress." Middle-class brick Victorian houses hugged the rough edges of shotgun houses and sidled up to busy railroad tracks during this time. The sounds of Blind Lemon Jefferson and Louis Armstrong echoed down shady alleyways, and steepled clapboard churches provided spiritual solace and hope.

It was on this CRM research project that I began to understand that archaeology, anthropology, history, and oral history, when forged together, can become a powerful theoretical and methodological tool. It was in interviewing members of the African American community in San Antonio that I began to comprehend the strength of collective memories and the tenacity of black traditions. I explored the recollections of the people who breathed life into this black neighborhood from the nineteenth to twenty-first centuries in San Antonio. Rather than remaining passive occupants of the neighborhood, the former residents came to life for me. Some sources confided to me that integration with its supposed intent to compensate for the biases of the past had actually destroyed the solidarity of their small compact community on San Antonio's east side. They had been dispersed into the anonymity of the majority white population. I realized that like many other outsiders, I also tended to mask the people I studied into homogeneous groups rather than understanding the fluid nature of their culture in relation to changing social and political environments.[7]

I had completed this assignment, published the required paper, and was in the process of completing requirements toward my Ph.D. in anthropology at the University of Texas at Austin in 1993 when Alice Fay and her people unexpectedly entered my life. A local consulting firm approached me about interviewing Black Seminole descendants in Brackettville, Texas, as part of a CRM project. It focused on test excavations on what was formerly the Fort Clark Military Post, established in 1852, now the residential community of Fort Clark Springs, located outside the small town of Brackettville. This rugged, arid south Texas landscape near the Mexican border has a conflicted past. The area was frequented in the nineteenth century by roving American Indian bands such as the Comanches and Lipán Apaches, whose territory and livelihood were threatened by early Spanish *vaqueros* and later a stream of determined Anglo-American colonists and military members.

Fort Clark, one in a line of U.S. Army forts in Texas established to defend settlers against relentless Indian raids, is a prominent backdrop to this story. In 1870, twenty years after arriving in Mexico and at the behest of the U.S. Army, Black Seminoles crossed the Rio Grande to form a detachment of Seminole Negro Indian Scouts in Texas. The scouts were instrumental in most of the patrols and all of the major campaigns emanating from Fort Clark until 1914. Off post, Alice Fay's ancestors lived in an encampment they called Las Moras or "the Camp," where multigenerational households of women raised their families while the scouts were absent for long periods of time.

A 1902 U.S. Army quartermaster plane table map of the Fort Clark Military Compound revealed that part of the encampment would be within the required excavations. Subsequent excavations revealed the shallow rock foundation of one of the Black Seminole families' homes. Archaeologists recovered an outside chimney and a charcoal-filled hearth, shown in historic photos of the houses. They also recovered artifacts such as buttons, twentieth-century ceramics, bottles, and military insignia typical of the late nineteenth and early twentieth centuries.

My job was to interview some of the Black Seminole old-timers and to correlate the information with the CRM excavations. I made an appointment to meet three of the elders: Miss Charles (Emily) Wilson and her relatives Ethel and William (Dub) Warrior, the foremost historians in the community. I was uncertain of what to expect, with questions lined up on my yellow legal pad and my requisite tape recorder ready. As I would learn later, William's nickname or "basket name," Dub, is derived from the African word *duba*, meaning "the branch of a tree" or "to look for or at something."[8] It is an appropriate nickname for Dub, both because of his consummate knowledge of his history and because of the fact that he is always diligently searching for new information about his people.

On the appointed interview day, the prim Miss Charles greeted me enthusiastically, prepared to relate her people's stories, honed by years of repetition. Her intense brown eyes reflected the depth of her memories. Dub, born in 1927, and still looking forty, sported a straw cowboy hat and bright Indian-patterned shirt. Sitting next to him was his attractive, vivacious wife, Ethel, also born in 1927, the granddaughter of the scout Billy July, Miss Charles Wilson's

Fig. 5. In a 1993 Cultural Resource Management (CRM) archaeology project, Macaw Consulting Company placed test excavations on what was the site of the Black Seminole encampment, Las Moras. This house foundation was recovered in the excavation. Inside the rock-lined feature, the remains of a chimney and hearth were found. Coals were burned on the hearth in the winter for warmth. Courtesy of Macaw Consulting Company.

uncle.[9] Miss Charles began to speak, her sing-song voice rising and falling as she talked about her valiant scout uncles and her remarkable mother, Rebecca July (Wilson), born in 1881. Miss Charles, the youngest daughter, armed with a master's degree in bilingual education and firm determination, continued her mother's efforts in keeping up the tradition of Seminole Days. When once asked why she continued it, Miss Charles proclaimed, "They were forgetting their history. They said they were Seminole but no one wanted to be Seminole. We talked funny. We didn't see any future in working and going to school. I decided that we would have to come back and eat food, sing spirituals. *Now* they are interested!"[10]

Dub occasionally interrupted Miss Charles with a historical fact, the telling of it flavored with his unique talent for the theatrical. His well-practiced stories focused on the Black Seminole men, especially their leader, chief John Horse—also known as Gopher John, John or Juan Caballo, John Cowaya, Juan Cavallo, and Captain Juan de Dios Vidaurri in Mexico.[11] I recall being somewhat uneasy, feeling like an intruder, overwhelmed by the larger-than-life heroic exploits of Alice Fay's ancestors and my unfamiliarity with Black Seminole history and complexities.

After the interview, I finished my section of the CRM paper, thinking at the time that it related the same old tired, jargon-laden story, certainly not original research; but it did meet the CRM requirements.[12] Today its yellowed pages probably sit in a cardboard box in some dingy corner of a Brackettville city hall basement, the pages providing nourishment for hungry cockroaches and silverfish.

My curiosity was aroused, however, and I followed up the interview with additional research into Black Seminole history. In a perusal of the literature, I became aware of well-researched, scholarly works such as historian Kevin Mulroy's 1993 book *Freedom on the Border* and Alcione M. Amos and Thomas P. Senter's 1996 compilation of the folklorist Kenneth Wiggins Porter's notes in *The Black Seminoles: History of a Freedom Seeking People,* among other publications.[13] These scholars broke ground in recording and studying a people little known or recognized. I began to wonder what I could contribute to this story of Black Seminoles.

I continued to attend the Juneteenth and Seminole Days events and to visit Alice Fay at the home of her daughter Raphaela—or Effie, as she is called—in Kerrville. Alice's vivid recollections only whetted my curiosity, and persistent questions filtered through my mind. Where were voices of women in this story? What role did they play on this ancient stage of wars, conflicts, and desperate flights to freedom? Their valiant chief, John Horse, remains the enduring topic of conversation at Black Seminole events today. He has taken on mythic proportions, a fusion of the fearless John the Conqueror, a legendary hero in African American culture, and the cunning trickster hero Brer Rabbit, both of whom defy slavery.[14] Hundreds of stories garnered from military documents and oral histories about John

Horse compete. Yet little is known about his brave sister Wannah (or Juana), who lost her two children to slavers in Indian Territory, or his devoted wife of forty years, Susan. According to oral accounts, when John Horse mysteriously died in Mexico City on a quest to receive written title to his people's land grant in Nacimiento, Mexico, Susan was so traumatized that she became paralyzed. The Black Seminoles gave her John Horse's silver saddle, one with stars and crescent moons that had carried him through the Seminole Wars in Florida, but Susan did not live long after this.[15]

While the men continued to regale visitors with their stories of warriors and battles, I listened to the everyday stories of women like Wannah and Susan—stories both humorous and sad of old "Aunties" and "Sisters," terms of respect applied to elders. It was in these food booths with women at Seminole Days, framing myself in their gendered performances, that this book about Black Seminole women was born. It was there that I became a friend, not just spectator. I also became a member of Alice's extended family over time, sleeping on a well-worn couch and participating in their gatherings and celebrations. As researcher Josephine Beoku-Betts observes of her own fieldwork, I was expected to keep in touch in a kin-like relationship. If I failed to call or visit, Alice's daughter Effie informed me, "My mama is real mad at you, wondering why you don't come to see her. She says she doesn't know a Shirley anymore."

Alice embodies the spirit of her female ancestors who lived in the shadows of slavery, conflict, and diaspora. She is one reason why I persisted in writing this book. In photos as a young woman, she is tall and slim, with a mischievous but sad smile, a smile that I would come to understand through the years. Her dark eyes dance when she talks, and her voice has the rhythm and cadence of a poet. Her memory, like a vast genealogical map, travels back and forth through time to her ancestors, somehow transcending the past and the present. Alice thinks of this remembering process as natural, but her memory has been cultivated and systemized for recall, an inheritance from her female ancestors brought from an African homeland.[16]

When I asked her why it's important to her to remember her ancestors, Alice confided to me that she was always curious about her people, but it was not until she was older that she realized the historical significance of being Black Seminole.

"Shirley, you know what I think about—the old people like my [maternal] great-grandmama Rose Kelly, going back to Mexico, lots of those things," she said. "My [paternal] great-grandmama, Clara Dixon, was in Mexico, too. She was pretty old. You know she was on my grandmama Rosa's [Fay] side. I remember she talks about [their leader] John Horse."[17]

The dimension of gender is an important dynamic in my attempts in this book to reveal the contours of Black Seminole culture through the voices of women. I want to honor these women who exist unknown between the pages of western history—women who wove their stories and history into their work as they read dreams, prayed, cooked, tended children, and toiled in the fields, all in the company of generations of other women. Their voices, both past and present, play an active role in this epic that begins in the early 1800s on the Florida frontier. There, blacks resisting slavery formed resistance communities of fugitives hidden in the remote depths of forests and swamps. These fugitive bands share commonalities with similar maroon communities that fought for their freedom in the Caribbean, South America, and elsewhere in North America.[18]

Syncretism, a term used to encompass the parallel idea of both retention and the adoption and transformation of new cultural elements, is a characteristic of the Black Seminoles of the past that continues into the present day. They took the cultures they came in contact with and made them their own. They created a culture and identity out of diversities. At critical junctures in their history, black women sought alternatives for survival in their African roots; their lives on plantations of Florida, Georgia, and the Carolinas; and exposure to Seminole Indian culture and Spanish/Mexican influences. They gathered up their inheritance of eclectic foods and transformed them into new ones on a gendered stage. Women nourished their biological families and welcomed adopted children into their beneficent households of multigenerational families. To foresee the future, these women prayed, fasted, and cultivated dreams through visions, basing their interpretations on age-old precedents. Through naming traditions, they nurtured their creole-derived Afro-Seminole language—the "broken language" as Alice Fay's elders called it, bits and pieces of languages brought from western Africa to the Americas. They delved into the distant past to honor their ancestors by bestowing African-derived names on their children. They did all this in the shadows of endless wars and conflicts. Within the heavy curtain of racism, they experienced the tragedy of seeing their kidnapped children—like Clary, Polly, and Sukey—wrenched from their homes and returned to the misery of slavery.

As a recorder of the women's voices, I feel the heavy weight of time, a pressing awareness of the dissolution of a cultural group—but then that is part of the story, too. I notice that fewer Black Seminole descendants attend Seminole Days events. This is especially true of young people, many of whom have no knowledge of their history except for vague smatterings of heroic stories about their chief, John Horse. Some descendants pretend to know about their history when I ask them. Older women like Alice, Miss Charles, and Ethel July Warrior echo my concerns. Besides these generational and gender issues, descendants engage in struggles to control monetary resources and ownership of information or take part in deep-rooted generational squabbles. The dissolution of spirit, fueled by an attenuation of interest in the past, is certainly not specific to the Black Seminoles. The present world engulfs all of us with its demanding immediacy.

My stories of Black Seminole women presented in this book are informed by the manifests of deportees on ships leaving Florida for Indian Territory.[19] Daniel Littlefield, Jr., the eminent historian of southeastern Indians in Indian Territory, included the removal lists archived in the Library of Congress in Washington, D.C., in the appendix of his 1977 seminal volume, *Africans and Seminoles, From Removal to Emancipation*. The National Archives in Washington, D.C., also houses microfilm copies of correspondence, annual reports, and other papers primarily related to the Seminole and Black Seminole emigration from Florida to Indian Territory that I cite in this book. The major lists of deportees that concern *Dreaming with the Ancestors* begin in 1838, the start of the main period of Seminole Indian and Black Seminole departures from Florida to Indian Territory on what is known as the Trail of Tears. In the case of the Seminoles and Black Seminoles, the trail was not over land but by ship across the Gulf of Mexico and up the Mississippi River. Also recorded in the microfilm copies are the names and ages of Black Seminole individuals, often grouped together as families with Seminole owners.

The portent of the lists for my future research did not register at the time, but one other thing did. In perusing the microcopy lists I realized that the names of many Black Seminoles I had read about were included on the removal lists of emigrants departing from Tampa Bay, along with the names of their Seminole owners, dates of departure, and, in some cases, their ages. In many ways this revelatory experience was the genesis of this book. I recognized a female name recorded in the sienna-tinged handwriting of the U.S. Army officer in charge of the deportation west. The name of a five-year-old girl, Rose, is listed with those of her parents, Tina and Carolina Payne, and her little brother, Bob. Looking at their ages, I realized the significance of my discovery. Alice Fay had related stories told to her as a small girl by her maternal great-grandmother, Rose Kelly. Alice had grown up on Rose's ranch, Guadalupe, nestled in the foothills of the eastern Sierra Madre Oriental in Mexico. Finding Rose Kelly's name as part of the Trail of Tears, entwined with Alice's cogent memories, make her a central character in this book. The discovery of Rose's name in the list also was an important turning point for me, as it no longer seemed appropriate to write a story embellished with scholarly words and stilted language characteristic of my professional writing as an archaeologist. As I sought my own voice to tell this story, I asked why the book couldn't have a heart and soul—just as the ancestral houses of the ancient Maya people I study and whose ruins I excavate are given hearts and souls by the placement of offerings in their rocky crevices.

A mixing of genres in this work allows for a more encompassing story of Black Seminole history and culture that bridges time and place, and that paints a vivid portrait of the women while evoking the ancestors who continue to dwell in the hearts of descendants like Alice Fay. The rhythm of her voice is as much a part of this story as her words. It has a certain pitch, phrasing, and intonation, the latter of which is a characteristic pattern of her speech. The performative aspects such as facial expressions, mannerisms, eye contact, and gestures expressed by Alice and other women also are part of this narrative.

As I embarked on my journey in writing this book, always sitting on my shoulders were the devils of uncertainty regarding my motives. The Black Seminoles are not my people; I am an Irish third-generation American, a Texan of academic and social privilege. Why did I want to wrap myself in the folds of their culture? Could I see through my own cultural lens to tell their story—just as I strive to understand the meaning of archaeological residues left by ancient people that go beyond my twentieth-century understanding? I heard the whispers of suspicion sifting through the canopy of oak trees on the old school campgrounds where Seminole Days and Juneteenth events take place. I knew the gossip in some cases was about my presence, but more directly, my intentions. Some of the women sat on their metal chairs under the ancient oaks and examined me behind veiled smiles. Some feigned surprise that I was interested in their stories. Indeed, Black Seminoles have become a hot topic in the years I have been associated with the group. The descendants are aware that the photographs and artifacts of their ancestors are bringing high prices on eBay, and suspicions are frequently voiced about those who hoard photos. Common at Seminole Days and Juneteenth, even today, are the glare of dueling TV cameras and the presence of reporters, curiosity seekers, and avocational historians.

Pangs of jealousy haunted me as I saw the descendants react more favorably to women of color; thus I determined they had a better chance at gaining acceptance and information. Not that black researchers have it easy: Beoku-Betts, despite her "inside status" as a black woman doing research among Caribs in Belize, Central America, another maroon culture, stresses that she still faced challenges based on her gender, profession, unmarried status, and nationality.[20]

But I found solace with Alice, her family, and friends in their shadowed booths selling tamales and fry bread at Seminole Days and Juneteenth celebrations as they discussed children and relatives. Voicing my discomfort at being a stranger in their midst, Alice Fay cheered me up with her affirmation: "Sugar, pay no mind to them. You better take care of yourself. That's what I tell you."

I recall one old man retorting to me, "Why are you talking to those old women? They don't know anything."

"Hmmp," responded Alice Fay, when I repeated the comment of the male elder. She rolled her eyes in indignation. "They telling you that? Well, they don't know *anything*. I *tell* you what the people was doing!"

Later I came to realize that some of the men were actually fighting for a voice among the women. Dub Warrior, now eighty-four and the fast-talking off-and-on president of the Seminole Indian Scout Cemetery Association, is still holding his own as a historian and spokesperson for the group. It is a good thing to have an alternate and informed male voice among all those old Sisters.

As an archaeologist, I often ponder over multitudes of invisible humans who linger on the fringes of history—the anonymous Maya woman who fashioned a polychrome bowl, the African queen who led men into battle. On one of my many journeys of self-reflection, I realized also that I could never truly understand the stage from which Alice Fay sees her world. Sometimes I became sidetracked in the vast labyrinth of names and genealogies and in what I considered to be the maddening paradoxes and ambivalences in Black Seminole culture that still overwhelm me at times. Alice was occasionally annoyed with my endless, often repetitive questioning. She could not understand how I connected all the dots between her conversations to tell this story.

Black Seminole women join other women of color who, if present at all in historical literature, have been traditionally cast as supporting characters. Their absence is an unfortunate truism of histories that value men's activities above those of women. Early chroniclers of the American frontier were of European origin, primarily white males who did not understand the lives of indigenous males, much less women. The U.S. military or government officials viewed history

Fig. 6. Young sisters pose in plaid dresses, circa 1898. Family members' dresses were often sewn of the same material as the cloth was purchased in bolts. Alice Fay reported that "we sewed everything by hand." Institute of Texan Cultures, University of Texas at San Antonio. Courtesy of Sandra Gay Kinney, Emily Eggleston (Williams), and Joetta Knight.

Fig. 7. Black Seminole women pose in fancy dresses, circa 1902. Institute of Texan Cultures, University of Texas at San Antonio. Courtesy of Sandra Gay Kinney, Emily Eggleston (Williams), and Joetta Knight.

through their own lenses colored by Manifest Destiny. The process of recording history is also by its very nature exclusionary because of the silence of women, especially those who lacked economic or social equality. Many people during these times, whether male or female, also were illiterate, and their stories are recorded only through oral traditions handed down from generation to generation.[21]

As Linda W. Reese, a historian, observes of freedwomen in Indian Territory: "Historians have been reluctant to add the factor of gender to the already complex interpretation of the multiple variables of race, gender, culture, region, and time. Finding the sources to document and give voice to the 'lived presence' of Indian freedwomen and discovering the boundary of the fusion . . . has proven to be a daunting task for historians."[22]

The stories of women I reveal in this book are but faint brushstrokes of a people far removed in time. Their remembrances are like the ephemeral human dust I sift through, the broken sherds that remain to tell part of a story. I only have these faint glimpses into the enduring presence of Black Seminole women, from Florida to the frontiers of Texas and Mexico, to those who live scattered across the United States today searching for their roots—homemakers, teachers, lawyers, mothers, grandmothers, businesswomen, and soldiers. I gaze at the sepia-tinged photos of Alice's ancestors and wish they could speak. In their starched white Sunday dresses, posing like plaster statues in front of thatched homes, or in their homemade cotton plaid dresses and the satin frills and flounces of young women's hopes, their stories are frozen forever in a snapshot of time.

What were these women's lives like as they took refuge with the Seminole Indians in Florida in the early history of our nation? How did Alice Fay's Florida-born great-grandmother Rose Kelly, and her mother Tina, survive the endless conflicts and wars thrust on them by the expansion of competing colonial powers as they fled from one home to another? How did mothers cope with the inhuman tragedy of losing children to slave hunters in Florida and later in Indian Territory and Mexico? Of losing their husbands on nameless battlefields?

Alice Fay's recollections guided me as I carefully excavated the strata of meaning in this story of Black Seminole women. She has been my muse—the reason I have persevered in writing this account of her people. I ponder on her legacy of words: "I wanted this story to be history for the youngsters. What do I tell you? We're missing our heritage. Women had to be all family. When I was young we was always together—all those old people. I want this story to be for all the people."

CHAPTER ONE

The Birth of the Black Seminoles

> I have no more land, I am driven away from home, driven up. The red waters, let us all go, let us all die together, and somewhere upon the banks we will be there.
>
> "Song of Sinnugee"

> Yesterday morning just before leaving the boat, I had an opportunity of speaking to a very matronly looking woman. The mother of two grown women and an infant, the infant being in her arms, and I took the occasion . . . to tell her that she would soon be happier than she had been, reminded her of their having lived more like wild animals than like human creatures, but that now they would begin to have houses and make gardens etc., and could bring up their children to something besides war. The old woman dropped her head and burst into tears.
>
> Ethan Allen Hitchcock

The story of Alice Fay's people begins in the 1700s on the threshold of the Florida frontier, where the Spanish and British vied for control. This land was peopled with scattered groups of southeastern Indians. The Black Seminoles' story during the period is a complex one, difficult to excavate. The deeper one goes in history, the fewer artifacts that remain to tell the story. Even when found, these artifacts provide only fleeting glimpses of Alice Fay's ancestors.

Florida as we know it today was divided into territories in the 1700s. Spain, realizing the potential military value of blacks in protecting its colonizing efforts in Florida, began to offer refuge to runaways from British plantations. Perhaps some of Alice Fay's ancestors were among the blacks that the Spanish sheltered near St. Augustine at Fort Mose (Gracia Real de Santa Teresa de Mosé), which in 1738 was the first legally sanctioned community of freed slaves in what is now the United States.[1] Historian Jane Landers reports that the first recorded runaways to seek refuge there were women, some of whom became astute entrepreneurs and learned to use Spanish law, custom, and gender to their advantage.[2]

Blacks also began to run away to seek sanctuary among Florida's native population. In the early eighteenth century, the great Creek chief Cowkeeper or Mikko Ahaya had begun to settle his people on the northern Alachua plain near St. Augustine.[3] Dissident bands of Creeks began to separate from the tribe and formed a confederacy, adopting the name "Seminole," which is derived from the Creek Simaló-ni or later Simanó-li, which translates to wild or undomesticated. Cowkeeper's descendants—Chief Payne and his brother (Old) Bowlegs (Eneha Mikko)—were among the Seminole chiefs in the 1700s who began to offer refuge to the black runaways who included Alice Fay's ancestors.[4]

During the eighteenth and nineteenth centuries, Florida became a pawn between colonial powers, with its boundaries fluctuating according to changes in its owners. In 1763 Spanish-controlled Florida was ceded to Britain, a slaveholding nation, which divided it into western and eastern Florida. Twenty years later in 1783, Spain reacquired Florida and continued to offer sanctuary to black runaways. However, financially unstable Spain could not protect its territory, which piqued the interest of land-hungry Americans. In 1821, on behalf of the United States, Andrew Jackson invaded Florida and established a new territorial government. Florida now consisted of widespread settlements of Seminoles, their black allies, other southeastern Indians, and lingering Spanish enclaves.

During these changes in sovereignty and boundaries, Seminole Indian lands continued to be a concentration point for black runaways. Although they are called slaves in the literature, the blacks enjoyed a relationship with the Indians quite different from the traditional chattel system characteristic of southern plantation bondage.

A more accurate description of their interaction is what Mulroy calls a servitude relationship, in which the blacks provided tribute such as livestock or crops to the Indians and acted as allies in conflicts such as the Seminole Wars. Some of the Seminole chiefs found that prestige was directly related to the number of blacks they owned or gave refuge to. Elite Indian women did not have roles in political affairs of the Seminoles, but they were able to inherit or serve as guardians over slaves and as such expected the same tribute relations with their slaves. Women such as Harriet Bowlegs, the sister of Billy Bowlegs (Holata Micco), inherited large numbers of slaves in Florida, many of whom—such as Teener Factor and her family—are part of this story. Some blacks were purchased or given as gifts, while others were freed or even purchased their freedom. Blacks owned property, carried weapons, and chose their own leaders. They lived in substantial wattle and daub pine cabins.[5] But, significantly, the fugitives resided in separate, autonomous, often isolated maroon communities; maintained their African-born traditions; and were defiant in retaining their freedom. Rose Kelly, Alice Fay's great-grandmother, was born into one of these communities in 1833. The remnant maroon communities in Texas today have traditionally called themselves Black Seminoles, and for that reason I also will use this more familiar term.

The Black Seminoles' division of labor in these Floridian communities in relation to the planting, tending, and harvesting of crops was based on the traditions of their African forbears and ancestors in the coastal areas of Georgia and South Carolina, and more recent exposure to southeastern Indians. Men cleared the land for planting, after which women tended the communal fields that often wound for miles around rivers, raising bountiful crops of corn, melons, beans, peanuts, pumpkin, rice, sugarcane, and tobacco. Expert farmers, the women tended orchards of hardy fruit trees—guava, peach, and lime. They raised hogs and poultry, and they foraged and gathered wild foods and herbs to eat and for medicines. Women processed animal hides for bedding and clothing, and they spun, dyed, and wove their own cloth. They wove baskets and in some instances made their own pottery or were involved in trading networks that provided goods such as ceramics, beads, nails, and tools. Terrance

Weik reports that arms, rum, and molasses and gifts such as clothing, food, and pottery were given to Seminoles and their allies, of which the women were welcoming recipients. Certainly the labor of maroon women also provided a substantial portion of the tribute to the Seminole chiefs. Women also were of value to the Seminole Indians for they were efficient trackers, traders, horticulturists, engineers, artisans, guides, and inventors, introducing skills acquired from plantation experiences such as spinning cloth and candle making.[6] Linguists, often women, spoke other languages like English and Spanish in addition to their African-derived creoles and the Indians' Muskogean language.[7]

The maroon communities' enduring relationships with Seminole owners in Florida reinforced long-term alliances and even friendships. Important maroon leaders such as Abraham had busk names and were given Indian or part-Indian wives, although it was not common.[8] Having multiple wives was a standard practice among prominent maroon males since, like their African forebears and the Indians, they practiced polygyny. Male leaders typically had concurrent relationships with multiple female partners, a practice that continued many years later in Mexico and Texas among the Black Seminoles. Multiple relationships also occurred among women. Historical accounts and present-day interviews reveal that Black Seminole women had relationships with different male partners, but they were sequential relationships, not concurrent.

In Florida, sometimes ownership and marriage merged into a protective relationship among Indian men and black women. One remarkable story illustrates this relationship as well as the uncertainties created by Indian inheritance laws. In 1821, a black woman, Rose Sena Factor, a widow, escaped from two Spanish owners in St. Augustine. She was pursued, but, as the legend goes, some Indians gave her a horse and she fled deeper into Indian country. By then Rose Sena Factor had given birth to a son, Thomas (Tomás or *Toma*). Both Rose Factor and her son Billy were captured by a half-blood Creek, and Rose eventually ended up with the Seminole chief Black Factor (Ninnywageechee), who gave Rose to his son, Sam Factor, for a wife. Sam freed Rose and her children in 1835, but upon Black Factor's death, his sister Nelly Factor, under Indian matrilineal inheritance laws, claimed all his slaves. A legal problem arose when Sam insisted that he was the rightful owner of Rose and her two children. Ultimately Sam prevailed—the U.S. Army declared Rose Sena Factor and her children to be his property. Sam freed Rose Sena Factor, her children, and grandchildren, who were presumably his progeny, in a formal ceremony, but this time he made certain that a Seminole Indian agent witnessed the event.[9]

As time passed, the clouds of profound political changes loomed over the lives of the Seminoles and Seminole allies, as exemplified in the case of Rose Sena Factor and Sam. As maroon and Seminole communities continued to flourish as allies in Florida, they could not escape the machinations of outside forces determined to take their land. In 1819 the U.S. government officially purchased all of Florida from Spain. With the Americans' success in taking over ownership of Florida came a wave of new settlers and dependence on a slave plantation economy, both posing a threat to the lives of Alice Fay's ancestors and their Seminole compatriots. In 1829, Andrew Jackson, the newly elected president of the United States, came up with a grim legal solution to what he perceived as an impediment to American settlement in Florida. The basic intent of his solution, the Indian Removal Act of 1830, was to deport the autonomous southeastern Indian nations—Choctaw, Cherokee, Chickasaw, Creek, and Seminole—to the newly created Indian Territory in the west.[10] The planned relocation to the Seminole Nation was riddled with problems, however, because of the determined Seminole and maroon resistance. The allies fiercely fought removal from 1835 to 1842 in a prolonged series of conflicts in Florida known as the Second Seminole War.[11]

As time passed, the bitter fighting forced Alice Fay's ancestors and their Indian allies to abandon their sturdy log houses, livestock, and the farms they had carved from the Floridian wilderness. Wright reports that soldiers attacking Seminole villages came upon "crops of corn and rice, about a foot high, along with potatoes and other vegetables and signs of large herds of horses and cattle."[12] Other military personnel reported abandoned cooking utensils, and the skins of cattle, bear, deer, and alligators. They also found piles of prepared coontie, a food staple made from the root of indigenous plants such as smilax and zamia palms.[13] The Indians and Black

Seminoles would cut up pieces of the stems and pound them in wooden mortars into a paste, from which they made flour for bread. The property, fields, and food staples of the two groups hidden in the depths of the pine forests and hammocks became fair game to the soldiers. Ethan Allen Hitchcock, a U.S. Army major general in the Seminole Wars and later traveler in Indian Territory, described the devastation of the two allies' property. He observed the capture of the Indians' cattle, and ponies loaded with dried beef and all their possessions as U.S. soldiers destroyed their fields.[14]

Families were often a hindrance to the maroon warriors in their long, often unexpected flights and raids. Maroon settlements were often remote and ranged from temporary brush shelters and refugee camps to communities located near farms, according to historian Michael Mullin. Such communities were often of short duration, and moved to other sites, subject to discovery by troops.[15] During these fractious times, black women banded together to nourish families while moving from hamlet to hamlet subsisting on scarce resources, always in fear due to the absence of men. It is probable that the women also bore arms. Some of the older women who had escaped from southern plantations had been born in Africa. In the face of such dire circumstances, they joined together in multigenerational, matrifocal households connected by a strong sense of their African heritage and a determination to live in freedom with their Indian allies. Like Indian women, they were captured and used as hostages in efforts to flush out their warriors. Threatened with the death of their children, some captured women were forced to betray the warriors' hideouts.

The uncertain life of Black Seminole women at the time is reflected in Rose Sena Factor's experiences, for her troubles did not end after her husband Sam freed her. In 1836, during the Second Seminole War, three of her children were captured by slave raiders. She escaped with one son, Billy, and returned to Seminole country in Florida where she became a large landowner and acted as an interpreter and courier for the Americans. As Andrew Jackson's "solution" became realized, and she and her children prepared to migrate to Indian Territory, a series of legal battles ensued when her former Spanish owners surfaced unexpectedly to claim her. U.S. Army authorities reimbursed the men for Rose because of her services as an interpreter. Finally, in 1841, at the age of fifty-five, she departed for Indian Territory three years after the main body of Black Seminoles had left.[16]

With the passage of time, identity among Alice's ancestors became more complicated as they navigated the tangle of previous owners, chattel slavery practices of the whites, and different inheritance rules. As a Spanish slave, freedwoman, black woman, and mother of Black Seminole children, Rose Sena Factor exemplifies this complication. At the time, the Indian practice of matrilineality was becoming influenced by a white patrilineal system of inheritance as the Indians became more acculturated to the presence of Americans. The Seminoles, like other southeastern Indian groups, calculated kin relationships through the female rather than the male line. A matrilineage was a subdivision of a clan or group descended from a common ancestor that formed the core of the Indian household, drawing together related females in a powerful, corporate unity. Under the matrilineal kinship system, the child of a Seminole Indian and a black woman was considered black and not accorded membership in a clan. The child of a Seminole Indian woman, however, was considered Seminole regardless of the race of the father because of the mother's assured bloodline.[17]

Although some blacks were adopted into clans, the Black Seminoles were not matrilineal, but older women among the group maintained an in-depth, complex record of genealogical ties that connected them to their ancestors. These ties are reflected in an endogamous tradition of preferred marriage patterns. Another African-derived practice similar to that of the Indians was the practice of matrifocality, well-honed by maroon women in the absence of men. In a matrifocal society, daughters, even when married, often returned to their childhood home and resided with a closely related female. The household included a number of other family members, collateral ties often spanning several kin relationships and generations. Black women created a network of support within their customs of generosity and cooperation that was crucial to their survival.

Determined to end the incessant wars between the Seminoles and Americans, Brig. Gen. Thomas S. Jesup, in charge of the U.S. Army in Florida at the time in 1836, realized the Indians would not capitulate and depart for Indian Territory until their maroon allies were assured of freedom. His controversial solution was to promise the maroons freedom—that they would never be separated from their families or sold—and land in Indian Territory if they surrendered to the U.S. Army.[18] Realizing the futility of continued fighting, Alice's ancestors surrendered to the U.S. Army, while others were captured and transported as prisoners of war. They represented generations of families owned by Seminole owners such as Micanopy (Miccopotokee, Mikkoanapa), the Bowlegses, and the Factors. Alice's simple words expressed her people's desperation: "They all went together to leave Florida to Oklahoma. . . . You know that they had to do something to be free."

Alice's ancestors surrendered to the U.S. Army at Fort Jupiter, Florida, in 1838, prior to removal from Tampa Bay. Fort Jupiter, a rough stockade surrounded by ditches and embankments of earth and trees, was located near Palm Beach, where the rich and famous cavort today, unaware of the tragic historical drama that preceded them. Twenty-six vessels waited, anchored at Tampa Bay and ready to transport the Black Seminoles to New Orleans, from whence they would travel to Fort Gibson in Indian Territory. The Seminoles and Black Seminoles left at different times and under different conditions.[19]

The departure of both blacks and Seminoles from their homes can be imagined from eyewitness accounts of other departing groups. Claudio Saunt describes the Creek removal, noting "thousands of whites moved onto their lands, notching trees to mark their claims. . . . The Indians lost cattle, horses, and other livestock. Others did not plant corn in anticipation of leaving. . . . Others walked hundreds of miles by foot, often without provisions and facing freezing weather."[20] As for the Black Seminoles, they traveled in wagons or by foot northwest from Fort Jupiter to Tampa Bay under U.S. Army supervision. One of them was the influential leader and interpreter, Abraham (busk name, Souanaffe Tustenuggee). Abraham was an advisor to Chief Micanopy, a large slave owner. He had been a leader of a large maroon community called Pilaklikaha or "Old Abraham's Town" where many of Alice Fay's ancestors lived and prospered. Archaeologists such as Weik excavating Pilaklikaha have recovered evidence that the maroons traded and adopted some Seminole cultural practices such as the green corn ceremony.[21] Abraham, fifty years old and concerned for the well-being of his family, had surrendered with his part-Indian wife Eliza and their children. He had lost all his personal property and certificate of freedom. Eliza bemoaned the loss of her household items such as cookware and blankets. Abraham reported, "I waited for Wann and Wann's father; and my father-in-law was sick; and had to be carried two miles on the black people's shoulders. I afraid he won't live to get to Tampa."[22]

Alice Fay's ancestors left Jupiter and crossed over rivers, dense marshes of razor-sharp saw grass prairies, and swamps. As they skirted the many lagoons shadowed by pine forests and oak-lined hammocks near Tampa Bay, they passed the deserted burial mounds of the Indians who had come before them, lying under curtains of gray Spanish moss hanging from ancient oaks. Tampa had been the scene of another momentous event in African American history. The Spanish explorer Hernando De Soto had sailed into the broad, shallow bay in 1539, accompanied by Africans, before he proceeded to move north in his illusory quest for gold.[23]

In 1838, three centuries after De Soto's trip, two thousand to three thousand Indians and black Indians were forced to depart from the bay for Indian Territory. The removal from Tampa began, but Jesup's solution was laden with problems that would haunt him later.[24] The blacks who had escaped to the Seminoles were vulnerable to slave claims by former owners, and Jesup, recognizing that the Seminoles would not depart Florida without their allies, gave orders that the members of the departing groups were to be transported to Indian Territory immediately. U.S. officials herded the blacks and Indians aboard steamboats, where they were packed in like stacks of luggage for the arduous trip to Indian Territory. A U.S. Army officer in charge of the removal of Seminoles and their black allies in 1838 wrote, "One-hundred-and-thirty Negroes were sent off to Tampa Bay day before yesterday."[25] The soldiers recorded them on removal manifests, sometimes by family and age, with the names of parents, their children, and their progeny, and their Indian owner.

If one reads the U.S. military letters from the time, it is evident that the correspondents were confused regarding the identity of these maroons, some of whom looked black but had Indian ancestry. Some correspondence from this time period uses the term Seminole "Negroes" to refer to them. This identity dilemma was not a problem among Indians, however, as argued by many scholars, for they had no such categories as "black" or "Indian" as determinants of race until later when acculturation occurred in contact with western influences. The important classification for the Seminoles among themselves was kinship ties as part of a clan or extended family that determined social and ceremonial relations.[26]

Alice Fay's ancestors by the late 1830s had survived together on the margin of bitter wars that they had no hope of winning. As a result they were doomed to forced relocations to Indian Territory by the U.S military to make way for white settlers. By the time of their departure from Indian Territory, the lives of her people had become entwined in a complex network of multigenerational kin relationships, endogamous marriages, and in some rarer cases sexual unions with Indians. These blacks had formed a community amid their allies with a clear idea of their identity as Black Seminoles or maroons of African origins, fighting defiantly to be free from slavery.[27] Mulroy calls them a maroon culture, their ethnogenesis or birth forged by a unique set of circumstances that are common to such communities around the world. This birth was not synchronic or a static process but involved "processes of destruction, formation, change and fissioning" as Weik argues. Ian Hancock, a well-known linguist, determined that the Black Seminoles are a distinct ethnic group, born out of the ashes of conflict.[28]

But their identity was further shaped, and transformed, by Black Seminole women who boarded those ships bound for Indian Territory with families and loved ones. Some of these women had lost children to slavers and their husbands to devastating wars. These were women who carried the names of their ancestors etched in their memories and curated their age-old traditions in the midst of these ashes.

CHAPTER TWO

A Community of Brethren

> It has been women's task throughout history to go on believing in life, when there was almost no hope, and they are unable to deal only with despair.
>
> Margaret Mead

Alice Fay and I have visited the Seminole Indian Scouts Cemetery in Brackettville many times over the years. I have followed her footsteps down the gravely path winding around the cemetery. As she lingered at familiar tombstones or markers, she would reverentially repeat stories of her ancestors to me, just as Miss Charles had shared her stories with me before she passed away. The surnames etched on the markers reflect the depth of genealogical connections among these women's people and their remarkable survival. Many of the markers bear surnames that are crucial to this story—Payne, Factor, Perryman, Bowlegs—the markers witness to a community birthed in the shelter of dense pine forests and palmetto hammocks of Florida before endless conflicts and forced removal to Indian Territory.

Some of Alice Fay's ancestors can be traced back to Florida as they boarded the steamships for Indian Territory, before later ending up in Mexico and Texas. Theirs is a remarkable story that begins with Alice Fay's great-grandmother, Rose Kelly.[1]

Around 1833, Rose, hereafter referred to as Rose Kelly, was born to Carolina and Tina. Carolina, thirty-four years old, was owned by or under the guardianship of Micanopy, the principal chief of the

Seminoles who owned many slaves. Twenty-four-year-old Tina was a slave of Billy Bowlegs, a nephew of Micanopy. Carolina, a Micanopy warrior carrying the surname Payne, probably lived at both Pilaklikaha, or Abraham's Town, and another village, Okehumpke, on the Alachua plain. He had met Tina, who lived in Pilaklikaha, and they had carried on a courtship and married amid the angry clouds of war. In 1833, their first child, Rose (Kelly), was born.[2]

Carolina carried a popular name that may have derived from the Gullah *Kele* or *Ke'lena*, words that corresponded with a geographical location. In 1835, Carolina participated in the Dade Massacre, which precipitated the Second Seminole War.[3] Like other Black Seminole males he was an expert in skirmishing against the U.S. Army in the Florida swamplands using guerilla-like tactics, skills that would lead to the eventual deployment of Black Seminole men to the Texas frontier in 1870 as scouts for the U.S. Army.

Carolina's siblings—Jesse (age twenty-two), Nancy (age thirty-seven), and Plenty (age thirty-seven) with wife Rose (age thirty-three)—and their children, at least twenty-five persons in all, also owned by Micanopy, surrendered with their families to the U.S. Army at Fort Jupiter, Florida, in 1838.[4] Like other deportees, they surrendered as a large family unit that reflects their generational depth while living among the Seminoles in Florida. The elder Plenty, after arriving in Indian Territory, was killed in a raid. Other members of the Payne family who were part of the exodus to Indian Territory included Titus and Ben Payne. Titus would be ambushed and murdered by hired assassins outside Las Moras, Texas, in 1876 while traveling with John Horse. John Horse would also be wounded in the attack.

Carolina's wife Tina bore a variation of the African-derived female name *Tena*, meaning "rival" or "young woman," or *Tene*, which corresponds to a day of the week among the Mendes of Africa.[5] After the death of her owner, Chief Payne, a prosperous planter and slave owner who was chief of Alachua or Payne's town, Tina was passed on to his nephew, Billy Bowlegs, who remained in Florida fighting the U.S. government in the Third Seminole War. So it is likely that Tina departed Florida under the guardianship of a relative, perhaps Billy Bowlegs's sister Harriet Bowlegs, the daughter of old King Bowlegs and granddaughter of Cowkeeper.[6]

An infant departing that day, also owned by Micanopy, Clara (Clary/*Kari*) would also become part of this story ending in Texas. She eventually married a Black Creek, Joe Dixon, in Mexico and gave birth to one of the prominent storytellers in this book, Alice's paternal grandmother, Rosa Dixon Fay. Alice Fay's recollection of her great-grandmother Clara is hazy: "You know Clara was my great-grandmama, Rosa [Dixon] Fay's mama," she said. "[Joe] Dixon is Rosa's daddy. . . . He was part Indian. . . . Clara's buried in Nacimiento [Mexico] but I don't know where. I don't remember her too much but she looked Indian." Clary, Rosa Fay's young daughter by Adam (Koonta) Fay, whom we shall meet later in Mexico, carried her grandmother's name.

Another family among the maroons owned by Micanopy who surrendered with Rose Kelly's family in 1838 is also a key player in this drama that eventually plays out on the border of Mexico and Texas. The wife of the well-known warrior and interpreter July, thirty-six-year-old Teener (*Tena/Tene*) Factor departed Florida with his parents, Lucy (*Lusa/Luse/Losi*) (age fifty-five) and Sandy (Sunday, *Sande*) (age sixty-five). Lucy was owned by Nelly Factor, daughter of the part-black chief Black Factor, and Sandy was owned by Micanopy. Theirs was a remarkable family of leaders. Both July and his brother August were prominent interpreters and negotiators who lived in Pilaklikaha and carried names reflecting African origins. Teener Factor also favored African names for her and her husband's eleven children. July's parents, Lucy and Sandy—born during the British occupation of Florida from 1763 to 1783, perhaps in Africa—may have fled Sea Island plantations, and this played a large role in the name retentions. Teener and July's family represents three generations of twenty-five or more persons on the list of deportees to Indian Territory.[7]

Their daughter Susan (Susa) later caught the eye of John Horse on one of his return trips from Indian Territory to Florida where he was serving as an adviser and interpreter for the U.S. Army. She became his bride.[8] John Horse was joined by his sister, Wannah, with her three children. Two of her children would be kidnapped in Indian Territory. Susan's fourteen-year-old brother Sampson (*Sambo*), the future father of Rebecca (*Beka*) July, would become an important member of the Black Seminole community many years later in Mexico and Texas.[9] The Factor and Payne families would be conjoined when July's younger brother, Thomas (Tomás), married Rose Kelly years later after the Black Seminoles fled from Indian Territory to Mexico in 1849. Thomas and his other brothers, Hardy (Hardie) (age twenty-six) and Dembo (*Daemba/Dimbu*) (age thirty) Factor, who survived kidnapping attempts in Indian Territory, would become leading advisors to John Horse in Mexico. In the 1880 U.S. census, then seventy-six-year-old Dembo would be listed as living in poverty in Texas at Fort Clark with his Florida-born wife, sixty-year-old Lucy (*Lusa/Luse*).[10]

Another family central to this story is that of Cornelia Perryman (Cordelia/*Kore-Deli* or perhaps mispronounced as Amelia). Like Rose Kelly's mother, Tina, Cornelia was owned by Billy Bowlegs. She departed from Florida at age twenty-six with her two small sons, Pompey and Isaac (Isaak). Her husband may have been the Black Creek warrior Sandy (*Sandi*) Perryman, an important interpreter and negotiator owned by Micanopy who was killed in the Seminole Wars. Many years later Cornelia would show up in the U.S. census as a head of a household on Fort Clark. She would be recorded as living with a younger son, James Perryman, born in Mexico, and her granddaughter, Eliza. Cornelia is the great-great-grandmother of two female descendants who contributed to this work.[11]

Another well-known Micanopy warrior, traveling alone, was the dashing twenty-five-year-old John Kibbetts (Kibbitt, Kibbett/*Kube/Kivet*), also known by his busk name, Sit-tee-tas-to-nachy, or Snake Warrior. Kibbetts was both a surname and given name that may also have been derived from a Seminole chief named Kapi'tca or Kub-bitche in Florida. John Kibbetts would have an unexpected connection to Rose Kelly many years later in Texas.[12]

Among other travelers departing Florida were fifteen members of the Bowlegs family, including Zack or Jack (age thirty-six) and his wife Nancy (thirty). Other Bowlegses are one-year-old Davis (David), owned by Harriet Bowlegs, and Friday or Rabbit. The three men show up years later as scouts at Fort Clark, Texas. Jack Bowlegs would later lose his entire family and Davis would lose his wife and

Fig. 8. Dembo Factor, who was born in Florida around 1816, is shown here as an old man before his death in Brackettville in 1891. Owned by Sally Factor, Dembo survived kidnapping attempts in Indian Territory. Later in Mexico and Texas, he took on a leadership role in the Black Seminole community. Institute of Texan Cultures, University of Texas at San Antonio. Courtesy of Sandra Gay Kinney, Emily Eggleston (Williams), and Joetta Knight.

some children during a devastating Indian raid in the Laguna region of Mexico. The census of 1890 reports Davis as a household head in the Las Moras community on Fort Clark, but in 1892 he and his sister Dolly and other Black Seminoles left Texas and settled in Indian Territory.[13]

These families are only some of many that gathered at Fort Jupiter to surrender to the U.S. Army in 1838 with uncertainty in their hearts. They who had been living in brush shelters and tents in trepidation now reluctantly boarded steamships at Tampa Bay with their small bundles of belongings, leaving behind children and relatives lost in the wars and the bones of their ancestors. They harbored fears of slave hunters as they traveled to new lives in Indian Territory. These people formed a core of multigenerational families who intermarried and shared traditions and a common history that cemented their bonds throughout their diasporas and inspired their determination to be free. The women—like Teener Factor, Rose Kelly's mother Tina, and Cornelia Perryman—who nourished these families whispered the stories of their brave ancestors to their children deep into the night as they traveled to new homes in Indian Territory.

Many of the deportees were related to John Horse or his family. He departed Florida and arrived at Indian Territory later in 1838. Eyewitnesses described Horse as dressed in ragged, mismatched clothing on the trip, in contrast to his usual jaunty flourish of ribboned skin breeches or *metasos*, a turban held in place with a beaten silver band, and bright hammered silver gorgets and silver buttons.[14]

Traveling with John Horse were his mother and two married sisters—one of whom was Wannah and her five children, whose former owner still claimed her. Later in Indian Territory, two of Wannah's children, Linus and Sarah, would be captured and sold. Despite efforts by the U.S. military to rescue them, she would never see them again. Her infant son Andrew, who later took on the surname of Washington, and another infant, Clara (Dixon), would one day later have a relationship in Mexico. Only vague descriptions of Wannah have been passed down. Some of the women interviewed by Porter in the 1940s recall that she was older than John. One elder related that they had different fathers. She was described as "white-yellow looking" with a "bright complexion, brighter than John's." Another

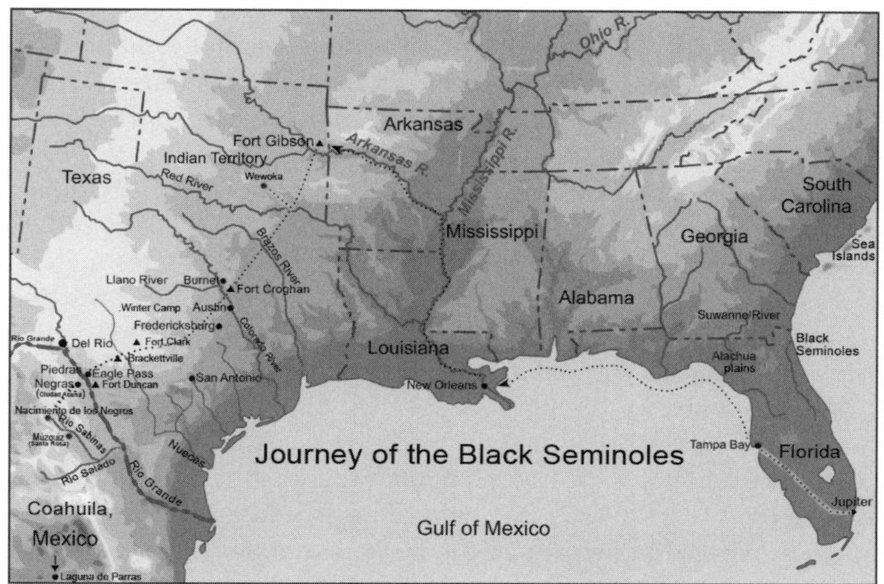

Map 1.

woman remarked that Wannah looked like a Cherokee woman with long wavy hair and that she dressed like one. Like John, she was probably of mixed racial heritage.[15]

Removal had a profound effect on the Indians, but among older blacks it carried an additional hopelessness despite the promise of freedom offered by the U.S. military. With removal came a realization from which they could not escape—recognition of the growing power of American racism based on skin color. The steamboats relentlessly kept shuttling their passengers to the West—Indian women berating their warriors for surrendering, black women mourning the loss of their husbands to war and their children to slavers. Some would die onboard the steamers to New Orleans and never reach Indian Territory. Among them were Bessy, Easter, Wann, and Fanny—unknown faces in the footnotes of history but mourned by their parents and relatives. Many of the casualties were small children who could not withstand the rigors of the journey. Some of the older people died awaiting deportation to Indian Territory and were buried in Tampa.

As they sailed along the coast in the Gulf of Mexico, Rose Kelly's people may have seen the vast cotton and rice plantations on which their black brethren were enslaved as chattel or the large, white-pillared mansions built on their labors. Her weary people crossed the swampy delta of the Mississippi River and passed the busy docks at the port of New Orleans. There they joined the thousands of Indians and blacks who awaited transportation up the Mississippi to the Arkansas River and Fort Smith, and on to their final destination, Fort Gibson. The U.S. Army provided tents for shelter or crowded the travelers into rudimentary stockades or transient camps while they waited for steamboats to transport them.

Former owners of the Black Seminoles, having received word of the mass migration, protested the hurried departure to Indian Territory ordered by General Jesup, complaining that he had no right to remove the blacks to the West before they could claim their slaves. Some desperate blacks painted themselves so they could not be recognized.[16] Claimants with valid ownership papers retrieved some of the unlucky blacks while the freedman status of others was challenged, a not uncommon occurrence as freedom papers were often lost or contested.[17]

By May 1838 there were 1,160 Indians and blacks awaiting boat transportation to Fort Gibson from New Orleans. Among the 249 Black Seminoles who departed New Orleans on the steamship *South Alabama* on May 22 were these close-knit, interrelated families—the Paynes, Factors, Perrymans, and Bowlegs. There were others who were related and whose names were recorded on the manifests but who cannot be traced to the Black Seminoles' eventual homes in Mexico and Texas. Rose Kelly and her fellow travelers ascended the Mississippi on steamships and reached Little Rock. They were alarmed when local authorities detained them briefly to accommodate persistent slave owners who were anxious to claim their former slaves. Claims by former owners were brought to the military and presented a dilemma. The Seminole owners refused to relinquish their slaves because of Jesup's order that enabled them to retain ownership if they moved to Indian Territory. Senior military authorities, wanting to be rid of the mounting problems created by the departing "Negroes," ordered the steamers to proceed to

Fort Gibson immediately. The migrating parties reached the fort on June 1, 1838.[18]

Politically naïve and uneducated, many of the Black Seminoles were unaware that the tentacles of slavery stretched all the way from Florida to their destination. They did not know that groups of runaway blacks owned by Indians, desperate for freedom, had already attempted to flee Indian Territory and escape to Mexico. The runaways had been pursued and caught. Nor were Alice's ancestors aware that the U.S. military had not established a separate reservation for the blacks in Indian Territory. Instead, they would be sharing land with factions of the slave-owning Creeks they hated, many of whom gained bounties by capturing blacks.[19]

Some of the new Seminole and Black Seminole arrivals, fearful of living among the Creeks, chose instead to camp in more friendly Cherokee country near Fort Gibson, where they remained for three years. The Cherokee Nation, though, also had slaves and eventually complaints arose that the blacks living with the Seminoles set a bad example. Detractors claimed the blacks were impudent, affected Indian dress, carried weapons, and did nothing but depredate and carouse.[20]

In 1839, Chief Micanopy, determined to maintain his status as befitted a Seminole chief in Florida, chose not to settle among the Cherokees. Instead, he led his people to set up households on the Deep Fork of the Canadian River in Creek territory. John Horse also set up a maroon community there but lived off and on at Fort Gibson. Because of Micanopy's status, and his ownership or guardianship of and relationship with these maroons, it is probable that Rose Kelly and her family, Carolina and Tina, among others, also initially made their settlements on the Deep Fork. An 1842 visitor reported that the Black Seminoles were prosperous, living as before in separate maroon communities, and still providing services and tribute to Micanopy as they had in Pilaklikaha: "The Seminoles, who have settled in the Canadian Fork, raise corn and rice; have 1,000 blacks among them, slaves for the most part, and stock a beef or two." It is reported that the Black Seminoles living at Deep Fork had at least one thousand head of cattle.[21] Obviously, this mutually beneficial relationship suited both groups well, and Rose Kelly's people must have felt some degree of security.

U.S. Army documents detail provisions allotted to other Indian groups upon reaching Indian Territory. It is likely that Rose Kelly's people also started out their new lives with tools, clothing, blankets, seeds, tents, knives, guns, ammunition, money, and annuities. The women were happy to receive blankets, calicos, and iron cooking pots. For sewing they were given needles, thread, scissors, and thimbles. Records of supplies and provisions to Indians such as the Choctaws, who arrived in Indian Territory in 1842, suggest that Black Seminole women also may have been provided with looms on which to weave cloth.[22]

Farming, though, was a demanding undertaking in this new land. According to an observer in 1844, it was "too cold in winter and too hot in summer for those who have been accustomed to the equable climate of Florida." Accounts of Black Creek descendants recorded by Saunt may provide additional glimpses into the Black Seminoles' uncertain lives in Indian Territory—there were droughts, famines, and floods. Insects ravaged their crops and they had to survive on wild plants.[23]

While his people were eking out new lives in Indian Territory, John Horse returned to Florida to assist the U.S. Army as a guide and interpreter. Stories relate that on one of these trips he met Susan, Teener Factor's daughter. Military records state that in 1840 Susan departed to Indian Territory with John Horse, along with one child, probably his progeny, although there is no record of the child's name.[24]

On another trip from Florida to Indian Territory in 1842, John Horse, then the primary interpreter for Chief Micanopy at Deep Fork, encountered his old friend, the well-known Seminole chief Wild Cat (Kowakochi, Coacoochee). Wild Cat had been captured in Florida with his warriors and eighteen blacks and was shipped in chains to New Orleans for transport to Indian Territory. The encounter was important, for Wild Cat would eventually play a large role in the future of the Black Seminoles.[25]

John Horse left Indian Territory and made additional trips to Washington as an interpreter in the government's attempt to persuade the remaining Seminoles to surrender. But his real, underlying objective was to seek a separate territory for his people. Unsuccessful in his mission, he finally returned to Indian Territory with a heavy heart in 1842.[26] The Black Seminoles continued to be susceptible to kidnapping, being sold, or re-enslavement under the strict Creek slave codes. Resentment also had begun to build against John Horse, even among some Seminole factions, as he had gained power and money by serving as a government agent in Florida. There were attempts to assassinate him.[27] "You know, they tried to kill him because he was trying to do good for the people," Alice Fay commented. "My great-grandmama Rose Kelly told me that. That's right."

In desperation, John Horse and several hundred of his people abandoned their homesteads, livestock, and wagons at Deep Fork and sought shelter at Fort Gibson. It is reported that John Horse hurried to get his family (wife, Susan, and two others) and his mother-in-law, Teener Factor, and her ten children, to safety at Fort Gibson.[28] Because of their common owners and relationship to John's and Teener's families, Rose Kelly's family probably joined them. While some maroons reluctantly abandoned their farms to leave Deep Fork for Fort Gibson at this ominous time, others decided to stay in Creek country rather than abandon their herds of cattle and homesteads. Wannah and her husband, the freedman Sam Mills (Colcocholky), had assumed they were free from slavers in Indian Territory because of General Jesup's promises in Florida. But after two of Wannah's children were kidnapped by slavers, she and her husband also fled with their three remaining children to the safety of Fort Gibson. The fort was under the command of a former adversary of the Seminoles in Florida, U.S. Army Lt. Col. Gustavus Loomis.[29]

When Wannah's former owner persisted in his attempts to claim her after she moved to Fort Gibson, U.S. military authorities there issued a proclamation demanding that he desist. He ignored the order, still insisting that he owned Wannah and her children and that he would only give up his claim for a price. By 1846 he had already sold two of her children to a Creek Indian who sent them downstream to be sold again. Witnesses related that the children were treated very badly. A Seminole chief claimed another of Wannah's children, Katy, but there is no other information about what happened to this child. Lieutenant Colonel Loomis appealed on behalf of Wannah's children and insisted they be returned to their mother if found, but he was not successful in rescuing them.[30]

Even under Fort Gibson's protection, Rose Kelly's people were still susceptible to slave raids by Creeks and even some Seminole factions. This was especially a concern for the women and children while the men were away during the long hunting season. The prominent maroon leader and interpreter August, July's brother, lost two sons to slavers. Slave hunters hounded Rose Plenty, Carolina's sister-in-law, four years after she lost her husband Plenty.[31] Her sons, by this time grown men, protested that their father had purchased their free papers in Florida. The U.S. Army threatened the guilty Indians with force if they continued to harass her. Chief Micanopy, her owner, pleaded to the U.S. Army for their safety, and finally the perpetrators desisted.

In another case, Clary Payne, also a relative of Carolina, was captured by a band of Cherokee and Creek Indians even though she was a free woman. She was carried off along with her children. Although Clary was ultimately rescued, her capturers beat her badly, and, according to accounts, she was never the same again.[32] Florida-born Noble, a thirty-year-old free black, had served with the U.S. Army officers as an interpreter under the condition that his family would be protected. Nevertheless, Creek Indian factions captured his wife and children and sent them to slavers in Louisiana.[33]

The profound changes in relationships between some Seminole factions and blacks once they reached Indian Territory or sought protection from Fort Gibson are difficult to explain. Wealthy Indian women such as Eliza Bowlegs and her relative Harriet, who is recorded as an intelligent woman who spoke English fluently, had ownership of many slaves due to matrilineal inheritance laws. In 1846, Harriet complained that she was impoverished and protested to U.S. Army authorities that her slaves had fled to Fort Gibson. It must have been an adjustment for Harriet to realize that in Indian Territory her slave-owner status had been compromised. However, she did not attempt to sell her slaves despite their reluctance to help her—she emancipated all of them upon her death. Unfortunately, researchers' understanding of the actions of elite Indian women is incomplete—these women did not keep records of their lives or those of their black slaves.[34]

Rose Kelly's family, Teener Factor's family, and the other families, including John Horse's relatives, lived for the next three-and-a-half years as squatters, protected by the U.S. military at the fort. Army officials expected the Black Seminoles to grow crops around the reserve to supplement their rations. The men cleared the fields and women planted and cultivated their crops outside the fort on the fertile terraces of the Grand River. The men were again absent on long trips across the Red River to the Texas plains where they hunted buffalo, deer, and other game, bringing the skins home for the women to fashion into leggings and shoes, or coverings for their beds.

Fort Gibson was undergoing new construction in 1845 because of its growing importance in Indian Territory, and the U.S. Army hired men such as Carolina to assist in the building. Thirteen-year-old Rose Kelly and her mother, Tina, like other women, got jobs washing clothes, cooking, or babysitting for the army officers' wives. Rose's family then obtained some extra rations—particularly dried corn, meat, and ammunition for hunting trips—which they typically shared with their kindred. However, by 1846 the construction was completed and their rations grew low.

As an old woman living in Mexico years later, Rose Kelly must have had distant memories of her teenage years at Fort Gibson—the crude log buildings on the high broad terrace above the wide stretch of the Grand River, the soldiers in faded blue uniforms, the palisade and whitewashed block houses, the sound of bugle calls, the gardens curling around the river. She may have recalled stories of unsuccessful escape attempts repeated in hushed voices around campfires deep into the night. While I was writing this book, Alice often surprised me with new bits of information about her great-grandmother Rose Kelly. These small unexpected accounts drawn from her data bank of memories were like precious artifacts to me in reconstructing her life and the lives of her people. I recall the memorable visit to Alice's ranch, Guadalupe, one day, when out of the blue Alice casually informed me, "Shirley, you know Rose Kelly wasn't like the others. She was special. She could read and write. She sure could."[35]

This was significant, for at the time Black Seminoles, especially women, did not have the advantage of schooling. Rose Kelly, as a bright young teenager, must have received some education while her family was living at Fort Gibson. Perhaps John Bemo (Talomas Mikko), a nephew of the Florida Seminole Indian chief Osceola, who opened a school in 1844, instructed her and others. A large congregation of blacks and even some whites came to listen to Bemo preach on Sundays. However, it is more likely that Lt. Col. Gustavus Loomis or his wife instructed the precocious young Rose. Despite his previous experience as a U.S. Army officer during the Seminole Wars, Loomis was sympathetic to the Black Seminoles, acutely aware of the way that they were victimized. Slave owners complained that he was teaching Negroes to read and write and had started a Sunday school that did not help their efforts to claim slaves.[36]

As Rose Kelly, now a teenager, was learning to read and write at Fort Gibson, the rash of kidnappings continued in Indian Territory. In 1846, her people suffered another devastating setback in their attempts to live as free people. The United States had become increasingly divided over the issue of slavery, and pro-slavery forces and corrupt Indian agents fanned the fires of dissent. In a Union divided, General Jesup's promise to the Black Seminoles of freedom upon surrendering was declared null and void. President Polk demanded that the blacks be returned to their former condition as slaves. Thus, the summer of 1848 was tragic for the Black Seminoles. U.S. Army officials ordered them, 260 in number, to be delivered to their former Seminole Indian owners, if those owners could be determined. By now, Micanopy, Carolina's benevolent protector who had harbored strong attachments to his blacks, had died and been replaced by a less-supportive, pro-Creek descendant.[37]

The U.S. military turned over the blacks, most of whom lived around Fort Gibson, to their former Seminole owners, who sent the men ahead to build cabins while the families stayed at the fort until the weather permitted travel. John Horse realized that the benevolent alliance between his people and the Seminoles had unraveled and he faced the grim future that lay ahead. Defying government orders in 1849, he led the Black Seminoles south from Fort Gibson to a tract of land near Wewoka Creek on the North Canadian River. Creek-influenced Seminole chiefs were outraged at this impudent act.[38] The Black Seminoles, though, defiantly assumed their traditional lifestyles and, again anticipating a permanent home, built sturdy cabins of split logs. The women's belongings as before were few—blankets or deerskins to sleep on, one or two stools, sewing implements, and iron pots or kettles. The men tended their livestock, took up arms, and prepared the land for planting while the women and children again communally tended their fields. Slave hunters, though, soon began circling around Wewoka like birds of prey; they knew that the settlement was outside the jurisdiction of the U.S. military.

In the meantime, John Horse had renewed his friendship with his old Florida friend, the politically ambitious and clever Seminole chief Wild Cat, who resented the fact that he had not been chosen as the primary Seminole chief. The collaboration of these two powerful, charismatic leaders soon gave a glimmer of hope to Rose Kelly's people. Wild Cat had ambitions of colonizing a Seminole settlement in Mexico, free from Creek laws. The Black Seminoles could fit within his plan, while providing a service to Mexico.[39] Reserves had been established in the United States for the Comanche, Kiowa, and Apache Indians, but they still defiantly crossed the Rio Grande regularly to raid Mexican towns such as Múzquiz (Santa Rosa) in Coahuila, thus discouraging border settlements on the southwestern frontier. Mexican government officials, desperate to end the raiding and encourage settlement, were aware of the reputations of Black Seminoles and Seminoles as warriors and scouts. The astute Wild Cat, cognizant of the predicament of the Mexican government, came up with a plan. He embarked on a series of trips between 1845 and 1846, traveling as far as the Colorado River in central Texas, on the pretense of hunting and trading. His real intentions, though, were to meet with Plains Indians and scout out the country as a home for Seminoles and Black Seminoles. Black Seminole descendants' stories relate that John Horse accompanied him on one of these hunting trips to Texas and they traveled across the Rio Grande to meet with Mexican officials. The officials assured them that their people would be granted citizenship and privileges accorded to white colonists if they settled in Mexico.[40]

Alice Fay related her own version of the story:

> They knew if they come to Mexico that they can't take them back to slavery. . . . Well, you know they was the leaders [John Horse and Wild Cat] and first went by themselves. John Horse finds out that there was no slavery in Mexico and so he comes back and talks to them and that's why

they all got together to leave. They got so friendly with the Mexicans. The Indians was killing them. So El Gato [Wild Cat] said, yeah, he'll send some of his people over there to help.

Rose Kelly's people, back in Wewoka, were encouraged by this report from Mexico and as a community began to discuss the possibility of escape. During the summer and fall of 1849 the men began to hoard arms and ammunition, sharpen tools and knives, refurbish saddles and tack, and fashion traps to catch game. The women and children spent months drying pumpkin, parching corn, and smoking meat. They gathered corn seed to plant crops along the way and patched blankets and old U.S. Army tents that had provided shelter at Fort Gibson. Rose Kelly's people planned with intense commitment, for John Horse had warned them that the journey across the plains of Texas to the Rio Grande would be long and perilous.

When visiting the Seminole Indian Scouts Cemetery outside Brackettville, Texas, today, one can see some of these original travelers' names—some of which are inscribed on rough wooden markers or engraved on marble tombstones. Sampson July and Dembo Factor are buried there. But the places where many lie are unmarked. Other travelers like Teener Factor and Cornelia Perryman and their families lie at peace in unmarked graves, perhaps there, or in the weed-choked cemetery in Nacimiento, Mexico, surrounded by ancient cedars. No one remembers now. Alice only knows that Clara Dixon and Rose Kelly are buried in the Nacimiento cemetery under some rocks.

The close-knit relationships between these travelers forged in Florida provided the foundation underlying the tenacious traditions and practices that are woven into the social fabric of Black Seminole identity today—and into this story of women. These travelers—whether well-known or only appearing in momentary glimpses on the lists of those leaving Florida—had prospered as extended kin groups within the closely related Seminole Indian networks of owners such as Payne, Micanopy, and the Factor and Bowlegs families. While absorbing some Indian customs into their community, the Black Seminoles had continued to commemorate the "internal landmarks" of Africa in their naming customs, language, and foods. As a distinct maroon community, sustained by their genealogical inheritance, generations of women archived these and imparted them to their children.

Nevertheless, the decision to uproot from Indian Territory in the mid-1800s was not an easy one for Rose Kelly's people. Their undertaking is an amazing story that underlies the ethos of the Black Seminole community today. Those who decided to leave were a close-knit group, a community bound together by generations of intermarriage, complex kinship ties, shared religious practices and language, and shared experiences in Indian Territory and Florida with roots in Africa. They were now anchored in their identity as maroons or Black Seminoles and swayed both by the power of John Horse's oratory and their desperation to raise their families in freedom.

CHAPTER THREE

The Big Trip

Escape to Mexico

> There is no power on earth that can stop men and women who are determined to be free at all hazards. There is no power on earth so great as the power of the intellect.
>
> Lucy Parsons

The chance to escape presented itself on an autumn day in November of 1849. The Black Seminoles' adversaries—Indian Bureau officials dominated by pro-slavery Creeks—had departed Indian Territory for Florida where they intended to persuade "hold out" Seminoles such as Billy Bowlegs to move west. Stories of Black Seminole descendants suggest that Rose Kelly's people, although not unprepared, upon receiving this information had to make a decision to depart immediately. Rebecca July related many years later, "My father Sampson July left in such haste that he left his wife and some of his children because the white people were about to seize them all and sell them as slaves."[1]

Alice's ancestors had gathered on many occasions under the curtain of night and, guided by their desperation, discussed Wild Cat's daring plans to escape to Mexico, where slavery was not practiced. The women prayed and read dreams to prognosticate their future, as were their customs.

As historian Tiya Miles observes of Black Cherokee runaways, the Black Seminole leaders like John Horse and the Seminole chief

Wild Cat also had some awareness of the geography of their escape routes.[2] Cartographer John Disturnell's Mapa de los Estados Unidos de Méjico, although inaccurate, was published in twenty-three separate editions between 1846 and 1858. Jacob De Cordoba's map of Texas, published in 1849 after annexation, was also well known at the time. Wagon trains heading south from Fort Gibson followed a well-worn trail, the Texas Road, through Choctaw and Chickasaw territory to the Red River. U.S. Army officials reported that Indians often waylaid travelers on the road and stole their supplies and horses. The so-called Comanche War Trail, a series of trails that zigzagged from the Red River to the Rio Grande, also was well known among the Indians because it followed buffalo routes.

Wild Cat and John Horse had sketched their own maps on their prior trips to Mexico. As expert trackers, they knew places to camp or hide, and the location of rivers, tributaries, lakes, and other water sources. They had gathered information about the weather conditions they might face and where slaver enclaves lurked. Based on previous trips, the two leaders could estimate travel time from one destination to another. They were aware of the land features, trails, edible plants, and times suitable for planting and harvesting a corn crop. They devised strategies to protect the women and children, knowing that Comanches prowled the Texas prairies looking for blacks, whom they would deliver to Creeks and Cherokees to resell at fifty dollars a head.

The timing of the Seminoles' and Black Seminoles' departure also coincided with that of traditional hunting parties in Florida that left in October or November to return in early March for the spring planting. It was likewise customary in Indian Territory for men to make long fall hunting expeditions beyond the Red River to Texas.[3] Early visitors to the area reported Seminoles—men, women, and children from Indian Territory—who had traveled 150 miles across the Red River into Texas to buy whiskey. Kickapoo Indians also traveled north to barter for liquor.[4] Wild Cat and John Horse hoped that because of the timing with traditional hunting trips pro-slave Creek factions would take little notice of their departure.

About 150 to 200 Black Seminoles, according to legends, banded together in a common resolve to make their way to freedom in

Mexico.[5] They were a community of multigenerational families bound together by years of endogamous intermarriage and a shared history of ownership by a small group of related Seminole slave owners. The names of many of the people who gathered on a crisp autumn morning in November to leave for Mexico are known from the emigration lists of departure from Florida, which documented when they left for Indian Territory. These same people can be accounted for years later in Mexico and Texas. Many of those departing were related to John Horse or his wife, Susan, and her family. Teener Factor does not show up again in the records, but her sons, Sampson (July) and Kistova, do in Mexico. July's brothers, August, Hardy, Thomas, and Dembo, former warriors in Florida, joined the group. Rose Kelly, and her mother, Tina, were among the departing, but Carolina would not be heard from again. The widow Cornelia Perryman and her two sons joined the Bowlegs family: Jack Bowlegs, his wife Nancy, and their four children, Davis or David Bowlegs, and Friday or Rabbit Bowlegs. Also embarking on the trip was the middle-aged, Florida-born John Kibbetts, who acted as second-in-command to John Horse. He was accompanied by his Florida-born wife Nancy. John Horse's sister, Wannah, departed Indian Territory with three children, grieving for her two children who had been kidnapped, realizing that she would never see them again. Parents gave last-minute admonitions to their children and bid tearful farewells to elders who could not withstand the rigors of the journey. The women in their long, handmade calico dresses and aprons wore their traditional headscarves; the men sported Seminole-style buckskin leggings, breechcloths, sashes, turbans, and silver gorgets. Their pack horses were loaded with bags of tobacco, corn, sugar, flour, knives, clothes, weapons and ammunition, cooking utensils, and agricultural implements, while other provisions were carried by women and children.

Departing on the same day as the Black Seminoles and leading the group of travelers was the gallant and charismatic Chief Wild Cat and his people—about one hundred Seminole Indians determined to find a home in Mexico where they would be independent from the hated Creek factions. Also joining the fleeing group were destitute Indians and other blacks owned by Indians who were lured by the promise of provisions, freedom, and land in Mexico. As they set out that morning on the momentous journey through Texas, Rose Kelly and her people wondered if they would make it to the Rio Grande, known among runaways as the Rio Bravo, the "Freedom River."

As they departed, Tina could not foresee that her daughter Rose Kelly would marry Thomas Factor, the younger brother of the great warrior July, Teener Factor's husband, when they reached Mexico. Rose Kelly would go on to give birth to nine children through at least three relationships. She would live to the ripe old age of ninety, and recount her stories to her little great-granddaughter, Alice Fay, many years later on her ranch, Guadalupe, in the foothills of the eastern Sierra Madre Oriental in Mexico.

The travelers probably avoided the well-traveled Texas Road that headed south along the banks of the Grand and Arkansas rivers because it was the heavily used main artery to the south. The road is reported to have been muddy and barely navigable at times. At some point, the group crossed the Canadian River, a tributary of the Arkansas that meanders across what is now Oklahoma. Early explorers thought that the river extended to Canada, thus the name. Deep gorges along the riverbanks would have made it difficult to cross.[6]

On my visits to Nacimiento, Mexico, where the group eventually landed, Alice would sit in an old metal rocker outside the ruins of her mother Nellie's adobe house and repeat stories about the trip from Indian Territory told to her by her great-grandmother Rose Kelly. I recall one day in particular—a postcard scene, the mountains above Alice's ranch providing a remarkable backdrop to her lavender print dress. The sun and the strong shadows played with the angles of her chiseled face as she began to recall her great-grandmother's words about the historic trip, her voice textured with nostalgia:

> You know, Rose Kelly was a bitty old lady, who was a young girl on the trip. I was about nine years old when Rose was with us on the ranch in Mexico. She lived with my grandmama Amelia and us. This ranch you see here was called "Guadalupe" 'cause that's what my great-grandmama Rose named it. You know, it was her ranch and Tina's. She'd tell me about the trip when I was little girl. She says, "We all gathered together in one place. They have to pick up some more people. They all

> have to start together." How do I know? Well I tell you, the old people would get together on a weekend [in Mexico]. The kids was not allowed. The old Sisters would go out to the ranch and talk about what they was doing and cry and cry. When night came they would put us to bed and they talk about the travel, the trip. My mama Nellie Fay had to work—wash clothes on a ranch like I told you. Rose Kelly probably wanted to talk [about her experiences], but my grandmama Amelia wouldn't let her talk to us. But when Amelia and Nellie go out, Rose Kelly would cry and tell me about the trip. She said they stay up all night long, travel part of the day—'cause they was scared the slavers would catch up and take them back. Lots of things I didn't catch 'cause I was too small. They had a ranch [in Indian Territory] and they had beasts like cows, horses, and all that she was talking about and they had to just get up and leave everything they had. It was real sad.

Alice paused in her reverie, her intelligent eyes heavy with memories. "I'd sit down and cry with her," she said. "Juan Caballo and Gato Del Monte was in front—you know—John Horse and Wild Cat." In her rhythmic voice, she continued to recall Rose Kelly's words about the trip that had become etched in her mind:

> She says they traveled hungry—no food, no sleep—days without nothing to eat. They walked and they had two or three horses, you know, where they packed all the things they own. . . . She tells me the women had to, you know, strain the water to drink with the kerchiefs. Yeah, you know, the things they wore on their heads [head scarves tied in the front]. They had to find good places to cross the rivers. They cook what little they have at night and for the next day and they all ate it together.

Many descendant stories relate that the two fleeing groups encountered trouble as they crossed the Red River, a wide, meandering stretch of water that receives its name from the color of the red clay it reflects. It was not easy to cross because of rapids and shifting shoals. To avert attention, the Seminoles and Black Seminoles had separated into two groups after crossing the Red River, according to descendants Kenneth Porter interviewed in the 1940s.[7] As the group crossed onto the thirsty Texas plains, legends relate that Creek posses were in hot pursuit.[8] A battle ensued, and Wild Cat and John Horse's group fended the posses off without a casualty. Certainly this journey to freedom for Rose Kelly's people evoked the biblical story of the Red Sea parting and the Israelites crossing to the Promised Land.

At the time, however, the hopeful travelers did not foresee living on the threshold of starvation, surviving the bitter cold of a sudden Texas norther, crossing turbulent rivers on makeshift rafts, losing children to illness, and facing the constant threat of slavers in pursuit. Theirs was a trip vested in courage. Had they known what lay ahead—hardships too bitter to understand—perhaps some would have turned back. But as a maroon community they had fought for their freedom in Florida and were determined to be free, a resolution underlying their identity as Black Seminoles.

As they wove their way on the maze of paths leading off of the eastern branch of the Comanche Trail, the travelers crossed into the vast, undulating prairies that extended into Texas, the home range of vast herds of buffalo and game, an area fraught with danger because of the presence of roaming Comanche bands looking for runaways. Rutted buffalo trails led to water sources such as creeks and springs as they traveled southwest. Behind every hill, lurking on every plain, were unseen pursuers who would find and follow their tracks. The Black Seminole leaders used diversionary tactics to shield their women and children, who normally did not travel on the winter hunt as did the Seminole women. As they headed south to cross the black loam prairies to the northern stretches of the Trinity River, the travelers were joined by additional runaways who had caught word of their escape.

While the two fleeing groups continued to split up on occasion, for protection from pursuers they sometimes banded together as they crossed the Texas plains.[9] One female elder, Molly (Mollie) Perryman, offered an interesting aside about Chief Wild Cat, who had taken a liking to her mother, Kitty (*Kitti*) Johnson, then a young girl:

> My mama came with Wild Cat, the Indian chief. They all came together, John Caballo [John Horse] and all. My grandmama loaned my mama, a little girl then, about 9 or 10 years old, to Wild Cat's family. Wild Cat's little boy, Billy, had liked her so Wild Cat took her . . . to nurse him. They

were Indian people, Mama says. . . . She always talks about how good they treated her. Mama and Billy came on a nice horse together; they always were in the lead.[10]

Molly Perryman was a favorite among Porter's interviewees. He describes her as "a very handsome lady who wears gold earrings with a kerchief on her head and smokes a short clay pipe. She has an elegant bearing and looks like an Indian or an aged Egyptian queen." Although he noted that she was a "remarkably intelligent woman," the racism of the time (the 1940s) is evident in his additional commentary: "if given the benefit of an education in early life [she] might have gone far, with her racial handicap."[11]

Rivers became the Black Seminoles' landmarks as they traveled south. They probably skirted the Elm Fork of the Trinity River and followed the Brazos River. According to legend, the soldiers of Coronado's expedition for the Spanish Crown were dying of thirst when they came upon the river around 1540. In gratitude, they named it "Los Brazos de Dios" (Arms of God). Centuries later, the French explorer La Salle crossed the lower reaches of river in the 1700s, seeking to establish a Bourbon Empire in what is now Texas. The upper reaches of the river had salty, bitter water that was not potable, and here, the Black Seminoles also faced the challenge of intermittent freezing winds and sleet, typical of Texas in late February or early March. Packs of wolves frequented the area; their cries at night reminded the group of Indian cries. Canvas tents issued to them at Fort Gibson by the U.S. Army were worn and torn and did not keep them dry or warm. The travelers huddled under crude brush arbors where the women boiled parched corn for their traditional food, *sofkee*, a type of hominy gruel, in army-issued cast-iron cooking pots. Women and children foraged for edible plants and captured small game like rabbits or squirrels while the men hunted deer, antelope, bear, or buffalo. The Black Seminole women dried and salted the meat of game caught by the men or mixed it with wild berries and fat to preserve it. They stretched the animal skins on sticks and hung them in the sun to dry.

Descendants' stories relate that the Seminoles and Black Seminoles reunited and made winter camp on Cow Bayou, a branch of the Brazos River below present-day Waco. Here they found clear springs and streams that were home to gar, catfish, and turtle. A small settlement of Hueco (Waco) Indians lived in the area. Flocks of turkeys and herds of wild cattle and buffalo roamed the area, drawing hunting parties. A band of Kickapoos camped nearby.[12]

Here, according to legends, the runaways, desperate for food, planted a corn crop while Wild Cat was out recruiting more Indians such as the Kickapoos to join their party, and they planned to linger in the area until it was ready to be harvested.[13] A trading post was located on the east bank of the river where Comanches reportedly came to trade dried buffalo meat, deerskins, and buffalo robes for beads and sugar.[14] Perhaps, because of the ideal location and with the two groups joined, they felt enough safety in numbers to linger in the area. However, because of the length of time required to harvest a crop (sixty to eighty days) and the presence of slave-hunting Texas Rangers in the area, it seems unlikely that this location would have been chosen to plant a corn crop. Mulroy, relying on military documents, is probably correct in asserting that the exact location of the group at this time is uncertain.[15]

Rose Kelly's people continued to follow the Brazos along the Balcones Fault, which extends in a long crescent shape from the Red River southwest to the Rio Grande. Chiefs Wild Cat and John Horse had old friends among the U.S. Army stationed in Texas, and they also were aware of a string of U.S. Army forts that stretched from north Texas to the Mexican border. Perhaps they considered these locations as they planned their travel, recalling the U.S. military's sympathy and assistance at Fort Gibson (see map 1).

They reached the lower, swift-flowing portion of the Brazos River in west-central Texas probably sometime in late March or early April. The river there winds its way south to the Gulf of Mexico through rolling hills of oaks framed by steep bluffs of limestone, which offered advantageous lookout points for pursuers.

The travelers crossed the lower Brazos on improvised rafts of logs tied with grapevines, and floated their pack animals in the swift current, often taking advantage of the flat sandbars in the river. Alice recalled her great-grandmother's account:

> Sometimes they'd swim across the river. You know, the horses would bring over the things and then go back to bring back more. Rose tells me that they tied the children on the horses. Sometimes the horses didn't wanna go. They worried about the children crying out. John Horse travels with them. He'd go off and then he'd catch up with them. The men, they had to stay back and fight with the Indians. It was pretty bad. There couldn't be no way where they could've been seen, they always was in a, you know, a place close to a mountain or something like that. They would try to find a place where they could hide until the men would find a way to go. . . .
>
> The people was always looking for a place to grow the corn. There was no food. There was no corn for the people but they prayed. They needed the *sofkee.* Rose Kelly tells me they hunt deer, turkeys, and other varmints. Sometimes they have to go into a town to buy corn or something. . . . But, you know, they all share the food what they had. . . . We'd stop and cook the corn and grind it. Put up on the horse. My mama Nellie had a great big old pot from Rose she brings on the trip. . . . The women, they was reading the dreams—all those old Sisters—it was so hard. You know they'd try to find out what was gonna happen. Rose told me that.

As Alice—and Rose Kelly, through her remembrances—demonstrates, the Black Seminoles are apt storytellers, and the grim nature of their trip was broken with humor and gossip, especially among the women, who tell ribald stories today at Seminole Days. Conversations with older women led me to think that gossip also focused on the wisdom of women and the fact that the men should heed their advice. One story told by women descendants focuses on an escaping party that camped one night. The men neglected to hobble the horses, leaving them loose as a means of thwarting Indian predators. The women, however, warned the men to tie the horses out where they would be safe, but the men did not listen to their sage advice. Indians were trailing them and knew that each night the Black Seminoles hobbled their horses. When the men changed their routine that night, the Indians took advantage of the situation. They slipped up and drove the horses away and then attacked and killed some of the people.

Descendants have recorded additional accounts of an unfortunate group of other fleeing blacks from Indian Territory who escaped white slave hunters but then were attacked and captured by Indians. In one instance, the Comanches captured an escaping group of blacks and ransomed them to slave-owning Creeks from Indian Territory.[16] Oral histories relate that various groups left Indian Territory at different times. One descendant, for example, was recorded as saying that his mother and father came in different groups to Mexico. There were probably many escape attempts that failed alongside those that were successful.[17]

After crossing the Brazos River, Rose Kelly's people reached the hilly area of south-central Texas that blends into the southern edge of the Edwards Plateau, a green ribbon of rolling hills and limestone outcrops. With the advent of spring, the Texas landscape would have come to life with a bounty of wild foods when wildflowers began to blanket the prairies and redbuds bloomed. Early travelers in the area report considerable quantities of oak, mesquite, and clusters of thorny acacias. Women and children warily foraged for wild grapes, *agarita* berries, and summer plums in the thickets guarding the edges of the plains. Wild pecan trees and beehives yielded their precious cargo to the hungry group. The travelers caught catfish and perch hiding in the secluded banks of small creeks with their bare hands. Familiar with both their Florida ancestors' and Indian methods of cooking root plants, they gathered the spiked *sotol,* similar to the Florida palmetto root, buried it, covered it with rocks, and started a fire on top to steam it. Then they ground it into a flour-like meal. The *sotol* is still gathered and cooked in a similar way in Nacimiento. One present-day Nacimiento woman informed me that the leaves, once cooked, taste like a boiled turnip.

Exhausted by this time, the members of the group had no knowledge of the uncertain spring and summer weather ahead of them in this strange land. The crucial point of their existence in Florida had been the cycle of the seasons—the rhythm of days, months, years; the planting of the corn crop and the harvest; the appearance of constellations such as the Pleiades, the seven grandchildren that signaled the onset of rain—this is how they understood time. In Mexico they would continue to tell time by the seasons. When John Horse departed to Mexico to petition for their land grant to Nacimiento, witnesses observed the time to be during harvest when the watermelons and corn were ripe.[18]

In the meantime, in Texas, the group still needed to plant a corn crop, but central Texas was also the home of bands of Comanches, and they knew if they made camp, they would be vulnerable. The worn travelers were also vulnerable to sicknesses, and certainly the older women like Teener Factor carried knowledge of a repertoire of survival techniques passed down by female ancestors. Gifted medicine women in the group could diagnose and treat physical illnesses, knew of the complex chemical properties of certain plants, and, through contact with Indian women, also were familiar with medical counterparts on the vast prairies of Texas.[19] Nevertheless, some of the older people did not make it to their destination across the Rio Grande. One female descendant recalled years later, "One old Black Seminole got sick and couldn't sit on his horse. He told everyone to go ahead and that he would catch up. We never saw him again."[20]

Perhaps traveling along the old Camino Real or San Antonio Road, a network of trails established by the Spanish, by the end of April the Black Seminoles may have crossed the lower stretches of the meandering Colorado River in what is now known as the Hill Country near Austin and San Antonio. Dense canebrakes and wild bamboo and tall cedars and cottonwoods lined the banks and provided some cover for the runaways.[21] According to legend, Rose Kelly's people were desperate, still with no corn to eat. In May Wild Cat and John Horse surprised a farmer in the small town of Burnet located in the hills near Fort Croghan and purchased several bushels of corn. The two chiefs also visited the fort to make appeals for food, and the officer in charge provided them cattle and food supplies.[22]

They continued their journey and may have camped on the Llano River, a tributary of the Colorado River, about fifty miles northwest of present-day Austin, where the Llano flows into the Colorado. As other travelers of that time report, the Llano was shallow with rapids flowing over sandbars bordered by large rock outcrops. The Black Seminoles found it brimming with catfish and trout and the surrounding hills teeming with bears and other game. Descendant stories relate that Indians and Black Seminoles again united when they made camp on the Llano, intending to grow a small corn crop while Wild Cat continued to recruit Indians to join them.[23]

Near the travelers' camp was the small German settlement of Fredericksburg, established in 1846, in proximity to Fort Martin Scott, which was established in 1848 to protect Texan settlers and travelers from Indian raids. At this point, legends relate that Wild Cat departed for Mexico to receive assurance that the Mexican government still wanted the group's services.[24] It is possible that the Seminoles and Black Seminoles felt safe in the area settled predominately by German freethinkers and abolitionists.[25]

Earlier travelers report this area of Texas to be richly timbered with post oaks and live oaks and to feature abundant game, springs, and rich farmland. Buffalo also were reported to be in the area by early travelers. According to descendant accounts, while the group planted a corn crop and waited for harvest, Wild Cat also met with other Indians in the area to persuade them to join his colony in Mexico and paid a visit to nearby San Antonio to meet with military officials at Fort Sam Houston.[26]

Stories passed down among the Black Seminoles relate that things were going well until one Friday afternoon in late May when Wild Cat, perhaps encouraged by the group's proximity to the Rio Grande about 150 miles to the west, slipped out to Fredericksburg with his son and the boy's nurse or playmate, a young Black Seminole girl, Kitty Johnson, and began to drink. When Wild Cat was running out of money, he attempted to sell her to pay the bill. Fearing Wild Cat's antics had attracted slave hunters, John Horse urged his people to head for the Rio Grande with haste. According to Black Seminole legends, Wild Cat had pulled this stunt on another occasion, trying to sell fifteen-year-old Clara Dixon, Alice's paternal great-grandmother, to a bartender for a barrel of whiskey.[27]

Alice didn't recall Clara Dixon mentioning much about the journey. "You know Clara was on the trip but didn't talk about it much that I remember," she said. "She would only visit the ranch for a few days—lived in town, like [her daughter] Rosa Fay, not on the ranch.

My grandmama Amelia would take me there. Clara was a little old lady. She's buried in Nacimiento like my Rose Kelly."

The outspoken Molly Perryman, however, did relate her version of this part of the trip to Porter: "They never stopped till they got to Las Moras Springs [near present-day Brackettville]. . . . [Wild Cat] was so drunk that he didn't know what he was doing. . . . John Horse liked his liquor . . . but he was the chief—he knew when there was danger and he mustn't touch it. There was John Horse always watching over his people."

The Black Seminoles hastily continued south across a broad expanse of monotonous prairies, crossing the Frio River and the shallow, meandering Nueces River, which had been first traversed by survivors of the ill-fated Spanish expedition of Cabeza de Vaca and the first African-born slave in Texas, the Moor Estévanico, in their momentous trip across Texas in 1534.[28] Only four years prior to the Black Seminoles' passage, the land between the Nueces and the Rio Grande had been hotly contested, with Mexico claiming that it, not the Rio Grande as the newly formed Republic of Texas maintained, was the boundary of Mexico.

Several versions of the legend circulate about this last leg of the Black Seminoles' trip as they approached the Mexican border in July of 1850. In one version, the travelers received word that slavers were on their way. The runaways were concerned but knew that their horses were still fresh since they had not run them. Wild Cat told the people to throw all their food supplies on the ground by the springs and to split up into two parties: the women and children with a few warriors in one group, and the rest of the warriors in another. They then stayed close to two U.S. Army posts located on the Nueces. In another story told by descendants, the group encountered a U.S. Army detachment in July under Maj. John T. Sprague, whom they knew from the Florida wars. The encounter took place at Las Moras Creek, later the site of Fort Clark and home to the Seminole Negro Indian Scouts. The springs and creek provided an inviting rendezvous for Indians, buffalo hunters, and traders. Jesse Sumter, stationed with troops camped at Las Moras Springs, recalled the Indians approaching the soldiers with a white flag and coming into the camp.[29] Sprague, sympathetic to their needs, gave them food, supplies, and a pass to travel to Eagle Pass on the Rio Grande, their final destination. According to one descendant story, though, the military subsequently betrayed the group and reported its presence to nearby slave hunters. The travelers retrieved their horses quickly and took off.[30]

A female elder related to Kenneth Porter that the men made a more visible trail to distract the slavers from following the women and children, who set off in a separate group—a tactic they had used before. They also drove some cattle over both trails to further confuse the slavers.[31] Then, Rosa Fay recalled for Porter, "With about 25 miles still to go to the Rio Grande, they saw slave hunters. John Horse wanted to stay and fight, but Wild Cat reminded him that they had women and children along."[32]

The weary travelers were terrified, according to accounts handed down from the participants. Alice Barnett recalled her mother, Eliza, who was raised by her grandmother, Florida-born Cornelia Perryman, repeating stories of the trip: "She says they were so scared they had to put cloths on the children's mouths so they wouldn't cry out."

The fleeing group was sighted near Eagle Pass, known originally as Paso del Aguila or the Pass of the Eagle, a dusty town of tents and makeshift buildings housing desperados, outlaws, gamblers, prostitutes, saloon keepers, and, worse of all, slave catchers. By the summer of 1850, when Rose Kelly's people passed through, the community consisted of 185 people of diverse origins. Across the Rio Grande was the little Mexican town of Villa de Herrera, later known as Piedras Negras.[33] A mile or two farther to the north was Fort Duncan, formerly Camp Eagle Pass, the southernmost fort in the line of U.S. Army outposts built to protect the Mexican border from Indian raids. In an ironic twist of fate, the fort also served as a point of departure for slave hunters traveling into Mexico to seek bounties for runaways.

Jane Cazneau was one of the curious spectators who gathered to watch the Black Seminoles pass through Eagle Pass on their way to the Rio Grande. She had arrived at Fort Duncan with her husband in 1850, the same year the Black Seminoles passed through. Known as a political activist and ambitious schemer and entrepreneur, she wrote under the pseudonym of Cora Montgomery. She also was a crusader for the American Nationalist Movement and decidedly pro-slavery. Cazneau provided a well-known description of the group's passage through the town:

> [Emerging] from the broken ground in a direction that we knew was traversed by any but the wild and hostile Indians came forth a long procession of horsemen. The sun flashed back from a mixed array of arms and barbaric gear, but, as this unexpected army, which seemed to have dropped down on us from the skies, drew nearer it grew less formidable in apparent numbers . . . some reasonably well-mounted Indians circled round a dark nucleus of female riders, who seemed objects of special care. But the long straggling rear-guard was worth seeing. It threw Falstaff's ragged regiment altogether in the shade. Such an array of all manners and sizes of animals, mounted by all ages, sexes, and sizes of negroes, piled up to a most bewildering height, on and among such a promiscuous assemblage of blankets, babies, cooking utensils, and savage traps, in general, never were or could ever be held together on horseback by any beings on earth but themselves and their red brothers."[34]

As they passed through the ramshackle town of gambling saloons, shanties, and adobe huts inhabited by outlaws, slave hunters, and desperados, Rose Kelly and her bedraggled people were reviewed by the cynical Jane Cazneau and a gauntlet of dusty residents. The Black Seminoles could see the winding green ribbon of the Rio Grande in the distance beckoning them onward. At the same time it offered hope of a new home just beyond, the travelers knew that slave hunters lurked in the group of onlookers and word would soon spread about their crossing.

CHAPTER FOUR

El Rio Grande, Rio Bravo, and Rio Bravo del Norte

> Now, women forget all those things they don't want to remember, and remember everything they don't want to forget. The dream is the truth. Then they act and do things accordingly.
>
> Zora Neale Hurston

Early Spanish explorers in Texas and Mexico, believing the Rio Grande to be several different streams, called it El Rio Grande, Rio Bravo, and Rio Bravo del Norte. Regardless of variation in what it has been called, though, over the years its dusty green waters have served as a gateway for bandits, desperados, horse thieves, and political refugees crossing into Mexico. In 1839, ten years before the Black Seminoles fled Indian Territory, some Cherokees fled south across the river after losing their homeland in east Texas during the "Cherokee wars" with Texas forces.[1] Today, the once mighty waters leading to the Gulf of Mexico have been tamed by the need for miles of irrigation canals and reservoirs for farmland. Now the Rio Grande is an entryway for desperate Mexicans, some crossing it illegally, others legally, seeking a better life to the north in the United States. What was it like when Alice Fay's weary ancestors crossed it in its full glory on a hot July day in 1850?

Frederick Law Olmsted, a prodigious traveler in the early 1850s, described in his journal the approach to Eagle Pass and Fort Duncan, both of which were on the eastern bank of the river, opposite the Mexican town of Piedras Negras: "The nearer we approached the great river . . . the more dreary, desolate, dry, and barren became the scene; the more dwarfed and thorny the vegetation, only the cactus more hideously large. Within six miles of the Rio Grande the surface of the ground surges higher, forming rugged hills, easy of ascent on one side, but precipitous on the other."[2]

The Black Seminoles reached the Rio Grande at evening, but, concerned that word was out about their passage, did not cross immediately. They waited for new information and advice from the Seminoles who accompanied them before finalizing their plans. Old-timers have related that they chose to cross at Lehman's ranch, across the river from El Moral and above Eagle Pass, because there were no rapids and crossing was safer. Other old-timers suggested that they crossed at different places. Alice Fay is very certain about the location of the crossing. I recall a particular situation when an old man, a stranger at Seminole Days, suggested another crossing site. Alice became very indignant, dismissing him with her fiery eyes. "*I* tell you where they crossed. That old man knows *nothing*! *I know* 'cause my great-grandmama Rose Kelly told me!" Alice continued to huff at the unsuspecting visitor who finally sulked away.

Writing in his 1842 journal, seven years before the group of Black Seminoles left Indian Territory, another traveler, Ethan Allen Hitchcock, described the Rio Grande as he was ferried across it from Eagle Pass to Piedras Negras.[3] His observations offer an additional glimpse into what Rose Kelly's people faced upon arrival at their destination. He noted that the Rio Grande is very turbid at this particular spot, with a wide sandbar and an abrupt bank forty to fifty feet high with a narrow beach below it. Mexican skiffs waited at the sandbars to ferry passengers across. He observed rudimentary shelters excavated into the banks of the river, with their entrances covered with brush. According to oral accounts, the river was high when the Black Seminoles crossed. Most of the people could not swim, so the two chiefs, John Horse and Wild Cat, decided to build rafts or skiffs as they had when crossing other rivers.

A descendant, Becky (Beckey/*Beka*) Simmons, described the crossing of the Rio Grande to Laurence Foster during one of his 1929 or 1930 visits to Brackettville. Her identity, however, has remained a mystery. Her description of the trip is similar to other versions told by descendants to Kenneth Porter.

Becky recalled,

> Now we were glad that we got away from the American race people [slavers], and we felt that we could be safe if we can get across the river. It was dark and about the middle of the night, so that we had to be a hurrying to get through with the crossing for we were so close to the American race people that we wanted to get away across the river soon. Soon Wild Cat says that he finds a good place. We [women] crossed first then the men crossed after us. There was a skiller (a raft) made out of three logs tied together, which we crossed on. It was a good ride, for the men took long sticks to guide the contraption across the river. I never would forget that time. Children about to cry out because they were sleepy and the old ones scared that they was going to start bawling (crying) out before we can get over. Wild Cat he is fast and quick. He does things quick. The Mexicans did not know that we were there.[4]

It was not an easy passage, according to Dub Warrior. "They had lots of trouble crossing the Rio Grande," he related. "Some couldn't swim. They had to hurry to make the rafts. Some drowned. The slavers were very close."

Rosa Dixon Fay, Alice's paternal grandmother, always the energetic narrator and female warrior, many years later repeated a story told by her ancestors: "Just at daybreak, as the last raft was crossing—the water wasn't dry on the feet of their horses—they saw the troop . . . on the opposite bank of the river; . . . [the soldiers] waved red handkerchiefs and called to them to come back, she announced defiantly. 'Yes, we'll come back all right . . . but we'll come back to fight!'"[5]

A total of three hundred people crossed that day, about July 12, according to Mexican documents. The group included not only Black Seminoles, Seminoles, and Kickapoos, but also Black Creeks, Cherokees, and other Indians fleeing with them. By the 1800s, Mexico was a land of mixed racial groups. A black in Mexico acquired status based on economic contribution rather than race. It is estimated that several thousand blacks were living in Mexico by 1850 when Alice's ancestors crossed the Rio Grande. Flight into the area was prompted not only by the proximity of Texas, but by the sparseness of settlement, which would have made recapture difficult if not impossible.[6]

According to oral histories, among the groups that joined John Horse's people were runaway blacks who were already in Mexico, and free mulattoes like the Shields, originally from South Carolina. Legends also related that Black Creek families such as the Wilsons, Warriors, and Daniels who had belonged to a Creek, Pink Hawkins, were already living in Mexico, speaking a dialect similar to Afro-Seminole. Miss Charles Wilson, one of the Creek descendants, related to Porter, "My great-grandfather, Tony (Toney) Wilson, was a medicine man who dressed like an Indian. My daddy, Billy Wilson, was part Creek." Porter reports that as late as the 1940s the Creek group maintained an independent spirit and wanted the Seminole Indian Scouts Cemetery outside Fort Clark to be titled "Seminole–Creek" rather than "Seminole." Some of the tensions that linger in the Black Seminole group today stem from these Seminole and Creek differences. According to Mulroy, the Neco family of Biloxi Indians—María, Nadra (Laura), and their brother, Isidro—was already in Mexico when Alice's ancestors arrived.[7]

At the heart of the community, though, was the presence of the older Florida-born women like Teener Factor. They resolutely continued to honor traditions of their African ancestors nourished in Florida, repeating stories of their deeds and diasporas, and passing down their religious practices and rituals to generations of women, curating these like well-worn artifacts at the core of their culture.

After the Black Seminoles crossed the river, John Horse traveled to San Fernando de Rosas (present-day Zaragoza) to confer with Mexican officials, and upon returning bore good news for his exhausted people, still fearful of capture when they were so close to the border. They could celebrate, for Mexican officials had promised that they would welcome them and give them title to land.[8] A female descendant recalled the occasion: "They crossed the Rio Grande down to Piedras, Grannie said. They cross over . . . the Mexicans called them all up to the big office and give them a lot to eat; they killed some cows, give them beans, flour and everything and made a treatment [treaty]."[9]

While awaiting official permission from the government to stay in Mexico, the Kickapoos, Seminole Indians, and Black Seminoles separated until they received confirmation of their land allotments. The Mascogos camped at various places, usually near the Rio Grande. Most of them stayed for a year at El Moral, Coahuila, near Monclova Viejo, about thirteen miles from Piedras Negras, but they were soon threatened by slave hunters. Alice's ancestors had anticipated Indian attacks but had not foreseen the constant threat from slave hunters in Mexico. Wild Cat's group settled at San Fernando de Rosas and then on land near the *colonia* of Monclova Viejo. The Kickapoos ended up at Tuillo, near Colonia de Guerrero, at the protected base of the hill, Buena Vista.[10]

All three groups were issued rations—corn, tobacco, sugar, beans, cattle, rifles, ammunition, farming implements, and money to start their new lives. In 1850 the Mexican government also officially gave the Black Seminoles something more lasting than supplies: the designation "Mascogos," a term still applied to the Nacimiento maroon community today. Rose Kelly's people had, for the first time, their collective identity recorded in official documents.[11] Over time, the Mexican government would influence the Black Seminoles' identity in other ways as well. However, the Mexican government had determined specific requirements of Rose Kelly's people before they were settled into their colony at Nacimiento. The Mascogos would agree to be baptized into the Catholic Church and receive religious instruction. Most Mascogos would only give lip service to the requirement to become Catholics. However, eventually, the women did appropriate some of Catholicism's traditions and rituals, which they deemed useful as blended into their own eclectic religious practices. At heart, though, the Mascogos remained Evangelical Baptists led by women with strong roots in African-derived traditions.[12]

Another edict of the Mexican government was the requirement that the Mascogos be assigned godparents and adopt Spanish given names and surnames. The acquired Spanish names and Spanish naming traditions would likewise become blended into the community's African-derived traditions of naming over time. However, the requirement to adopt Spanish names created some confusion in a people that often used only one name, such as the two brother interpreters July and August. Added to the Mascogo naming tradition was the Mexican custom of a child carrying the father's surname, followed by the mother's maiden name.

With the Mexican government's requirement for the Mascogos to take Spanish names, the surname Factor, carried by Rose Kelly (at that time) and her husband Thomas, became González. Of the members of the original Florida-born group, the surname Bowlegs became Bully, and Perryman became Flores. July became Julio. The Payne surname became Váldez. There are differences of opinion on the naming substitutions, for Porter states that Factor became Aldape. The surname Fay became Alvarez. Alice emphasized, "They all had to change names." The Mascogos also adopted the custom of adding the surname of the mother to that of the father.

These substitutions, though, seem to have created even more ambiguities in the Black Seminoles' naming traditions, for they were often assigned arbitrarily, were not translations of the English surname, and were often duplicated.[13] The Mascogos found it to their advantage to use English names when crossing the border. Many Black Seminoles living in Mexico or Texas continue to use or refer to people with both Spanish and English names. This system of multiple names often befuddled me as I sought to ascertain the identities of various people. Alice Fay would discuss different individuals in the Black Seminole community, often using both of their names interchangeably and assuming I knew who they were without informing me.

More than a century before Alice and my conversations, after their arrival in their new homeland in 1850, the Mascogos had barely managed to plant a corn crop before Mexican military authorities summoned the men for a two-month campaign against Indians. The corn crop failed, and the women and children faced starvation alone and in fear as they were still living close to the Rio Grande and Eagle Pass, where vigilant slave hunters congregated. The Rio Grande had not turned out to be the river of paradise either the Seminoles or Rose Kelly's people had anticipated.[14]

Wild Cat was concerned for the Mascogos, for they and the Seminole Indians were still living as allies in many respects as they had done in Florida. He and John Horse, concerned for their families, continued to plead for new, safer land. Mexican authorities finally recognized the danger and in late 1851 granted Seminoles, Mascogos, and the Kickapoos land, four *sitios de ganado mayor*, or 26.5 square miles in the Hacienda de Nacimiento located in the Santa Rosa Mountains at the headwaters of the Sabinas River. The Mexicans gave them seeds and agricultural equipment.[15] Miss Charles said, "They told the Mexicans they wanted land, and if they got some they would fight the Comanche and Apache for them. . . . The Mexicans agreed, and the Seminoles did a fine job for them, they were good fighters, horsemen."[16]

Alice told me, "They look around and they like Nacimiento and that's when the governor gave them Nacimiento."

The Mascogos still were in danger, though, for the Hacienda de Nacimiento was situated at the base of the Santa Rosa Mountains on the south end of a pass that was the main corridor for Indian raids into Mexico. Nevertheless, Alice's people had reached their destination: a new home in Nacimiento, Mexico, and land they could call their own with potential for farming and raising livestock. Although Seminoles and Mascogos lived apart, according to Mulroy, the two allies continued their tribute relationship from Florida, the blacks providing agricultural products.[17]

The Mascogos' time was not their own, though. When plagued by incessant Indian raids, Mexican officials called the men into service with their Seminole allies, enticing them with the promise of money and rations, and with the additional potential of keeping the plunder and livestock captured from the Indians. With the men engaged in long campaigns, the ever-present danger of Indian raids weighed heavy on the women's minds. For safety they banded together in multigenerational compounds of "stick" houses and arbors as they had in Indian Territory and Florida. Rose Kelly and her family, including her daughters Sara and Amelia, her mother Tina Payne, and other children by now—were among these households. The practice of matrifocality, as this way of living is called, was a pragmatic African-derived tradition, well honed by maroon women living in Florida,

Indian Territory, and Mexico in the absence of men. Matrifocal tendencies were characteristic of other enslaved blacks in the Americas. In a matrifocal society, daughters, even when married, often return to their childhood home and reside with a closely related female. The household includes a number of other family members, their collateral ties often spanning several kin relationships and generations. Women created a network of support within their customs of generosity and cooperation that was crucial to their survival.[18]

The women drove their horses and livestock into sheltered enclosures at night for protection. Alice's brother, Henry, on one of my trips to Nacimiento pointed up to the mountains. "You know all those old people would wake up the children and go hide up in the mountains when the Comanche came," he said. Alice's ancestors glanced over their shoulders as they toiled in the fields, fearful of raids not only by Indians but also by slave catchers who regularly organized kidnapping expeditions into Mexico. Dub Warrior recalled, "Well after awhile the Seminole Negro even had to whip the Texas Rangers . . . they teamed up with some slavers and came down illegally. We whipped 'em and they ran back across the Rio Grande."[19]

In addition to homes and enclosures for their livestock, Alice's ancestors learned from the Mexicans how to build acequias—irrigation ditches—to bring water from the Sabinas River and springs to irrigate their house gardens and fields. During the men's long absences, it fell to the women to communally maintain the acequias and to plant, tend, and harvest the crops.

I recall an excursion Alice and I made along the banks of the Sabinas River that ran through the Nacimiento land. She had told me that the old people had lived here. Early observers in the area described riverbanks lined by magnificent trees laden with wild grapevines and ferns clustered in clear pools of water. However, this was not the case when Alice and I visited—there were only dry clumps of topsoil and weeds. Peeking out in places were small pieces of colored glass bottles and sherds of mid–nineteenth century transferware dishes and white bowls. Apparently, the Mascogo women, despite their insularity and in some cases poverty, had access to such wares, probably only a few pieces that also were popular among middle-class families.

Approximately two years after the Black Seminoles arrived in the area, they apparently saw some advantages to moving a few miles downriver in close proximity to the hill of Buena Vista, which provides a backdrop to what is now Alice's ranch, Guadalupe, today. On changing the location of their settlement, Rose Kelly's people left these artifact clues to their history behind. Perhaps the move was for safety from Indian attacks, for many families settled in the town of Nacimiento, building small jacals. They still shared communal farmland. Other land was portioned out for ranches, such as Rose Kelly's where her family raised livestock. On one visit to Alice's ranch, she pointed out the remains of a jacal foundation on the edge of the arroyo, which provided a rugged descent to the springs and creek below from her ranch. Around the scattered rocks of the foundation were pieces of lead-glazed pots traditionally used for cooking *frijoles*, or beans. Alice pointed to a herd of goats at her ranch during another visit and remarked, "You know they had beasts, goats, and horses here. My grandmama Rosa Fay, she lived in town though."[20]

The Mexican state of Coahuila was famed as a slave refuge and word soon spread that a large group of blacks who had settled in Nacimiento, twenty miles from Santa Rosa (Múzquiz), were giving refuge to runaways. Over time, more runaway blacks or *cuarterones* (people of mixed blood) joined the Mascogo colony or came to live nearby.[21] The teenage Rose Kelly may have been the first member of the group to marry in Mexico. She wed twenty-six-year-old, Florida-born Thomas Factor, brother to August, Dembo, Hardy, and July (Teener's husband). Beth Dillingham reports that as late as the 1960s it was customary for the couple to get permission from the bride's mother, in this case Tina.[22] Marriage ceremonies sometimes were conducted with Bibles even though the person conducting the ceremony could not read. A ceremony could consist of something as simple as the groom chasing the bride and catching her. The union of Rose Kelly and Thomas, on the heels of escape from Indian Territory, may have been celebrated with a "jumping over" ceremony. During one of Foster's visits to Brackettville from 1929 to 1930, an elderly lady living there, perhaps the same Becky Simmons he mentioned earlier, reported on the "jumping over" ceremony.

> The occasion of marriage was one of great interest to the community. The whole community attended the ceremony, at which there were two groups of persons, both of which formed a circular line. At the head of each line was the father of each family, or the next ranking male relative. The bride and groom were the next persons in line. The rest of the people in the lines were close relatives of the persons to be married. When the bride and groom were ready for the marriage, a stick was handed to the groom's father, who in turn placed one end in the hands of the bride's father. The groom then jumped over the stick, and immediately afterward, the bride jumped also, and the ceremony was completed. . . . The relatives of the bride and groom always furnished a great deal of food for the occasion, and there was much merrymaking. For the most part, these marriages occurred in Florida. A few were known to have taken place in Nacimiento. No such marriages were known to have occurred in Brackettville. There are only two persons now living who remember when the "jumping over" was practiced. Both of them agree that in later days nobody used the "Jumping Over" Ceremony.[23]

We cannot know what the ceremony might have meant to couples like Rose Kelly and Thomas Factor or their community and why it was continued despite the vast geographical and temporal differences. This ceremony was popular among enslaved blacks and its continuance by the Black Seminoles many years later supports the deep-rooted traditions inherent in their culture. The meaning of the jumping over ceremony has been debated by scholars. Herbert Gutman, a scholar of African American culture, reports one ex-slave's belief that the ceremony guaranteed that the couple would remain married. Gutman suggests that this ritual arose from tension among ex-slaves whose marriages were not sanctioned or legalized by law. Regardless, the act of "jumping over the broom" acquired symbolic importance.[24]

After descendants like Rose and Thomas were united in marriage through the jumping over ceremony, a big feast would have been prepared. Tables set up on plank boards would have been brimming with pots of traditional foods—the staple corn-based *sofkee,* a hominy-like gruel, and *tettapoon*, a kind of sweet potato pie, prepared by a network of close-knit female kin. Women climbed or rode mules up in the rugged Santa Rosa hills behind what was then Rose Kelly's ranch, Guadalupe, to gather palmetto hearts to grind on their wooden metates to make the traditional coontie flour for fry bread, as Alice Fay would continue to do in Nacimiento many years later.

After Rose and Thomas married, Rose gave birth to her first child, Sara, in 1852.

As Alice recalled:

> You know, Auntie Sara was the first baby in Mexico. Then there was my grandmama Amelia. . . . Sara was my favorite auntie. She was different from the other women. Sara was tall—a big woman . . . light too. You know, she named me after her daughter Alice who died. . . . Auntie Sara raised me for three months when my mama Nellie had the chicken pox in Nacimiento, and then I went to live with her until I was a goodly little girl—about fifteen years old. Then they took me to my grandmama Amelia 'cause Nellie was out working. . . . When I stayed with Sara in Mexico she was a *partera*—you know, a midwife. She would go way up in the mountains and help with babies. She didn't have nobody with her, but she wasn't scared—not my Auntie Sara.

A pregnant woman turned to a midwife, usually an older experienced woman, for advice about proper foods to be eaten, medicinal herbs, and how to care for herself. Foster observes that midwives were relatively untrained in the 1930s. The mortality rates were high in Nacimiento, especially during birth or a few weeks after the birth of a child. The death rate was lower if the breast-feeding period was extended. Foster mentions mothers' habit of chewing food for the baby, sometimes until the child reached seven years. When Foster asked how many pregnancies they recalled, many of the women responded that they did not remember.[25]

Sara, at twenty years old, married Charles Daniels (*Chalow*), the son of the Black Creek Elijah Daniels, whose family had preceded the main body of Black Seminoles into Mexico along with other families such as the Wilsons and Warriors. He and his father later served in the Seminole Negro Indian Scouts. After many years of marriage and children, the couple separated. Charles remarried while Sara moved back to Nacimiento, probably to live with her sister Amelia and Rose

Fig. 9. *Right to left* Sara Factor Daniels, the daughter of Rose Kelly and Thomas Factor, at around eighty years old with her niece Annie Cole in Brackettville. Sara was the first child born in Mexico in 1850. Benson Latin American Collection, University of Texas at Austin. Photo by Mary Louise Thompson.

Kelly. While visiting Nacimiento in the 1940s, Porter reported that Sara was living with her granddaughter Mary Griener and John Horse's handicapped grandson. Mary operated a little café and guesthouse that Porter visited. Later, Sara returned to Brackettville, Texas, where she lived for thirty-three years in a little frame house with her niece Annie Cole until she died at age 113.

Sara's legacy to her group was a long line of descendants. Kenneth Porter concluded after his visits to Mexico and Texas in the 1940s that a large part of the population of Nacimiento and Brackettville were Sara's descendants (see fig. 9).[26]

Around 1855, five years after the Seminoles' and Black Seminoles' arrival in Mexico, the Mascogos' old ally Chief Wild Cat died in a disastrous smallpox epidemic. Some of the Seminole Indians then departed for Indian Territory. Although some of the Mascogos were infected, the majority did not get ill. By 1856 the United States finally recognized a Seminole Nation in Indian Territory and the majority of the Seminole Indians still in Mexico moved back to Indian Territory, what is now the state of Oklahoma.[27] For the Mascogos who remained in Mexico, more bad news arrived in 1859 when a Mexican government official rode up one day and ordered them to relocate to the Laguna, home of the valley known as Parras de la Fuente in southwestern Coahuila, an area continually ravaged by Lipán Apache and Comanche raids. The Mascogos did not know it at the time, but possession of their prime farming lands in the Hacienda de Nacimiento was being sought by wealthy landowners.[28] Alice said there was no other option for her ancestors but to leave. "My people had no choice," she stated, throwing up her hands. "What could they do? My great-grandmama Rose Kelly tells me the trip was hard to Parras. They didn't wanna go."

After John Horse complained that his people lacked the necessary resources to fight Indians, Coahuila governor Santiago Vidaurri gave them ammunition and money but warned the Black Seminoles to stay away from the non-Mascogo blacks. With growing resentment, the Mascogos, who were subject to the beck and call of the Mexican government, departed Nacimiento in April of 1859. Alice Fay's ancestor, Felipe Alvarez or Philip Fay, led the group as it traveled three hundred miles south to the Laguna.[29] As usual, the women traveled with few possessions, cooking utensils, and, of course, their treasured wooden metates to their new home. Surrounded by mountains and known as the "Oasis of the Desert," Parras de la Fuente was a way station on the route from Eagle Pass to the gold mines in California. Legends relate that the Black Seminoles' departure from Nacimiento was so hasty that they left their corn crop behind. Alice recalled stories she'd heard of their trip: "The men ride horses and they had wagons for the women and children. But some of the women ride horses too. They sat on the side of the horse [sidesaddle]."

I would hear this refrain about riding horses from the women many times over the years of my research. I began to understand riding horses, as a masculine symbol, was a source of empowerment. The carts or wagons the women normally rode signaled dependency and domesticity.

Rose Kelly was twenty-six years old when she left for Parras de la Fuente with her husband Thomas, her mother Tina, and extended family. According to oral traditions, *cuarterones* and blacks from the nearby black community Rancho del Rincón traveled with the group on separate wagons.[30] Three members of the Gordon family—the runaways Albert, Henry, and Isaac—also are reported in descendant stories to have joined the group in the Laguna. These three men will re-enter this story later through accounts from Isaac's descendant, Genevieve Payne.[31]

Alice Fay has her own version of her people's journey from Nacimiento to the Laguna in 1859. "The Governor wanted someone to get the Indians," she said. "We moved to Nacimiento but then we had to go back to Parras to civilize those Indians. So we was stationed at Parras and stay close and the Indians get bad again. They was wild. That's how we called them. They [the Black Seminoles] . . . had to get up and leave."

The Mascogos and those with them divided into two groups or bands once they arrived at Parras de la Fuente. One band stayed at Hacienda de San Marcos, but the principal community resided in small bands at Hacienda El Burro. No archival documents exist to trace the group's more specific movements in Mexico since the sources were burned during the Mexican Revolution.[32]

An observer, Samuel Jerome Spindle, while traveling on a wagon train expedition near Parras in August of 1861, came across the Mascogos, both men and women gathered for the annual Festival of the Grapes, Fiesta de la Uva. His observations reveal the Black Seminoles' attachment to Indian customs through their clothing.

Spindle related:

> We had just succeeded in cleaning out the spring when we were joined by Gopher John (John Horse) and five of his Negro followers. John is a character out of history as well as in it. . . . He entertained with sketches of his life during the Florida War, as we lay scattered around on the grass. . . . They had left the train for the same reasons that we had. John told us he was then in the service of Santiago Vidaurri [then governor of Coahuila and Nuevo León], that those six Negros would fight 20 Indi-

> ans but the same number of Mexicans would run from five Indians. He evidently considers himself superior to the lower class of Mexicans.
>
> The next day—John and his Negros are still here. They still retain some portion of the Indian dress and have the Indian voice. They speak the English, Spanish and Seminole languages. John has visited New York, Philadelphia, Washington, and Cincinnati and is very fond of talking of any of the distinguished men who showed him any attention while on the trip.[33]

Spindle would have another encounter with John Horse and his company in Parras on August 24:

> One of the first men I saw upon arriving . . . was Gopher John, the Negro whom I spoke of having met on the route to Durango. He was accompanied by many of his men and women who came down to spend the eight days of feasting [during the annual festival of the grapes]. He was making himself conspicuous and really seemed to be looked upon by the Mexicans as their equals. It, of course, naturally followed that the Negros considered themselves superior. The boys told John that I was their captain upon which he made me an Indian speech, called one brother-officer and concluded by saying that he would like to drink with me. I sent and bought him a bottle of Mescal and I think it pleased him equally as well, that I suffered him to drink my share of it. He wore his Indian ornaments consisting of a number of half-moons of silver on his arms and breast.[34]

The same year, 1861, the Mascogos were denied permission from the Mexican officials to return to their land in Nacimiento. By the time Spindle encountered the Mascogos in Parras de la Fuente, Rose Kelly's people had lived in Mexico for eleven years. There were around 350 people in the group now, including non-Mascogo *cuarterones*, although it is uncertain how many of these were accepted into the group. Over the next five years, life became even more dangerous and uncertain due to incessant Indian raids in this part of the country. Dividing up into small bands made the Mascogos more vulnerable to Indian raids; women and children, often working in the fields, were attacked and killed or captured while the men were away. Old-timers who Porter interviewed in the 1940s recalled that the Indians also would ride up and kill or steal livestock.

Jack Bowlegs, who departed Florida and Indian Territory with Rose Kelly's family and kinfolk like Teener Factor, Cornelia Perryman, and their families, lost his family members in a single Indian attack. Black Creek Abbie Wilson lost her son and husband in another Indian raid. Dolly July told Porter the story of her mother crying when her brother died from an arrow wound after a long period of suffering. Indians raided Black Creek Dick Grayson's camp and kidnapped his son, who was later rescued. Unfortunately he died soon after that from wounds suffered in captivity. In the same raid, his brother Bill Grayson lost his wife and children. Pursuing the Indians, the Mascogos fought a heated battle.[35]

These are only the recorded incidents that have been passed down through time in the oral histories of descendants that bear witness to the terrors that Rose Kelly and her people faced. Dub Warrior repeated a story to Porter told by Rosa Dixon Fay about her mother, Clara Dixon, that may have happened during one of these raids. Clara reported that the men departed to fight Indians, leaving the women in a wagon train, under the care of a "handicapped" boy. A party of Indians attacked them and killed some of the women.

As the Black Seminoles struggled with setbacks as a group, Rose Kelly, Alice's great-grandmother, faced her own losses. By the time she was in her late twenties, she suffered a terrible tragedy—the death of her husband, Thomas Factor. According to her daughter Amelia (Valdez, Kelly), who repeated the story of his death many years later, he suffered a wound in an Indian raid and, after lingering on for four or five months, died in great pain. But this more heroic story is contradicted by Nellie Fay, Amelia's daughter, whose version may be closer to the truth. She insisted, "Thomas Factor was not shot by Indians. A Mexican he was working for shot him. . . . Grandmother Rose told me so."[36] Whichever version is correct, Rose Kelly was left alone in Mexico in a matrifocal compound comprised of her mother, Tina, and a number of children with no means of support.

Political strife soon also affected the Mascogos' situation in Mexico, in part instigated by the Mascogos' ambitious military overseer, Santiago Vidaurri, who controlled Nuevo León and Coahuila as a self-appointed governor. Benito Juárez, a reformist leader and later president of Mexico, led the War of Reform (1858–61), a confrontation between conservatives and liberals in Mexico. Juárez championed equal rights for Indians and better access to health care and education. The power struggle between him and Santiago Vidaurri added more uncertainty to the lives of the Mascogos. Vidaurri denied permission for the Mascogos to leave Parras. Adding to their problems was an invasion by the French, determined to claim an empire in Mexico. By 1863, during the American Civil War, they installed Ferdinand Maximilian as emperor of Mexico, and French imperialist military operations began in the Laguna region in 1864.[37] A year later, the French forces burned the Mascogo homes in the Hacienda El Burro. Rosa Dixon Fay, a young girl at the time, recalled the French attack on the hacienda to Porter:

> My brother Toby was in bed with the smallpox when they were burning the house next to us. The soldiers were running from one house to the next with torches, putting them to the thatch. I ran out to find someone to help me move Toby, but they didn't burn the colored people's houses or kill any of them because John Horse, with his son Joe Coon and Dave Bowlegs, went out to talk to them.

According to Rosa Fay, the general said, "I've heard of you and have orders not to harm you. Don't stay here among the Mexicans, where you may be confused with them, but go back to Nacimiento."[38]

Eventually the forces of Mexican president Benito Juárez (Juáristas), led by Gen. Porfirio Díaz, defeated the French imperialists, and they began to withdraw in 1866. Maximilian surrendered in May of 1867 and was summarily executed. The Black Seminoles, with hopes to return to Nacimiento, wanted to reestablish title to their original grant given in 1852. Legend has it that John Kibbetts personally met with Juárez and was granted permission for his people to leave Laguna de Parras and return to their land in Nacimiento. A large group of Mascogos led by John Horse decided to stay in Laguna through 1870, but John Kibbetts's band returned to Nacimiento. Kibbetts's granddaughter, Julia Payne, recalled riding with him and her grandmother, his wife Nancy, away from Laguna.[39]

Kibbetts's group soon encountered problems, for they discovered a large group of Kickapoos and some black squatters now occupied Nacimiento, having moved there during the Black Seminoles' absence. Kibbetts traveled to the former capital of Coahuila, Monclova, to talk with Mexican officials, complaining that the Mascogos not only had outsiders camping on their property, but had been deprived of their original land grant by a duplicitous official. President Juárez finally confirmed the Mascogos' title to Nacimiento in 1866 in a written document.[40]

During the next decade, political uncertainties continued to plague the Mascogos as their land was claimed by outsiders who argued the Black Seminoles had deserted Nacimiento while living in Parras. Meanwhile, incessant Indian raids continued to require the men's services. Smallpox struck the community again. The Mascogos had no choice but to tend their fields and gardens as before but now in desperation, for cycles of devastating droughts invaded the land. Wheat and corn crops failed. The Sabinas and their acequias were dry. Rose Kelly and the other women, or "Sisters," continued to find solace in their age-old traditions, fasting, praying, and reading dreams to prognosticate a better future and keep their community together. One of their taunting topics of conversation was whether their lives would have been better if they had stayed in Indian Territory. But events across the border in Texas would soon change the future of the Mascogos in dramatic ways.

CHAPTER FIVE

Rose Kelly Moves to Texas

> I've thought about men and women, and I always thought a man was bigger and stronger. A man is sensible, and knows more, and he's smarter than a woman. . . . I was that way for a long time until I got gray hair, then I found that a man is way behind and a woman is way ahead, because a woman can do all kinds of hard work too. I found out that they have many sufferings and they can stand them.
>
> Son of Old Hat, Navajo

As their relatives in Nacimiento struggled with droughts, Indian raids, and revolutions, the Black Seminoles who had stayed in Indian Territory were thriving in the Seminole Nation in the 1860s after emancipation. Encouraged by this situation, the Mascogos led by John Kibbetts and John Horse became determined to move back to Indian Territory, with the ultimate goal of removing to the Seminole Nation. First, though, they would have to return to the United States. One thing working in their favor was the attempts by the U.S. military to attract settlers to Texas. These attempts were thwarted by continued, incessant Indian attacks. John Kibbetts left Nacimiento for Texas with the intention of negotiating an agreement with the U.S. Army for the Mascogos to cross over to Fort Duncan to assist in border defense. Commanding officers at Fort Duncan were aware of the Black Seminoles' reputation as warriors and welcomed their request to cross the border. The Mascogos camped at Fort Duncan near Eagle Pass pending U.S. Army negotiations to approve their request. As part of the agreement or "treaty" negotiated in 1870, the Mascogos agreed to serve as scouts in a new army detachment: the Seminole Negro Indian Scouts.[1] This move was predicated on Kibbetts's plan that the U.S. Army officials eventually would grant his people permission to move back to Indian Territory or to receive land in Texas after they concluded their scouting duties.

One descendant recalled her people rejoicing in this arrangement:

> I was just a young girl but old enough to remember when an American officer and some soldiers rode up to my grandpa's house at Nacimiento. I wondered what it meant. He was on a mule, had a flag to show he was friend. He took up that flag and come right to my grandpa's house, say we mustn't fight 'cause he comes friend. . . . Grandpa [Caesar Payne], he put his hand to his mouth like this . . . and he whoop, "Woo, woo, woo!" That's the way he calls the people together. Peoples all come and the man explains he want help with fighting Indians on the other side in Texas, wants scouts for American army. He say he give all the men $25 in silver every month and everybody women and children too plenty of rations. Every child get rations, same as others, good rations. All of us went right away, took our stock, everything.[2]

The Florida-born chief John Kibbetts, now a middle-aged man, still a respected leader in the Black Seminole community, more personally reenters our story here and Rose Kelly's life. By July 4, 1870, John Kibbetts had brought his band across the Rio Grande and assumed leadership of a Seminole Negro Indian Scout detachment at Fort Duncan. The men and their families, about 75 to 125 in number, settled five miles from the post on Elm Creek.[3]

Julia Payne described their excitement about their good fortune in gaining work, new homes, and supplies: "at Fort Duncan they gave us nice wall tents on the hill until we could move down into the bottom and build mud houses . . . we never lacked for rations in those days . . . [we] had so much food we had to throw it away. Every eight days they'd drive up two or three beeves and kill them right there."[4] John Horse's sister Wannah and her children joined the group at Fort Duncan, presumably because of her oldest son Andrew

(Washington), who was a young child when they left Florida and became one of the first scouts.

Among the first contingent of scouts, besides sixty-year-old Kibbetts, was his contemporary Hardy Factor (and Hardy's sons Pompey and Dindie), also born in Florida; eighteen-year-old Adam (Koonta) Fay; and George Washington, Wannah's younger son. The 1875 U.S. Army census lists thirty-seven women and forty-eight children at Fort Duncan. Possibly among them were Adam's teenage wife, Rosa Dixon Fay, and her mother, Florida-born Clara Dixon. By 1871, Kibbetts's group was joined by the Black Creek Elijah Daniels's band, and the number of scouts increased to eighteen. During the next three years other kinsmen who had lived in Mexico at Matamoros, Tamaulipas, and Laguna de Parras joined the group. The number of scouts increased to thirty-one by the end of 1871.[5]

Among the families listed in the U.S. military census of 1875 was that of Rose Kelly. Perhaps she had followed her oldest daughter, Sara, who was married to Pvt. Charles Daniels at the time, to Fort Duncan with the expectation of working as a laundress or cook on the post. The census reports a family of seven, headed by Rose Kelly, who was then around thirty-eight years old, living at Fort Duncan. Included in her household were four generations of women: her mother, Tina, then sixty-five; her own daughter Amelia, who was in her twenties and is Alice's maternal grandmother; and a group of seven children by different mothers: Nancy (age nine), Kibbetts (three), Lizzie (two), and Willie (two).

Amelia was the mother of Lizzie, Alice recalled. "Amelia has a child, Lizzie [*Losi*], and her daddy was Henry [William] Miller or Jesu Pilau," she remarked. "He wasn't Seminole though." Miller had joined the Seminole Negro Indian Scouts as a cook while at Fort Duncan as a young man, so he received rations that undoubtedly were shared.[6]

At some point Rose Kelly's life had taken a mysterious turn. She had dropped her Factor surname by marriage and taken on the surname Kelly (Kelley), presumably because of another relationship. Alice added to the mystery of where this name came from by informing me that Rose's daughter, Amelia, also took on the Kelly surname, as did her daughter, Lizzie. Who was this mysterious Kelly?[7]

Always curious about her people's often unpredictable naming patterns, I queried Alice over and over trying to grasp a logical explanation. Finally, my research led to an explanation derived from Rose Kelly's Gullah roots. Although Porter argues that the Kelly name is a derivation of Carolina or Kelina, it is probably derived from the African-derived Gullah name *Kele*. The most likely candidate is Kelly Wilson, one of the Black Creeks who preceded Rose's people to Mexico. Kelly was a favorite name, used alternatively as a given name and surname (like July and Fay, along with others), typical of the Black Seminoles' naming customs brought from Gullah backgrounds. This system of redundant and reversed given and surnames was maddening to me at first, compromising my efforts to identify various actors in this story. As the inscrutable Alice Fay informed me: "Those old people. They was real tricky."[8]

Kenneth Porter surmised that Rose may have given birth to a child as a result of her relationship with the Kelly whose name she took. Porter had became interested in a 1930 account by J. Frank Dobie, the noted Texas historian and folklorist, about a gold mine and a fourteen-year-old boy named Willie Kelly. Willie, according to legend, mysteriously disappeared after finding gold in Mexico. Porter speculates that Willie Kelly was Rose's son by the mysterious Kelly. Thus, Willie was the younger half-brother of Rose's daughters Amelia and Sara.[9] Alice Fay supported this idea in her recollections while, again, surprising me with another revelation about Rose Kelly's life. Based on her account and Porter's interviews, it appears her great-grandmother had another relationship, with someone else: "Rose takes up with [John] Kibbetts at Fort Duncan," she said. "They had a kid named Kibbetts. Willie Kelly and Kibbetts Kelly, they was Rose's kids."

Kibbetts Kelly took his father's surname as his given name and carried his mother's Kelly surname, another example of the Gullah-derived tradition of alternating given names and surnames. His father, John Kibbetts, was married to Nancy Kibbetts, also born in Florida, and she was very much alive at the time of John's relationship with Rose—in fact, still married to him upon his death in 1887. Black Seminole men still practiced polygyny in Mexico and Texas as they had in Florida and Indian Territory. It was not unusual for a male to have more than one family at one time, even in the same town if he could afford it.[10]

One of the most unusual Black Seminole women, JoAnn (Johanna) July, has a connection to Fort Duncan. She had crossed to Eagle Pass and Fort Duncan with her family in 1871, presumably because her father was one of the first enlistees. JoAnn was a horse-breaker and is the subject of a well-known interview conducted in Brackettville when she was seventy-seven. She was forced into horse-breaking after her father died and her brother ran away. At eighteen she married a scout and moved to Fort Clark. Due to his abuse (he tried to shoot and rope her), JoAnn ran away to Fort Duncan and never went back to him. She knew nothing about housekeeping, sewing, or cooking, but could hunt and trap in addition to riding bareback and breaking horses and mules. The soldiers at Fort Duncan could not believe that a woman was breaking horses and acting like a man. JoAnn said that she was used to "hard ridin'" as she had been chased by Indians during one of her trips to Fort Duncan.[11]

Dub and Ethel Warrior discussed JoAnn one day during one of my visits to Brackettville. We sat on the screened porch of their little house, one of the original buildings on old Fort Clark. They called the building the "camp." When I asked about the name "Johanna" given the woman by her interviewer, Ethel told me, "Her name was really JoAnn, though." It was probably derived from the Gullah *Wanna.*

Dub told me, "Yeah, she was my great-aunt. We called her Aunt Chona. You know she looked just like Rosa Fay." He mused over the identification of JoAnn's three husbands: "I don't know who they were. . . . Old man Adam Wilson taught her to break horses. . . . She used to go to the church and talk about her dreams with all those other women."

A Brackettville old-timer, Alex Longoria, remembered JoAnn: "I called her Miss Juana. She was always with John [July]. When she got older, she became a cook up at the fort. Her husband I think was Jerry Daniels. He was so strong he could knock out a horse with his fists."[12]

By 1875 Fort Duncan was being phased out and the scouts, including some new recruits from Mexico, were transferred to Fort Clark, Texas. Rose Kelly and her large family probably returned to Nacimiento as there is no record of them in the U.S. census rolls at

Fig. 10. JoAnn (Johanna) July, also known by her basket name, Chona, was a horse-breaker. She married three times. One marriage was to the scout Charles (Cobo) July, by whom she had a son, John. She is shown here in Brackettville processing corn with a pestle in a wooden mortar. Prints and Photographs Division, Library of Congress, ppmsc 01144.

Fort Clark during this time. John Horse and some of his people had stayed in Mexico, choosing not to join the scouts. Other Mascogos like Adam Fay and his wife Rosa Dixon Fay, and John Kibbetts and his wife Nancy, began to relocate to Fort Clark in 1875 as it became the Black Seminoles' home base until 1914. During this time, the scouts continued to perform exemplary duty in the Texas Indian campaigns under military leaders like Lt. John Lapham Bullis.[13] They formed a separate military unit of the U.S. Army and re-enlisted for brief periods of time. The men were paid the equivalent of a private's wages and, in some cases, the salaries of noncommissioned officers, but it was difficult for their extended families to survive on the rations provided. One officer, Lt. William Shafer, after a visit to the Black Seminole camp commented, "several . . . persons had eaten nothing that day and none of them had more than a little refuse corn." Some of the scouts were forced to move back to Mexico between reenlistments because they could not support their families.[14]

Fort Clark stood on the easternmost tip of the Edwards Plateau, beside the springs that give birth to Las Moras Creek. The creek, lined by lush groves of mulberry and pecan trees, flows to the Rio Grande twenty miles away. It played a central role in the lives of Rose Kelly's people. They established their village, Las Moras or "the Camp," about a mile from the fort along the banks of the winding creek. There, the Black Seminoles drew on their repertoire of agricultural skills brought from Florida, Indian Territory, and Mexico. They used the creek to irrigate the communal gardens winding around their encampment. Despite a cycle of floods and droughts typical of south Texas, their gardens grew lush on the creek terraces at the same time that their relatives in Nacimiento suffered a siege of devastating droughts.

The houses in Las Moras were typically built by lashing wooden poles together and filling the gaps with small stones, called chink, and mud. They were small, with low doorways and windows. As in Mexico, roofs were covered with woven grass or river reeds. Photographs indicate that on some houses, cloth tarps were stretched across sections of the roofs, presumably to keep out rain and cold winds. The dwellings resembled Mexican stick houses but also displayed stylistic traits like wattle and daub fireplaces attached to the front. These fireplaces were an architectural feature carried over from the Black Seminoles' houses in Indian Territory.

I was curious about the fireplaces because Alice had told me the women cooked outside on open fires, both in Mexico and Las Moras. I later found out that the fireplace hearths were meant to keep the homes warm in the winter. As Alice explained, the members of her family gathered around the embers at night (see fig. 5).

Houses also featured a thatched arbor or *remada*, which was used for storage of saddles and other equipment. Bags of food such as parched corn or dried pumpkin were hung from the top beams.

Fig. 11. A family and typical chink-style house in Las Moras. The fireplace of the house is built of branches daubed with mud and small stones. Among other people, the photograph shows a woman with her two small children in the forefront, dressed in their Sunday best, under the thatched remada or arbor next to a saddle and riding equipment. Institute of Texan Cultures, University of Texas at San Antonio. Courtesy of Warren H. Outlaw.

Families ate and slept under the arbors in warm weather, just as their Kickapoo neighbors in Mexico continue to do today.[15] Typically the wooden mortar and pestle used by the females would be leaning against the house next to a flat pole bench. Water was stored in a wooden barrel, and some food was stored in tins.

The 1902 U.S. Army survey map of the fort provides some details of the Black Seminoles' camp, Las Moras. The map, photographs, and descendant stories indicate that in some cases the houses were clustered in a compound, sometimes connected by one or more crude brush arbors. The camp was composed of these groups of extended families of related kin and adopted members. The clear, shallow waters of Las Moras Creek wound their way around these residents' communal fields of corn, melons, squashes, sugarcane, and rice that flourished on the creek's black loam terraces. Rose Kelly's

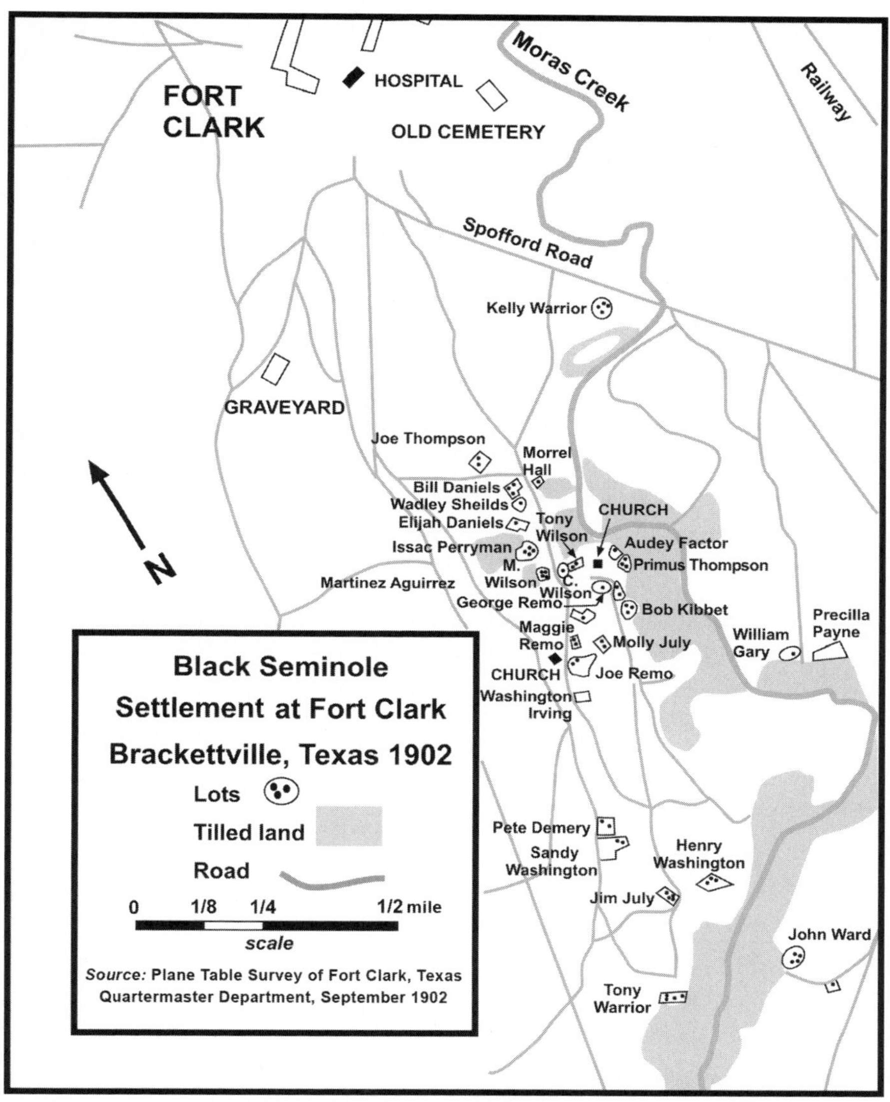

Map 2. Spellings are according to the 1902 survey.

Fig. 12. U.S. Army Third Texas Infantry soldiers stationed at Fort Clark during the Spanish-American War in 1898 join a possible Fourth of July celebration with members of the Black Seminole community. The musicians play guitars, banjos, harmonicas, and tambourines. Seated in the front is Prymus Thompson, ancestor of Ben Thompson, father of Nancy Williams and Ophelia Benson. Prymus joined the scouts in 1877 and served several enlistments until 1889. In the background is Leah Perryman, wearing a festive straw hat, accompanied by her husband Isaac. Institute of Texan Cultures, University of Texas at San Antonio. Courtesy of Sandra Gay Kinney, Emily Eggleston (Williams), and Joetta Knight.

descendants gathered water there in oak barrels that they loaded onto mule-driven carts, and they drove cattle across the banks of the creek to feed on the Fort Clark land. Descendants said the community congregated on the cool green banks to have picnics, witness joyous baptisms, and join in musical events.

I had the unexpected opportunity to visit the old site of Las Moras at Fort Clark in the summer of 2009. My guide was Russell Nowell, the president of the Fort Clark Historical Society at that time. Guided by the 1902 map of the village, we attempted to locate some of the house foundations in the thick brush and five-foot-high cactus clumps that flourish on the rich, anthropogenic soils typical of human living residues. We drove over vestiges of an ancient Indian campground, scattered with broken pieces of chert and mounds of burned rocks characteristic of a cooking process that the Mascogos still practice in Mexico. A plant such as *sotol* was placed in a pit, covered with hot rocks and dirt, and left to cook overnight, after which the starchy root was processed into flour.

Traces of the long irrigation ditches leading from the creek that the Black Seminoles maintained to water their fields were still evident. Huge, enveloping oak trees formed a shaded canopy over what were the rock foundations of the jacal homes. I examined the ruins of the house Molly Perryman (also known as Maggie July) lived in for a few artifacts that could offer clues to her life. The thirty-six-year-old Molly was the widow of John July, a scout who had died in 1900. Later, Molly married scout Ignacio Perryman. Molly had lived at Fort Duncan as a young woman in the 1870s. Although her maiden name was Bowlegs, she had been a member of John Kibbetts's extended household, and, according to Dub Warrior, she was married from Kibbetts's house. Included in her household according to the 1900 U.S. census were her children Laura, Annie, and Pompey; other extended family members had Spanish surnames.

Broken glass bottles and small sherds of dishes and kitchenwares provided evidence of women's household activities and remnants of treasured objects in Molly's home. Nearby, one of the ancient oaks was decorated with a large, heart-shaped cutout, perhaps fashioned by a young man to impress his sweetheart, lending pathos to the scene. Outlines of latrines were detectable; one depression was decorated with a large wagon spoke. A stock tank carved out of bedrock and a corral indicated by a row of upright wooden stakes conjured up images of cows and goats herded through the compounds and over the creek. My guide showed me the location on the creek where they crossed. I was disappointed to learn that the foundation of one of the old chink churches shown on the 1902 U.S. quartermaster plane table survey map lay under the manicured Fort Clark Springs Golf Course.

The 1902 map of Las Moras shows Theresa Wilson's household next to her sister Molly's. Theresa (Cressy/*Kresi*) Wilson, fondly remembered by Alice Fay and Genevieve Payne, is listed as a household head in the 1900 U.S. census. At forty years old, she was still listed as a household head in the 1910 census.

Fig. 13. Annie July, daughter of Molly (July) Perryman and her first husband, scout John July, poses with a basket of flowers next to a large doll, also holding a basket of flowers. The scene is similar to the occasion when Rosa Fay's little girls, Sally and Clary, admired Vida McKellar's doll, Sunflower. Institute of Texan Cultures, University of Texas at San Antonio. Courtesy of Alice Daniels Barnett.

The compound of twenty-eight-year-old Margaret (Maggie/Rena) Remo is also shown on the 1902 survey map near Molly's home. In the 1900 census Margaret is listed as married to Joe Remo, a Black Creek descendant and scout, with three dependents. However, on the map he has a separate household. Between the Remo households lay the second Baptist church in the camp, east of the creek. Rena was also married to Jim July, Rebecca's brother, at one time.

Precilla (Silla) Payne also headed up a household, and the map shows that she had extensive fields that followed the curves of the creek.

John Kibbetts's son, Robert (Bob)—a half-brother to Kibbetts Kelly, John's son with Rose Kelly—headed up a large compound composed of extended family members as well. In 1902 he was married to Phyllis, a well-known reader of dreams, one of three daughters of a Biloxi Indian woman, Nadra (Laura/Nedra) Wilson, who married Adam. Oral histories relate the story of Nadra and her sister María Neco, who were in Mexico and joined the Black Seminole group (see fig. 14). The two women and their brother, Isidro, were Biloxi Indians, purportedly the only survivors of the tribe that had lived in Mississippi. Penny Factor told Porter in the 1940s that "the rest of the tribe join hands and walk into the Red River and drown they selves—all except Willy Wilson's mother [Nadra] and her sister [María] and brother." According to legends, when the Biloxi had to leave their homes they buried gold at the foot of trees and marked the spot with an ax.[16]

Nadra married the scout Adam (Ned) Wilson. María moved to Mexico, and their brother, Isidro, deserted the scouts in 1880 and returned to Mexico. According to Dub Warrior, "When John Horse left for Mexico he didn't have enough money to go. He stayed with María and her husband Iglesias. They gave him money to continue the trip. You know Alice Fay is a relative of Iglesias."

Nadra's daughter Leah (Lear) and her husband Isaac (Isaak) Perryman lived in a sizeable compound with their extended family in the center of Las Moras. Shown on the 1902 map, adjacent to Leah Perryman's compound was the home of her other sister, Mary (Wilson) Shields, the wife of scout John Shields. Nadra was reported as living with them in 1910, by then a widow. Nadra eventually moved

Fig. 14. Nadra (Laura), a Biloxi Indian woman, and her older sister María, wearing a dark shawl, pose in front of their adobe house, probably in Mexico around 1910. Nadra's husband Adam (Ned) is seen in the right margin of the photo wearing a bowler hat. The young boy in front of Nadra and María wearing a hat is Nadra's grandson, Willie. Institute of Texan Cultures, University of Texas at San Antonio. Courtesy of Warren Outlaw.

Fig. 15. Leah (or Lear), second from left, was one of three daughters of Nadra and Adam Wilson in this circa 1890 family portrait. To the right of Leah is her husband, Isaac, a scout and son of Florida-born Cornelia and Sandy Perryman. The couple had seven daughters and one son. Standing to the right of Isaac are two of the daughters, Nellie and Louisa. Lucinda or Lucy, standing to the left of Leah, is a niece. Daughters Della, Carolina, and Edith are not pictured. One of the boys shown here is identified as the couple's only son, Jake, probably the Jacob listed in the 1900 census. However, in the 1910 census, additional family members were noted. Institute of Texan Cultures, University of Texas at San Antonio. Courtesy of Sandra Gay Kinney, Emily Eggleston (Williams), and Joetta Knight.

to Brackettville, where she lived with her children for forty years, reaching the old age of 103.

Although not shown on the 1902 map, the 1900 U.S. census lists Cornelia Perryman, one of the original travelers from Florida, with two sons. The 1910 census reports Cornelia still as a household head, living with her middle-aged son James after the death of his wife, Teresita. Cornelia was raising two grandsons and an eleven-year-old

Fig. 16. Mary (Wilson) Shields, Leah Perryman's sister, daughter of Nadra, circa 1900. She married John Shields, a scout who served from 1894 until the scouts were disbanded in 1914. Her second sister, Phyllis, a well-known reader of dreams, married Seminole scout Robert Kibbetts, son of John Kibbetts. Institute of Texan Cultures, University of Texas at San Antonio. Courtesy of Sandra Gay Kinney, Emily Eggleston (Williams), and Joetta Knight.

great-granddaughter, Eliza Payne, the mother of Alice Barnett, who lent many of her stories to this book.

Cornelia's son James (Jim) Perryman was among the Seminole scouts who were involved in an 1873 raid on Lipán and Mescalero Apaches and Kickapoos near the town of Remolino in Mexico. Among the forty prisoners captured and brought back to Texas was a young Lipán Apache woman, Teresita (Marcia), along with her elderly father, Chief Costillitto (Costilietos). Costillitto had a history of fighting the U.S. Army in his younger days. Charles Daniels, a Black Seminole scout, reported that at Remolino his group captured sixteen women and children and only one male. Of that male, Charles said, "he was as just good as a child because he were not able to use a gun in his hand: just barely could get along with himself—an old fellow. He gave his name as Costillitto."[17]

James Perryman married Teresita in a ceremony performed by the commander of the scouts, Lieutenant Bullis, with a Bible. Known as a good tracker, Teresita later served as a guide for the scouts before dying in 1881 (see fig. 17).

The family compound of the seventy-year-old Black Creek Elijah Daniels shown on the 1902 survey map was probably home to his son Charles, who had divorced Rose Kelly's eldest daughter, Sara, and was living with his second wife, Mary, a Mexican woman.

Jim (James) July, the favorite brother of Miss Charles's mother, Rebecca July, is referenced on the 1902 survey map as well. Married to Rena, he is shown with a substantial compound and acreage located at the southern end of Las Moras near the home of Henry Washington, a descendant of Wannah, John Horse's sister. Jim probably lived here with his aged parents, seventy-year-old Florida-born Sampson and Mary July.[18]

The 1900 U.S. census classifies the relationships of some members of these families as "something other than a direct relationship," which reflects the presence of adopted children, polygynous relationships, and extended families living in matrifocal households, an enduring characteristic of Alice Fay's people. Even though some of the households are noted on the map with male names, it is probable that the households were run by women in the men's absence

Fig. 17. Among the forty-two captives taken in Mexico during the 1873 Remolino raid led by Col. Ranald S. Mackenzie were a Lipán Apache chief, Costillitto (Costilietos), and his daughter Teresita. The Seminole scouts were in charge of escorting the captives back to Fort Clark. Costillitto and Teresita are shown here in the doorway of a Black Seminole home. Holding a rifle, Costillitto wears a tall fur hat over his long braids, a calico shirt, vest, breechcloth over gathered pants, moccasins, and a shell pendant. Teresita wears a long calico dress. A Black Seminole woman stands in front of the home's chink fireplace. Teresita eventually married scout James Perryman, son of Florida-born Cornelia and Sandy Perryman. Legends relate that she later guided scouts on several expeditions into Mexico. Her son Isaac married Leah Perryman and her son Warren (Juan) became a leading figure in the Protestant church in Brackettville. Daughters of the Texas Republic Library.

during scouting trips or when they were working on ranches. During this time, in groups of multigenerational households, women communally tended their large fields, which wrapped around the creek, and shared the fruits of their labor. Women tended their free-ranging livestock—their hogs and goats—and chickens as they had done many years before in Florida. The gardens adjacent to their homes, behind pole fences, were shaded by fragrant fruit trees. As Alice Fay would say, "They all did it together, those old Sisters."

Times were tough, though, for Rose Kelly's people. Lt. F. H. French, the scouts' leader at the time, wrote in his diary that Sergeant July and other scouts on the post were always out catching wild turkeys or other game and selling them to the soldiers to supplement their rations. After picking up the scout wages from the quartermaster at Fort Meyer, Lieutenant French paid off the scouts' debts at the local store before he distributed their pay. While the scouts were away on scouting trips, their wages were distributed to their wives or other female relatives. This probably afforded the women some control over how the meager salaries were spent.[19] The women were expected to clean and check the men's saddles and bridles and other gear, prepare food for them, and pack their saddlebags before they left for their lengthy trips following Indian raids. Women also took in washing, or hired out as cooks or laborers on neighboring ranches while grandmothers took care of their children.[20]

By the early twentieth century, the Fort Clark Black Seminole community clearly reflected its mixed heritage. Only a few families could claim to be "mainline," a term the older people often used, and some elders still do, as a marker of genealogical history, pride, and identity for those who could trace their lineage to Florida on both sides. When Alice introduced me to her friend Gertrude Vázquez, for example, she prefaced the introduction with "Gertrude, you know, is mainline." When I inquired of Alice as to the meaning of the term, she shrugged her shoulders and told me impatiently as if I should have known by then, "Well, they was the old ones, and their daddies and mamas come from Florida. They were Seminole. Both sides. I'm a Seminole." Noting that Black Seminoles often refer to themselves as Seminoles, I asked Alice's brother, Henry Fay, about the meaning of mainline and he told me the same thing: "Mainline people means that they had Seminole mamas and daddies. . . . You know there are few of the old Sisters left—Gertrude and her sisters. Old Seminoles were full mamas and daddies—both Seminoles. Now my people are crossed with Spanish. Most people talk English, but parents never did teach."

Knowing that runaway blacks, Mexicans, and Indians such as Nadra and Teresita married into the Black Seminole group over time, I was curious about the persistent use of the term mainline by Alice and some of the older women today since their genealogy is mixed with that of other blacks and Creek, Lipán Apache, and Biloxi Indian ancestors. When I inquired about the term, mainline, Yvonne Best, a descendant of John Kibbetts, informed me at a Seminole Days event, "You know that my people were mainline. . . . They called the people who weren't Seminole *buckra*."

Porter remarks that the older Black Seminoles distinguished between those born into the community and males who became Seminole by marrying Seminole women in the early 1940s.[21] The former was the preferred identity code. He comments, though, that these criteria were relaxed by the succeeding generation. Certainly recalling ancestral relationships became more difficult over time among the women. Alice's recollections, for instance, cover four generations of ancestors. Kinship, though, even if not always genealogically correct, still appears to serve as an ideal organizational principle in determining interpersonal relationships and stature, especially among the women. Those old Sisters gained power from that knowledge.

While some of her relatives were living at Fort Clark, Alice's paternal grandmother, Rosa Dixon Fay, had moved back to Nacimiento at this time. She shared a home with a passel of children and her husband, Adam (Koonta) Fay, who had left the scouts in 1884 after being one of the first to enlist at Fort Duncan. Although life was a struggle in Nacimiento, it was apparently preferable to the situation in Texas. From 1891 to 1893 she and her family worked on the McKellar ranch. She expressed an uncharacteristic bitterness about her later situation to Porter in a 1940 interview, after she moved back to the States, probably because of her age and for economic reasons. "Colored people have more of a chance in Mexico," she said. "If I had a son who could work I'd go back right away." Porter reported that Rosa, although eighty years old then, did not seem to be a day over sixty, a woman in her prime (see fig. 3).[22]

As Indian hostilities subsided, in part due to the scouts' presence, the future of Fort Clark became uncertain, and the men were reduced to routine garrison duties. Even by 1884 many of the scouts like Adam Fay had been due to be discharged, and only the pleas of sympathetic U.S. Army officers convinced the authorities to keep twenty men in the detachment until 1892. The whole community lived on their meager wages. The remaining scouts again left their families to participate in operations against Mexican revolutionaries and bandits operating on the Texas border.[23]

If Rose Kelly's family returned to Mexico during the 1800s, they would have found that the Mascogos' ownership of Nacimiento was in jeopardy because there was no written title from former president Juárez, who had given them the land in 1866. Mexico also was racked by continued political unrest and revolutions. By 1881 a new owner had claimed the Hacienda de Nacimiento, contending that the Mascogos had abandoned the property while they were living in Parras. John Horse, by now a weary old man, embarked on one last quest for his people. In 1882 he traveled to Mexico City, legends say. He purportedly was accompanied by his son, Joe Coon, and Florida-born Hardy Factor as they ventured to the city to petition their old benefactor, now President Porfirio Díaz, for their land. John Horse never returned, though. He died in Mexico City.[24]

In 1884 the Mexican government ordered the Nacimiento land to be divided between the Mascogos and the Kickapoo Indians who had settled there while Rose Kelly's people were living in the Laguna. However, in the ensuing years, the boundaries of their grant became uncertain, and the Mascogos, not familiar with the machinations of government, arrived at the conclusion that they had been robbed of part of their original grant. Every time the land was surveyed, they believed the boundaries had been changed to their disadvantage. Rosa Dixon Fay proclaimed, "First they cut us off at the wrists, then at the elbow, then at the shoulder-bone; finally at the breast-bone."[25]

Back in Texas, by 1903 the number of scouts had been reduced further, and those remaining performed menial chores such as fixing fences and general maintenance. The women continued to support the military community as cooks, laundresses, or babysitters, but some sought jobs in the nearby, growing town of Brackettville or on nearby ranches. The Black Seminoles in "the Camp" supplemented their diet by hunting deer, pigs, and small game like raccoons, armadillos, and wild turkeys. By 1914 Las Moras encompassed 225 acres with 207 people—113 adults and 94 children. An additional 31 people from Nacimiento were reported to be temporary residents. That same year the U.S. Army determined that the Seminole Negro Indian Scouts were no longer needed and disbanded the unit.

Their earlier unsuccessful attempts to receive land in Indian Territory had been a profound disappointment to Alice Fay's ancestors, but they had held hope that they would receive the land on which Las Moras was located. Despite military correspondence that favored such an allotment, the land on which Las Moras was located was sold. This marked a bitter end to the Black Seminoles' hopes of ever having land of their own.[26] Alice Fay recalled her grandmother Rosa Fay talking about the Black Seminoles' eviction: "Rosa tells me the U.S. military didn't need them anymore."

Miss Charles related, "I was 4 years old then, and I remember them grabbing our things and throwing them in the wagons. . . . We had to get up and get out. We moved down into town as best we could, hoping that something would be worked out. We had to do things we didn't know anything about, like paying rent."[27]

The seeming violation of an illusive treaty promising the Black Seminoles land for their service still imbues descendants' conversations on Seminole Days and other celebrations. The treaty has never been found, and Porter believes that Black Seminoles confused it with land grants to Nacimiento in 1852 and 1866, and therefore the document never really existed. Alice Fay, however, surprised me one day with a version of the treaty story I had not heard:

> Well, there was a Black Seminole lady who thought the reservation was for her. She went to the general and said that the Black Seminoles were fighting and drinking. He sent people to tell them to get off. She thought *she* was going to get the land. The general said if one gets off the land then all get off. So . . . she didn't get the land. But she caused us to lose the land.

The recollections of three Black Seminole women—Ophelia Benson, Nancy Williams, and Gracie Lasky—who lived in Brackettville and are all now deceased, bring color and texture to this story of

Fig. 18. This photo shows one of the abandoned compounds on Las Moras after the scouts were disbanded in 1914. It consists of two chink houses and an improvised lean-to, probably part of a compound. The foundation of another house appears in the foreground. Small stones are visible between the interwoven branches that formed the skeletons of the houses. The roofs of both dwellings are thatched. The chimney is visible on one house. To the side of the houses are the remains of the collapsed brush arbor under which their inhabitants slept and ate. Institute of Texan Cultures, University of Texas at San Antonio. Courtesy of Warren H. Outlaw.

women, the mysterious treaty, and the loss of their land. Ophelia and her sister, Nancy, are descendants of Sara Daniels.

On the day I interviewed them at Seminole Days, Ophelia's face and lovely, kind smile were shadowed by a lavender straw hat. Her speech was colored with vibrant memories. Nancy, her older sister, was petite and dark, and spoke with a low, monotone voice. Nancy had arrived at the Seminole Days festivities in her spiffy black-and-white vintage Chevy Impala, driven there by Dub Warrior. Like her sister, Ophelia, she was dressed to the nines, wearing a hat and dress to match her car. Nancy's daughter Gracie, dressed in blue, oversaw the two older women and added some levity to the conversation.[28]

Fig. 19. *Back, left to right* Alice Fay, Sandy (Fay) Wilson, and Gracie Lasky, and *front* Gracie's mother, Nancy (Thompson) Williams, at Seminole Days in 1997. Sandy's father, Garfield Wilson, fled from Pancho Villa's armies in Mexico and was rescued by Rosa Fay. Nancy Williams and her younger sister Ophelia Benson are descendants of Ben Thompson. Both women are also great-granddaughters of the Black Creek Charles (Chalow) Daniels and Rose Kelly's daughter, Sara Daniels, who is Alice Fay's great-aunt. Photo by Shirley Boteler Mock. Author's collection.

In response to my question about the treaty, Ophelia explained, "You see there was an uprising and they had to leave the Camp [Las Moras]."

The pragmatic Gracie chimed in as Alice, also in attendance, nodded in agreement: "The government put them off because they wanted the land," Gracie said. "We thought we had a treaty. I think we did have a treaty. I may be dead but I think that they will find it. That is our land. It belongs to us Seminoles. There are a lot of things that trouble me that I don't understand."

Ophelia rolled her eyes and looked at Gracie, her niece. "Well, *someone* got the money," she said. "Somebody was smart enough to get the money for the land. But they didn't give it to any of us!"

Gracie looked askance at her. "Shh . . . don't say that!" she said. "When they [the U.S. military] moved off the post, they even dug up all the military in the cemetery and took them to Washington!"

Despite the admonition from her niece, Ophelia continued her story: "We thought we had a treaty. Somebody else was a little bit smart. Some day after I have died, I think they'll find it."

Black Seminoles were not the only ones who were angry at the forced removal from Las Moras by the U.S. military. According to one Brackettville old-timer, Else Sauer, "It was and continues to be my belief that the land was given to the Seminole scouts at the time they were brought to Texas . . . to assist the U.S. Calvary. . . . The scouts lost this land in 1914 when the U.S. entered World War I."[29]

As I visited old Fort Clark on many occasions and looked at the century-old rock houses that cluster around the former military parade ground, I thought of the ghosts of U.S. Army generals Robert E. Lee, William Sherman, Jonathon Wainwright, and Phillip Sheridan, who were once stationed at the remote post. The elegant rock home of Lieutenant Bullis, the scouts' leader for ten years, is still there on the post. Today a small community of civilians has taken the officers' place, residing in the old rock houses surrounding the parade field like soldiers. The houses are now air-conditioned and decorated with American flags and a bevy of outdoor decorations and plants. When I drive around the parade ground on visits I think of Black Seminole women like Rebecca Wilson, who tended the children in these houses, washed their clothes, and cooked their meals.

In the early days of my research the site included a tolerable restaurant. Today, the stables are still there, but travel appears to be mostly by golf carts. Sprawling beyond the houses on the parade field are rusting trailers, modern houses, and apartments, some of which sit impudently on the remains of the Black Seminole encampment, Las Moras. A museum is quartered in the former post guardhouse, with only one section dedicated to the Black Seminole scouts. In one small glassed-in space, I saw an old iron kettle and a finely woven basket and lamented that they were the only material possessions that were preserved.

Some Black Seminoles, disillusioned, returned to Nacimiento following their departure from Fort Clark. Others, like Miss Charles Wilson's family, had already purchased property and made homes in nearby Brackettville. Her family was wealthy compared to the other members of the group, largely because of the enterprising ways of her mother, Rebecca. She was known among the whites in Brackettville as the "Mrs. Vanderbilt" of the "colored" community because her family had a big car and nice house.[30]

Miss Charles related fond memories of her childhood in Brackettville, often shortened to "Brackett," to me at a Seminole Days event. "It was a good life," she said. "We bathed in the creek and cooked in the fireplace before stoves. We cooked Mexican foods as part of the tradition of Mexico. Toys? If we didn't have dolls, they'd carve faces on sticks for us. We played marbles, baseball, made-up games, and used broken plates to play kitchen."

Whether they were children at the time like Miss Charles or adults, a strong sense of community still prevailed in the first decades of the twentieth century as Alice's ancestors spread out to homes in Brackettville or on nearby ranches. Men continued to supplement their diets by fishing or hunting and spent free time playing ball or other sports. Women repeated the traditions of their forebears and maintained small gardens outside their clapboard and chink houses in town and tended goats, chickens, and hogs. Like their ancestors who fended off illness as best they could while traveling from Indian Territory to Mexico, Black Seminole women continued to draw on age-old traditions handed down from mothers and grandmothers. Alice Fay enthusiastically described a litany of the herbal remedies used by her female ancestors:

> We have *curandero* [healers]. We have weed doctors too. We used to take the teas like lemon, mint, *romero* [rosemary or *Rosmarinus*]. You know we used altamisa [*Artemisa vulgaris*, or grass of the San Juan plant] to help when your blood was sweet [diabetes]. We used Palma Christi by mixing the leaves with grease and we put it on the forehead for a headache. *Ruta* [*Herba rutae* or *Ruta graveolens*] we use when we was sick. The

> women, they used weeds like *salseman, senis, sabinis,* for the babies. Corn silk and *ajo* [garlic] was used too. . . . We learn all this from our mamas and grandmamas.

Ethel Warrior shed further light on medicine among members of the community during one of my visits with her: "We didn't have doctors," she said. "We used a spiderweb for a cut on the hand and bleeding. It would close up and leave no scar." She laughed, adding, "We'd use a mud pack from the pig's pen for mumps. . . . We'd kill a polecat or a skunk and use the fat for a baby's cold. Rub the baby down."

However, there were no medications for tuberculosis, the illness that Rebecca July and her daughter Dorothy finally succumbed to in 1960.

Into the twentieth century, women still found time to continue another communal tradition handed down from their female ancestors: quilt making. Alice recalled,

> Well, when they wasn't planting, the women would make quilts all summer long for the winter. We learned from our mothers. No, there was no pattern. We'd use the old clothes we couldn't wear. You know, we'd put it together. There would be women on each side and sometimes we tied it to a tree. You know I took a quilt to Washington [the Smithsonian Folklife Festival] and they give me $500.00 for it. It's all right. They are just too much work for me now. My mama Nellie made lots of quilts—star, lazy, block quilts. When she died I washed them, but they burned with my house when it caught fire.

Ethel Warrior described in detail how the women made quilts. "Every summer the women got together early to make quilts—all summer long," she said. "They wouldn't really use a pattern. They'd just use the old clothes that they couldn't wear—make different colors. The women would get together and have quilt parties. The children would help because school was out."

The women gossiped and shared stories and materials as they worked together on their quilts in their matrifocal households, and taught their daughters the value of thrift and patience.

Louise Thompson recalled making quilts with the women who raised her: Nancy Williams, whose stories about dream reading grace this book, and her maternal great-grandmother, Mary (Mirah) Thompson Bowlegs.

> She [Nancy Williams] was the person who taught me about quilting and I was her helper. I was the person who cut out the pieces and picked out the buttons. She would save buttons from clothing, you know old clothing or whatever, and she would put them in a can. And when we were ready to do a quilting project, and she was deciding on what type of quilt we were going to make, she'd let me do the sorting of the buttons for the quilt. Where they have the cording [tacks] in the quilts, sometimes she would put buttons just as a decorative effect.
>
> Well, lot of the quilts they made during that time that I remember were not made with a lot of emphasis on designs. You see, they were made mainly for warmth and durability, and they were made from whatever materials that were available.[31]

Each piece of fabric sewn in a quilt reveals a history and, like a genealogical record, calls up the name of an ancestor and a story. Stitched together in different ways, pieces of an old frayed and faded dress conjure up memories of a grandmother, or material from a kerchief brings to mind a child. Some stitches are subtle while others are broad and bold. As they worked on quilts, the older women spoke with each other in their Afro-Seminole language. They continued their insular naming customs and they talked of their dreams and pondered over them to find a meaning. Quilt making among these women, like other traditions, was a way of remembering and reinforcing their history and unique identity as Black Seminoles or Mascogos.

CHAPTER SIX

Ancestors in the House

> In these families of coastal Carolina, as in those of so many African Americans, the woman is the central and most stable member of the household.
>
> William S. Pollitzer

Just as measured stitches fastened together pieces of fabric in Black Seminole women's quilts of many colors and textures, a community of Black Seminole women held together the African-derived traditions inherited from their ancestors that invested their identity. One of these traditions mentioned previously was the female-led matrifocal household. This setup in the home served many purposes, but one was foremost: the survival and welfare of the family and community, by creating community-wide networks of support and reciprocity. The matrifocal unit occupied a central position in Black Seminole culture as evidenced by eyewitnesses in the 1930s, 1940s, and 1960s, and my own conversations with the older women. The African-derived practice took precedence over the conjugal union or nuclear family as a norm.[1]

The matrifocal unit could consist of children from conjugal unions but also extended to networks of consanguineous kin, collateral ties often spanning generations and adopted members. The insularity of the Black Seminoles and their endogamous practice of marrying partners within their group according to custom or even cultural pressure in the late nineteenth century and the twentieth century also factored into the practice and makeup of the household. The infusion of new military to Fort Clark beginning in the late nineteenth century also brought new partners for women into the community. Regardless of outside relationships, if a man or woman was a Black Seminole descendant, he or she was considered family and part of this corporate group. As Alice had told me, "They was all family," meaning that they descended from the original Black Seminoles who had departed from Florida.

The group's Seminole Indian allies also practiced matrifocality and were matrilineal in that membership in a family group or clan was inherited through the female line. Matrilocality also was a characteristic kinship pattern, meaning that the offspring of a mother, both male and female, lived in the mother's house, forming a clan group. These consanguineous ties provided a model for alliances and marriages between clans and ordered female labor in communal tasks such as farming. The Black Seminoles were not a matrilineal society, nor did they consider themselves Seminole. However, Dillingham used Porter's works and the genealogies and patterns she gathered in 1965 and 1966 in Nacimiento to propose that, although bilateral, the community still exhibited a matrilineal bias.

Dillingham observed that children would adopt their mother's surname and retain it after marriage. She also observed a matrilineal tendency in inheritance practices in which land and households were passed down through the female line. Porter, though, ascertains that the retention of the mother's surname occurred after the death of a spouse, as with the case of Alice Fay.[2]

The leading role of women in the Black Seminole community also extended to other members of the family and relatives in the Texas and Nacimiento communities, in that they often resided with a closely related female, usually a grandmother. Florida-born Cornelia Perryman's household in Brackettville in 1880 included her widowed son, James, formerly married to the Lipán Apache Teresita, nieces and nephews, and a granddaughter, Eliza Payne. Five generations of Alice's ancestors lived at Fort Duncan in the early 1870s: Rose Kelly, her aged mother Tina Payne, her own daughter Amelia, her daughter Nellie, and various grandchildren and other relatives.

Rosa Dixon Fay, Alice's paternal grandmother, adopted at least six children apart from her biological children while her family barely survived in Nacimiento. However, this pattern of matrifocality also may be attributed to practicalities, considering the frequent absence of the men from Nacimiento for extended periods of time while they were fighting Indians in Mexico and working jobs on ranches. Later in the 1960s, Dillingham reported that the majority of the migrant workers were young men who left their families, only to return once or twice a year for visits.[3] This pattern continues in Nacimiento today with the incessant droughts.

I recall on one of Alice and my visits to Nacimiento that we noticed a young woman with a newborn standing in the shadowed doorway of an old adobe with no windows. She had been watching us. Not wanting to be intrusive, I asked Alice if it would be appropriate to go and talk to her. She replied, "Why, sure, honey, that's OK." The young mother with bundled infant invited us inside. There was only a bare mattress and chair. I asked her where her husband was. She was very shy and told us that her husband was away working. Alice smiled and asked her, "*¿Cómo es viejo es su bebé*? How old is your baby?"

"*Tres meses*," the young mother replied, indicating three months.

I asked Alice and her friend, Gertrude, who lived in the village, how the young woman supported herself. Alice nodded her head and replied, "Her people will take care of her. You know everybody takes care of everybody here."

Gertrude nodded in agreement: "Yes, *mama*."

The matrifocal unit of women, exemplified in Rose Kelly's household of four generations of women, was the stage on which traditions were played out and passed on by women, whether through culinary traditions, their Afro-Seminole language and naming traditions, mortuary customs, or spiritual beliefs and practices. As with the Seminole Indians, this extended household was a corporate group that organized tasks and scheduled and carried out agricultural pursuits.

The practice of matrifocality can be traced to the Black Seminoles' Gullah heritage, for these relationships were anchors for survival among enslaved blacks. Knowledge of family roots and social memory can be identified among slaves living on southern plantations. According to Gutman, "Negroes clearly knew when and to whom they were married and who belonged to their families. . . . Slaves incorporated elements of the traditional lineal orientation of their West African forebears into their belief systems."[4] Jane Landers reports that the blacks living at Gracia Real de Santa Teresa de Mosé in Florida established complex kin networks over several generations in the 1700s.[5] Slaves, whether in informal liaisons or official marriage, often were kept together as a family unit by owners to discourage flight. Historian Kathryn Braund remarks, "There is evidence to indicate that many Creek slaveholders tended to buy, sell, or trade black families as a unit."[6] Keeping family members together made for higher productivity, contributing to stable family relations and preventing slave escapes. Gutman similarly argues that the concept of family among enslaved blacks was imbedded in kinship.[7] For slaves—as for Black Seminoles, whose lives were disrupted by wars and slave hunters—knowledge of family genealogies served as a means of keeping in touch with their history and relatives, and perpetuated their values and traditions. Even after emancipation, kin relations did not disintegrate.

A similar complex of kinship networks of multigenerational families was typical of Rose Kelly's people, and the networks were enhanced by their years of living together among a few families of elite Seminole owners in Florida. The manifests of those departing for Indian Territory illustrate this generational depth: Teener Factor, her husband (and his siblings and parents), and her family representing four generations, all owned by Nelly Factor; Rose Kelly's father, Carolina, who departed with his four siblings, Plenty, Titus, Isaac, and Nancy and their families, one of many sets of descendants belonging to Micanopy; Clara, a baby, who would become the mother of Rosa Fay, and Friday Bowlegs, also owned by Micanopy. These families lived together in Micanopy's village Pilaklikaha in Florida and probably later at Deep Fork in Indian Territory. Carolina's wife Tina and daughter Rose and Bob were slaves owned by Billy Bowlegs, as was Cornelia Perryman and her family. In the Bowlegs family, Jack, his wife Nancy, and one-year-old Davis were owned by Harriet Bowlegs.

These interrelated families had surrendered together in Florida and departed from Tampa on the same boats in 1838 with apprehensions about their future. They had shared the misery of losing children in Florida and in the future would lose more family members in Indian Territory. Together they would choose to leave for Mexico on that fateful 1849 trip with their chief, John Horse, to whom many were related. And later in Mexico they would suffer through devastating Indian raids. Finally, in Texas they would lose any hope of Black Seminole land and a home.

Audrey Lawson Brown's ethnographic work among the members of the modern Afro-Baptist church in rural Florida identifies a similar strong tie with ancestors and matrifocal past. Brown also relates that one's prestige is linked to one's descent from the founding families of the community. Women controlled this status through their knowledge of the genealogy. Descent also determined the inheritance practices and care of children.[8] This aspect of organization is similar to the Black Seminoles' concept of "mainline" status, discussed earlier, in which descent from the original Black Seminole families from Florida is considered an ideal. As Alice related with pride, "Well, they was the old ones, and their daddies and mamas come from Florida. They were Seminole. Both sides. I'm a Seminole." The status is also conceptualized as descent from common ancestors, for ultimately all Black Seminoles descend from a few core families and are related through the practice of endogamy, or marrying within their group.

Ultimately, once Nacimiento was formally granted to the Mascogos by the Mexican government in 1850, another layer of complexity was added to the Black Seminole's multifaceted story. Under restrictions imposed by the Mexican government, the lands could not be sold and were to be inherited only by Mascogos. If a female member of the group married a non-Seminole, as happened with frequency through time, this law insured that the land stayed in possession of the woman and her bloodline. Intermarriage with Mascogo females was and continues to be one way for *mexicanos*, at least unofficially, to obtain Nacimiento land.

However, Dillingham reports that in 1938 the state distributed some of the irrigated usufruct land, formerly communally owned land, to individual families and their male heirs. By the 1960s conditions in Nacimiento had altered, with notable trends in assimilation to Mexican culture. Dillingham noted that half of the adults in Nacimiento classified themselves as African American while the other half considered themselves Mexican, with full rights in the community. Some Mascogos rented cropland to the Mexicans as Henry Fay does today.[9]

In my conversations with Mascogo women, they typically referred to the ranches in Nacimiento as an inheritance handed down from a particular female ancestor. Alice, in reminiscing about Rose Kelly, emphasized, "Guadalupe was my great-grandmama's ranch. That's the way it was. It was Tina's first, then Rose's, then Amelia's, and then Nellie's ranch. They all lived there. Now it's my ranch but Henry runs it."

Ophelia Thompson Benson also echoed Alice's litany: "You know Guadalupe [Rose Kelly's ranch] belonged to Nellie Fay and my grandmother, Mary Bowlegs, Sara Daniels's daughter. They all was family—mainline. Nellie ran the ranch, though. I remember she brought my grandmother some money."[10] Later, curious at Ophelia's revelation that her family also owned Guadalupe, I asked Alice about the relationship between the two families. Alice, of course, with her genealogical template, remembered it well: "Well, their mama Mary Bowlegs came out of Auntie Sara's daughter Nancy. They never did live on the ranch, though."

The 1902 survey map of Las Moras outside Fort Clark also shows men as the primary household heads; however, family makeup was flexible and ever changing in these multigenerational compounds as the census takers observed, dependent on which person happened to be present when the information was recorded. The censuses of Fort Clark also list members of the family household with different surnames. Rosalyn Howard's observations of the Black Seminoles living in the Bay Islands similarly reveal household compositions that change for brief or extended periods of time.[11] Further demonstrating that flexibility, in recent years the men have taken on a more active role in childrearing, which affects who is at home. Brackettville women such as Ethel Warrior have reported that during the summers the children are sent to stay with the men working on the ranches.

The extended matrifocal family provided the basic socialization unit for children, a means for education and guidance. It also made possible assisting older kin and caring for the infirm, promoting mutual welfare of family members, and it worked as an agent of social control.

Foster discusses the extended matrifocal family as a "basic law enforcement agency" in Africa that carried over into the Americas: "It was the strength of the extended family that in part explains the absence of elaborate policing mechanisms and penal institutions in pre-colonial Africa." He contends that this structure was re-created in America as an adaptation to the realities of slave life. This unit acted in cooperation with a larger kinship network of members as seen in the small village of Nacimiento or Las Moras on Fort Clark.[12]

Traditionally, it was common among the Black Seminoles for a child to be sent to live with a childless relative, to provide for the aged female grandparent. The grandparent in turn imparted education, guidance, and discipline to the grandchild, and ultimately a sense of the child's cultural identity and ancestors who traveled from Florida.

Stories about Susan and John Horse tell of their raising other children who were given to them. The couple had been taking care of a little girl when John mysteriously died in Mexico City. According to oral tradition, Susan became so ill that one of her brothers, Sampson July, Rebecca July's father, raised the little girl. One also may recall the story of Julia Payne, daughter of Benjamin Shields and Kitty Johnson, who was given to her grandparents, the old-timers John and Nancy Kibbetts, to raise with the expectation that she would help them as they aged. Upon their return to Nacimiento from the Laguna in 1865, Julia rode on horseback sitting in front of her grandmother.[13] Alice's Nacimiento friend, Gertrude Vázquez, raised Frances, the biological child of her younger sister Lucia. Frances, a quiet and shy woman, was able to take care of Gertrude in her old age and has now inherited her adobe house and property in Nacimiento.

Alice Fay's experiences growing up on her mother Nellie Fay's ranch in Nacimiento in the early 1900s reflect this matrifocal focus. Her life in Nacimiento was immersed in a network of female kin, as she was raised by her grandmother Amelia and great-aunt Sara Daniels while her mother Nellie left to go work, just as many years later her own children were raised by Nellie. The tradition of placing children in the care of older relatives in the matrifocal unit allowed younger women like Alice Fay to be able to barter their domestic skills and work outside the home on ranches or military forts.

Alice attested, "You know, Nellie's mama, my grandmama Amelia Valdez, raised me. You know, she was out of Rose Kelly. Auntie Sara raised me too when I was just a little one when I had the chicken pox. Nellie Fay had to go out and work on ranches 'cause we didn't have no food."

Nellie later returned to Guadalupe to raise Alice's children while she left for Texas to work on ranches. Nellie was an astute businesswoman, as Alice's youngest daughter Effie recalled from her days of living with her grandmother. Her memories point to this age-old tradition of grandmothers raising their grandchildren in later times:

> The *granitas* [grandmothers] took care of the family. My grandmama Nellie took care of a couple of nephews at the ranch. Everybody took care of each other. There was no welfare then. . . . Nellie was wealthy and had tons of guinea hens and ducks and turkeys. Her ranch was full of animals—cows, horses, donkeys, and goats. She always wore white, and she made sure our clothes were clean and starched. . . . I lived with my grandmama when my mother was out working. She always took care of those less fortunate. She would help everybody.

Nellie also exhibited to others the laudable virtue of generosity so characteristic of Alice's female ancestors. Alice's old friend Gertrude Vázquez had fond memories of Nellie Fay that she related to me on one of my visits to Nacimiento. After her husband passed away in Nacimiento, Gertrude fell on hard times because she had no children and no means of support. Gertrude recalled, "Nellie would sit in her chair with her cane in her hand. She used to help me, give me *lots*

Fig. 20. Nellie Fay, Alice Fay's mother, at around eighty years old, stands in front of her adobe house on her ranch, Guadalupe, in Mexico. One of Alice's grandsons remarked, "If you look at that picture, there is my grandmother. Granita [Alice] is the spitting image of Nellie." Institute of Texan Cultures, University of Texas at San Antonio. Photo provided by Mike Davis.

of groceries. I would help her at the ranch. She would *really love me* and was really nice to my husband when he was live. Amen, mama."

Nancy Williams, the eldest of the two sisters I interviewed in the Black Seminole community in Brackettville, told me, "You know Nellie was my godmother. You always stayed on the main line with her. She didn't like people to overstay their welcome. Nana Rosa Fay, too. If it was getting late you had to go home. Mama Rosa Fay raised our daddy Ben Thompson, when he was young."[14]

However, Alice expressed ambivalent feelings about her childhood and being raised by her grandmothers because they were so strict. Sometimes her face lit up and she told me that they were very nice; other times her brow furrowed, and she told me that those old people were really mean: "They was real strict. They was something else," she said. I could see the pain in her face and I pictured her as a young girl living in fear of punishment for a minor infraction. Alice pondered disconsolately over the memory. "Nellie was always helping everybody in the village, but we children was on our own," she said.

When Alice's mother grew old and ill, Alice returned from her work as a cook at Fort Clark to take care of her, fitting her people's tradition of helping the infirm. Alice recalled:

> When my mama Nellie got old, she got cranky. She would say "fix me this—fix something to eat," and then not like it. I say to my mama, "What can I do? Everything I cook I learned from you." Then when she got sick, she says that she hurt me so bad [with whippings] when I was little. She says to me, "You know what I did. I want you to forgive me." I sure remember that. My mama, she wanted to be buried in her wedding suit so when she died I bury her in it. The casket, only thing not in it is her shoes. Nellie told me, "Burn them." I did. She was 103 years old, my Nellie.

Many of the functions of the matrifocal family unit crisscrossed with the practice of polygyny, also characteristic of the Black Seminoles' African ancestors, the Gullah people of Georgia and the Carolinas, maroon cultures, and the southeastern Indians.[15] Among Black Seminole men and women sexual relationships did not always include formal marriage. Because of the practice of polygyny, many of the males had other concurrent families and were not often dependable as providers unless they were wealthy. John Kibbetts, for example, carried home a larger paycheck and more rations than other scouts and perhaps this is why he was able to support Rose Kelly's extended family at Fort Duncan as well as his own. Obviously, his wife Nancy, who also lived on Fort Duncan, knew of this relationship.

Some of the wealthier men in Brackettville even purchased houses for, and concurrently supported, multiple families headed up by women. This polygynous tradition was in part perpetuated by the men's absences for long periods of time and the fact that males regularly crossed back and forth between Texas and Mexico. The convenience of dual passports facilitated multiple relationships—even after the Seminole scouts' disbandment in 1914.

Men used women's economic vulnerability as a way to extract sexual favors, but Black Seminole women also had serial short- and long-term relationships for economic reasons. Women's relationships, however, were never concurrent, nor did they affect the family unit. The male population among the Black Seminoles had dwindled in the early twentieth century due to fatalities suffered in the Indian conflicts in Mexico and that some men returned to Indian Territory, which left women with a diminished marriage pool. Watching their families face hardships without rations or male assistance, women like Rose Kelly at Fort Duncan probably resorted to consensual relationships with men. As Alice told me in her matter-of-fact way:

> Those old people, they were really all running together. The women had different men. Well, the first time [she] would sleep with the same man—you know they didn't mingle too much with the outside men. They stayed with a little group. They married cousins. . . . You know the people didn't have marriage. . . . They just lived together. . . . My grandmama Amelia never married. Amelia had a thing with a Vázquez. Then she had Uncle John and Helen. Henry Miller or Jesu Pilau was another man she took up with. He was a cook—the daddy of Lizzie. He was part Creek. You know that Nellie Fay's daddy is a Mexican German.

Despite the complexity of these kinship ties, the women's conversations revealed to me the importance of recalling genealogical connections, even if the parents were not married formally. The older women I interviewed easily recalled the generationally duplicated names, Spanish names, and nicknames—or "basket" names, as they were called among their Gullah ancestors living in the Sea Islands off the coast of Georgia and South Carolina. Children from different relationships suffered no stigma and were welcomed into matrifocal households of women related by blood or marriage, or were adopted. As Porter observed in the 1940s, the terms "stepchild and "stepparent" were not part of the vocabulary of the "Seminole Negroes." Nor were women criticized for bearing children out of wedlock or conceiving them by different fathers.[16]

Both the men and women I interviewed were uninhibited in talking to me about these concurrent and sequential unions. Indeed, these relationships are often the center of jokes and laughter among descendants. At the same time, these relationships did not distract from the reputations of well-respected Sisters in the community or their inclusion in the matrifocal household. Multiple relationships among both Black Seminole men and women at least in the past were a way of life, and there were no recriminations against the children of these unions. Alice found out as a child that her mother Nellie Fay had another relationship with a Warrior before her marriage to Adam Fay, and that she is not really a Fay but a Warrior:

> My mama, Nellie, got with Bill Warrior before she married Adam [Abram] Fay. He left her, so that's when she married Adam. I was sixteen years old when Nana Rosa [Fay] tells us about this—my brothers George and Roosevelt, too. You know, I have another sister, . . . she went by July, and a brother who ended up in the pen. My daddy, Adam Fay, he got with some woman.

This sister and her family and descendants were considered members of Alice's extended family.

Similar stories flowed from other Black Seminoles: another elder told me the story of her Brackettville grandmother, whose husband brought back a son from Mexico. She accepted the child as her own and the child took her surname. Another descendant related the story of one man who had three families in Brackettville. Alice continued, "You know Amelia married again and then she had my mama, Nellie. Nellie was bright 'cause her daddy was a Mexican German, Leandro Valdez. He had a big family with lots of children in Mexico, though."

One female elder, Alice Barnett, shared her story about her father's relationship with her mother, Eliza Payne, born in Mexico in 1888. Upon the early death of Eliza's mother, Florida-born Phoebe (*Phebe*), Eliza was raised by her grandmother, Cornelia Perryman, also born in Florida and one of the families introduced earlier. Alice Barnett related,

> My papa was the best-looking man. He worked on a ranch in Ozona and would come back to San Antonio to bring money to my mama. She couldn't get a job except washing and cleaning. She had all those kids, you know. . . . Molly, Tina, Happy, Curly, Noble. She sure loved him . . . till the day he died. She was such a good woman. I hardly knew my daddy because he was always gone. . . . When he came to town, he'd bring another woman with him and break my mama's heart. . . . All I remember about those men was that they was like wild Indians—just wild. . . . Then my daddy was shot and it disfigured his mouth. But he still had all those women and had another family. One time my mama went after the woman with an iron. Daddy had to stop her. . . . He had another woman with him when he died.[17]

Offering further insights into her family's situation, and her aunt Tina's life and efforts to help, Alice Barnett commented:

> My mama Eliza's sister, my auntie Tina, was married to Curly Jefferson, a Seminole scout. She left him and moved to Oklahoma with her little son Roosevelt to get a better life. Tina used to send my mama and her little sister Molly packages. Molly was my favorite auntie. . . . You know my mama was so poor. It was hard. My daddy wouldn't even help her with that little shack of a house with all those kids.

The matrifocal households in Nacimiento and later in Texas also incorporated an African-derived practice that Gutman calls the "symbolic kinship," in which fictive kinship bound members together as a community.[18] Special terms of endearment crossed familial lines—terms you hear sprinkled throughout the women's conversations—appellations like "Aunties," "Sisters," and "Mamas" as Alice and Gertrude mentioned on numerous occasions. Foster

Fig. 21. *Left to right* Eliza Payne, mother of Alice Barnett, and Molly Payne Perryman, daughters of Phebe (Phoebe) Payne, granddaughters of Florida-born Cornelia and Sandy Perryman, in Brackettville circa 1920. Eliza married Sarah Daniels's son Sam. Institute of Texan Cultures, University of Texas at San Antonio. Courtesy of Alice Daniels Barnett.

Fig. 22. Tina Payne Jefferson, second from left, poses as part of a musical group in front of the Lone Star Barber Shop in Oklahoma circa 1920, following her divorce from Curly Jefferson. Tina is sister to Eliza Payne Daniels and Molly Payne Perryman, daughters of Phebe (Phoebe) Payne and grandchildren of Florida-born Cornelia and Sandy Perryman. Tina's son Roosevelt, born in Brackettville, is the child standing on the chair next to her. The tall man on the left is probably Tina's second husband, for they are shown together in another photo taken in Oklahoma. Institute of Texan Cultures, University of Texas at San Antonio. Courtesy of Alice Daniels Barnett.

traces these kin-like relationships back to slavery, in which such ties developed as the norm for social relations in order to replace the kin networks from which they were taken in Africa. These collateral kinship relationships created enduring and extensive networks of cooperation as mooring posts for survival.[19] Sidney Mintz and Richard Price have expressed their opinion that these kinship terms were an organizational structure for social relations—part of the slaves' adaptation to replace the blood-related kin networks they had known from Africa.[20] The terms are important as honorifics in everyday social, kin, and status relationships among both men and women even today. "You might not be no relation but that's the way they called each other," one descendant reported.

Irma McClaurin, an anthropologist who spent time among the black creoles in Belize, found that this practice of fictive kinship, also characteristic of maroon cultures, extended to her as a black woman from New York. She was readily accepted by the group, the members of which insisted that she must have had a Belizean ancestor, or alternatively, that her ancestors were from the same place in Africa. However, they came on different ships.[21]

A matrifocal unit tendency continues to be part of the Black Seminole female tradition even today. Alice's daughters, Effie and Carmen, have a grandchild, niece, or nephew living with them from time to time. Alice raised grandchildren in Mexico who, even if from different partners or generations, are very close to each other today.

Thus, Black Seminole identity was like a well-polished heirloom, carried on these disaporas and etched with the names of ancestors, that found a place of honor in the matrifocal household. Kinship, even if not genealogically correct with the passage of time, still serves as an organizational principle in determining interpersonal relationships and prestige. Through deaths, illnesses, marriages, desertion, and divorce, Alice's family reflected other families, who continued the perpetual cycle of mothers and grandmothers raising the children of their own children—a cycle that became institutionalized into a matrifocal unit of cooperation for mutual survival. As Foster observes, "It was an efficient economic mechanism."[22]

As I reflect on my conversations with Black Seminole women, I often regret that I was not able to magically tie all these genealogical links into a coherent whole that encompasses their history in some succinct way. I fashioned elaborate genealogical charts in my mind but then found out the Pompey I thought was married to Molly is not the right Pompey, for this was a popular name, carried down. Or I discovered that there are two Molly Perrymans, two Adam Fays, and two Pompey Perrymans. Dub Warrior and I have spent many hours poring over notes; in his mile-a-minute explanations he often dashed my hopes when I showed him my charts of ancestors. I realize what an impossible task it is to unravel his people's tangled web of hybrid genealogical and cultural connections and relationships.

But I like to think that Cornelia Perryman, Teener Factor, and Rose Kelly, and her mother Tina, lived in close-by matrifocal households and often shared stories of their remarkable journeys, perhaps over a steaming pot of *sofkee* or as they tended their fields of corn together.

As Alice has grown older, her memory still retains a large genealogical scaffold of these ancestral names and how they were related to each other. This retention is a crucial part of her and her people's identity, maintaining these ties with the original families. It is embedded in their culture. Prominent on this scaffold of ancestors is Alice's paternal grandmother, Rosa Dixon Fay. She is remembered by descendants even today for her generiosity and as a spiritual leader among Mascogo women in Mexico during troubled times.

CHAPTER SEVEN

Nana Rosa Fay

Life on a Ranch in Mexico

> Clara lived in a universe of her own invention, protected from life's inclement weather, where the prosaic truth of material objects mingled with the tumultuous reality of dreams and the laws of physics and logic did not always apply.
>
> Isabel Allende

As some scouts and their families—like that of Rose Kelly at Fort Duncan—made their home in Texas in the 1870s and 1880s, others ultimately returned to Mexico. There, daily life interwove tough times due to incessant droughts and local political uprisings with hard work. The women continued to nourish their eclectic religious traditions and raise extended families in matrifocal households. One of the families ultimately returning to Mexico in the 1880s was that of Alice's paternal grandmother, Rosa Dixon Fay. All of the present-day Black Seminole elders remember Nana Rosa, as they call her affectionately ("nana" was a term of affection among the Black Seminoles for addressing elderly females). Dub Warrior recalled that "Rosa had such a pretty, smooth face. She always wore long dresses."[1]

Born around 1856, Rosa was the daughter of Florida-born Clara Payne and the Black Creek Joe Dixon (see fig. 3). Joe Dixon had been one of the original scouts at Fort Duncan in 1870. Of Rosa, Alice recalled, "She was a real little lady. Rosa named [her daughter]

Clary for her great-grandmama, Clara Dixon. Rosa, she didn't want to live on a ranch, though, and lived in the town."[2] Rosa Dixon married Adam (Koonta) Fay, one of the original scout enlistees at Fort Duncan in 1870. By then he was seventeen and she was around fifteen years old. But after twenty-one enlistments (August 1870–August 1884) Adam Fay left the scouts and he and Rosa evidently returned to Nacimiento in Mexico. Eight years later in 1892, he and Rosa and their large family began working on the McKellar ranch.[3] As a result, the story of Rosa Dixon Fay and her family is enhanced through the 1892–94 memoirs of Margaret Maud McKellar (1873–1963), one of seven children in the Australian David Harkness McKellar family.

The McKellars lived in Coahuila, Mexico, from 1891 to 1893. Maud's father had purchased the old Navarro land grant, part of Hacienda de Nacimiento, and other adjacent ranches as an investment, initially intending to raise sheep. The ranch had a long history of owners. It had been passed down from the original owner, Fray Carlos Sánchez de Zavier, to the Navarro family in 1879. The Navarros sold it to John Willet of the United States, and he sold the ranch, consisting of 247,195 acres, to David McKellar.[4] The new ranch property, Hacienda de la Mariposa, lay twenty-seven miles north of Santa Rosa (Músquiz) and about three miles from the Nacimiento community. Maud's memoirs describe the McKellar family's experiences in adapting to Mexico in 1892, when she was nineteen.

Rosa Fay and her family worked for the McKellars over a two-year period. Maud recorded many firsthand conversations with Rosa Fay, her children, and the other Mascogos such as the Black Creek Bruner family, Monday (*Cudjo*) and Friday Bruner, working on the ranch. Rose Kelly's daughter Amelia (Kelly, Valdez) and her family also were employed by the McKellars.[5]

During the McKellars' tenure on the ranch in the early 1890s, the Mascogos were caught in a series of local uprisings. Troops (*pronunciados*) under Venustiano Carranza—president of a nearby *municipio*, and future governor of Coahuila and president of Mexico—were fighting local militias under the ambitious Col. José María Garza Galán. Galán, governor of Coahuila, wanted to be reelected in 1893. He was an unpopular governor and Coahuila ranchers organized an armed resistance to oppose his "reelection." Troops of both sides ravaged the Mexican countryside, looking for any male they could conscript with promises of weapons, food, coffee, and tobacco. The men working on the McKellar ranch were caught in the middle. If conscripted, they were given dilapidated and outdated firearms. As a result, the McKellar family was besieged by Mascogos begging to be employed, even without pay, to avoid conscription by Galán's troops. "You know," Alice said, "some of the men put on dresses so they wouldn't get caught."

Monday and Friday Bruner were among the Mascogos affected by the fighting. "Monday proudly exhibited a bullet hole in his straw hat," Maud wrote, "to show he had been involved in a fight with militias." But Monday also reported their reluctance to be involved in the conflict to Mr. McKellar: "And we didn't know for what we was fightin like that, and there weren't no ammunition, so we just all we lit out and we runned. Yes Sir." Another boy on the ranch was so terrified of being conscripted that he asked Mrs. McKellar if he could chop wood, saying that he was scared that the soldiers might jump out of the trees to get him and that he might not see them coming.[6]

Over time, the McKellars employed several Mascogos before they hired Rosa Fay and her family. One was a washerwoman from what Maud called the "Negro" settlement. The young woman's identity is unknown, but Maud's account of her permits a glimpse into the attire of a young Black Seminole woman at the time. Maud noted that she was "resplendent in a blue and white calico dress adorned with many frills and flounces, a gorgeous erection of a hat, and a very scarlet sunshade to protect her very black complexion." Maud's memoirs also offer evidence of the bias against Mexicans among Black Seminoles. The girl assured "a beautiful hand at washing" and was promptly hired. She had commented that she didn't wash for the Mexicans because "they had no style."[7]

Eventually, the washer girl married and left. Her husband, Mrs. McKellar learned, was in jail in Múzquiz for cattle rustling. Mrs. McKellar then hired another Mascogo, the young Sophy (Sophie/*Soki*/*Soke*) Washington, as a cook, whom she described as quite satisfactory. Sophy was the child of Clara Dixon by Andrew Washington, Wannah's son. Both of Sophy's parents had been infants upon departing Florida in 1838. Perhaps this was a second marriage for Clara. Clara and Andrew Washington are reported in the 1880 census as living in Brackettville with Sophy as a child, so they evidently moved to Mexico later when she was older.[8]

Sophy Washington also left her job as washer woman to marry. Mrs. McKellar then hired Sophy's half-sister Rosa Dixon Fay, who was nearing forty years old, commending her as a "valuable acquisition, . . . a hardworking, industrious little woman."

Maud wrote of Rosa Dixon Fay:

> She had a large family (thirteen children), including several adopted children, who proved an endless source of amusement to us. Once a week they would arrive from Nacimiento . . . Mrs. Fay with two or three of the youngest children perched on one scraggly horse, and her husband (a handyman) or one of the older boys on another with two or three more children, the remainder being left at home in charge of numerous relatives.[9]

The names of Rosa's children reflect those of her ancestors, again illustrating the African-derived tradition of double naming or generational reuse of names. Rosa's daughter Clary was the smallest of her children, according to Genevieve Payne, who grew up in Mexico with Alice Fay and remembers Rosa Fay.[10] Two of Rosa Fay's other children, Sally (*Sele, Sali*) and Adam (Abram), had a different father than Adam (Koonta) Fay, according to Dub Warrior.

Ranch work for Rosa Fay's family involved helping provide the McKellars with food, for which they were paid. Rosa and her family would bring eggs to the McKellars, each one carefully wrapped in corn shucks, like small treasures. The men caught and brought wild turkeys and other game to the Australian family. Undoubtedly, Rosa's family gathered these prized food items to sell while their own meals consisted of a simpler menu of items grown in their gardens or fields. Rosa's children all held some sort of job on the ranch. Sally, the oldest daughter, was placed in charge of the kitchen, which brought with it additional responsibilities.[11]

Maud writes about Sally's ignorance of kitchen matters; all the kitchen utensils bewildered her, as well as the use of soap to wash the dishes—but she added that Sally was quick to learn and soon took over.

Sally told Maud,

> The first time I comed here I didn't know what nothing was, . . . and I was that scared I never said a word but just kept looking round the kitchen at all the things. Then when you all done gone out I picked up the little tin opener, and I done ask Nana [Rosa], "what kind of little spoon am that?" And she told me, "Don't touch child, that a kind of little knife." And then I saw the colander, and I thought for sure some bad person done that; and I ask Nana, "For what they put all them holes in that good basin?" And she told me, "Hush up, child, that ain't a good basin, that just to cook with." And over to de Nacimiento we never washes the dishes with soapy water.[12]

With Sally's job came the bonus of sleeping in the kitchen. It also brought her little siblings into the kitchen when they accompanied Nana Rosa to the ranch. The children saw such a visit as an opportunity to take advantage of Sally's position in the kitchen and acquire food beyond the beans to which they were accustomed. When stores of food arrived at the ranch from Eagle Pass, the children delighted in spilled sugar and dried fruit and biscuits. Sally gave them scraps but reprimanded them when they asked for too much. Three of the boys were often recipients of Sally's admonitions, especially young Adam or Abram, whom she scolded for coming into her kitchen in improper attire. "Abram, take off your hat when you comes in the kitchen," she told him. "Ain't you got nuff sense to know to take off your hat yet?"[13]

Maud's family obviously had trouble understanding the Afro-Seminole spoken by Nana Rosa and her family. Likewise, the Mascogo family had trouble comprehending the strange speech of the Australians. Maud writes about a conversation between Rosa Fay and Mrs. McKellar: "'They don't understand you, ma'am, when you talk polite,' . . . explained Mrs. Fay as she apologized to Mother one day for she had spoken to one of the boys and received only a bewildered stare in reply. . . . 'Make you bow to the lady, honey,' she [Rosa Fay] would prompt them quickly if any of us stopped to speak to the children." Maud described how the children would duck down and draw one foot backward "with a vigorous scrape."[14]

From her new exalted position as a confidant to Maud and her nine-year-old sister, Vida, Sally expounded to them on the "uncivilized" people at Nacimiento who did not understand the English language spoken by the McKellar family and the ignorance of her little brothers. One of the offenders was five-year-old Dickey. Sally warned, "There now, Dickey, Miss Vida don't understand you don't talk good." She confided,

> When I was a little child I never knowed how to talk good, and one day they tooked me to see a lady and she say, "What little girl is you?" and I told him [her] "I dunno ma'am." And she say "is you little Indian?" and I told him "I dunno ma'am." And I told him, "no, ma'am I'se little nigger" 'cause I never knowed nigger was a bad word. And she told me, "no child, you ain't a 'nigger', you're little colored girl."[15]

Sally left an impression not only on the McKellars and her siblings, but on her niece Alice Fay and Alice's daughter Effie. "I sure remember Teta [aunt] Sally," Alice recalled. "She wore long skirts and she wore one of those cloths around her head—like the real old people." Effie has mixed feelings about Sally. "She was really strange—very old fashioned and strict," Effie said. "Even my grandmother Nellie did not fool around with her—especially when she got older."

Besides providing a peek into the work and daily life of the Mascogos during the early 1890s, conversations between the McKellar family and Rosa Fay's on the ranch provide glimpses into the eclectic nature of the Fays' religious beliefs and traditions. Maud McKellar recorded a discussion between her younger sister Vida and Rosa's young daughter Clary that provides insight into beliefs in magic and taboos that permeated the conversations of Alice Fay's ancestors. Little Clary spent a lot of time attending to her hair, Vida observed. In seeing her scissors, Clary exclaimed, "Oh, Miss Vida, let me see if them cute little scissors can cut my hair?" Clary then cut two small tuffs of hair and proceeded to bury them. When asked by Maud as to why she buried her hair, Clary responded, "That's so I know where to find him again, . . . cause when you die you have to come back to earth again, and gather up all your old hair fore you can go to Heaven. And if you don't bury it maybe some get burnt up, and then you be a poor thing walking about hunting and hunting and never go to Heaven."[16]

Hair—its maintenance and stylistic appearance—represented Clary's identity. Her cut hair, according to her people's customs, represented part of her body and if found by an evil person could be used to harm her. Thus, Clary needed to dispose of it correctly. When I mentioned this account of Clary's concern with burying her hair to Alice, she surprised me with her answer: "Sure, my people dig a hole and put the hair in it. Yeah, we put it in a little hole 'cause if you didn't a bird might get it to build a nest. If he did then you would have a bad toothache."

Maud also provides a glimpse into the Mascogos' eclectic religious beliefs. Clary told Vida that when she got frightened she put on her "picture." Vida looked at the small square picture of the Madonna that Sally wore around her neck and asked whether it was meant to keep Clary from being scared. Sally answered, "Yes, m'am; that little picture sure keep you safe from everything. When I gets scared I runs and puts on my picture, and then I ain't scared no more."[17]

Clary's picture is similar to a Catholic scapula—a sort of amulet or relic for protection, usually adorned with an image of the Madonna or a saint. Its use also is similar to the West African practice of wearing a protective amulet called a *sebeh* or *grigr*, except in this case the scapula is probably a remnant of the Mascogos' exposure to Catholicism in Mexico.[18] Maud's conversations also reveal the Mascogo belief in prognostication that carried over into the reading of dreams and the departure of the Catholic priest from Nacimiento. Sally reported to Vida that "we don't have the priest in our church no more; cause he got mad when Clary been prophesying things, so have church of our own."[19]

Clary had "spells" or "fits" that her family attributed to eating mulberries. When Vida inquired about the prophesying, Sally responded, "It was before you came here, Miss Vida, and the times was awful hard then, as vittles was fully scarce, and we just had nothing but beans; and when Clary eats just beans, and no bread nor nothing he [she] gets fits, and then he [she] talk fully strange, all out of the Bible! And one day he [she] had an awful bad fit, and he [she] say there going to be a big flood."[20]

The spells may have been a genetic disposition to epilepsy, an illness that affects the sensory system, causing symptoms such as seeing lights and hearing sounds, and jerking or stiffening of the body. Rosa Fay's younger daughter Mary tried to explain Clary's fits to the curious Vida: "Clary, he eat lots and lots of mulberries fore the rain fall on them, then the wind it blow on Clary, and Clary have a fit."[21] Angry at hearing Sally's continued interpretations of this occasion, Clary retorted:

> Never say nothing bout a flood, . . . just say that all the peoples must take up their things and go to the mountain and pray. And so nearly all the peoples at Nacimiento they took their things and went way to a hill, where we always goes to pray, cause it got a cross on the top . . . the Brunos, Monday and Friday and Elsie and them all . . . and then we had no more vittles, so we comed down.[22]

Sally continued to report on Clary's "fits" and how they affected the presence of the Catholic church in Nacimiento: "And Nana Rosa took Clary to the priest . . . and the priest told her lick 'that child good' and Nana say, 'No, she ain't going to lick Clary when the poor child can't help the fits.' . . . So the priest he say that Nana can't have no more of the church, so we have our own church now."[23]

With the departure of the disillusioned Catholic priest, Rosa Fay's family apparently created their own traditions, fashioned from the multicolored cloth of their diasporas from Florida to Mexico. Sally described their eclectic brush arbor church in Nacimiento to Vida: "It ain't a very good church, cause it just an old roof of trees, with no sides; but we has lots of crosses, and we prays and sings. And we are awfully particular; we have lots of days to fast, and never picks flowers or nothing on Sundays." Sally also told Vida, "We don't have dolls for our church, . . . we has crosses, and when we gets a new cross we puts a lil white dress on him, and goes down to the river singing hymns, and dips him in, and christens him and then we hangs him in the church."[24]

Sunday was a day on which no work was done. Mary reported to Vida that one Sunday some of the children had gone down to the river to get nuts. One brother told on them, and Nana Rosa waited to lick them until the next day after the Sabbath.

Permeating the Fay and McKellar children's interactions—whether regarding Sally's work in the kitchen, Clary's fits, or how good of a church her family had, in her eyes—was the reality of the Fay family and other Black Seminoles' poverty in comparison to the wealth of their employers. Maud's recollections reflect the competitions between Rosa Fay's two little girls, Clary and Sally, to hold and dress Vida's porcelain doll named Sunflower, known for her beautiful hair. In one instance, Vida was playing with Sunflower, and the Fay girls were hovering around, admiring the doll's pretty clothes edged with lace. They fought over who got to touch the precious doll. Sally begged Vida to let her help put Sunflower away and to "tidy up you things." Clary, meanwhile, also implored, "Please give me Sunflower to hold for you . . . I just be awful careful of him." Sally indignantly responded to Clary's request, asking why she wanted to hold Sunflower when she wouldn't hold her youngest brother, baby Sammy. Clary responded, "I don't like to nurse Sammy cause he fully ugly . . . but I just like to nurse Sunflower all day, he so pretty."[25] Maud McKellar observed that, despite their poverty, the children of the Fay family adhered to strict rules of honesty laid down by their mother, Nana Rosa Fay. When anything was thrown away like a scrap of cloth or piece of string that they wanted, the little girls brought it back to the owner and asked if it was really meant to be thrown away. The girls treasured these precious scraps and fashioned hats and mended clothes out of the discards.[26]

The Fay children also invited Vida and her family to visit Nacimiento, providing insight into their celebrations and recreational activities. Sally reported, "Some days when we have plenty of vittles we have lots of fun over there. The peoples cooks and cooks for a long time, about a week. Then they dances and dances and eats and eats and dances for about three days."

Vida inquired of Sally whether they did anything but dance and eat. Sally replied quickly:

> Oh, yes, ma'am, they has kinds of races. Sometimes they has chicken races, and that am fully cruel. They get a poor little chicken, and one man holds it under his arm and gallops off on a horse; and then the rest they gallops too, and they pulls the chicken to see who can get it away. And they pulls that poor little chicken's legs and wings till the poor thing is clean all teared up, and sometimes they pulls the head off. Yes, they does, Miss Vida, the truth. And they won't kill it first, cause one time I had a beautiful chicken, and Isaac [Sally's brother] he say let him have it to race, and I told him, "No less he kill it first; and he say, "No that ain't no fun when the chicken dead." Sometimes when they has races they makes so much noise, and shooting guns, I just gets plumb scared to death, and then I puts my picture [religious medallion] on.[27]

The Fay family's good bounty came to an end after two years of working for the McKellars when Mr. McKellar was murdered in 1893 and the family left Mexico as a result. Perhaps one motive behind the crime was that Mr. McKellar had fenced in his extensive holdings, through which ran the Sabinas River. His fences may have interfered with the watering of stock belonging to Mexican ranchers. Officials never determined the culprit.

When the McKellar family departed, Sally became the recipient of all of the McKellars' clothes that could not be packed due to space restrictions. Sally remarked, "Lordy! If Miss McKellar going to give me much more clothes I dunno to goodness how I'm going to wear them all." Her wise mother, Rosa Fay, replied, "Sally, child, when the good Lord let you have lots of clothes you ought to save them up child. Maybe the hard times come and then you be awful glad that you have so much clothes."[28]

Maud wrote that Rosa Fay's family, along with some of the Mascogo men, gathered to say good-bye to the McKellars as they departed Mexico. Nana Rosa told Mrs. McKellar, "Good-bye ma'am, we won't never forget you alls, though I guess you aren't going to come back to old Mexico no more when you once get to the lovely States." Maud added, "Poor Sally, with a straw hat perched back to front on her head and two or three of our discarded kitchen aprons, one on top of each other, stood looking utterly woebegone and quite at a loss to express her sorrow, till we finally drove off, when her feelings found relief in an unmistakable sound of woe, as she buried her face in her superabundant aprons."[29]

For Rosa Fay and her large family, this departure was a sad occasion indeed, accustomed as they were to the rare amenities and entertainment that the ranch had provided and the Fay children's friendships with the McKellar children. One of the oldest men from Nacimiento expressed the Mascogos' devastation at the departure. He recalled the kindness of Mr. McKellar, who lent the Mascogos wire they could not afford to replace their brush fences and prevent cattle from eating their corn. "Mista MaKellar was the only friend we poor colored folks had—we call him our father."[30]

Sally, like her mother Rosa Fay, later gained employment as a cook on another ranch near Nacimiento. In a later letter to Kenneth Porter, Mrs. Sara (Scott) McKellar reported that Sally, as she grew to be a young lady, received criticism from the community for she had left her husband and taken off with a "Chinaman." Porter noted that Rosa Fay purportedly asked, "Sally, what will your children be?" Sally shook her head and replied to her mother, Rosa, "But I sure do love that Chinaman."[31]

Alice recalled, "Later Sally moved to Laredo, Texas, with her kids."

Maud's journal entries reveal Rosa Fay's qualities of forthrightness and honesty that endeared her to the Mascogo and later Brackettville Black Seminole community. She was eighty-two years old when Porter interviewed her there, a half-century later, in the early 1940s. He observed that her features showed a great deal of Indian blood. "Even in her eighties, she was as vigorous as a woman twenty or thirty years younger," he noted. "She had a hopelessly paralyzed son, and displayed tremendous strength and energy in carrying him and moving him to change his position."[32] Porter expressed pleasure that Rosa Fay knew a lot about John Horse's character and personality. She had a talent for "vigorous phrase" as he put it, because she was outspoken and descriptive in her conversations.

Like other Black Seminole women in Nacimiento and Texas, Rosa Fay lived under difficult circumstances but managed to take on the responsibility of raising both her own family and other relatives in her matrifocal household. She deftly took on multiple roles as cook on the McKellar ranch and religious leader throughout her lifetime, while passing on the traditions of her forebears to her descendants. All the older women I interviewed had fond memories of Nana Rosa Fay as a respected leader in the Black Seminole community. The threads of this continuum of strong women are interwoven into the twentieth century with the appearance of a determined young woman following in the path of her remarkable mother and sister. This woman's leadership continues to have a profound impact on her people.

CHAPTER EIGHT

Miss Charles Wilson, Female Warrior

> I used to want the words "She tried" on my tombstone. Now I want "She did it."
>
> Katherine Dunham

One cannot write about Black Seminole women without discussing Miss Charles July Wilson. Like Yaa Asantewaa, the African Ashanti queen mother in Ghana who led a rebellion against British colonialism, Miss Charles fought battles, but through words and actions instead of with a gun and sword. Miss Charles's mother, Rebecca Wilson, born in Texas in the early 1880s, was the only daughter of Florida-born Sampson and Mary July among eight children. Many of Rebecca's brothers became well-known scouts, from whom she received lots of attention. Rebecca, like her daughter Miss Charles, was tall and willowy, with coppery skin and reddish hair. Rebecca's given name may have been of biblical origin or handed down from her Gullah ancestors' *Beka*. Porter reported that "Mrs. Wilson" was the first Black Seminole he encountered on his first visit in 1941, and he recounted her friendliness and willingness to communicate and provide contacts.[1]

Rebecca only received a grade-school education but was determined that her two daughters—both born in Brackettville, Dorothy in 1906 and Charles in 1911—would go off to high school and college, despite criticism from conservative factions in the community that did not believe that women should go to school. Rebecca also had a son, but the boy, Miss Charles's younger brother, was killed in an unfortunate accident on Fort Clark while running an errand. He fell into a quarry pit while delivering some money and Miss Charles suspected that someone had pushed him and stolen the money he had received for the errand.

Not only was the Black Seminole culture still entrenched in age-old conservative traditions in the early 1900s, but women still bore the burden of raising large extended families in their matrifocal enclaves and putting food on the table while men were away scouting or working on ranches. Children were needed at home to help with the chores and to tend to the gardens and livestock, not to go to school.

When Laurence Foster visited Brackettville in the 1930s, Rebecca was in her prime, forty-nine years old, and a well-known community activist. Miss Charles, whom he did not interview, was around twenty years old and probably away attending school.

I am fortunate to have had interviews and many ongoing conversations with Miss Charles in Brackettville over the years when she was alive and "kicking up," as Alice Fay would say of her friend until her death. Always prim and proper on occasions such as Seminole Days or Juneteenth or for my interviews, Miss Charles usually favored long, bright-colored dresses, white pumps, and a string of pearls. Her thick-rimmed glasses hung on her nose precariously and she often wore a red or salt-and-pepper wig. As she talked, her voice was low but had a singsong quality to it.

Rebecca July started Seminole Days and Miss Charles took up the challenge to continue it. The occasion on September 19th every year is intertwined with her mission of passing on her people's history and her concern that the young people will not remember it. "You know my mama started Seminole Days," Miss Charles said. "It's a chance for everybody, especially the young people, to come out and learn about our history. . . . Everybody comes and has a good time."

Miss Charles and Dorothy were the first Black Seminoles to get a college education. Miss Charles always attributed her success as a student to her mother's persistence. "My mother Rebecca was really the moving force . . . in us . . . going to school," she would stress on many occasions, using words that became a mantra dedicated to Rebecca's accomplishments.[2]

> Some thought she was aggressive. . . . It was the influence of my granddad, Sampson [Rebecca's Florida-born father]. . . . [O]ur ideas were just different. . . . [S]ome others felt keeping family together was more important than sending kids away. . . . Mother was a very good leader, and if they [Black Seminoles] thought she was right they would follow her. The role of women and men in Black Seminole culture . . . it was equal. . . . [T]hey didn't do anything without discussion . . . that was part of the culture.

Always the optimist, Miss Charles reflected on favorable memories of her childhood in Brackettville in many of her interviews:

> It was a good life. We bathed in the creek and cooked in the fireplace before stoves. We cooked Mexican foods as part of the tradition of Mexico. Toys? If we didn't have dolls they'd carve faces on sticks for us. We played marbles, baseball, made up games, and used broken plates to play kitchen. . . . I walked to school with my little lunch in a pack, cornbread and red tea. It was a long walk for a little girl.

When highlighting positive traits in relation to education, she stressed that "it was the Indian in us" that helped her family members be successful. "My mother wanted us to go to school," she remarked. "I guess that was an Indian trait too, she wanted us to have an education, and she wanted the finer things."[3] Interestingly, Miss Charles Wilson's family is listed in the 1920 census as Indian, while other relatives are listed as black.

After the Black Seminoles were moved off of the fort in 1914, women like Rebecca had to find jobs babysitting or cooking for the officers on the post. Rebecca, acclaimed for her cooking, had catered for the soldiers and decided to open up a small café in Brackettville. It was very successful. Miss Charles helped her but contended that she was not a good cook, prone to burning the food: "We had to do lots of work. Everything was too much for me. I couldn't cook. I had to depend on my mama to make corn pudding. I couldn't make it."

Fig. 23. Rebecca July Wilson, Miss Charles Wilson's mother, appears here in a rare photo of her as a young woman. She was born in Texas in the early 1880s. Institute of Texan Cultures, University of Texas at San Antonio. Courtesy of Sandra Gay Kinney, Emily Eggleston (Williams), and Joetta Knight.

Rebecca was also a midwife, in addition to being a successful businesswoman. Miss Charles reported that the other Black Seminoles considered her family uppity. Unlike other families, the Julys had a fashionable wagon to travel in. Miss Charles reported that they had a parlor in their house in which to receive visitors. It had nice wood floors as Miss Charles described it. A photo of her mother, Rebecca, taken around 1900, reveals a handsome young woman posing in a dark ruffled dress.

Miss Charles stressed in many interviews that she didn't start out aspiring to become a teacher. She would laugh at her ignorance of practical matters. "I don't know, but it was something I didn't want to do," she said. "Mother said I was too cranky and she didn't want me teaching anyone's children!" Miss Charles began to babysit children of U.S. Army officers stationed on Fort Clark to earn extra money. She told me that babysitting made her sad because she became too attached to the children, but it did help her to get used to children.

Despite Miss Charles's initial reluctance about teaching, her older sister, Dorothy, set an example for her. Dorothy had been a good student, and she graduated from Huston-Tillotson College (now University) in Austin in 1936. Then she started graduate work at Prairie View College (University) outside Houston. Dorothy later was hired to teach at the Carver elementary school in 1941, the first Black Seminole to do so. All of the other teachers had been African American. In 1942 African American troops were stationed at Fort Clark and the government demanded that a new grade school, with first through twelfth grades, be built to accommodate the new families. Dorothy later taught the seventh and eighth grades at the Brackettville (still segregated) school and became a principal in 1945. Eventually she also became a high school coach in Del Rio and Austin.

Dub Warrior shared a photo with me of Dorothy. In it, she poses with one of her high school classes circa 1948 in front of the old one-room clapboard schoolhouse. A pretty woman, like her younger sister, she appears prim and fashionably dressed in a white suit, wearing white gloves, a straw hat, and high heels. Like Miss Charles, Dorothy was tall and had copper-colored skin.

After babysitting children at Fort Clark, Miss Charles reconsidered her perspective on teaching and began to substitute in the black elementary school. She recalled, "I liked doing this and decided to teach. . . . My mama, Rebecca, convinced my daddy [Billy Wilson], who was often gone working on ranches, to let me go to school and so I did."

Following Dorothy's footsteps, Miss Charles left Brackettville for Austin and finished a degree from Huston-Tillotson College in 1942, majoring in elementary education and library science. Later, she also completed a master's degree in education at Prairie View College and returned to Brackettville. After moving back, she was aware that the "colored" school needed a teacher. Miss Charles knew that by taking the job she would be going against the conservative factions in town who did not believe in education. "[T]he family didn't want me to teach there," she recalled.[4] An additional incentive to becoming a teacher in the community was the fact that her people were forgetting their history. "Nobody wanted to be Seminole," she explained. "We talked funny—that Afro-Seminole—broken language."

Miss Charles soon had problems because many of the children did not attend school during the pecan season. They sold the pecans to earn money. "My mama Rebecca warned me to be patient with the children," she emphasized. "Children had to pick crops, and allowances had to be made."[5]

During his Brackettville visit in the 1930s, Foster observed the lack of education in the insular community, noting, "The vast majority of the older persons have no schooling. Of the seventy-eight persons above thirty years of age, not one has any education above high school, and only one of this group has attained a high school education. . . . Only thirty-nine of the seventy-eight can read and write and they all can speak Spanish and English, although of poor quality."[6] Foster also reported that "American race" women, a term used by the Black Seminoles meaning outside blacks born in the States, had obtained more formal education and had lived in more locations than Black Seminole women:

> Women of the "American Race" people averaged 3.8 places lived in while the Seminole women averaged 2.4 places lived in. It is rather significant to note that 47.8 percent of the Seminole women of Brackettville have never lived in any other place than Brackettville; if we add the town of Nacimiento, in Coahuila, we find that 84.4 percent of them have never lived in any other place than those two villages. . . . Twenty-eight women had not even been outside of the State of Texas except to go to the two neighboring Mexican towns.[7]

After pausing to reflect on her past, Miss Charles often repeated her stories of trying to impress the importance of an education on her community. As she talked, her passion for teaching was revealed in the intensity in her voice:

> As a teacher . . . and I could see that . . . you have to fight with them [Black Seminoles] now to get what you want done . . . they don't see the need. I think that was the problem [they were afraid of education], but then they are growing out of it. I think it's just a Seminole characteristic. . . . One [person] was for progress and the other just wanted to stay with the old ways and we went through a lot.

Miss Charles stressed that she had to find new ways to get the children to stay in school. "We had regular Friday get-togethers, with children singing or doing recitations, storytelling. . . . [T]hey [the children] got to where they could play . . . sports, and it helped school attendance." She laughed. "It worked out, I never flogged anyone! . . . Some children cried, but I felt comfortable. They finally found out I wasn't going to beat them to death."[8]

Even though Miss Charles did not intend to teach English to Spanish-speaking students, she felt compelled to learn Spanish. "Black children came from Mexico not speaking a word of English and the other children would laugh at them and I wanted to hit them on the head," she said.

Lillie Mae Dimery, who would later teach school in Brackettville, recalled, "When I was small and they told me I was Seminole Indian, I was really ashamed of it . . . the way they talked, the Gullah language, I was ashamed of it. . . . I didn't know nothing about the Seminoles . . . but Miss Charles, when we was in school, she would tell us stories about them, and we would say, 'Well, tell us more.'"[9]

Miss Charles revealed with pride that she found some creative ways to teach the children: "I used pictures, a few Spanish words. . . . They spoke the broken language [Gullah] mixed up with Spanish, the Black Seminole creole, like Brer in rabbit stories. Got criticized for it. The elders probably had a hard time. . . . We did a lot of singing . . . they liked to sing, singing in Spanish and English," she continued with intensity in her eyes. "I don't know how I had the patience to do that but I did it." The Black Seminole children from Mexico had more motives to improve their material lives, according to Miss Charles.[10]

After teaching elementary school, Miss Charles decided to serve as principal for two years at the segregated high school in Brackettville. While working as principal she started a parent-teacher organization and a mothers' club. Miss Charles was proud of her accomplishments. "The blacks had their own school, a nice rock building," she said. "Whatever books they gave us were leftovers, but that was all right. We had a pretty good superintendent."[11] Miss Charles's continued efforts to educate the Black Seminole children paid off. She received high marks from one of the former principals of the Brackettville Public Schools. She recalled with pride that the state inspector of schools couldn't believe the good attendance she commanded as a principal at her school. She did not pad the rolls as some principals apparently did to get more state funding, remarking, "I'm too afraid of jail!"[12]

As Miss Charles continued her career, her life witnessed change brought to her community by outside forces. The advent of World War II soon had a profound effect not only on the segregated education system in Brackettville, but also on the Black Seminoles' contact with the world outside the small town. Fort Clark became a home base for soldiers, including the all-black Ninth U.S. Calvary, from 1941 until 1944, when twelve thousand soldiers awaited their deployment to the Pacific. This influx of black soldiers with families created the need for a new, larger school in Brackettville. The U.S. government demanded an integrated school be established with grades one through twelve.

Strife over civil rights had bypassed the Brackettville Black Seminoles, who considered themselves different from other African Americans in that they had not been enslaved. Their isolation from other African Americans had insulated them from direct contact with the problems arising from segregation and Jim Crow laws that were taking place farther from the border in Texas. Miss Charles said that leaving Brackettville to visit relatives in California and mixing with other races as a result affected her and her sister Dorothy's attitude about segregation. But for some Black Seminole residents of

Brackettville, the influx of African American soldiers and families to the community provided the first time that they met outside "black" people. Miss Charles reported,

> We didn't experience bitter segregation in Brackett you know. Brackett just has been a more or less integrated town . . . being so small that they just got to knowing everybody—that colors didn't just make any difference. It was so small you knew whose house you could go to for one thing. . . . Now we could have a funeral and there was no segregation, they would come in this house. . . .
>
> Segregation I tell them . . . we'll just have to accept . . . that's the way it is, that's the way God made us and that's the way . . . the white people seem to want it so to keep peace. We'll just stay you know, you just go along and study just as hard as you can . . . and maybe one of these days it will happen that we can all get to school together.[13]

This lack of discrimination is a common theme in my conversations with Black Seminole women. Porter comments that one characteristic of Black Seminoles is their ease in dealing with whites. The remembrances of Ethel Warrior reflect an idyllic life. An old-time resident, she recalled, "In Brackettville we had Spanish living next door and a white living across the street . . . another one over here. And everybody knew everybody. The children played together. . . . The only thing, we had to go upstairs at the movies . . . and we went to separate schools."[14]

One effect of the infusion of large numbers of new black soldiers was a change in the gender dynamics among the Black Seminole community. The black soldiers not only provided a glimpse of the outside world, but they were better educated and provided a broader pool of possible marriage partners for the women, along with the some financial stability.

Miss Charles reported on the drama that was beginning to unfold in Rebecca July's little café, a popular eatery among the whites on Fort Clark. Miss Charles recalled that when her mother heard about the arrival of the black Ninth U.S. Calvary soldiers, she worried about possible trouble. Some of the black soldiers protested the idea of allowing whites in the café because of their own experiences with segregation. In an animated manner, Miss Charles recalled her mother's response to the soldiers' argument:

> My mother was not a violent person but she grabbed an old butcher knife. And she told them [the black soldiers], "Now look . . . they are coming in here. You can go or stay . . . but they [whites] are coming in to eat. Now you are welcome to stay if you want to but you're not starting anything in here." . . . They said, "Well, we don't want them in here." My mama said, "Well this isn't your place. Now soldiers, you are welcome to come back, but right here I don't have segregation."[15]

Miss Charles laughed. "Well they stayed," she said. "But some of them were a little fearful. It was new to some of the blacks."

Porter ate in Rebecca Wilson's café during one of his Brackettville visits. He remembered sitting and eating at the counter with everyone else, surprised to find that the café was integrated. Later, he held a meeting at Rebecca's café, as he wrote in a letter. Blacks and whites gathered around a table to talk. A white nurse joined the group, and her boss later reprimanded her for her impropriety of referring to blacks as "Mr. and Mrs. So and So." The boss told the white nurse, "We don't call Negroes Mr. and Mrs.," Porter wrote, adding, "The white nurse then replied[d] candidly, 'Well I do.'"[16]

Miss Charles recalled that following her mother's clarification of the rules in her café,

> There was no trouble after that. . . . Everyone was just one color. But the Ninth Calvary broke all the rules of integration and segregation. . . . When the soldiers came [in 1941], well that enlightened people . . . but no problems occurred and we got along fine with them. They just wanted to be soldiers. We just thanked the Lord that nothing happened. The chaplain was a big help because he was black. . . . Some [soldiers] were nice and others were hostile. A couple of stores would not allow black troops in—crazy people—but after a while they relented . . . because the black soldiers had lots of money and they [store owners] said they hated to see them go.

A new elementary school was built in Brackettville to accommodate the new arrivals and integrated in stages, not finished until around 1965.The old school building and adjacent lot were to be taken over by the city. During this time Miss Charles was away visiting some relatives in California. She recalled, "I came back. We had just bought new chairs for our school when the trouble started. They were trying to take them away. . . . You know I had to help all the children get ready for integration."[17]

Miss Charles decided to organize her people to persuade the city to sell the old school building to the Black Seminoles. She pointed out to the city officials that the parent-teacher organization had worked hard and put money into the building: "My mother Rebecca worked very hard to get this place and the other people too, but she was a very good leader and if they [Black Seminoles] thought she was right they would follow her."

"Well, the whites didn't see how the blacks could afford to buy the school. . . . How did they raise the money?" she added, laughing in triumph. "Well, they sold chicken suppers. The bank loaned us the money. It took a number of meetings with the city before they agreed to sell the building to us. I had to talk a lot more."[18]

Miss Charles continued her service in education at Brackettville High School as a teacher and librarian until 1979. Neither she nor Dorothy ever married, possibly because with their college educations and independent ways they set high standards for a marriage partner. "We didn't have time to get married," Miss Charles explained. "There was always another meeting. We did something [with the students and parents] just about every Friday night."

By the late 1900s, Miss Charles was beginning to show the first signs of Alzheimer's disease, but she continued to be a fixture at the annual Black Seminole celebrations. In many of her interviews she began to repeat the same information in her schoolteacher voice, as if on autopilot. She continued to hold center stage at Seminole Days as travelers from all over the United States listened spellbound as she repeated stories of her brave Seminole scout uncles and her life as a young girl in Brackettville. Reporters from television stations and video producers stood in line to interview her about her people, with the little frame schoolhouse where she had taught in the background. In her many interviews she would voice her concern about passing on her history.

"Maybe our kids will suddenly get interested before I'm gone, but as of now I don't see it happening," she said. "The kids don't want to learn about where they came from, they want to watch television."

Eventually Miss Charles had to leave her snug, little frame house in Brackettville. She went to live in a niece's home and later was moved to a rest home in Kerrville, leaving the mementos and photos of her ancestors she had reverentially gathered around her. Every nook and cranny and table of the house was garnished with some little treasured knick-knack or newspaper article she had kept over the years. A photograph of Rebecca had always held a place of honor on the white tablecloth draping her dining room table.

I recall visiting Miss Charles in Kerrville, hoping that she could answer some of the questions I had not thought to ask in previous interviews. She was dressed in her usual prim attire and glad to receive visitors. But the answers to my questions evaded her, and in her authoritative teacher's voice she began to repeat her age-old stories.

One of my times with Miss Charles over the years that stands out was a visit to the Seminole Indian Scouts Cemetery. Dressed all in white and wearing a big straw hat tied with a scarf, she guided me on our last tour down the winding gravel path through the cemetery to her family plots, as if on autopilot. "Let's see," she said as we viewed the graves. "It is mother, sister, William, my daddy, and then my little brother is buried way down there. . . ."

She was distracted momentarily at Dorothy's marble tombstone: "I started this plant with one little sprig," she said. "Look at it now." She bent down to retrieve a vagrant sprout and then proceeded to wander among the other graves, almost ghost-like as her white dress reflected the burning sun. "Let's see, here is my mama's favorite brother, Jim. . . . He lived next to her . . . and there is my granddaddy Sampson. . . ."

Her frail voice trailed off in memories. "I haven't been here to look at the registration book. It's been so hot . . . I need to pick up here." I followed her as she walked over to the guest book, resting on a wooden pedestal. She proceeded to turn the book's yellowed pages, brittle from the incessant sun. Frowning, she said, "We'll have to change this."

Today, the graves of her vibrant mother, Rebecca, and her sister, Dorothy, who passed away in 1960, are overgrown with the progeny of the little sprig—scraggly juniper bushes that drape themselves over the concrete borders. On my last visit pots of faded plastic flowers in glass vases had been overturned and irreverently scattered by the wind.

Miss Charles was released from the murky shadow of Alzheimer's disease in 2006 at the age of ninety-six. She now rests in peace in the Seminole Indian Scouts Cemetery, joined with her loved ones. One of the last speakers of Afro-Seminole, the matriarch of Seminole Days, she was sung to the heavens in the Black Seminole tradition.

I recall a statement Miss Charles made at the 1992 Smithsonian Festival of American Folk Life that provides a lasting tribute to her life:

> Today there are few of us left who know our history and speak our language. It may be that too much time has already passed to get those things back. Some of the young people leave our small community and return to Brackettville only to visit. But perhaps this recognition of who we are and what we have done may stir in their hearts a sense of pride and may move them to learn from us while they can, and they may yet pass on our story to their own children. We have given our loyalty and our skill to our country, and we have contributed to its history.
>
> I can rest now, knowing that this has been recognized at last, and that future school children, both American and Seminole, will learn about the part we have played in the growth of our great nation.

Today Black Seminole children attend school on a joint campus that includes elementary grades, a junior high, and high school. The old school building and grounds Miss Charles fought for so valiantly now provide a venue for Seminole Days and Juneteenth celebrations, due to her determination. Many of the old-timers recall fond memories of attending school there under Miss Charles's tutelage. Descendants from all over the United States return and bring their family photos to display, hoping to identify some of their ancestors and share stories. On those occasions the old schoolhouse becomes a theater for members of an enduring community to pay homage to all their ancestors and to re-create their unique history.

CHAPTER NINE

Those Old People Liked to "Kick Up"

Out of the huts of history's shame
I rise up from a past that's rooted in pain. . . .
Leaving behind nights of terror and fear
I rise into a daybreak that's wondrously clear
I rise, bringing the gifts that my ancestors gave,
I am the dream and the hope of the slave.

Maya Angelou

Most of Alice Fay's life is about remembering, her stories filed in the archives of her fertile mind. As the years have passed she has shared her memories with me, whether at official celebrations, in Nacimiento, or at the homes of her descendants. Many of her stories began to unfold in 1997 during my visits to Kerrville, in the Texas Hill Country northeast of San Antonio, where she lived with her daughter Effie (*A'fi/A'fe*) and granddaughter, Barbara. Effie was working two jobs—as a nursing home attendant during the day, and as a caregiver at night. Effie has the rare ability to care for children and the aged and infirm with grace and a sense of humor.[1] With her diverse responsibilities, she stands as a modern-day reflection of the multiple roles women of her culture have taken on for centuries. Effie is proud of her seven children, most all of whom have achieved the middle-class dream through hard work and opportunities not accorded to their grandmother, or *granita*, Alice Fay.

When I visited Kerrville, Alice would always be waiting for me on the front porch of their little white frame house. I asked her what she thought about while she sat there, and she gave me that little sideways smile, her eyes glowing with the reveries of the past. "You know what I think about," she said. "The old people—going back to Mexico—lots of those things." She confided that she was always curious about her people and their history, but it was not until she was older that she realized the importance of their recollections. She told me:

> You know how I remember all those stories, Shirley? Those old people would get together and talk [when I was a child] and I would listen through the keyhole. My mama, Nellie, would say, "Alice, you sure are tricky." I say to her, "Mama, I just wanting to know how you got here." She would put her arm around us and say, "We suffered—pay no mind to what we say." After she died I thought about all that—what my great-grandmama Rose [Kelly] told me, too.

Many of Alice's memories are wrapped around experiences related to her female ancestors in Nacimiento, where she was born to Nellie Fay in a little stick house in 1916. She grew up on Guadalupe, the ranch of her great-grandmother Rose Kelly, which had been passed down from Rose's mother Tina (Bowlegs), wife of Carolina Payne. As one of the original Mascogos arriving in Mexico from Indian Territory in 1850, Tina's family had been given the land by the Mexican government. Alice's stories upon my visits always were textured with nostalgia about her life in Mexico nestled in the comfort of her female ancestors. She is indelibly linked to this place of meaning, the root of her and her people's history in Mexico for more than a century. To present-day descendants, many of whom have not even visited Nacimiento, the village still stands as a symbol of freedom inscribed in their minds.

On my early visits to Kerrville Alice repeatedly expressed her intention of returning to Nacimiento. Effie told me that her mother once attempted to walk to the bus station, determined to go to the Mexican village, but her family intercepted her. I became swept up in the middle of the drama as Alice often used me as ballast to get the attention of her daughter. On one occasion she announced to Effie,

"Shirley and me, we're gonna go down to the ranch [in Mexico]. Well, right now I am thinking if I had a way to go and fix it up. They say, 'What's you gonna do there by *yourself*?' I say to *them*, 'You don't have to bother *no* one!'"

Effie knew her mother was unhappy in Kerrville and wanted to move closer to her friends and relatives across the border, but finances were a problem. One day, during a visit with her oldest daughter, Carmen, in San Antonio, Alice related the story of how she finally had a showdown with Effie about moving to the Texas border city of Del Rio. Her face showed determination as she motioned me to sit down with her, like a co-conspirator at the kitchen table. "Well, you know I did it," she said. "I rented a U-haul-it. My great-grandchildren helped me. I started packing my things. When Effie comes home she sees all my stuff in the truck. I say to her, 'Effie, I tell you I was going. You see that [pointing to the truck]? Do you believe that? My stuff's in the truck. I'm ready to go.'"

Effie finally got a break on a house in Del Rio where there was room for the whole family. Of course, living within breathing distance of Mexico made Alice Fay very happy with the prospect of returning to Nacimiento. As the years passed, and health problems cropped up, her threats to run away to Mexico became fainter, but occasionally Alice would attempt to engage me in this impossible endeavor.

Determined to find a way to go to Nacimiento, not only to fulfill Alice's dream but to see the village for myself, I commandeered the use of an ancient white van from my university museum, the Institute of Texan Cultures, for a foray into Mexico. I received funding from granting agencies and I also forged a collaboration with the Texas Historical Commission and their staff archaeologist, Michael Davis.

I recall my ebullience on the day I called Alice, still in Kerrville at the time, and told her that I had made arrangements to go to Nacimiento. There was silence on the phone as she processed the idea and then the familiar enthusiastic refrain, "Well, let's go then. Let's kick up." By that expression, Alice meant "let's get going."

On the day of departure from Kerrville in late spring of 1996, Alice was waiting on the front porch, her bag by her side and her big black purse in her lap—a purse that I learned was her constant traveling companion. After admonitions from Effie about minding her high blood pressure, we climbed in the van like co-conspirators and embarked on our journey.

We "kicked up" in the van and headed south toward the border about two hours away. The route from Kerrville to the border became a medium for Alice's narrative about her childhood on the ranch in Mexico and her limited education and its repercussions. The journey also proved revelatory for understanding Black Seminole women's unique roles in their small community, Nacimiento. Through Alice's remembrances of them along the way, we were accompanied by her female ancestors, in spirit. Traveling to Nacimiento was not just an excursion, then—it became a prologue to the historical drama that inspired this book.

Our trip began over a smooth stretch of four-lane highway dotted with monotonous housing developments, gas stations, and fast-food joints trailing out of San Antonio. We drove through a litany of little towns hugging the road—beginning with the quaint Alsatian town of Castroville, located in rolling hills, founded in 1843 by the entrepreneur Henry Castro. The Black Seminoles skirted the edge of the community and nearby Fort Scott Martin in 1850 as they fled Indian Territory to freedom in Mexico.

Next on our road map, Hondo, a farming community founded in 1881, boasts the now-famous warning sign on the outskirts of town, "This is God's Country, Please Don't Drive Through It Like Hell." We continued our journey south through the Texas Hill Country as irrigated fields of corn, cotton, and other crops give way to strands of gnarled live oaks, mesquites, and pastures that surround the town of Sabinal, known for its annual Wild Hog Festival. The town is situated on a section of the former Comanche War Trail, which began on the High Plains of Texas and ended in Coahuila, Mexico. It actually encompassed a number of trails, the southeastern section traveling through Las Moras Springs, near present-day Fort Clark, a landmark in the Black Seminoles' flight to Mexico. Continuing south, one can almost miss the little Alsatian town of D'Hanis. The old town, hidden off of Highway 90, is dominated by the ruins of St. Dominic church and its cemetery founded in 1847, three years before Alice's ancestors passed this way.

Only one hour away from Del Rio is the city of Uvalde—a crossroads of history where the landscape of Texas begins to meet that of Mexico. Fort Inge was established nearby in 1849 to combat the incessant Indian attacks. We rattled on past vast stretches of a monotonous backdrop of live oaks, junipers, mesquite trees, and grasses. We passed iron-gated ranches with mythic names and desolate scrubby land dotted with beat-up trailers, where hunting blinds rise up unexpectedly out of the scrawny brush and desperate, old windmills refuse to concede to time. We drove across bridges spanning what had been creeks but were now dry arroyos with old Spanish names—Big Perido, Little Perido, Pinto, Seco, and Ranchero. Rose Kelly and her people crossed these watery landmarks on the last stretch of their flight to Mexico, and as we headed southwest, I reflected that Alice and I were joining them as fellow travelers in the timeless cycles of history.

The scenery began to blend into an endless flat canvas of gray brushstrokes of chaparral, low-slung acacias, blooming cacti, and junipers on bedrock soils. Just when it seemed we would never see another town, a white water tower appeared hovering over old Fort Clark, which lay luxuriant in an unexpected oasis of green. To the right of the highway huddled the small, one-blink town of Brackettville, with a rich architectural heritage of adobe, "chink," and clapboard houses, now deserted. Some of them were once the homes of Black Seminoles like Alice's grandmother Rosa Dixon Fay and great-aunt Sara Daniels, after they were forced from their nearby village, Las Moras. Guarding the town is the typical imposing rock Texas courthouse that overlooks a small town square.

Brackettville, or "Brackett," was founded in 1852 by Charles Brackett. It officially became Brackettville in 1873, a year after the Black Seminoles arrived at Fort Clark. The citizens pinned their hopes on the community becoming the hub of a projected railroad, but by 1882 the railroad was built ten miles south of town, relegating Brackettville to relative obscurity with the exception of nearby Fort Clark, founded in 1852. To the west of the fort is a prominent hill, Las Moras, which looms like a sentinel in the distance and served as a landmark for Comanches, Apaches, and other Indians who crossed the area.

Alice and I turned through the visitor gate into Fort Clark and drove around the quadrangle surrounded by imposing limestone houses typical of early Texas forts—homes of famous generals such as Albert Sidney Johnston, Robert E. Lee, George S. Patton, Phillip H. Sheridan, George C. Marshall, J. M. Wainwright—a hero of World War II who was captured in the Philippines, and Col. Ranald MacKenzie. Both Sheridan and MacKenzie supported the Black Seminoles' petition to have land of their own in Indian Territory. We stopped at the Fort Clark Springs restaurant to eat lunch before heading south to Del Rio and the border. Alice, lost in thought while we waited for our food, informed me, "Shirley, you know after my mama Nellie died, I came over here to cook at the fort. It was a hard time with my kids."

When Alice and I first began to travel together, she was at obvious unease on occasions like this when we stopped at a restaurant or store. She speaks both Spanish and English with fluency, but cannot read either. Taking literacy for granted, I had not realized the full impact of her not being able to read and write. I learned to ask her what to order, and her standard request became "I want beefsteak ranchero. You ask me, I tell you! *Ranchero del filete de la carne vaca*!"

When I first met Alice, she was very quiet, but she became bolder as we traveled together over time as her demands for beefsteak indicate. Alice Fay has painful memories of her lack of education and the ways it has made seemingly simple activities like reading a sign impossible. She related to me one terrifying incident she experienced on a trip:

> One time I was going to visit my granddaughter in Alexandria, Louisiana. I end up in Tennessee. I couldn't read the sign. . . . This man says, "Where you going?" I say, "Alexandria, Louisiana." He says, "My God you're way off! You're in Tennessee. You was supposed to get off at 5:00 P.M. It's 1:00 A.M. now. He say to the man [bus driver], "This lady was supposed to get off. . . . Don't worry, we'll get you back." I'm so scared. I cried. I don't know what to do. . . . He got me back on the right bus. . . . See what you have to go through if you don't know how to read and write.

Alice's lack of education mirrored that of other Black Seminoles at the time, especially in Nacimiento. When Laurence Foster visited in the 1930s, Alice was in her late teens. He reported that the headmen of the Mascogos in Nacimiento contended that education would detract from the Indian characteristics of the children and discouraged it. Black Seminoles valued their "Indianness" as a factor of their identity, and some elders favored this identity even believing that they spoke an Indian language.[2] But today Alice equates not being educated with being blind:

She emphasized to me,

> You know on the ranch I don't get to go to school like the other children. They didn't believe we go to school. I didn't learn to read and write. My brother George and I only got to go to school for two weeks in Mexico. Only Henry Fay goes to school. Shirley, education means lots to me now. It's just like you can't see. Like you are blind when you can't read or write or count. My grandkids went to school and college. I'm proud of them. I think about this when I talk. I think about my oldest granddaughter. I'm talking and she says, "OK, Granita, it is not like that but like this." She makes me feel bad because she has education and I don't. My grandkids went to school and college. I'm proud of them though.[3]

Alice's childhood friend Gertrude Vázquez, who also is unable to read, shared similar concerns on my visits to Mexico. "Me, I can't be too old," she said, meaning that being old restricts your travel. "Travel somewhere and get lost because don't know how to read. When I need to take some medicine, I cannot read the bottle." She continued, "No, I don't learn to read and write. That's what I would like when I was younger. We don't speak correct English."[4]

Things changed for children in Nacimiento after Gertrude and Alice were well past school age. In the 1960s there were about 250 people living in approximately sixty households in Nacimiento.[5] The Mexican government began sending in Mexican teachers and requiring school attendance. Still, for children on ranches, it wasn't a guarantee that they would acquire all the education needed for daily life. Carmen Vázquez, Alice's oldest daughter, explained:

> When we was growing up on the ranch there were lots of kids. So the people talk to the president from Múzquiz [nearby town] and he helped them and they built a school, Escuela de Benito Juárez, and send a school

> teacher out there in Nacimiento. My grandmama Nellie takes care of us in Mexico, and she didn't want us to go to school. There was always chores to do. When I came over here [Texas], they would talk about me as that "wetback" at work. That time I didn't have my citizenship and nothing ready, so I just let them talk, and when they come on a lunch break, we was talking and I said, "Well, I'm leaving 'cause I'm a wetback." They laughed looking at me, and they say, "You're not a wetback," and I say, "Yes, I am, and when I get my citizenship, I'll let you know that I belong to Texas."
>
> So they never say nothing no more, but they was talking to themselves that you know wetbacks come from Mexico. They don't work for anything. I just keep on going, but sometimes I feel bad 'cause lot of people say some things. Well, I feel bad too because my English is not correct, but there are lots of people that have been very nice, that they say they understand my English very well. Sometimes it makes me feel bad like when I first started working, and this nurse's aide was working there and they was talking about words that I don't know, can't catch on what is it. I can get a better job if I can read and write. And I need to go to school to learn English. But I haven't started yet, so that's what I'll do.

As Alice and I left the fort and the memories it inspired and headed south in our van, Alice pointed out the old clapboard Mt. Gilead Baptist Church to the right of Highway 90, standing forlorn upon a hill, its steeple toppled and its windows black holes. Tall cedar of Lebanon trees still faithfully guarded the old building—the church where Alice's ancestors prayed, fasted, and shouted in a circle to the Lord. She sighed, "Shirley, I used to go to that church when I worked on the fort here. Lots of those old people did." Legend has it that when the Black Seminoles were forced out of their homes on Fort Clark in 1914, they moved their church from Las Moras to this hill in Brackettville.

The church with its steeple had become a landmark on my frequent trips from Brackettville to Del Rio. I always imagined a sea of fervent worshippers led by women singing, shouting, and dancing in joyous abandon to the Lord and anxious faces of little children in white frocks eager to go out and play. I saw them streaming out of the doors after services, followed by their "Aunties" and "mothers" who sternly admonished them for small infractions.

Alice and I continued driving south until we reached the sign marking the road to the Seminole Indian Scouts Cemetery. We turned off to make a short visit. After parking the van, Alice and I walked down the familiar winding gravel road. She pointed out some of her ancestors' graves to me. Crudely etched names on some of the markers lent pathos to the somber setting. On one grave marker the surname Warrior was spelled as Wroyer. We saw a fresh grave piled with dirt and decorated with an American flag and bright plastic flowers.

Four neat, whitewashed graves at the Black Seminole cemetery are distinguished by white, metal grating around them and their granite tombstones. Two United States Medal of Honor winners—scouts Adam Payne (Paine) and Isaac Payne—are buried here. Sgt. John Warrior (Ward), born in Arkansas, and Pompey Factor, descendant of Teener Factor and the warrior July, rest in the other two graves.

I recall one of Miss Charles's comments when we visited the cemetery one day outside Brackettville. "That cemetery meant a lot, a whole lot . . . to us. See, the whole thing was land we could call our own."

Alice and I paused at the marble tombstone of the popular and beauteous Molly Perryman (1865–1951)—a favorite informant of Kenneth Porter. The marker reads "Mother at Rest." Alice pointed out the tombstone of her favorite aunt. It states "Sarah [Sara] Daniels, 10 Mar 1852–20 Jan 1949, 'Her Memory is Blessed.'"

As we came to the oldest section of the cemetery, I inquired, "Alice, is John Horse's wife Susan or his sister Wannah buried here?"

She mused over my question squinting in the sun as we paused, "Well, you know a bunch of the old people have graves in the cemetery, but there is no marker now," she said. "My grandmama Amelia is buried there, too, but I don't know where. Part of the people is in this cemetery; some is in the one in Mexico." She added, "I'm pretty proud about it. What little I know I got from them . . . about traveling so hard and running from slavery."

Porter described Alice's grandmother, a young Amelia Valdez (Kelly), who had moved from Mexico to Brackettville, in a 1943 interview, noting that "a rather distinguished and very intelligent-looking woman, she expressed herself easily and well."[6] I had read

Porter's description of Amelia to Alice, and she shook her head quizzically, saying:

> Amelia, she didn't like dark people, though. I don't know why. We don't have no pictures of Amelia. You know, she was so strict like my mama Nellie Fay. I have to get up at 4:00 A.M. in the morning [on the ranch in Mexico] to tend the goats and the beasts [cows and horses]. It was so hard. But I have to take care of myself. I have to do everything. I have to milk the cows and sell the milk, make the cheese, get the water, and clean the corn. The women all milk the cows and go off to sell the milk.

Alice's face took on an expression etched with painful memories as she continued:

> Amelia was Baptist. That was the only church then. She was strict. Those old ladies was so mean. . . . We couldn't iron on Sunday. Amelia says to me, "The Lord said on a Sunday you pray or go visit—or stay home—no iron and no singing." . . . Amelia wouldn't even let you sweep on Sunday. She say to me, "You're gonna rest your carcass." Saturday they'd do all the cooking. I thought I was smart. I got this iron out one time—Amelia, she saw it, and she was mad and threw the iron. She says to me, "Who put it on the fire? You put off that dress [for a whipping]!" . . . They wouldn't whip you with your clothes on. I tell you, you never do it again. . . . I don't care who it was, they could correct you. The elders say, "You gonna get in big trouble. . . . Don't want to hear you talk about so and so because they are older than you. You don't be moving around." No, we don't have a happy life when I was brought up. You know I don't have shoes until I was fifteen years old. . . . Amelia goes to the Kickapoo village to buy moccasins for us. When I was a big girl I still got moccasins. When it rains we walked barefoot.

Alice frowned in memory. "One time I was mad and went to the lady I know in town to ask her for shoes like the others had," she said. "I slopped the pigs and cleaned the pens for her. I just wanted some shoes."

I asked, "Alice, what did you do for clothes?"

> Sometimes we get on a *carretón* or mules or horses to go to Múzquiz to get some things . . . and buy big things [bolts] of cloth. Everybody had the same thing—you know, like stripes and plaids. That's why everybody looks the same in the photographs. Some would add something to make it look different. The material made drawers, slips—all. We'd make the clothes by hand—with needle and thread—no sewing machines.

As we made our final round through the cemetery to return to our car, I turned back. The graveyard's worn markers conjured up the spirits of enduring ancestors in a theater of tombstones. I recalled the exuberance of Gracie Lasky, daughter of Nancy Williams and related to Alice through a common ancestor, Rose Kelly. Gracie's poetic words when she talked about the Black Seminole Indian cemetery reflect the memories of many Black Seminoles:

> When you go down to the cemetery something special happens. You are overwhelmed. Your heart fills up. As soon as I walk on the ground, everybody who is gone and dead is with me. The voices are all around me. They walk around and they are glad to see you. They are waiting for you. When you think of all the people that was. They are all gone. . . . I am so proud of my family. The Lord gives us strength what the Aunties have left for us.[7]

Alice and I climbed in the van to continue our journey, intent on reaching the Mexican border before mid-afternoon. It was thirty miles away. Traveling south, we passed through a never ending featureless expanse of land covered with a an array of desert plants—mesquites, thorny acacias, bushes of gray-leaved sage, spiked yucca, oregano bushes, and giant century plants flaunting sprouts of white flowers waiting to bloom. Ocotillo plants spread out their limbs with purple blooms. The early settlers used the limbs of this spindly plant to brace the walls of their houses and to make corrals for sheep and goats.

This parched landscape would have been a perilous part of the Black Seminoles' journey, for they could have been spotted by an Indian or slaver from miles away on the flat horizon. As we approached the outskirts of Del Rio, we passed a sign pointing to

San Felipe Springs, where Rose Kelly's people stopped, aware that it was also a watering hole for Comanches and Lipán Apaches on their way to Mexico. Later, San Felipe would be one of the Fort Clark outposts of the Seminole Negro Indian Scouts, meant to stop raiders from Mexico from stealing livestock. With only a short distance to the border the Black Seminoles did not linger.

This area of Texas always brought back fond memories for I had spent time around Del Rio years earlier giving tours and studying the rock art found in the numerous rock shelters lining the Rio Grande, Pecos, and Devils rivers. Years before I, and many years after Alice Fay's people, arrived in this area, the Seminole Negro Indian Scout detachments out of Fort Clark made temporary bivouac headquarters in one of the large shelters on the Pecos River as they scouted for Comanches.

The ancient Indians who lived in the steep canyons etched by the Pecos River and Rio Grande created vivid paintings on their shelters that the Black Seminoles would have encountered in their travels. Here Indian women had also left their mark on the history of the area, traditions handed down through generations. They painted enigmatic designs on small river pebbles that they carried up into their shelters and fashioned baskets, nets, and woven mats with highly polished bone awls and needles, artifacts preserved in the dry climate of the shelters for thousands of years. I wondered if these women, like Alice's ancestors, also traveled to the world of their departed ancestors to read dreams and to recall their stories to their daughters.

Alice and I drove through the city of Del Rio and crossed the greenbelt that leads to the border crossing. We stopped at the U.S. border patrol station, where two starched officers checked out our van. On the other side we saw lines of dusty cars laden with families guarding bulging boxes of souvenirs crafted by Mexican artisans. Lines of weather-stained trucks and buses piled with lopsided boxes and worn suitcases were waiting to return to the United States, undergoing rigid inspections by the border patrol.

Passing inspection, we drove across the bridge over the Rio Grande and headed for the narrow, crowded streets of Ciudad Acuña, a bustling gateway to Mexico. A sign—*Bienvenidos a Coahuila, Tierra de La Amistad, Ciudad Acuña*—welcomed us. On the other side of the bridge we waited at the Mexican border station for another inspection. As we waited at Acuña, Alice told me a story about a border crossing at Eagle Pass that provided new insight into her feisty temper as a young woman:

> You know, Shirley, I remember a guy at the border at Eagle Pass crossing. . . . He said he was from Múzquiz. He always was picking on me. He would take my suitcase and throw it down and say, "You can't go over." . . . The man used to call me names and say the black people, Las Negras, look like donkeys—*burros*—and things like that. "Don't tell me I can't go," I say to him.

Alice clenched her jaws and continued:

> Well, I get tired and I told him, "You know what I'm gonna have to do—change coming this way. . . . One of these times we're gonna get into a big trouble and I don't have no people down here to defend my part. I think that he is gonna to try to attack me, or I'm gonna to try to attack him. . . . I just tell him what I have to tell him and I leave—and I never did see him again 'cause I never did go to Eagle Pass again—started to cross at Acuña.

As the two of us traveled together over the years, I came to realize other obstacles my friend encountered as a black woman. On one occasion, Alice and I were on our way to Nacimiento with a video team from my museum. The video producer stopped in the old colonial city of Múzquiz (former Santa Rosa), Coahuila, twenty miles from Nacimiento, to visit a female friend who lived in a little pastel house on a shady *callé*, or street. The other passengers unloaded from the van and traipsed into the house, anxious to be out of the grueling heat. Alice surprised me, though, by remaining seated in the van. I noted her rigid posture and stubborn look. Her face was like stone. I asked, "Alice, are you going in?"

Finally, her chin resolute, she murmured defiantly:

> I'm not going in there. 'Cause of what happened. . . . Well, I come to Múzquiz with my friend and we go to a house . . . a Mexican house. She knows the lady there. We knock on the door. The lady look at me and tells me to go in the back door. She [my friend] could go in the front. I was so mad I left—well because they didn't like us, say they hate us because we was black, and sometimes we would be going through the street and they were standing up in the door calling us, uh . . . Negras.

She sighed and crossed her hands on her lap. "You know, I have lots of relatives in Múzquiz, but they don't want to know me," she said. "They just don't like blacks."

Minutes later, the owner of the house rushed out to the car and said, "I am so sorry. *Mucho gusto en conocerle, Alicia. Bienvenido a mi casa.* Please come into my home. *Tanto gusto.*"

I recall Alice looking at the woman and giving her a luminous smile. I saw the dignity in her face return as we climbed out of the van to join the rest of the group in the house.

We returned to the van after inspection at the Mexican border station and continued to travel south. Alice sat like a statue in the front seat, unaffected by the heat and undisturbed by my frustration at the numerous speed bumps that popped up outside dusty little border towns—Nueva Rosita, San Juan de Sabinas, Palau, Morelos—resembling cardboard boxes stacked up along the highway. Large, belching power plants hovered over the flat landscape, lending an ominous aura to the flat blue sky. As we approached another village, Alice motioned me to stop the van, her eyes surveying the landscape. "Shirley, you see those trees over there?" she said. "The river is close by here."

I knew she was talking about the Sabinas River, which winds around Nacimiento and slinks by other little villages in its serpentine travels. We got out of the van and I followed Alice to the bank of the river, lined by narrow ribbons of cypress trees. Gnarly grapevines clung to their outspread branches.

She shaded her eyes and scanned the creek, low that year due to another drought. "You know, it must be real bad in Nacimiento," she fretted. "They can't grow the crops now. It's sad, 'cause my people had the corn, beans, pumpkins . . . all of that. It's all gone now." She continued to worry as we climbed back into the van to continue our journey as it was growing late. "I wonder if Henry [Alice's brother] is taking care of the corn on the ranch," she mused. "Probably he isn't doing it."

Farther south, we began to approach cloud-hung mountains and hills, the Sierra Hermosa de Santa Rosa foothills of the lower eastern Sierra Madre Oriental—the Santa Rosa hills or *colinas*. This was the place where Alice's ancestors had lived—where young Rose Kelly settled down with her new husband, Thomas Factor, and where she bore her children. Tailings from copper mines trail down the slopes, like jagged scars. Alice looked up at the rugged mountains as if she were spotting a deer, her treasured memories kindled. She pointed,

> Shirley, you see that? That's where they used to hunt and kill deer and bear . . . the old people. That's where my mama Nellie and the other women went to take hot baths from the water. . . . It was called "Las Hermanas." My mama Nellie would go up there when she didn't want to go to the doctor—Amelia, Sara, and Rose, too . . . everybody went there. The men, they didn't go . . . only the women. . . . I did it too.[8]

We reached the outskirts of Múzquiz and made our way through a maze of ancient cobblestone streets into the center of town. Hearty bougainvilleas in shades of red and magenta hung from brightly colored stucco houses with terra-cotta tile roofs. We located an inexpensive hotel off of the main road, Juárez Street, named for former Mexican president Benito Juárez who confirmed the Nacimiento land grant for the Mascogos in 1866.

Múzquiz was settled by the Spanish Crown in 1735, part of a line of military outposts or *presidios* that extended from San Antonio, Texas, to Sonora, Mexico. The Spanish intended for the forts to deter Comanche and Lipán Apache Indians who regularly crossed the Rio Grande to raid small settlements in Mexico. The town was well-known as a refuge for runaway blacks.

Nacimiento de Los Negros lies twenty miles from Múzquiz; an obscure sign points the way today. The original land grant was valued because it included the San Javier de la Escondido springs, waters that flow into the Sabinas River. The springs are now on land occupied by the nearby Kickapoo Indians. They were given title to the land in 1852 but did not occupy it until later.[9]

In the early days, Múzquiz could be reached from Nacimiento only by horseback or on mules over rough trails. A new scraped gravel road makes the trip shorter, but during the dry season it is faster to cut your vehicle across the gravel banks of the Río Sabinas. Alice and I decided to take this shorter route, and we drove up to a gate, where two small boys of the neighboring *ejido*, Morelos, stood as the designated gatekeepers. We handed them a few coins as passage and took off down the road.[10]

After a few miles Alice's sharp eyes lit upon a clump of woods and she motioned me to stop. I didn't see any foundations but weeds and a few trees. She told me, "That's the Perry Church, Shirley. Yeah, his name was Henry Perry, the man who had the church. Another preacher is Kelly [Colley, Keli/*Kole*] Factor. He [Kelly] was an old guy who didn't wear any shoes. Those guys run from something they did over here [Texas] and had to go to Mexico."

Coincidentally here, Kelly Factor's name illustrates the Black Seminole tradition of switching the given name with a surname over time.

It was late in May as Alice and I drove into Nacimiento, and thousands of yellow butterflies fluttered around us like snowflakes. They clustered together on plants growing along the road, resembling a large yellow flower in bloom. When the McKellars first arrived in Coahuila to establish their ranch La Mariposa, they were similarly greeted by clouds of butterflies. I had traveled through Mexican towns before, but this visit to Nacimiento had an intimate quality because of the presence of Alice Fay.

Clouds of dust raised by trotting horses hovered over the adobe houses, which seemed to vibrate in the unforgiving sun. The powdery dust gathered on tall clumps of weeds and was thrown in clouds on the fence posts. Alice gaily waved out the window of the van to friends and cried, "It's Nina!" People shouted back "It's Nina! It's Nina!" and waved excitedly from the fields. That is how I learned that Alice's nickname, or "basket name," is Nina. The nickname may have its origin in the Mexican name or could be derived from the Gullah feminine name *Nina,* meaning, among other things, the fiery one, a gift, or something new.[11]

Nacimiento was considerably smaller than I had anticipated. From Porter's glowing descriptions, I had expected to see blooming fig and peach trees and well-tended, lush gardens of sugarcane, beans, wheat, and corn. The town reveals the typical Spanish colonial grid pattern, its two parallel streets lined with compounds of adobe houses. Some of the houses abut small, concrete-block additions. Many of the adobe houses were abandoned; like worn artifacts they allude to the passing of a vibrant community. More affluent families have adopted different styles of houses that are gaily painted.

An occasional rusted pickup truck covered with dust or a worn-out SUV hunkered by the road awaiting its owner. Foster, on his visits in the 1930s, estimated the population in Nacimiento to consist of three hundred individuals or twenty-one families.[12] Porter, almost a decade later, described the Nacimiento community as larger, with 518 inhabitants. He reported seeing well-irrigated, fertile fields in Nacimiento, better tended than those of the adjacent Kickapoo Indians. There was a jail, grocery store, butcher shop, saloon, and a small theater. Transportation was by foot, horse, or a bus held together with baling wire that offered wooden planks for seating. Porter observed that men still wore trousers, jackets, and fringed deerskin moccasins.[13] Alice laughed, "I sure remember that rickety old bus with the wood seats. Yeah, when I was young we rode horses or we walked or caught a ride."

By the 1960s, Beth Dillingham reported that the community was much smaller, about 250 people living in approximately sixty households. There were two schools, one run by local residents with lessons conducted in English, and the other, with required attendance, run by the Mexican government. She observed that both the residents' food preferences such as *sofkee* and mode of dress still reflected Seminole influence.[14]

Bartering was a method of exchange. "We always did that—exchange corn for the pigs or milk," Alice said. "My grandmama Nellie though, she had cows, not goats. I would butcher the calves. Sometimes the people would work in the fields for like meat or something."

By 1965, stock raising and, to a lesser extent, farming were still crucial to survival in Mexico. Residents kept chickens, goats, cows, and pigs. Mules, horses, and oxen provided transportation for the community.[15]

As we continued to drive down the main street of Nacimiento, Alice became very excited at the prospect of seeing Gertrude (Gertrudis) Vázquez, her old childhood friend. We drove up to the front of an adobe house, distinguished by a sprawling rosebush and traces of white stucco—lingering reminders of a better time.

"There's Gertrude's house, Shirley," Alice said. In an aside she confided, "You know that Gertrude is a Factor, too. My husband Luis was Gertrude's uncle. Her husband was murdered you know." Alice's daughter Effie had told me he was murdered on New Year's Eve, right in front of the church.

Alice informed me that Gertrude had healing hands, and specialized in treating sprained ankles. "She rubs the oil over and over and then it gets better, you know," she said. "If it is broken then she tells them to go to Múzquiz."

Gertrude had already heard through the grapevine that we were in town and came out of her house to hug Alice enthusiastically. The tops of large white tennis shoes met the hem of her gaily printed dress. Gertrude is very dark in contrast to Alice and shares the distinctive low hairline of the women in the Vázquez family. Her mischievous face is lined with deep wrinkles and her deep-set black eyes twinkle like black coals. At times, like other older women, she smokes a little brown rolled cigarette.

Gertrude is royalty in the Black Seminole community. As an elder she was invited to Washington, D.C., along with Alice, Miss Charles Wilson, and Ethel and Dub Warrior to be an honored guest at the Smithsonian Institute Festival of American Folklife in 1992. The event focused on maroon cultures and the women provided a cooking demonstration for visitors. More recently, Gertrude was invited to Tallahassee, Florida, and Florida A&M University as a guest during Black History Month festivities.[16]

She invited us into her home, in which she runs a little *tienda*, or shop, selling cold drinks and candy. We took a seat on some worn, carved wooden chairs. I noticed a framed certificate from the Smithsonian next to a photo of Martin Luther King, Jr., and a Norman Rockwell drawing of a white family at prayer. Typical of Gertrude's speech are the phrases "Yes, ma'am" and "Yes, mama" and a distinct emphasis on certain words. Speaking the English of her forebears is a point of pride with her, distinguishing her from Spanish-speaking residents in the village today.

After I commented on the Smithsonian certificate, Gertrude, leaning on the counter in her store, told me emphatically:

> I live here, until the good Lord remember me. I go to the United States but I come *right* back to Nacimiento because this *here is* where I was born and raised. . . . I'm proud that I am living in Mexico—Nacimiento—years ago what lots of us people here who could speak English. Lots of people come from different places—drop to my door—speak to me in Spanish. I speak to them in English! *Yes, ma'am*!

Gertrude raised her voice and frowned. "'You speak English?' they ask me. 'Why sure.' I live here but my old parents speak *English* to me. . . . Yes, ma'am, I answer to them in English but I can't read it. I speak English, thank you ma'am, but not Spanish!"

Gertrude continued chatting with us as a young boy came in with change to buy a soft drink. As the proprietor of desultory treats, she rattled around in her ancient refrigerator and handed him the drink. He scuttled off after she gave him change.

I asked the two old friends, "When you two are together, what do you talk about?"

Alice smiled and hugged Gertrude. "We talk about our young days—when we used to court and have boyfriends," she said. "Go to the dance and have good times."

"Yes, ma'am," Gertrude murmured. "We have good times."

Alice laughed with a twinkle in her eye. "We just catch them old boys and chase them around!" she said.

Alice lifted the hem of her pink dress and pretended to dance with an imaginary partner who twirled her around. She continued with the devil dancing in her eyes. "We used to jump out of the window to go to the dance," she said. "We used to have dances and it used to be the time we find boyfriends and husbands. We'd go home to get dressed after the fast—then go to the dance for a day and night. I sure liked to dance. . . . Yes, ma'am!"

Gertrude's response emphasized the difference between her dancing and that of a religious figure or Sister of the church. She grimaced as she looked at Alice. "Me, no!" she said. "I am no Sister for a praise house, but I can sing and pray, dance and pray. Sister who serves God *cannot* dance."[17]

Alice persisted in her bedevilment. "Reason why I going out because they no let me go," she said. "Yes, I put on this wide skirt and loose coat. We used to go to the church house. When we get to the dance later, we take it off."

Gertrude frowned in disbelief. "You remember what *they do* over there?" she asked.

I had heard through the grapevine that Alice was one of the best "fun" dancers in Nacimiento as a young lady. She told me that she used to sneak out of her adobe house or "jump out of the window" to go dance at the nearby Kickapoo Reservation. "We'd spend a whole day up there, good time," she said. One day she pointed out the trail to me that she used to take.

Effie laughed later when I repeated her mother's story during Seminole Days. "The Kickapoo had rain dances that were religious," she said. "Sometimes they would let us join in. Mama would go out and dance all night. I didn't ever go. . . . I used to hate it when we went to Seminole Days because I wouldn't see Mama for two or three days. She would be dancing."

In response to Effie's comments on that occasion during Seminole Days, Alice looked up defiantly and pointed proudly to the concrete dance ground at the old school yard where they gathered on Seminole Days. "Yeah, you see that platform right over there? There I was dancing!" Alice's granddaughter, Tommie, repeated a similar story. "Granita would make us outfits and take us down to the Kickapoo camp to dance," she said. "She made them of bright material and sewed on bottle caps to make noise."

Gertrude's only daughter, Frances, and her children occupied another room of the adobe tienda, separated by lace curtains. Frances, a pleasant-faced woman who is very shy, came out to meet us and show us her embroidered tablecloth. Gertrude dotes on her daughter and grandchildren. In an aside, Alice confided to me, "You know that Frances is her sister Lucia's daughter—not Gertrude's.

When Frances was born Lucia couldn't take care of her, so her husband gave her to Gertrude." This mode of adoption is an important facet of Black Seminole culture, in this case ensuring that the childless Gertrude will always have someone to care for her.

Gertrude led us back to a compound of three adobe houses nestled off of the main road. She motioned us to sit down on some worn chairs under the spreading branches of a clump of old salt pines. Beyond us in the distance, on a clothesline stretched between two trees, gaily colored quilts waved like flags. A lonely century plant fought for space in a carpet of short grass that had been mowed by goats. Two small goats threw graceful shadows on the grass as they frolicked, unaware of their ultimate fate as *barbacoa*. One kid lay somnolently in the sun.

I remembered that Kenneth Porter reported that the Black Seminoles hung goat meat, wrapped in gunnysacks, on lines to dry. The women also made rugs from goatskin to cover the packed earth floors in their adobe houses.[18]

The day grew unbearably hot as noon approached, and found us sitting under the salt pines. The two friends begin to talk furiously, sharing stories that I could hardly understand. I listened as they discussed the whereabouts and deaths of old friends. I was distracted by the nearby adobe houses that appeared to be abandoned. Alice, sensing my unspoken questions, asked Gertrude to show me around her compound.

Alice pointed, "Shirley, you see that peach tree? We used to have lots of those when I was growing up. There're all gone now. It's sad. You know, we had lots of big melons, too—all kinds."

The two old women surveyed the landscape. "No water to grow," Gertrude sighed.

A stray cow wandered into the yard, surprising me at its lack of supervision. I then recalled that among the Seminoles and their black allies in Florida it was customary for the livestock to roam free.

Gertrude, walking in a clumsy gait in her tennis shoes with turned-up toes, went up to one of the houses. "That house belongs to my old grandmama Hannah Wilson and my mama, Mariah [Jesusita Valdez] Wilson," she said. "Those two old ladies lived here." I noted that Gertrude used the Wilson (Black Creek) maiden name of her mother, Mariah, instead of the Flores of her father, Jesús Vázquez. Using their mother's maiden name rather than their father's name was a trait carried by some of the older women.[19]

We strolled around the compound to a third adobe house, and Alice took over the role of tour guide. "Shirley, her brother Adam—or the chief, Chago—you know, lives there, but it is Gertrude's house. It sure is."

Gertrude yelled at Adam outside in Spanish and huffed, saying something under her breath that I could not understand. Gertrude apparently was the boss of the compound even though Adam, called Chago, was the chief.

This brought up another question. "Who polices the community?" I asked. "What did the people do when someone started trouble?"

Gertrude looked at me sternly and growled a "humph," which I found out later is another of her characteristics. "We don't need *no* police in Nacimiento. No, *ma'am*!"

I sensed that I had asked a sensitive question, but I knew that Porter recorded the presence of a jail in Nacimiento in the 1940s.[20] Alice, who would have been in her twenties when Porter visited in the 1940s, told me, "Only one jail when I was here, and we put in people who fight—even womens who would get in on it."

Gertrude added with authority, "Well, the commissioner, the *capitán*, just tells them [the people fighting or committing crimes] to stop. Or they cuff them, too. Every year you just say that you are going to be the leader and you are. . . . Yes, mama."

I found out later that Adam or Chago, as required by the Mexican government, presides over a council of elected representatives who handle village matters, also keeping records of births and other vital statistics.

Gertrude and Alice then proceeded to have a side conversation about those Wilson boys who were always fighting. Alice acted it out. "You know, we just cuff them, Shirley," she said. "The old women do it—those old Sisters."

Even Alice's grandson, Lewis, who lived with her in Mexico for seven years off and on, remembered the power of the older women. He related:

> Women ruled the village. If there were any problems, they talked to my *granita* Nellie. There were no crimes because they were afraid of those old ladies, especially Nellie. Chago treated her like a male. He just was like an administrator but she was the boss unless the problem couldn't be solved, and then they had to call in the people from Múzquiz to the Camp. . . . You know we called Nacimiento "the Camp."

Alice's younger brother, Henry Fay, agreed:

> Those old women—any of them, wherever you were—could beat you if you were bad. Didn't matter. . . . They'd hit you on the head with their cane—those old grandmamas, Sisters—no matter what. They would get you, no matter what. If it was Sunday, then they would get you for Saturday. They would even hit me in front of my mama Nellie. . . . Nana Rosa asked me to get coal for her pipe, and if you didn't do it right, she'd bob you on in the head with her cane.

Herbert Foster, a scholar of African American culture, discusses the extended family of women as an agent of social control among people of African origin. This structure was re-created in America as an adaptation to the realities of slave life. The extended matrifocal family of females operated as a "basic law enforcement agency. It was the strength of the extended family that in part explains the absence of elaborate policing mechanisms and penal institutions in pre-colonial Africa."[21]

In the Black Seminole context, the "basic law enforcement agency" consisted of the older women who could ostracize members of the community who failed to conduct themselves in a proper manner either socially or spiritually. This realization was part of my journey of learning about the power of women over the morals and traditions of the Black Seminole community in Alice Fay's generation and earlier. Like their female Gullah ancestors, those old "Sisters" had an elaborate system in place for solving grievances, claiming jurisdiction, and enforcing punishment.

Interestingly, this role of Black Seminole women as arbitrators of justice in Mexico and Brackettville is in marked contrast to the roles of their kinsmen in Indian Territory. There, law enforcement rested with the male freedmen, called Seminole Light Horsemen, an agency established during Reconstruction.[22]

Of course, men were often the targets of the old women's wrath as they posed on their gendered stage of law enforcement. Exasperation with the men ran strong in conversations with the older women. When I inquired what the men did as members of the community, the women always shrugged their shoulders in a kind of conspiratorial silence. Alice usually gave out a dramatic sigh and her friends shifted and rolled their eyes. Since they knew that I was writing down their stories, I suspected that they performed this age-old drama sometimes for my benefit.

Alice put her hands on her hips and looked at me disapprovingly when she had guardianship of some information and was questioned. "I tell you, the men worked the fields and planted the corn," she said. "I tell you, Shirley, only the womens go to church. The men, they stand outside drinking and talking. The women do it all. They take care of everything."

Alice and I wrapped up our visit with Gertrude, for the sun was casting long shadows on the hills beyond. As we left, I thought that no wonder the woman, matriarch of her compound, had emphasized, "We don't need *no* police in Nacimiento." Seemingly, the women's job was to make some sense of order in the community from the chaos created by men. Their control over the community was further enhanced by a powerful spiritual component and their genealogical knowledge derived from their multifaceted past, and to some degree this is true today. All those old Sisters like Rose Kelly and Rosa Dixon Fay prayed and read dreams with their ancestors—as did their female ancestors before them—to guide their community through troubled times.

CHAPTER TEN

Return to Nacimiento

> Everything that explains the world has in fact explained a world that does not exist, a world in which men are at the center of the human enterprise and women are at the margin "helping" them. Such a world does not exist—never has.
>
> Gerda Lerner

In 1997, Alice and I made another trip to Nacimiento. Alice's brother Henry Fay had been visiting in the United States during our previous visit to Mexico, and Alice told me that he was home this time. Again driving south across the border, we arrived in Nacimiento early in the morning. Dark-skinned cowboys, their faces shaded by requisite straw hats, were heading out to tend their cattle. The clank of cowbells followed them—a male sound, competing with the raucous sounds of strutting roosters crowing. Cattle ownership was traditionally a sign of prestige and wealth in Creek and Seminole Indian communities in Florida. Wealthy Indians like Micanopy became wealthier because blacks were adept at raising cattle.

Alice and I took an alternate route that morning to Henry's house as I was interested in seeing other houses in the village. Some of the houses lining the road seemed to have more prosperous owners than others. One white stucco house sported windows with bright red shutters and lace curtains. The dusty, screened windows were shut tightly, suggesting an absentee owner. A tall, chain-link fence surrounded the house.

We drove by a concrete-block house painted bright blue, its roof made of corrugated tin. A water tower loomed overhead. A swarthy cowboy in an old khaki army shirt and a stiff straw hat was sharpening his axe in the shadow of his saddle, hanging on a wooden pole. We stopped and got out of our van to observe his task. His small children were playing tag around the saddle. He looked *mexicano,* but I wondered if he were part Mascogo or had married into the group, so I asked him.

"Yes," he explained. "*Soy seminole de la parte de mi madre.* I am part Seminole on my mother's side."

We noticed an adobe house where three little girls sat on the doorstep, staring at us and giggling. Alice and I walked over to talk to them and asked, "Do you want to stay in Nacimiento when you get older?" Two replied, "We don't want to be here. We would rather be in another place."

The third little girl in a blue dress shook her head. "I want to be here," she said. "I like everything here—the trees, the rivers, and because we all have fun."

"What do you call yourselves?" I asked. They answered, "We call ourselves Negras mixed."

"What do you think about the history of your people?" I asked.

"Many years ago mixed blacks came to this land," they said.

"Who taught you your history?" I queried again.

They replied, "Our mothers. Well, you know, we weren't born yet." Then they said "good-bye" and ran into the house.

As Alice and I continued our walk down the main street, a mule-drawn cart of water barrels passing us on the road suddenly distracted me. Alice, always anticipating my questions, told me, "We call them *piperos*. We got the water from the river and put in those barrels."

"All my old parents, they had to walk or ride the *carretón* [wagon]," she continued. "When they would come to Múzquiz from the ranch, they would get two oxen and put a *carretón* on to ride. You know, when my grandmama Amelia and I visited Oklahoma, we went in a wagon like that but some of the women went horseback."

As we continued down the street, Alice waved her hand and motioned for me to stop at one abandoned adobe house. The house was surrounded by a packed surface of dark-brown earth with not a blade of grass in sight. Thick, white stucco hung like icicles from the roofline over the rust-colored adobe bricks, their edges rounded from the rains. The windows of the house, like those of other houses, had no glass in the frames.

Alice smiled. "You see that little house, Shirley? It's my house," she said. "It's about Henry's age—about seventy years old. . . . My brother Henry, he was born in that little house. . . . My mama Nellie lived here in town for a little time in this house. My mama had someone to make the [adobe] bricks. . . . You know adobe is good for sleeping 'cause it's cool. In the winter it's warm."

"Then Nellie lived on the ranch, too?" I asked.

"Yeah," Alice answered.

Knowing the remoteness of the ranch, Guadalupe, I understood why Nellie chose to live occasionally in Nacimiento.

Alice continued, "My [paternal] grandmama Rosa [Dixon] Fay lived here in Nacimiento too, 'cause she didn't have a ranch."

Still trying to understand their often confusing inheritance practices, I asked, "Do you own that little adobe house now, Alice?"

She looked at me querulously. "Well, *sure*! My mama Nellie gave it to me."

I asked Alice to pose in front of the house for a photo. She laughed and positioned herself in her print dress in front of a fence pole, looking back at the house proclaiming proudly, "This is my old house."

Vacant spaces for windows stared blankly at us and I thought of curious children's faces peering out many years ago—anxious to get away from the switch or cane of a grandmother or admonitions of an old Sister. To the side of the house a woman was hanging laundry to dry. The clothes fluttered in the brisk wind. A small trailer home was perched next to the house.

"Alice, who lives next to your house?" I asked.

"Oh, she's my cousin and will, you know, make sure my old house is okay from the kids and things like that," Alice said.

"But the land is yours, right?"

"Well, the land is all our people's and if you want to build a house you just . . . you know . . . just ask."

During a later conversation at her granddaughter Merry's house in San Antonio, Alice informed me that someone else had moved into her old adobe house. Merry overheard the conversation and voiced her objection to her grandmother's apparent generosity. "*Granita*, how can they do that?"

Alice threw out her hands in exasperation. "Well, you know I don't live in it and the land is all the same [belongs to all the people] . . . well, you have to live on the land so you can have it. If not, then others can."

I later would find out that another relative had moved into the house. More disturbing to Alice's family was the rumor that Henry, her brother who ran the ranch, had given or sold the ranch to someone. Alice's brother lived in the town of Nacimiento with his two children and was barely scraping out a living on the ranch in the drought-ridden area.

Alice and I continued our trek down the main street of Nacimiento. Behind many of the adobe houses I noticed little abandoned jacal-like structures. Alice, ever the tour guide, again anticipated my next question:

> Shirley, those are houses where the old people lived. We call them "stick" houses, *jacalitos*. . . . My great-grandmama, Rose Kelly, lived in a stick house on the ranch. She didn't like to live in town, and so she was always out on the ranch. . . . I was born in one of those on the ranch. . . . We used to make fire inside 'cause it would get pretty cold in those stick houses—a big pot of coals to keep us warm during the night. We all slept around it. . . . Then we move into that little adobe house we just saw.

Like bleached skeletons, these old stick structures linger around the village, some repurposed as storage sheds or outhouses. The roofs are covered with old tires or pieces of plastic.

We got in the van and drove farther down a side street. Getting out of the van, Alice continued her tour narrative as we walked. I noticed a fine new stick house next to an old rundown adobe house. I was impressed with the craftsmanship, especially in the woven grass roof, and wondered about the owner. I expressed my admiration of the house to Alice. "Who lives there?" I asked.

Alice looked very strange, her eyes downcast. "That's Doonie's house—she built it," Alice said. She pretended to ignore my continued requests to meet the owner.

Suddenly a large woman burst out of the adobe house and approached us. Her clothes were ragged and dirty and she seemed to be very agitated. I assumed this woman was Doonie. Alice, for some reason, was reluctant to talk to her and started to get back in the van. She looked embarrassed and told me, "Doonie is—well—always looking for money."

Doonie was persistent and followed us and hung onto the van door, but Alice fended her off. Later, after I wore her down with repeated questions about the mysterious Doonie, Alice finally explained. She folded her hands on her lap, obviously ill at ease. "You know, Shirley. She is a woman—you know—who wants to be a man. She's the only one."

So that was the story of Doonie. Whether she was an outcast due to her eccentric behavior or due to homosexuality, I still do not know.

Climbing back in the van, we continued our trip to Henry's house in town. He had promised Alice that he would take us on a tour of the farm and the ranch that morning. Alice informed me, "His daddy's name was Rafael Dudan, a Spanish. They [Mexicans] went to Nacimiento to go planting with the older people."

"Why does Henry then carry the Fay surname of his mother instead of Dudan?" I asked.

"You know, my mama Nellie got with this Dudan," Alice answered. "She was pretty old. They took on other partners. Well, like before Adam Fay married my mama Nellie, he was with a Miss Hattie from Brackett." Adam (Abram) Fay was the son of Rosa Fay and Adam (Koonta), illustrating the Black Seminole custom of generational name-saking.

As we drove up to Henry's small concrete block house on the edge of the village, his two small children ran out to greet Alice and wove merrily around her legs. The children were by his third wife, a shadowy figure in Alice's memory, who died young. Alice's posture and facial expression upon mention of her name suggested that she obviously did not approve of the union. Henry sauntered out of the house. Alice, her face full of smiles, hugged him. "Henry is my favorite brother," she said.

Henry resembles his mother, Nellie, with a long angular face and prominent nose surmounted by large, black-rimmed glasses. He is tall and lanky, with a cowboy swagger. His skin is light in contrast to other descendants living in Mexico. His lean, well-muscled body made him seem much younger than his seventy-two years and explained why he had the reputation of being attractive to women.

Leaving the children at the house with a relative, Henry climbed in his pickup, and we followed in the van. His truck—ingeniously held together with baling wire, duct tape, and frayed rope—proceeded to rattle down a rutted dirt road lined with large clumps of blooming cactus, mesquite chaparral, shrubs of wild huajilla with fragrant white flowers, and cenizo, sporting purple blooms amid its silvery gray-green leaves. After a few miles Henry suddenly pulled off to the side of the road and stopped.

Alice pointed out the window. "You see? That's my farm, Shirley. They plant wheat, barley, corn, and fruit trees. The men clear the fields and the women keep the fields and take in the crops. . . . They was all doing it together, but the women they did most of it."

I didn't see anything looking like a farm—only thick brush and dried corn stalks standing in an empty field of dark cracked earth with deep furrows. Again I recalled Kenneth Porter describing the big ears of corn, lush fruit trees, and beans and melons he saw on his visits to Nacimiento in the 1940s.

Henry got out of his truck and took off through the brush, leaving us under the canopy of a scraggly oak tree. Alice surveyed the dried-out farmland with intensity, and shot out an angry aside to me. "Henry is not taking care of the farm," she confided. "That's just like Henry. . . . Henry is just lazy." She shook her head disapprovingly. As we waited for a long time in the shade of the tree, my mind was teeming with questions.

"Alice, tell me about how you farmed and what you planted."

She answered readily:

> Well, I'd walk from the ranch to the farm to get corn or food for the beasts [livestock]. I'd put a towel on my head and hit the road. . . . All

> the women, they would get together and take out the crops. . . . We go from one field to another until we get done. . . . We grew tomatoes, oats, wheat, squash, melons, and pumpkin. . . . We grow white and yellow corn and sometimes let it dry on the vine. . . . They plant the corn in April or May and we pull it in June. . . . We put another crop in December and took them out in the spring. The women then would break the corn. We did it right here. . . . We had an old plough and pulled it by a mule. It was hard. . . . We trade corn with the Kickapoo for deer or bear meat. The wheat we take to the mill. . . . We take the pumpkin and skin it cut it in strips and lay it on to dry. We all do it together.

As with Alice's farm in Nacimiento, the Black Seminoles, as in Florida and Indian Territory, practiced communal ownership of the farmland in Mexico. "The farm was all ours," Alice said, meaning it belonged to all the Mascogos, descendants of the original settlers.

Coming from my culture of property ownership and related legal issues, I was still having difficulty understanding her people's practices of land tenure and ownership. Particularly difficult to understand was the idea that a ranch could be passed down by generations of women as the women's conversations related, but at the same time ownership of some of the land was communal.

The practice continued in Las Moras. Florida-born Sampson July, Rebecca Wilson's father, was a more liberal force in the community in advocating private ownership of the communally owned land. According to his granddaughter Miss Charles, he broke with tradition in maintaining that individual ownership of land encourages hard work and self-reliance.

Foster reported that in the 1930s Black Seminole women did most of the work in the fields. He observed that the men considered themselves to be "Indians" and enjoyed drinking and riding horses, an observation echoed by Beth Dillingham, who visited in the 1960s. She also observed this pattern in the division of labor in agriculture during her visits. She reported that in some cases males hired laborers to till the fields, considering themselves, like their Indian counterparts, to be above agricultural tasks. This pattern later carried over to the Black Seminole community that moved to Fort Duncan and Fort Clark in 1870, and farmed at Las Moras.[1]

Alice, still waiting for Henry to return from his mysterious mission, echoed Beth Dillingham's observation: "The men, they didn't like to farm," she said. "They liked to raise the beasts. The women had to do all the work. The children, you took them with you—tie them on your back; yeah, I did—Carmen, Herbert, and the others. . . . It sure was hard, but I did it." Lifting her shoulders, Alice demonstrated with a flourish how she carried her children on her back. "You know, the women and children also raise goats, chickens and pigs, and sell milk and cheese in Múzquiz," she said. The women's contributions to the economy bolstered their status and provided them some independence from reliance on the men for financial support. At the same time, raising goats depleted the land even more over time, making it impossible to grow crops.

Three acequias, or irrigation canals, like the ones at Las Moras, carried water to the Mascogos' fields and two others ran along streets to provide water for household uses and gardens. A chosen male oversaw the acequias and made certain the water was apportioned equally to villagers. The community also drew water from five functioning wells and transported it in barrels by burro or foot to the village.[2]

"Now only three of the wells have water, and the people are fighting over them," Alice said. "You know, when we planted the crops we cleaned out the holes [acequias] that go from the river then. Not now. Now they're all gone because nobody plants anymore."

Cyclic droughts continued a relentless onslaught on the farms, returning in 1940, 1943, 1947, and 1969, according to eyewitnesses. Harvests diminished from two or three a year to barely one. Only a few paltry corn or bean crops survived. In summer, the weather was hot and dry, and in the winter, freezing winds swooped down from the mountains and blew through the community's chinked jacals. The poor growing conditions caused the Black Seminoles to re-evaluate their means of survival.[3]

"That's *right*. The people had to stop farming and look for work," Alice said. "My mama Nellie went out to work on a ranch, and I stay with my Auntie Sara and my grandmama Amelia." Amelia and Sara were sisters, daughters of Rose Kelly.

One Nacimiento resident complained, "A lot of people quit work around this place on account of the droughts. I mean, you can't grow nothing. The rivers run dry and your beasts are laid out—and so a whole lot of people just go out [leave]."

The droughts still continued into the twenty-first century. During a devastating dry spell in 2004, parched winds blew through the homes in the village of Nacimiento, sweeping and scouring the residents' land. Henry had to take his horses over the mountain because there was no hay. Desperate to feed his cattle, he scorched cactus pads to burn off the needles so the cattle could eat them. He was badly burned and nearly died when the butane torch he was using caught fire. Alice and her daughter Effie left for Mexico to bring him back to convalesce at their home in Del Rio. All Alice's anger at Henry about how he managed the farm and ranch dissolved with this experience.

Alice continued her story in her sonorous voice as we continued to wait for Henry to return:

> We had a little stick house on the farm, stayed there a few days and then went to the ranch and in town and stayed a few days there. When it rained we'd stay in the stick house till it stopped. Sometimes we'd walk all the way from the ranch to Múzquiz. Took all day, and we got back at night. There was no cars then—just mules or horses—but we walked anyway. . . . One of my cousins had a big field of marijuana in the hills above the ranch. I had to come over here [from Texas] to live when Nellie died, but there was just me on the ranch. There was some people coming and looking for my cousin. To get to his ranch they come by Guadalupe. I was scared out there. That's why I moved to Texas the first time.

Observing my growing concern about Henry's return, Alice paused to assure me that "Henry is checking on things." Our conversation ended as he appeared out of the brush, explaining that he was checking on his cattle. He climbed in his pickup to continue the journey to the ranch. We traveled down a winding, red-gravel road, colored by ancient volcanic eruptions. Low-lying mesquites, huisache, and more clumps of cactus flaunting vibrant crimson tunas dominated the terrain while majestic mountains formed a canvas-like backdrop to the bright red soil. Every now and then we saw a group of cattle shyly peeking through the mesquites. Alice smiled at them and explained, "Some of them are my beasts. They have two notches in their ears."

Alice's ranch, Guadalupe, suddenly appeared, low on the horizon; the burned ruins of the old adobe house that she had described to me many times lay forlorn on the landscape like a timeless artifact nestled in the maternal embrace of the verdant Santa Rosa hills. Here Alice had lived as a small child amid the protective circle of women—her great-grandmother Rose Kelly, her grandmother, Amelia, and her mother Nellie. The land on which the adobe rested had been given to Alice's great-great-grandmother Tina Payne, by the Mexican government in the 1850s, the same land she handed down to her daughter Rose Kelly. The story of Alice's ancestors and her descendants' memories took on a new meaning here during our visit to Guadalupe.

Alice's grandchildren had lived in the adobe house with her during the summer months and laughed and played in the freedom there. Here they had listened to Alice's stories about the bravery of her people at night. "You know my mama Nellie. She built the house," Alice said. "I send her my money from working. I raised Effie and Carmen in that little house."

In a conversation, Alice's daughter Effie recalled, "Yes, we all lived in that adobe. We had to be careful because there were snakes under the tin roof of the house. They liked to get pigeons. My grandmother Nellie would get out there with a stick and get them down. We were afraid one would fall in her pocket of her apron."

In 1976, after Alice had moved back to Texas, her adobe house burned down, the fire devouring with it any possessions she had ever owned. Now the thick walls of adobe bricks are crumbled with age, the plaited roof gone. No longer are the windows hung with lace curtains, nor the kitchen permeated with the pungent smells of pork tamales, *tettapoon*, and *sofkee*.

Alice lamented to me, "My pictures, my nice wardrobe, my clothes—everything gone. You know, Shirley, when my house burned, my mama Nellie has lots of pictures of all the people. I didn't know who they was. She has one of those books when they was showing the slavery. I want my kids to see it. But I had to go on. I had children, and there was nothing I could do. That's when I move back to Texas and get a job."

Adjacent to the adobe ruins was a very small, concrete-block structure that Nellie had built later to accommodate a stove and other possessions. It, too, was in disrepair.

The two structures overlooked an arroyo and as Alice and I looked down I noticed a small, limpid, spring-fed pool and creek below. Alice walked to the edge to look down to the bottom. "You know, we had to wash clothes way down there [the creek] on a board—didn't have washboards," she said. "It was hard, but we was used to it. My mama Nellie carried buckets of water from down there for her garden and her roses—Amelia, too. When she couldn't go, we have to go down to there with the buckets and bring up the water."

Alice's daughters and granddaughters recall going down to get buckets of water under the watchful eyes of Nellie and, later, their *granita.* Effie laughed, "We all used to fight and stand in line for the small bucket. They were all different sizes. No matter what—if you got to the top and spilled the water, you had to go back and get more water."

I followed Alice as she scuffled around the ranch compound pointing out things to me. As if she were still living on the ranch she lingered over a little withered pepper plant that Henry had failed to water.

Guadalupe was now a desolate place, but when Alice visited the ruined adobe, her mother's lime and peach trees flourished in her eyes. She pointed to a spot in the landscape, her photographic memory alert: "My mama Nellie had her little garden over there," she said.

I saw only large clumps of cactus in the hard, red soil. Alice smiled and pointed to a little circle of tied sticks. "Shirley, see my stick fence over there by the house? I keep my little goats there."

To the side of the adobe ruin was a little stick house with a tarp roof, now used for storage of ranch equipment. "My grandmama Amelia lived in that stick house, too," she said. "She learned me how to cook, wash, sew."

Alice pointed to the ground next to it. "You see over here, Shirley. Amelia had another little stick house. It was pretty old."

I recognized scattered stones from the rock foundation of this second, earlier stick house and a few broken sherds of a bean pot jumbled with pieces of metal. Alice said, "You know, my mama cooked frijoles in those little pots—add some chilies and a little salt and water, and cook for a long time. That's right."

Knowing of the large families characteristic of her ancestors, I asked Alice how they all fit in the little stick house. She looked at me in surprise. "There wasn't no problem," she said. "At night we all sleep around the fire and the rest of the time—well, we was always working outside."

Alice paused during our tour of the ranch to reflect on the memories vividly painted in her mind. Then she pointed up to the distant mountains, saying:

> I was nine years old. On the ranch we would be out there [in the mountains]. A bunch of us, we'd go up into the mountains and spend a day up there and come back down in the evening. We was young and it wasn't a long walk. Shirley, I herd the goats up there too. My mama tell me to go there so they can eat. One day the goats spread all around and the little dog was lying down. I look up, and there is a black devil—just like that! Looking at the goats. Couldn't move. Couldn't cry. "Lord, have mercy." I say, "What have I done? What did I say bad to my mama Nellie? What I gonna do?"

Alice's face became animated, lost in this terrible childhood memory but amused in recalling her adventure.

> I run home screaming. I was worried my mama would whip me 'cause of the goats. My Uncle John is up there riding a little donkey. I was screaming and crying because I know the old devil was out there. I knew my mama would whip me. I tell Uncle John that his face was looking at me! . . . Uncle John, he told my mama, Nellie, that a black bear had gone up there. My mama, she says, "Go get my gun and get that bear!" Uncle John went to the house to get a gun and he went and shot that old bear.

After our visit to Guadalupe came to an end, Alice and I followed Henry's truck back to town and his house. Alice was planning to cook lunch for us before we headed back to Múzquiz. Henry slouched over the tile counter in his kitchen, pouring a bucket of water from the well over a pot while I plied him with questions.

Never at a loss for words, Henry began to talk about the "elderlies" as he called them, a term often used by other descendants for the early settlers. Alice occasionally nodded her head as she fussed in the kitchen, indicating her approval. Sometimes Henry glanced nervously at Alice to make sure that she did not consider his comments inappropriate.

"You know I was born in Nacimiento," he began. "My first job was herding goats. Finished school and went with my brother George to the U.S. I go back and forth. Nellie died and then my sister Alice went to the States. After George passed I take his place here."

There, in Mexico, life had been different when Henry was growing up—though not necessarily easy. He relayed the story of his strict upbringing by women in Mexico:

> My mama Nellie talked English but it was different. You say that they speak Afro-Seminole. Some killed in the Mexican Revolution around 1910. Some went to Fort Clark. They's all over now. Back then they had a respect for the old Seminoles. My grandmama told me to do something and I did it. She says, "Get some water—get me fire to light my pipe—feed the pigs." She hit with a cane if you didn't do right. We was always afraid. . . . Sunday morning and evening we go to church—embarrassing. I don't like it because my mama was always looking at me—couldn't breathe. Most people stopped going to church after the old-timers die out.

Alice hugged him with a forgiving smile. "Henry *was* pretty bad," she said.

When he eventually crossed the border to work on ranches and in the oil fields of west Texas, Henry faced discrimination—stories he fleshed out for us as we prepared for lunch:

> Weren't lots of places in Texas I could go in. Couldn't go in the restaurant. One place the cook said that we can't feed no niggers. Had to go in the back door or wait outside to get food. We go to the back door, and they bring us a hamburger or something with rotten lettuce. We couldn't order a steak or nothing. Black people couldn't afford them.
>
> One morning the cook told Mr. George our boss that we can't feed those people—"no niggers here. Niggers go in the back." If you put your

> food on their table, they would pack you out. Mr. George, he puts his gun on the table and says you're gonna feed these people.

I asked Henry, who had ultimately returned to Nacimiento despite venturing back and forth into the States for work, "What about your children? What about their future?"

His face reflected his concern about the situation as he answered:

> I would say for my kids no future here. They need to go to school. It's just living—work and eat here. No big future. I'm seventy years old and I take care of the cattle and come home, go to sleep at noon. Then I take care of the farm the rest of the day. It is so dry . . . no food for the animals. I'm going to have to take the horses over the mountains where they can feed. . . . It'll cost me some money to take the horses over there.

Henry Fay pulled me aside and pointed up to the mountains behind where Alice's ranch lay.

> Shirley, do you see those mountains up there? The old-timers lived up there at Buena Vista in pole [stick] houses . . . lived there a long time until 1856. You know, on the side of the hill where they could watch for the Indians. The Indians would ride up on their horses and ambush the old people plowing in the fields or slip up on the horses at night and steal them. When they [the Indians] came down, the women ran with the children to the caves up there. If the Indians came, you know John Horse and the men would stop them. They built their little pole houses up there and a little pole church my grandmother Rosa Fay called Mt. Zion. The people called it [where they went] the Canyon de los Negros."

Henry returned to his duties in the kitchen as Alice oversaw his progress with a pot of boiling frijoles. Alice fussed as she slowly patted out corn tortillas, but, as usual, she did it with a theatrical posture, looking at me to make sure I was paying attention. Henry continued to talk a mile a minute while his two small children tumbled all over the plaid couch. He was oblivious to the noise but Alice scolded them. Henry's well-worn saddle, bridle, and harness occupied a corner of the small house, but there were no other pieces of furniture except for the kitchen table and chairs. We all sat down to eat in the kitchen and the meal was delicious, replete with Alice's pork tamales and thin tortillas. Alice and I stayed to clean up, and at dusk we said our good-byes and left for Múzquiz, despite Henry's entreaties for us to spend the night. We departed Nacimiento as the ageless sun made another dramatic retreat over the purple mountains.

On my last visit to Del Rio to see Alice in 2005, she and Effie were furious with Henry again. This time they reported that he was selling parts of Alice's concrete block structure adjacent to the adobe ruin to a distant relative.

Alice lamented, "I have my grandmama's old stuff up at the ranch—and my big cooking pot for *sofkee*. I can't believe it. Henry sold all my stuff on the ranch, even the roof of my house."

When I visited Alice at her daughter Carmen's new home in San Antonio afterward, I asked Alice about Henry. She threw out her hands in resignation.

"No, I can't be mad at Henry," she said. "Yeah, he sold all my stuff, even the roof, but I'm not mad at Henry. You know the good Lord will work it all out."

On the occasions of my visits in Mexico I had enveloped myself in Alice Fay and her stories that centered on her ranch, Guadalupe, in Nacimiento. She lives through her memories of her people bound together in an identity of Black Seminole or Mascogo nourished by years of diasporas to seek freedom: those maroon ancestors who departed Florida for Indian Territory—her great-great-grandparents Carolina and Tina, their daughter Rose Kelly, Carolina's siblings and their families, John Horse and his sister Wannah and their families, Teener Factor's large family and her husband July's brothers and parents, Cornelia Perryman and her sons, and the Bowlegses—all were bound in generations of kinship vested in their African origins and their lives on Sea Island plantations, and nurtured by years of affiliation with their Seminole owners. Later, these close-knit families collaborated in a desperate trip from Indian Territory to freedom in Mexico. However, their lives in Nacimiento continued to be shattered by uprisings and bloodshed. The story of one of these devastating conflicts, the Mexican Revolution from 1910 to 1920, is recalled by many of the Mascogo elders.

CHAPTER ELEVEN

Two Old "Sisters" Talk about the Old People

> The conversation of friends is the nearest approach we can make to heaven while we live . . . so it is in a temporal sense also, the most pleasant and the most profitable improvement we can make of the time we are to spend on earth.
>
> Rachel Russell, 1636–1723

From unlikely situations and unexpected conversations with Black Seminole women in Mexico and Texas, stories told by Alice Fay, her relatives, and friends merged over time. Like artifacts that are revealed in an excavation unit, they join together in a context pointing to their use during a specific time period or in a particular way. These spontaneous stories all fold into one larger story of Black Seminoles during the Mexican Revolution from 1910 to 1920. One cannot talk about Alice's people in Nacimiento without casting them as unwilling participants during this time. The McKellars and Rosa Fay and her family experienced this dissolution earlier, in the 1890s, on the McKellar ranch in Coahuila. But the Mexican Revolution affected everyone, whether wealthy landlord, middle-class worker, or impoverished peon.[1]

Alice Fay was a young girl at the time of the revolution, but her great-grandmother Rose Kelly, her grandmothers Amelia Valdez and Rosa Fay, and other female relatives were caught up in the dark clouds of chaos created by dictatorships and revolutionary figures such as Pancho Villa, Porfirio Díaz, Victoriano Huerta, and Emiliano Zapata. The controversial Villa took control of the northern part of Mexico, which included Coahuila. As the violence escalated over ten years, some Mascogos fled to Texas, others tried to avoid conscription, and others chose to fight the Villistas. The women in Nacimiento banded together in a network of large matrifocal families and tended their fields and livestock. With the men gone, always lurking in the women's minds was the unpredictability of the political antagonists and their soldiers. Guerilla bands roamed across the country destroying and burning villages and stealing food.

Many of the stories surrounding the Mascogos in Mexico during the revolution have not been told—that is until I had the fortune of meeting one of Alice Fay's old friends, Genevieve (*Ninfa*) Payne, at her home in Kerrville. On one of my visits to Alice there in 1998, prior to her move to Del Rio, she had informed me that Genevieve had some stories to tell me about her people during the Mexican Revolution. An avid storyteller, Genevieve shared recollections that point to the bravery and fortitude of her ancestors at this time, including her mother, Mirtes Gordon Payne, and her father, John Payne. They are evocative stories that provide powerful testimony to the courage of Mascogo women.

"You know Genevieve grew up in Mexico, and her mama was kidnapped by Pancho Villa," Alice said unexpectedly, immediately getting my attention.

"Is she home?" I asked in excitement. "Can we visit her today?"

"Why, sure, Sugar," she replied. "Genevieve knows we're coming."

After we arrived at her tiny frame house in Kerrville, a spry Genevieve greeted Alice and me and motioned for us to come in and sit down in her living room, which was gaily decorated with a Christmas tree and lights. She was preparing to leave for Kansas to visit her daughter for the holidays, and the house was full of potted plants lined up to await a caretaker. Her children and grandchildren peered at us from photos placed between the plants.

Genevieve's family shares a history befitting an epic western movie. She was born in 1926 to Mirtes and John Payne. Mirtes and John raised a large family in Nacimiento, Mexico, six members of which are still alive.

Alice Fay, again in that computer data bank of her mind, repeated to me the genealogical history of the family. "You know, Genevieve and I grew up together in Nacimiento," Alice said. "Our ranches was close together. She's out of Pompey Factor—her great-granddaddy. . . . My daughter Carmen and Genevieve are cousins." She laughed, "You know Genevieve and I are related on both sides."

Alice nodded her head as I tried to assimilate these facts. I recalled that Pompey Factor was a descendant of Teener Factor. Not only was Pompey a Seminole Negro Indian scout, but he was also a famous Medal of Honor recipient.

Genevieve started out her conversation by identifying her ranch in Mexico. She talked fast—very fast—and her words seemed to dance off my notebook as she started her story:

"Our little *ranchería* was called Barancas Azul," she began. "Barancas, right on the Sabinas—right next to Alice's ranch, Guadalupe, but across the arroyo."

I recalled the arroyo below the cliff on Alice's ranch and the little stream below where they drew water in buckets to water Nellie's garden.

Genevieve looked at Alice fondly as she reminisced, "You know, my mama called Alice's mama Nellie 'Corazón.' They took a pecan, broke it in half, and each took a half to show they was like sisters. They would help each other make quilts—sing old songs—talk about years ago—make *sofkee*."

"Genevieve was raised on *sofkee*," Alice said with a sly grin.

Genevieve chuckled. "We two played together on the ranch on Sundays," she said. "We'd slide down the hill and jump out of the trees. . . . We used to go to dances. On Christmas we go to church—woo-woo—drink mescal and sing and shout. I never did fast, though. . . . All those old people worked too hard."

Alice changed the subject to catch Genevieve up with all the news. "You know, Auntie Sara [her great aunt, the daughter of Rose Kelly] was in a nursing home. Last place I want to go." She sighed, apparently thinking about the future.

"How's Miss Charles?" Genevieve inquired.

"She still gets around," Alice replied.

Our conversation was interrupted momentarily by the jangle of a phone ringing. Speaking in Spanish, Genevieve told her friend on the phone that Alice had gotten married.

"¡*Vivo y coleando*!"

After Genevieve hung up, the two women grinned mischievously and told me that they were looking for *chulos* (boyfriends). Genevieve inquired, "Do you know any old buffalo soldiers? Maybe I'll find one in Kansas when I visit my daughter? ¡*Un macho tiene huevos*!" The two women laughed together in an age-old female conspiracy.

Looking around at the Christmas decorations in her little room, Genevieve quickly changed the subject again, lamenting, "Christmas is so sad. I get to think about all those that was living."

Alice nodded her head in agreement and there was quiet for a moment as they reflected on their ancestors. By now I had given in to the unexpected turns and twists of their conversation and decided just to go with the flow. Alice always talked freely, often revealing new information, when she was with an old friend.

Genevieve showed me a photo of her husband of forty-three years wearing a black cowboy hat. "We had eight children," she said. Shaking her head, she added, "That man sure drank a lot. Buried him in his black cowboy hat—that's what he wanted. He was part Indian, but he wasn't Seminole. He tried to get me to move to Mexico but I wouldn't." Genevieve put her hands on her slim hips and frowned. "No! I wouldn't let him stick me out there on a ranch in Mexico with all those children. They couldn't go to school then."

With no prompting from me, she continued her fast-moving family history at a gallop:

"My mama was Mirtes Payne [1885–1968]. She was a big black woman and she had a hard time in Mexico. . . . After mama died I paralyzed my whole side. You just have to hold out. . . . She was the daughter of Isaac Gordon and a lady named [Susan] Sukey Factor. My grandmama Sukey [born in 1845] was a slave in Indian Territory and escaped. She spoke that 'broken language' [Afro-Seminole], you know."

Alice nodded in agreement: "She was pretty old when I knew her, Sukey Factor . . . like my great-grandmama Rose Kelly. Sukey was

Fig. 24. John and Mirtes Gordon Payne, circa 1916, on the porch of their home in Brackettville after leaving Mexico. Mirtes was the daughter of Isaac Gordon, a black runaway who fled to Nacimiento, and Sukey (Susan) Factor, a descendant of Florida-born Teener Factor and July. John was son of Rena Remo and Plenty Payne, a descendant of Florida-born Plenty Payne, who was Carolina's brother and Rose Kelly's great-uncle. Institute of Texan Cultures, University of Texas at San Antonio. Courtesy of Genevieve Payne.

on the trip [flight from Indian Territory]. . . . She passed away early on. . . . She died at Christmas. She had a heart attack sitting in her chair—Nana Sukey did."

Genevieve continued to describe her mother: "My mama Mirtes was real strict. She had fourteen children . . . two little girls and one boy would die later. She had to be strict with all those kids. Later, I came to Brackett and went to school. I washed dishes in Miss Charles's mama Rebecca's café."

Later, at Alice's eighty-ninth birthday in Del Rio, I met Genevieve's brothers John and Fred Payne, and her sisters Beatrice and Lorraine

Payne. Lorraine had told me "My nickname is Babita or Bita [*Bete* or *Biti*]. . . . Everybody had a nickname. They named me Lorraine for my older sister who passed when I was young."

During our visit, Genevieve, the vivacious one of the sisters, began to further detail the story of her Mascogo ancestors, how they came to Nacimiento, and their role in the 1910–19 Mexican Revolution when Pancho Villa's efforts at conscripting the men struck fear in the heart of the Mascogo community in Coahuila. She began her story,

> There were two brothers, Isaac and Albert—he was the oldest one. Isaac was my granddaddy who married Sukey. Albert escaped from his plantation owner in Alabama to run away to Mexico. He crossed the Rio Grande and reached Nacimiento where the Seminoles was happy to see him. Albert liked it so much that he went back to Alabama to get his brothers Henry and Isaac. The plantation master almost beat Albert to death for running away, but he was telling his brothers that they could still run away to Mexico when his back was healed. So they started out to Mexico and they hide by day and travel by night, to avoid the white people. . . . They had reached Texas when one day Albert says, "If we can make it to that motte [a patch of brush] we'll be all right." It was nine or ten miles to the brush over open prairie, but they made it all right and there in the motte, standing up against a tree, was a brand-new rifle and on the ground beside it a pile of cartridges. The rifle was just standing there—a brand-new rifle. "Now we're all right!" Albert said. "Now we can fight!" Well they [slave hunters] caught them somehow at Eagle Pass and they was put in jail.

Genevieve paused briefly and continued:

> The jailer said they better make it a good meal because next morning their owner comes to claim them. Well, they start digging in the dirt floor with their hands. They find a little piece of iron to help. They dig till daylight and crawled out. They took off running. They was chasing them with bloodhounds. Woo! Woo! They cross the Rio Grande and went into Mexico and join the Seminole.

As she described her maternal grandfather, Isaac Gordon, Genevieve's voice took on a sharper tone. She grimaced, "I didn't like my granddaddy Isaac [Gordon]." she said. "He was mean. He said, 'Run do this, run do that.' I was scared of my mama Mirtes's people."

"How did your parents meet?" I asked.

"My mama met my daddy John Payne in Nacimiento," she said. "My daddy John's parents was Rena July Remo and Plenty Payne but he was raised by Joe Remo. His grandmama was Kitty Wilson, you know mama of all those sisters—Molly [Mollie July] Perryman, Penny Factor, and Cressy [Theresa] Wilson, and Julia Payne. His cousin was Monroe and they fought together against Pancho Villa."[2]

Genevieve laughed, "Molly [Maggie/Perryman] was my great-aunt. . . . She was the nicest lady. You know Molly had all those children with different last names—Kelly, July, Wilson, Warrior. I can't remember all of them."

Molly seemingly regretted her many relationships. "She told me when I was growing up, 'Now don't jump the fence like I did,'" Genevieve said. "I remember I was embarrassed."

I knew that both Molly and her sister Theresa (or Cressy) later headed up household compounds on Fort Clark in 1902 (see map 2). I asked Alice and Genevieve about the two sisters. Alice nodded her head wisely. "I sure do remember Cressy, too," she said. "She was mild and had blue eyes."[3]

From her living room, Genevieve continued her story as Alice and I listened:

> Well, he [John] my daddy came there [Brackettville] and my auntie Cressy felt sorry for him. She was my favorite aunt. She says his stepfather, Joe Remo, would work him to death, so he hadn't been inside a schoolhouse. He always had him doing stuff. . . . Well, one Christmas John's stepfather sent him to Oklahoma to work. John come home for Christmas and goes to Brackett to see Auntie Cressy. She was going to Mexico, and she asked him to go.
>
> Well, at Christmas he saw all those Mexicans and blacks dancing in Mexico. He got scared. He didn't speak Spanish, but he learned real quick. . . . He said, "Don't you know what is freedom? I'm not going back to Texas!" Well, Aunt Cressy gave him a mule and a mare. She gave him land. He farmed and ranched and moved out to the La Lela [ranch]. Everyone owned the farm. He built a little house. A year after that he

Fig. 25. John Payne and Monroe Payne pose with cartridge belts crossed over their chests. Both fought against Pancho Villa in the Mexican Revolution from 1910 to 1920. John's daughter, Genevieve Payne, related that the Mexicans called him El Pájaro, which "means bird . . . because he was so fast." Institute of Texan Cultures, University of Texas at San Antonio. Courtesy of Genevieve Payne.

saw this tall black woman and then wanted to marry her. That was my mama, Mirtes [see fig. 24].

The years between 1910 and 1920 were a troubling time for Genevieve and Alice's ancestors in Coahuila, Mexico. Even the remote Nacimiento community could not escape the widespread, tumultuous Mexican Revolution and its repercussions. Some Mascogo men were conscripted into guerilla bands led by the notorious Pancho Villa or other revolutionaries. These stories of the Mexican Revolution vary in the collective memories of the older Black Seminole women like Alice and Genevieve, but each elder who lived in Mexico has one tale, usually connected to the notorious Pancho Villa.

With the onset of the Mexican Revolution, Genevieve described how John Payne had escaped from Villa and his ragtag "army" to join the opposition forces. Genevieve continued:

> Villa was running, and he was a crook. He took girls in Mexico and keeps them. His men come into Nacimiento and take all the stuff in the store . . . in the fields . . . all the food. He was mean. He slapped one of the women. We knew the Villistas because they would cut the tops of their ears when they joined Villa. My daddy, John, joined the *federalistas*. "*Ya se van siendo bola.*" They sung to the music, *La Cucaracha . . . Porque veine* Pancho Villa. . . . They sang, "*Tierra y libertad*!"

Genevieve paused, then went on, drawing us into the drama of her family.

> I hated those songs. My daddy John was dark and skinny—brown—his hair was white. He was so good in the war [the Mexican Revolution] they called him El Pájaro . . . that means bird . . . because he was so fast. There was lots of trouble everywhere and the Villistas was always calling him looking for him. . . . There was a young girl, Ida, going to have a wedding. A Villa soldier fall in love with her. She was so scared. *Besa de senonta*. My mama Mirtes sent Alice's cousin Sophy [Sophie Washington] to talk, but the soldier wanted Ida.[4] The soldiers came in to Nacimiento from both sides . . . you know that main street. They was shooting at the

> house and killed four or five people. Well, my daddy [John] was going to milk the cows, and the women yell to him that soldiers was on both sides of the road. My mama, Mirtes, she said that he jumped on a horse and she hit it with a broom. He jumped the fence, and they never saw him. He took to the brushes because he knew the way. It was sure a fast horse! Another time they was shooting at the house [see fig. 25].

Alice interjected, "You know Nana Rosa Fay's brother, Monroe, he fought for the *federalistas* [or *federales*] against Villa too. My Uncle Andrew Fay didn't want to join Pancho Villa's men. He puts on a dress. He says that he's gonna get some water. He got a horse and didn't stop till he hit the border."

Genevieve continued her story:

> They couldn't catch my daddy or the other men. So Pancho Villa's soldiers came into the village and took families. . . . Woo, woo. . . . My mama was home with four children. They take her and my grandmama, Sukey. They take them to Múzquiz for a hard trip and put them on a train and then tried to put them on a boat and take them to an island . . . the Isla de Maria . . . Veracruz. *Cien de bajo.* Mama had a baby with her . . . about two or three. The baby, . . . a little girl, died so they threw it into the sea.

Genevieve's mother and relatives were not the only Mascogo women captured by Pancho Villa and taken to Veracruz. Villa had hoped that their men, like John Payne, would surrender upon learning of the capture of their families.

Alice Fay interrupted Genevieve's story: "Bill Griener's mama was captured, too. She lost two little girls," she said. "I remember they take Clary too [Rosa Fay's prophetic daughter]. . . . My great-grandmama Rose Kelly, . . . she went to my Auntie Lizzie's house [Amelia's daughter] to hide so that's why they didn't find her!"

"Sandy Wilson and his mama, Mary [Maria] Wilson [Rosa Fay's daughter], was captured, too . . . a five-year-old, and his two sisters, Rosie and Lucy. . . . Their daddy was Garfield Wilson and he was running," Genevieve added. "Elsa Payne and other women was there. It was a hard time with my daddy still running."

In the midst of this conflict in 1914, the United States seized Veracruz in a dispute with the conservative dictator Huerta. This action would bring Genevieve's mother, Mirtes, to the forefront of the political drama, for through her efforts the Mascogo women were freed by the Americans. Genevieve recalled that Mirtes had some education:

> Well, my mama Mirtes could read and write a little. She always says that writing was important to us and we needed it. She had bad handwriting but she wrote a note. There was a Spanish man where they were in jail trying to help. The soldiers made all the women give their names so he said to write a letter. So she was writing, and when the Spanish man came back she gave him a message in her shoe.

Genevieve pretended to put a note in her shoe before continuing:

> He gave it to the Americans. In the next two or three days they was free. They go by boat to Galveston and then San Antonio. Then they was in Brackett. By this time my mama lost another child. My mama's mama [Sukey] was there in Brackett. She didn't even know they was kidnapped. Later, my daddy John, he goes back to Nacimiento to look for his family, and they was gone. Then he came to Brackett. He didn't know he lost two little girls. They stayed awhile, but my daddy wanted to go back to Mexico.

Genevieve's brother, John Payne, named for his father, told me on another occasion, "My mama and daddy took a wagon all the way from Brackettville to go back to Mexico—with all us kids."

Genevieve sighed as she reflected on the past and a father she loved.

> My daddy John Payne died in Múzquiz in 1929. He came into town and was riding a gentle little horse . . . we called him Pony. It was getting late—about 6:00 P.M. He was on this way home back to the ranch, and he decided to go through that trail. . . . His horse stepped in a hole and fell on him. He couldn't move. He was in such pain. All he could think about was the good Lord. He had too many close calls running from Pancho

> Villa. People was coming from the field. . . . He kept calling. . . . Some folks passed that way but couldn't hear him. Pony was standing there. After they found him, he lasted nine days. They took him to Múzquiz but it was too late. He's buried in Nacimiento. My mama, Mirtes, is buried in Brackettville 'cause she moved there after he died. She was eighty-eight. She was always ready to help people even if she had only a little.

As Genevieve finished her story I recalled that her mother Mirtes's tombstone in the Seminole Indian Scouts Cemetery is engraved "Grandmother."

Their memories may falter in some cases, but the women's stories continue, some focusing on rescue attempts. One story details a dramatic rescue by Alice's paternal grandmother, Rosa Dixon Fay. Her son-in-law Garfield Washington, when running from Villa, had to escape Mexico to Texas. His wife, Rosa's daughter, Mary Fay Wilson, who was a child on the McKellar ranch, and children Sandy, Rosie, and Lucy were left in Mexico without support. Garfield went to work on the Shahan ranch to make money to bring his family over. He asked Rosa to help. Rosa Fay, living in Brackettville at the time and knowing her relatives were destitute, determined to rescue them. As stories go, she took the train from Brackettville to Palau, Mexico, and brought Garfield's family back across the border to Texas.

Other stories of the revolution are left to the vagaries of old age, but Genevieve and Alice's acute memories reflect the diasporic history of the Black Seminoles, conjoined in purpose. Despite their growing diversity through outside marriages and Mexican influences, Rose Kelly's people still remained a maroon community, continuing to fight and preserve their culture and hold onto their African-born traditions. Despite the geographical boundaries and incessant conflicts, the Nacimiento and Brackettville communities remained bound in identity by genealogical depth and a firm resolve to be independent.

The shadows grew longer as the two old friends continued to reminisce in a stream of conversations at Genevieve's house, talking of ancestors whose names sounded familiar but eluded me because of their repetition. Finally, Alice sighed and I knew that she was tired and it was time to depart. As we left the house and walked through Genevieve's rickety little gate, Alice commented on the plants in the front yard. Her grandchildren had told me, "Granita is always getting plant cuttings. She tries to get corn from a little stick."

To the side of the old chain-link fence was a wilted plant. The two old women talked about it as if it were a person. "It's a good plant," they pointed out to me.

Their words were sprinkled with some Spanish words and a few conspiratorial laughs. The lively Genevieve told me she picked the leaves and put them in alcohol.

"It's good for arthritis . . . like marijuana," she said. "Its name is the *ruta* [rue]. . . . Woo, woo. I'm surprised the police haven't found it. I keep it in a jar and I just rub it on my legs and woo, woo, the pain just goes away."

Alice smiled and nodded her head in conspiracy. "It sure is [good]."

Later, curious about the *ruta* plant, I looked it up in a botanical book. The scientific name is *Rutaceae,* a small plant with a pungent odor. It is an herb of ancient lineage, probably brought to Mexico by the Spanish, who inherited it from the Romans. It can treat more than eighty-four ailments from earaches to menstrual pains and hysteria.

As Alice and I left, I told Genevieve that we would see her in Kerrville in June.

Alice retorted defiantly, "Well I'm not gonna be here. I'm gonna be in Mexico or Brackett. I've had enough! Well I just wanna be by myself. I hate it! Gonna rent a house in Brackett, have someone come stay with me. Can't go to Mexico now."

As we drove away, I looked at Alice and again saw that steely resolve in her face, mirroring the decades-old determination of her female ancestors like her great-grandmother Rose Kelly and her grandmother, Rosa Fay. And I could understand the passage of time that lurked in the depths of her mind—between her virile youth in Mexico and the vicissitudes of old age. I reflected on the poignant story of Mirtes Payne, and other brave Mascogo women, who survived with their families in this theater of tumultuous hardships and revolution in Mexico. As Maggie Kelly, a descendant of Rose Kelly, speaking Afro-Seminole in Brackettville in the 1940s, said of her maroon people, "*We nuh duh people whey duh gi'up.*"[5]

CHAPTER TWELVE

The "Broken Language" and Those "Basket" Names

> Yes, I remember grandma Hannah—and my grandpa Calina. They were Ibos. My grandpa told me how he got here. He was playing on the beach in Africa and a big boat came near the beach. The men in the boat took down a flag and put up a piece of red flannel. The children got close to the water to see what they were doing. Then the men came off the boat and caught them and when the old folks came in from the fields there were no children in the village. They were all on the boat. And then they came here.
>
> Phoebe Gilbert, an Ibo descendant living on Sapelo Island

My research with Alice's ancestors has been a slow but gradual process of enlightenment, like a series of archaeological excavations that turn up a montage of clues to decipher, which then reveal stories about the people who lived there. These tantalizing clues led to new revelations that fueled my determination to finish this book. As I wound my way through the many contours of Black Seminole culture over the years, I grew more amazed at the depth and resilience of Alice's people's cultural practices. Every conversation revealed another strand in this fabric of practices woven in Africa and rewoven in the Americas. Included in those strands is what Hancock calls the Afro-Seminole language, which he determines is a form of creole the Black Seminoles spoke. Naming conventions also are a significant part of this heritage and reflect practices among the freedmen in Oklahoma and the Gullah of the Sea Islands, even today. The elder Black Seminoles called the Afro-Seminole language the "broke" or "broken" language. In reality, though, it was not "broken." Like Gullah spoken among the blacks living on the rice plantations on the Sea Islands of South Carolina and Georgia, it was a language with its own grammar, vocabulary, and phonological or sound systems. Hancock determined "that Afro-Seminole is almost identical to the conservative Gullah of a century ago . . . but it doesn't have the non-English sounds which Gullah has. . . . [M]ost of the vocabulary is the same as in other English-derived creole languages, and has nearly the same pronunciation as well." Mulroy determines that its lexicon was English-sounding words with the influence of African, Spanish, and Muskogee words.[1]

It is important to understand the relation of Afro-Seminole to Gullah because the retention of this language throughout the diasporas of Alice Fay's people played a prominent role in their identity as "Black Seminoles." The eminent African American linguist Lorenzo Dow Turner in the 1930s recorded the Gullah used by former slaves in South Carolina and Georgia in discussing their traditions and daily lives. He determined that Gullah was derived from African languages spoken by slaves brought to the Americas in the eighteenth and nineteenth centuries. His observations lifted the shroud of ignorance and led to a new, revitalized view of African culture in the Americas. He recorded more than three hundred loanwords from various African languages in Gullah and, significant to this chapter, almost one thousand African personal names used by Gullah-speaking people. His documentation countered commonly held assumptions that the Gullah dialect was a form of baby talk used by slave owners to facilitate oral communication between themselves and slaves. Turner pioneered a significant breakthrough, for he proved that the Gullah language, like the Afro-Seminole of the Black Seminoles, was a language with its own grammar and vocabulary.[2]

Race constructions were complexly intertwined in the slave experience and exposure to Indian culture. The Black Seminoles living with the Seminoles in Florida and later in Indian Territory, Mexico, and Texas did not realize that the language they were speaking was of African origins and Gullah roots. Some had learned English from their lives on plantations or Spanish from former owners in Florida. During their lives with the Seminoles, some learned to speak the Creek Muskogee language. This association with the Indians colored their conversations and syncretic traditions. Historically, some Black Seminoles have referred to the unique language they spoke as "Seminole," just as they often refer to themselves as "Seminoles."

I remember talking to one old, red-suspendered veteran—Melvin Daniels—at the Seminole Indian Scouts Cemetery. Melvin was a descendant of Black Creek Elijah Daniels and Alice's great-aunt, Sara Daniels, Rose Kelly's daughter. He made a conspiratorial aside when in the midst of a group of people, including a black researcher who had accompanied me to Seminole Days. I overheard him say under his breath, "I have a *cabrito* [meat of a young goat] in the car. But it's only for the Seminoles."

According to Foster, one or two old women claimed to be Creek or Mikasuki when he visited Brackettville in the 1930s. He reported that the Black Seminoles called their language Creek and suggested that perhaps some of them could speak Muskogee. As noted previously, the men wore Indian dress—such as burnished silver bangles and hunting shirts—in Mexico and after they moved to Texas, according to descendants and eyewitness accounts.[3]

A descendant interviewed by Kenneth Porter in the 1940s told him that Wannah's (John Horse's sister) son, Andrew (Washington), and his wife, probably Clara, Alice's great-grandmother, "prayed in Indian."[4] One descendant recalled her parents speaking a strange language that she could not understand. Miss Charles Wilson recalled the elders chanting. "It was like an Indian chant," she said. "De-hey, de-hey—like that. I couldn't understand them and asked my mother [Rebecca July] what they were saying. She didn't know either." However, Miss Charles, despite her recollection, was one of the last speakers of Afro-Seminole in the Black Seminole community.[5]

Alice Fay, as usual, provided a succinct explanation to clarify how Afro-Seminole came to be considered an American Indian language among her people. She relayed the key role of the language in their identity—their language was separate from that spoken by other African Americans. The Black Seminoles' belief that their "broken" language was Indian is also based on the fact that they realized that their English was different from the standard "black" English. As Alice Fay said when describing their language, "Others talk that *colored* talk." "When we come over here [Mexico], they only couldn't understand what we was saying," she said. "Some people think we're speaking Indian. Our language was broken Seminole—that's the language we raised up with. My grandmama and great-grandmama and others talk like that. We call ourselves Seminoles, the way we talk. We call it the broken language. Some of the elderlies they speak Seminole."

The Black Seminoles clung to that Indian identity because of their history with the Seminoles, with whom they had fought for their freedom and surrendered in Florida, but they also seem, even today, to cradle the two-sided relationship. In the days of racial stereotyping and bigotry against blacks in the United States, certainly a connection to Indians as noble vestiges of a western American panorama was appealing, rather than an association with slavery.

The WPA account of JoAnn (Chona) July by a white interviewer clearly illustrates this tendency of outsiders to stress the Indian connection. The interviewer describes JoAnn as a colorful girl with dominant Indian blood who goes barefoot and smokes a rolled cigarette: "Her love of horses, her wily and daring ways, her bright dresses and ornaments were that of an Indian. Her quick darting eyes, aquiline nose, thin lips and high cheekbones showed more Indian blood than Negro. Her horsemanship was her pride. . . . Johanna lived the life of a carefree Indian boy. She scorned a saddle, preferring to ride bareback and sideways."[6]

Cherokee heritage, in particular, was mentioned by descendants, often associated with admirable qualities like intelligence, and was considered to be an advantage. Hair also was used as a racial signifier. John Horse was reported to have "good" hair—Indian hair, or straight hair.[7] His sister, Wannah, was said to dress like an Indian. Woodward, a historian, observed among other black Indians that "Indian blood is frequently invoked to account for cherished traits of rebelliousness, ferocity, and fortitude."[8] In his 1930 visits to Black Seminole communities, Foster even remarked on this trait of assigning a wild or untamed quality, noting the members of the communities were fond of calling themselves Seminoles.[9] One female descendant I interviewed, Alice Barnett, Florida-born Cornelia Perryman's great-great-granddaughter, attributed Black Seminole men's propensity toward multiple partners to their Indian blood. "Those old men were wilder than Indians," she said. "They were—woo-woo—just like Indians!"[10]

Katja May, a historian of southeastern Indians, observes that such irrepressible Indian blood is a recurring topic in the slave narratives, and that part-Indian slaves were considered "sassy." May relates a conversation with an interviewee who said that her mother, a Black Creek, was captured but none of the whites wanted her because "she was so spirited." Indians were more prone "to fight when provoked, and significantly, part-Indian slaves were said to be more 'respected' by white owners." Part-Indian African Americans also had a reputation of being proud, hard-working, and likely to escape.[11] A former slave related that certain people did not like her papa "because he wasn't so black, and he had spirit, because he was part Indian."[12]

Miss Charles, as mentioned before, attributed her family's focus on education to "the Indian in us." "My mother wanted us to go to school. . . . I guess that was an Indian trait," she said. "[S]he wanted us to have an education, and she wanted the finer things."[13]

The Afro-Seminole language they called Seminole has been a double-edged sword for the community in that while it was a key factor in forging the Black Seminoles' identity as they were merged into an English-speaking population over time, it also marginalized those who spoke it. Miss Charles Wilson discussed the problems of the "broken language" in teaching the young children in Brackettville. "When I speak *Seminole* to my friends," she said, "the young folks say it's just *bad* English, but I beg to differ with them." She explained in her Afro-Seminole, "*Dem nuhlika'we duh talk lika'dis.* Them no like we do talk like this."[14]

The conversations of Rosa Dixon Fay and her family on the McKellar ranch in the 1890s, and comments made by Alice Fay a century later, reveal a few extant characteristics of the Afro-Seminole language. Sara McKellar, a daughter-in-law of the McKellar family ranch owner, David Skene McKellar, corresponded with Porter from the late 1940s to the 1950s about the Mascogos on the ranch. She reported that Amelia, Alice's maternal grandmother and daughter of Rose Kelly, spoke the "broken" language constantly, but it was seldom used by the younger generation.[15]

Turner describes two Gullah conventions that were revealed in the Afro-Seminole speech of Black Seminoles in Mexico. The first convention, known as a double subject, is the practice of opening a sentence with its subject and following it with a personal pronoun. Porter also observed the use of "he" as a universal third-person singular pronoun in the conversations he recorded in Nacimiento.[16] The conversations of Rosa Fay and her family, recorded by Maud McKellar, reflect the double subject and the use of a pronoun without regard to plurality or the sex of the referent. For example, Sally Fay, Rosa's daughter, reported, "Clary, he [she] eats lots and lots of mulberries."[17] Occasionally Alice's conversations may reflect this carryover of double subject. A pronoun will sometimes follow the noun, as in her statement, "You know Clary, she read the dreams like her mama Rosa."

The second convention is there is no distinction of voice in verbs. Afro-Seminole, like Gullah, is noted for the use of one verb for all tenses.[18] Alice's conversations sometimes reflect this, for she may use the same verb, such as "come" or "run," for past, present, and future voice. Rosa Fay's conversations on the McKellar ranch illustrate this convention. For example, Rosa Fay replied to Sally, "Sally, child, when the good Lord let you have lots of clothes you ought to save them up child. Maybe the hard times come and then you be awful glad that you have so much clothes."[19] Porter also observed that a few old parents, especially Rosa Fay, concluded sentences with the Gullah word *enty*, a corruption of something like "Is that so?" in reply to a statement that surprises the listener. By the 1940s, Porter said that little of the Black Seminole language was still in use.[20]

This exposure to the Afro-Seminole language was all a learning curve for me, but I had lots of help from the older women. On one occasion in Brackettville, the ever-helpful Ethel Warrior gathered some of the older women together to discuss their language and traditions. The conversations flowed freely as the women played off of each other's memories, demonstrating the ways in which their language and identity are linked. The occasion was a competitive stage on which women had the opportunity to relate personal stories that had never been revealed. Alice Fay, always the director of the drama, spoke up first, as usual, stressing that the broken language could carry a stigma.[21]

> When I first came over the border, I used to talk that broken language like I was brought up. I don't know. People would tell me that they don't understand me. My great aunties Hanna [*Hani/Hanu*] and Sara Daniels, they help me and tell me how to talk to get a job on Fort Clark when I cross. . . . That was after my husband Luis left me and I have to leave Mexico to feed my children. My mama, Nellie, kept my kids on the ranch. But those ladies told me not to be ashamed—that was my language. I remember that pretty good.

Gracie Lasky shared her own recollections. "My grandmother, Mary July Bowlegs, was very strict," she said. "She wouldn't let us speak that language . . . 'that broken language,' she would say. She wanted us to speak English and Spanish. She was very polite."

Ethel Warrior echoed, "My grandmother didn't want me talking Seminole either."

Ophelia Benson interjected:

> Everybody [outsiders] would whisper about us. They'd say, "Oh, they must be from Brackett" 'cause we'd get off the sidewalk and let them on. We was used to segregation you see. . . . My mother did not want me to speak the language—the "broke." She would correct me. Being Seminole made me mad! My daddy wanted us to go to school. He said, "Mexico is such a poor country—whatever you raise you eat." I was always afraid to go over to Nacimiento—that they wouldn't let you back. The old ones crossed all the time. When they came over here, they would just use their English names that they brought with them.

Some descendants like Lillie Mae Dimery also expressed their shame in speaking the broken language. "When I was smaller and they told me I was Seminole Indian, I was really ashamed of it," she said. "'Don't call me Indian,' I'd say. 'I'm not *no* Seminole.' The way they talked, the Gullah they used, I was ashamed of it. . . . But it's a thing to be proud of. I just didn't know that then. I didn't know the history, what we had, what it was all about."

Genevieve Payne reported a similar experience. "They'd [outsiders] make fun of us 'cause of the way we talked," she said. "Tell us to get back up in the saddle. Evelyn July, a first cousin of my daddy John [see figs. 24 and 25], would help me with the [English] language."

"Do you still speak the broken language?" I asked the women.

Gracie laughed, "I'd get with Ethel and we'd talk. 'Where you going?' I'd say."

The vivacious Ethel responded, "I's gwine to store."

Gracie slapped her hands together in the spirit of the moment: "Well, I sitting here on my ass doing nothing!"

The women all chuckled at this rather common black vernacular way of speaking. They were too young to actually remember details of the old people's language, but they put on a good act for me.

In a conversation, Anita Daniels, a descendant of Sara Daniels, recalled an added layer of complexity when it came to speaking—or not speaking—Afro-Seminole. While some outside people looked down on those who spoke the language, it was a two-way street, for some Black Seminoles shunned them if they didn't speak the language, just as they criticized those who chose to marry outside their endogamous community. The language clearly was tied into their identity. "My daddy Ernest left home but would take me on his trips back to Brackettville," she said. "The Daniels line was Cherokee [actually Black Creek]. My Seminole aunties would sometimes shun us because they said we were too American. They said we forgot our roots and we couldn't speak Seminole." She continued in a different tone, "My relatives [Black Seminoles] were peculiar, though. They didn't care for black-skinned people. . . . They would say now, 'Don't talk that colored talk. I didn't understand it.'"[22] By this statement, Anita echoed Alice Fay's earlier sentiment that African American Vernacular English or the African American language spoken by some blacks of that time period was quite different from Afro-Seminole. Clearly, then, some Black Seminoles cherished the Afro-Seminole and spoke it among themselves, which was another way to differentiate themselves from other African Americans. Being able to speak it was considered to be an insider's privilege, part of being Black Seminole, at least in the past.

Compounding all these African-derived language traditions exemplified in the broken language or Afro-Seminole is the fact that the Mascogos in Nacimiento each carried an additional Spanish given name and surname and spoke Spanish as well as English. William Pollitzer reports that blacks brought to the Sea Island plantations spoke more than "one native tongue" and also knew English languages.[23] When discussing different people, Alice Fay would add to my bewilderment by easily switching between the English and Spanish names without informing me. "Shirley, well, that was the way," she explained patiently. "We have different names so we can cross the border."

Alice's Fay's surname, Alvarez, is the Spanish substitution for Fay given to her family when they crossed into Mexico in 1850. Alice very seldom uses the surname of her second husband, Tomás Lozano. She explained it to me: "Over there [Mexico] it's my daddy's name Fay. That's how they call me. That was the way. That's right."

As I talked to the women over the years, I was overwhelmed at the depth and resilience of their African-derived cultural practices. Even though they did not realize those practices' deep origins, they cherished them. Besides the continuation of their Afro-Seminole language and its characteristics, later spoken only among themselves on certain occasions, another Gullah-related, entrenched tradition, as noted earlier, was their naming practices so characteristic of the Gullah people of the Sea Islands, and even continued today among the freedmen of Oklahoma.[24] When I began this book I pored over documents, trying to correlate the names with dates and historical events noted in the lists of deportees from Florida, the Seminole Negro Indian Scout enlistment registry at Fort Clark, and the U.S. census records. Despite my frustration, I could not know that these repeating names, a tradition that harked back to Africa, would become part and parcel of this story that I would try to untangle.

As illustrated in many of my conversations with the women, Black Seminole naming customs were redundant and complicated, again partly as a result of being nourished in close-knit endogamous communities, bonded by polygyny. The maddening generational repetition of names and use of Spanish names took me down many dead-end alleys as I tried to grapple with the task of distinguishing some of Rose Kelly's people, and to make genetic connections in order to unravel stories of the key Florida-born families and their journey later to Texas. As Adams cogently observes, lineages were not so much a family tree, but were made up of many strands: biological relationships, the extended family, and adoptions. She emphasizes that the unexpected is true of the naming system.[25] Moreover, the handed-down names were often spelled differently as witnessed with the given names and surnames Kibbett, Kibits, Cubit, Kibbetts, Kibbets, and Kibets. This was due in part to the fact that the Black Seminoles were an oral society and some in the early days could not read or write. Many of the names also were recorded differently by English-speaking outsiders.

Rose Kelly's people named their children in freedom, in multigenerational extended family units, when they were living side by side with their Seminole allies in Florida. Black Seminole women, as the custodians of genealogy, had the bloodlines etched in memory for instant recall, despite the complications of extramarital relationships and children born out of wedlock. Porter observes that the women named the children, both by tradition and the fact the men were often away fighting, scouting, or working on ranches.[26] Ethel July Warrior's comments concurred with his observation when I queried her as to whether this practice was characteristic of her people. She replied, "The women gave ninety percent of the names. The men were gone. The grandmother would name you. A man would name himself for his father and his father." Based on his research of ex-slave narratives, linguist John Inscoe coincidently reports that Gullah mothers usually named their children.[27] These practices explain the vast labyrinth of names handed down from generations, according to specific rules etched in Africa, only some of which can be ascertained today.

Turner's list of names and explanation of Gullah naming practices brought new insights into my challenge to understand this entrenched genealogical template.[28] Robert L. Hall also traced the linguistic, economic, and cultural ties shared by large numbers of enslaved Africans, showing that despite the fragmentation of the diasporas, many ethnic groups retained enough cohesion to communicate and transmit units of shared culture.[29]

Alice's brother, Henry Fay, had warned me of this characteristic of his people at the start of my research: "Fifteen or twenty of those old people would all have the same name." My optimism was quelled as I realized he was correct. Alice introduced new actors in her stories with identical names, like Rose and Rosa, and initially I did not realize that the names were repeated from different generations or were even for different people. Pronunciation also factored into my understanding of names mentioned in my conversations with the women. When I read the names as an English speaker, I accommodated them to my language—just as the WPA interviewer did in changing JoAnn to Johanna. JoAnn probably is a derivation of Wannah or Juana. I patiently drew endless, often futile, genealogical charts as my research progressed, dealing with the frustrations of different generations, spellings, and pronunciations. As time passed with acculturation and distance from Gullah-derived names, it appears that the Black Seminoles adopted new versions of given names and abbreviated versions. It also appears that the women in particular chose to name their daughters with more English-sounding names, evident in the names of Ophelia Benson and the sisters Genevieve (Ninfa) and Lorraine (Babita) Payne. However, the women also continued to carry African-derived "basket" names or nicknames, as discussed later in this chapter.

The survival of African-derived naming conventions detailed in Rebecca Bateman's seminal research among Seminole freedmen in Indian Territory echoes the complexities of Black Seminole genealogy in Mexico and Texas. Bateman focuses on three traits: namesaking; the double naming system, in which given names can be transmitted as surnames and vice versa; and the practice of reversing female and male names in succeeding populations. Following the linguist John Thornton, she determines some of these traits to be a characteristic of the African Kongolese system. In addition to these traits, the use of basket names was also a resilient African-derived naming tradition still carried by the Black Seminoles today.[30]

Turner observes that his Gullah informants in the 1930s did not remember the meanings of these names, but, like the Black Seminoles continued to use them in naming practices because their ancestors had used them.[31]

The son being named after the father or grandfather or uncle, even a distant relative, was a Black Seminole name-saking custom if one looks at the census records and other documents. The Black Seminoles drew from an inherited repertoire of names connected to the ancestors through a genealogical recall, those connections often stretching back many generations. For instance, Plenty Payne, a Seminole Negro Indian scout, carried the name of a distant relative, Carolina Payne's brother Plenty. He and his wife Rose named two of their sons Caesar and Wan, two names carried from Florida that would be repeated through generations. Three Cuffys (Cuffie/Cuffee/*Kufi/Kufiya*, meaning Friday)—two belonging to Chief Micanopy—were present on the lists of Black Seminoles departing Florida, and their names were still repeated in the 1980 Brackettville census. Women also named children for their aunts or grandmothers. Clary, Rosa Dixon Fay's daughter, for example, was named for her Florida-born grandmother.

There were four Adam Fays. The elder Adam Fay (Koonta) married Alice's paternal grandmother, Rosa, and their son Adam (Abram) Fay married her mother Nellie. I found out there were three Pompeys, two Ben Wilsons, three Roosevelts, four Carolinas or Kelinas, three Sandys, two Rabbits, and two Mondays.

Porter observes that the Factors, a large family with generational depth, showed strong African influences in the names. Lucy and Sandy named three of their boys August, July, and Dembo.[32] Dembo (*Daemba/Demba, Dimbu*) and his wife, also named Lucy (*Lusa*), then named a son Dindie (Dindy, *Dimi* or *Dimbu*). Teener and July provided some of their children with African-derived names: Sukey, Kistooa, Norata (*Or'rite*), Kuntusse (*Kunta/Kuta*), Rosenta, and Pond. Other names with possible African counterparts or their derivations were Nellie (*Nili*), Jenny (*Jeneba*), and Nanny (*Neni*). Teener's daughter Nanny also favored this convention, gifting her male children with the African-derived names Cuffee and Kibbett. Their son Sampson (*Sanson/Sambo*) later took his father's given name July as his surname, presumably as the oldest son to honor his father rather than using Factor carried by other members of his family. Sampson was a popular name, for there are three Sampsons on the lists of deportees leaving Florida for Indian Territory. July as surname was passed down by Sampson to all his descendants.

Another relative, Hardy (Hardie/*Arti*) Factor, and his wife Esther (*Hester*) continued this tradition of generational recycling of African-derived names in naming one son Hardy and another Pompey. Molly Perryman's son Pompey carried the name of the Medal of Honor winner, Pompey Factor. His given name, also spelled as *Lomprey, Fom-pey, Pom pi, Pompie,* or even *Conte,* and pronounced as Pom'pi among the Black Seminoles, coincidentally was the name of a Roman general. It has been argued that such English classical names were terms of derision imposed by slave owners as a source of amusement. However, Inscoe also points out that sometimes the names that appear to be classically derived are not terms of derision, but are actually a "misinterpretation of African words."[33] Pollitzer observes that the name Pompey may be derived from the Mende name *Kpampi,* meaning a line, course, or red handkerchief.[34] The name of Florida-born Caesar Payne and the Black Creek Caesar Bruner, rather than mimicking the name of a Roman ruler, may have been rooted similarly in a Gullah name, *Cosar,* variations of which appear on the departure lists to Indian Territory.[35] The given name of the present-day Evangelical Baptist minister in Nacimiento, Zulema Vázquez, has an African counterpart, *Sulima*.[36]

It is likely that historians Jerome Handler and Jo Ann Jacoby are correct in arguing that slave owners may have assumed an "English sounding equivalent" to an African-derived name. The retention of certain names also may have depended on how easily they were pronounced.[37] Certainly enslaved blacks realized correlations in pronunciation between their African-derived names and English names bestowed by owners, and manipulated their African name with an easily understood, equivalent English name. This way they retained their former identities and enduring African-derived naming traditions without the slave owner's knowledge.[38]

Inquiring as to the name of a slave, an owner may even have heard the African or Gullah name as an English name. The Gullah names passed down among the Black Seminoles such as *Sari,* for example, then likely became the English Sarah or Sara. Fiba or *Phibba,* one African name for a girl born on Friday, then became Phoebe or Phebe; *Abb*, the name for Thursday, became Abby; *Kete* became Katy or Kitty; *Mali* became Molly; and *Pene* became Penny. Nellie, the name of Alice's mother, draws on the Gullah feminine name *Nali* or *Nele*. Alternatively, the name also may emulate that of a prominent Indian female such as Nelly Factor.

Significantly, among Rose Kelly's people, the adopted English surnames carried by Indians such as Factor and Payne were consistently handed down only as surnames, unlike African-derived given names, again pointing to the deep roots of this tradition.

Thornton's research with Angolan archives reveals that some of the given names carried by slaves to the New World also were of Christian origin; this particularly referred to saints' names, which were often combined with African names.[39] This fact may also explain the popularity of names such as Mary and Sarah or Sara among the Black Seminoles over time, but even these names may have African-derived equivalents such as *Mara* or *Sari*. Perhaps Alice's ancestors, in these coincidences, realized that such overlaps attached a power to these names, making possible competing origins still valid. For instance, Rose or Rosa carried by Rose Kelly and Rose Seña Factor may be of Spanish origin or alternatively derived from the Gullah *Risa*.

Even names seemingly unrelated to African or other origins may have deeper roots than immediately obvious. Rose Kelly provided her second daughter with the nontraditional name Amelia, which struck me as unusual at first, given her predisposition to bestowing African-derived names on her progeny. Thornton, though, reports that Amelia may be related to an Angolan-derived baptismal name, *Ame*, passed down through generations among slaves on a South Carolina plantation. Three of *Ame*'s descendants display a generational depth in naming their first female child *Ame*. That name, also, is passed down to subsequent children.[40] Due to different pronunciations, it is possible that the name Cornelia or Cordelia was derived from Amelia.

The source of Alice's name Fay, carried by her father Adam (Abram) Fay and grandfather Adam (*Koonta*) Fay, may have been Fa'i, the Gullah name of one of the maroon women owned by

Seminole chief Cowkeeper. Fay also was the name of an eighteen-year-old passenger on a steamboat leaving Florida.[41]

Name-saking and the double naming practice, in which surnames become given names and vice versa, are well documented among the freedmen in Oklahoma by Bateman, with many of the names found in the Dawes rolls. Bateman notes that Thomas Payne married Clara and they had six children, among whom were a male Carolina and a female Rose. The sons took both Thomas and Payne as surnames. Carolina had two wives and nine children, two of whom used Carolina as a last name. Later generations continued this pattern with the names Rose, Clara, Flora, and Carolina.[42] The prominence of the names Carolina (Kelina), Clara, and Rose is interesting considering the names' use over time among the Black Seminoles. Flora and Thomas also were popular names in the Black Seminole community in Mexico and Texas.

Among the freedmen, the given name Renty (Grayson) became a surname as have Noble and Pompey. Dindy (*Dindie*) also is a given name that became a surname among succeeding generations.[43] The given names Renty, Noble, Pompey, and *Dindie* are repeated among the Black Seminoles over generations, but because of the lack of written genealogical records it is difficult to document their exact historical sequence.

One example of this practice among Alice Fay's ancestors is in the given name of John Kibbetts's son, Kibbetts, by Rose Kelly. Washington was used as both a given and surname—Washington Kibbetts and Kibbetts Washington. Clara Dixon's son, Dixon, bore the surname of her first husband, Dixon. The names of two old-timers, Willie Fay and Fay Willie, provide additional examples of this pattern. When a popular barbecue café named Fay Willie's opened up recently in San Antonio, I could not resist inquiring of the proprietor as to his heritage. Curious about my question, he looked at me and said, "Why sure, I remember my mama said she was black Indian but I never thought about it."

Rose Kelly's married surname, probably derived from *Keli* and its many variations, also follows this African-derived tradition of alternating as a given name and surname over generations. Kelly (Carolina) Warrior carried Rose Kelly's surname Kelly and her father Carolina's given name. A Kelly (Cheo) married a Black Creek, Victoria Wilson, in the late 1900s, and one of their sons, Pompey, carried Kelly as a surname. Kelly also was carried as a surname by Alice's family's descendants such as Ira, Fina, and (Margaret) Maggie Kelly—the same Maggie Kelly who operated a popular café in Brackettville until it closed in early 2000. Another relative of Alice Fay, Tina Factor Kelly, carried two African-derived names. In her male descendant Kelly Factor, as with Kelly July, the surname reverts back to a given name. More recently, a Kelly Fay served as caretaker of the Seminole Indian Scouts Cemetery.

Another characteristic of the naming tradition Bateman observed among the freedmen is the rotation of male and female names over time. However, this practice is rare among the Black Seminoles.

At first I did not realize that another tenacious African naming tradition, the use of African-derived basket names or nicknames among the Black Seminoles, would pose additional challenges to my attempts to make genealogical connections. The continued popularity of African-derived basket names among Black Seminoles, even today, is complexly interlinked with their former insularity and intermarriage as a group but also an integral part of their identity as nourished by women.

In the 1930s Turner observed the Gullah roots of basket names: "Most of the Gullah people use two kinds of given names. One is English, and they call it their real name or true name and use it at school, in correspondence, and in their dealings with strangers. . . . The other is the nickname, also known as the pet name or basket name." Turner noted the nickname was "nearly always a word of African origin," used by the Gullah "among their friends and acquaintances." "In fact," he added, "so general is its use that many of the Gullahs have difficulty in recalling their English given name." The basket name is an alternate name, not an abbreviation or reduction of a specific name as it is in English nicknaming practices. It was perhaps originally used among enslaved blacks to establish an identity other than that imposed by an owner and to help retain their African conventions.[44] Slave responses to slavery included subtle modes of passive resistance and contestations perhaps undetected by their owners. Zora Neale Hurston calls this a "feather-bed resistance," by which they deceived their masters by using methods to parlay their ideas that owners could not detect or understand.[45] The use of basket names may have been one of these conventions.

During one of my visits to Nacimiento, Henry Fay provided his perspectives on this practice: "They came over here running from slavery. They was like one family—those old-timers. I didn't know their real names till I was old. Didn't know my sister's name was Alice. It was always Nina. Those old people had names like Koonta and Keshe [*Kasi* or *Ki'ese*]. They don't know what their real names were. I know if I had to fight like they did I couldn't make it."

Alice Fay's litany of basket names floated in and out of her stories about the old people, the "Aunties" and "Sisters"—Susan became Sukey, Theresa became Cressy, JoAnn became Chona, all names found on the lists of their ancestors departing Florida. Alice Fay also would insert basket names into our conversations, assuming, in that vast computer template in her head, that if she knew of whom she was speaking, then I also did. It was only after many years that the clouds started to lift from my name-cluttered mind. I realized that Alice and her friends often used basket names when talking to each other or among close friends, but when referring to lesser-known people they used the more formal given name. Alice's youngest daughter, Rafaela, goes by Effie (*A'fi*), a name used to salute a female born on Friday or *A'fe* meaning companion. "Afe" also appears among the names on the enrollment lists for migration from Florida. However, among the basket names I also observed maddening, inconsistent twists and turns typical of the Black Seminoles' naming practices, as viewed by an outsider. For instance, one of Rose Kelly's descendants carried the name Caro or Kelly Wilson but also was known as Carolina and Kelina.

These evolving revelations piqued my curiosity as I attended many social occasions with the older women in Brackettville and elsewhere. One occasion was Alice's eighty-seventh birthday in her Del Rio home, celebrated with Effie, Ethel and Dub Warrior, and her other relatives and friends. Alice was enjoying all the attention and the new gliding chair she had received for her birthday. Dub had brought a plump red scrapbook to compare notes with me and was intent on spitting out names like an auctioneer.

"Well, Mary, Sampson's wife, came from Florida. Besides Fay they had Kalina, Cato, John, Jim, and Bill," he said. "Jim married Rena (*Rinah*) Wilson, John married Molly (Bowlegs) Perryman. Bill married Dolly (Ward) Warrior. Dolly and Bill's son was John July number two."

Dub continued in a rapid, staccato-like fashion. I tried to listen intently because I knew that he expected me to remember all the connections. The rapid scrawls in my notebook were illegible. In the midst of the gregarious group, I seized the opportunity to bring up my problems with the Gullah nicknames and immediately received attention.

Ethel Warrior exclaimed, "Everybody had those nicknames!"

I asked, "Ethel, what is your nickname?"

She laughed embarrassedly. "Mine was . . . well, I don't like it so I won't tell you!"

Everyone else in the group smiled in conspiracy because they knew the name. I couldn't even get Dub to tell me Ethel's nickname. Later, though, I found it in the obituary of her recently deceased sister, Mary Hall Williamson.

Basket names also factored into the use of Gullah-derived day and month names. However, again the Black Seminoles put their unique twist on the tradition. Monday Bruner (Bruno, Bruner), for instance, who worked with Rosa Fay on the McKellar ranch, also carried the traditional basket name of Kudjo. His son, Friday Bruner, also carried the basket name of Rabbit. Another Friday Bowlegs, a key figure in the Mascogo community in Nacimiento, also carried the basket name Rabbit. Johnson Ajibade Adefila discusses some of these naming practices recorded in the 1930s Georgia Writer's Project, observing that a number of people were named for the weekday or month in which they were born.[46]

I am not the only victim of the Black Seminole elders' confusing naming practices. At a recent Seminole Days event, young members were invited to give testimonies at the Seminole Indian Scouts Cemetery on Sunday morning. One teenager gathered up her courage in the midst of some of the older women. She remarked that she and her peers wanted to learn the stories about their ancestors so they could teach them to their children. She asked the elders in the group to please write down their real names.

"When we come here, we see the real names on the tombstones—Sampson July, Penny Factor, they are all there—but we grew up only knowing your nicknames until we were old," the young woman said. "If we knew the names, then it would be easier for us to remember the history."

Alice, not understanding the request, got upset at this disclosure, thinking that the young women were negligent in not knowing the people attached to the nicknames. She chided the young people, saying, "Who you talking about? You mean you don't know them?"

Pointing out the older women around her, Alice accused the girls of forgetting: "See over there—Mimaw [probably *Mema*], Cookie [*Koki*]. They're still here!"

Many of the members of the younger generation of Black Seminoles think of the language only as a relic of the past, though, not having experienced the shame and indignity of being marginalized because of it. Soon no one will even remember the language, for the Sisters who spoke it among themselves are gone. The language will vanish like an artifact covered with the sands of time.

I recall another conversation with some children on the campgrounds in front of the old schoolhouse during Seminole Days. When asked what they thought about being Seminole, a little girl spoke up: "I like to come here every year but I don't know what a Seminole is. When they talk about it in school everybody looks at me." She pointed to a small boy dressed in a red soccer outfit. "He's a Seminole but he doesn't know it yet." Then the children ran away, relieved to not have to answer any more questions about being Seminole. Some do not know their history, and others do not understand that the retention of those names perpetuates a distinct historical consciousness underlying their identity.

Rose Kelly's people tenaciously held onto and nourished these bits and pieces of naming practices from Africa as they wove their way through their diasporic journeys. A name then was more than a mere identification tag; it was an historical record of their diasporas and suffering. Black Seminole descendants are all related to the travelers who boarded the steamships from Tampa for Indian Territory in 1838 and who later embarked on a desperate, yearlong journey through Texas to freedom in Mexico—John Horse and

Wannah, the Factors, the Paynes, Bowlegses, and Perrymans. These travelers brought with them the African-derived language and naming practices that re-created and transformed the bonds of kinship that anchored them in their identity as Black Seminoles—a kinship both genealogically and culturally defined. This identity was also nourished by the Black Seminole women in their homes and communities through a spirit of reciprocity—of cooking, serving, and sharing their traditional foods.

CHAPTER THIRTEEN

THE "SISTERS" MAKE THE *SOFKEE*

CASA DE LA COMIDA

Sufkee [*sofkee*] Recipe
3 cups of dried corn
½ cup of sugar
1 teaspoon of cinnamon
½ teaspoon salt

Cover the corn kernels in water and soak overnight. After soaking, boil over medium flame for 10 minutes, drain, and remove to large wooden bowl. Smash the kernels with a metate or pestle until a coarse puree is formed, the husks are separated from kernels, and the centers of the kernels are exposed. Add 5 cups of boiling water and the salt. Cook. Add sugar and cinnamon to the corn puree and mix well. Serve hot with cinnamon sprinkled on top.

Ethel July Warrior

Beyond African-derived language use and naming practices, the extended matrifocal Black Seminole household provided another stage on which women like Alice Fay and her female ancestors acted out and transmitted cultural values and traditions: through stories and food preparation. In this context they also perpetuated their value as women.[1] Over the years, generations of maroon women in Florida, Indian Territory, Mexico, and Texas, whether in flight or

Fig. 26. Alice Fay and Ethel July Warrior make Seminole fry bread at the Smithsonian Institute Festival of American Folklife in 1992. The event focused on maroon cultures, and Alice and Ethel provided a cooking demonstration for visitors. Institute of Texan Cultures, University of Texas at San Antonio. Photo courtesy of Dub and Ethel Warrior.

in a settled community, gathered under the shade of brush arbors outside their homes to proudly prepare the food that they had communally sown and harvested for their families in the tradition of their female ancestors. They hung twisted strands of pumpkin or squash and bunches of garlic and herbs like rosemary and oregano from their arbors to dry. They tended hogs, poultry, and goats and wrapped deer or other meat in cloth and draped it on pole racks nearby to salt and dry in the sun. Outside their homes, they stored harvested ears of corn from their communal fields in wooden cribs. Alice's ancestors like Rose Kelly and Rosa Dixon Fay tended gardens near their jacal homes of bright red chilies, tomatoes, and cabbages in the shade of fragrant peach and fig trees. They drew buckets of water from the acequias or irrigation ditches and the swift-flowing rivers to water their gardens. The foods they grew became olfactory props on a stage of action and social memory, with scripts passed down by generations of women.

Black Seminole women traditionally had few material possessions, so not only food but its accouterments such as iron cooking pots and wooden mortars and pestles, patinated with age, acquired significance as gendered symbols. Using them conjured up stories of their female ancestors. Small sherds discovered in my brief archaeological surveys in Nacimiento and in Las Moras, Texas, revealed that Black Seminole women had access to pottery such as white ironstone, transfer, and sponge wares typical of the early nineteenth century. Perhaps they only had one handed-down piece attained through trade, but such a small treasure represented a connection among women to the outside world.

Regardless of which tools or materials they used, *la cocina* was more than a kitchen. It was a veritable landscape that extended outside the matrifocal household as women banded together in their timeless spirit of reciprocity to prepare foods for family, community events, and church occasions. Food was infused into religious proscriptions, baptisms, funerals, marriages, child-rearing practices, and seasonal celebratory occasions such as Christmas, New Year's, and Easter. Adhering to their ancestral traditions in the kitchen was another facet of being mainline among Black Seminole women.

Although, like their African and Sea Island ancestors, Black Seminoles grew rice, it was not a staple like corn. The lives of Black Seminole women were inscribed in fields of corn. It is probable that in the men's absence the women determined the proportions of crops such as corn and beans to plant in the communal fields, the suitability of the soil, the scheduling of various tasks, and the possibility of seasonal fluctuations. Sisters who read the dreams would prognosticate the success or failure of a crop. Corn was central to Black Seminole rituals, as it also was to the Seminole Indians in the busk or green corn ceremony, a period of reconciliation and regeneration based on the planting and harvest of corn. The sun's daily journey, the positions of stars, and the life cycle of corn were linked together among Alice Fay's ancestors in a worldview based on veneration of the processes of birth, life, death, and rebirth. Black Seminoles, in their characteristically creative way, wove these corn-related rituals of the Indians into their own Christmas and New Year rituals steeped in evangelical Christianity and synchronized with exposure to Catholicism.

Corn was also the key ingredient in the traditional southeastern Indian dish *sofkee*, a hominy dish or corn soup adopted enthusiastically by the Black Seminoles in Florida. It was made by boiling dehulled corn kernels for several hours. Women first used a mortar and pestle to separate the hulls.[2] Sometimes they added meat, berries, or other vegetables to the kernels, or, as Ethel Warrior recalled, mashed the kernels and added cinnamon and sugar. According to early observers, scarcely a household existed without a *sofkee* pot. As Gertrude Vázquez, Alice's childhood friend in Nacimiento, said, "The women clear the fields, take the corn, and beat the *sofkee.* Yes, *mama.*"

Cooking *sofkee* was a tradition carried on their diasporas. The Sisters took the "raw" and the "uncooked" and, like alchemists, transformed foods into cultural artifacts of identity and pride. Matriarchs such as Rose Kelly kept steaming pots of *sofkee* bubbling on open fires nearby as nourishment for the corporal body and even spiritual well-being of family and community. "You know on the ranch we ate it out of bowls," Alice said. "We used to make bowls out of white dirt—like clay. We dug it up and made a bowl and then beat up egg white and smoothed it on—made the pot smooth. Then put in hot water and it was okay. Yeah, it worked pretty good."

A high-protein food, corn can be stored for long periods of time by first parboiling or parching it. Rose Kelly's people loaded bags of parched corn on their horses in their exodus from Indian Territory to Mexico. One oft-told story relates that upon arriving in Mexico, the Black Seminoles didn't like the food but preferred their traditional southeastern Indian *sofkee.* One elder reported, "The Mexicans would give them a tortilla, give them some of those red beans; when they got out of the house, they'd throw them down."[3] Alice's face displayed her pride when she recalled, "They had a hard time getting used to Mexico. But they learned to cook Mexican food better than those Mexicans—*barbacoa, parrillada* [barbecue], *caldo de gallina y de verduras.*"

Alice and her family shared some of these popular Mexican foods with me on my visits over time, but I recall one visit in 2001 when I became part of the *cocina*. I arrived in Del Rio on a Friday night before Juneteenth as Alice and Effie were making tamales to sell in their food booth the following morning. Lingering smells of oregano, *comino* (cumin), and roasted chilies filled the small kitchen. Alice, sitting at the kitchen table and looking very serious, agreed to let me assist and patiently demonstrated how to spread the *masa* (a corn paste) evenly over the thin corn shuck, spoon on the pungent meat filling (*relleno*), and roll each tamale into an identical tight bundle. Alice worked with precision honed by generations of female ancestors. As I began working, she kept glancing over at my pitiful efforts. Spying my fat, ragged tamales, she finally declared, "Shirley, nobody gonna buy those tamales you make." So chastised, I was given the task of rolling up the tamales with the younger children.

Alice rose early the next morning to steam the tamales in her huge metal pot before the family departed. We loaded up Effie's van with children and grandchildren and many pots of food—including two southeastern Indian favorites, fry bread and *tettapoon* (sweet potato pie), before heading to the old school grounds for the festive occasion. I was reminded of Alice's ancestors, with cooking pots, bags of dried corn, wooden mortars, and animal traps tied onto their mules and horses on their trip from Indian Territory to Mexico.

We had already missed the opening Juneteenth parade that winds down the main street of Brackettville on Saturday. Floats typically carry young beauty queens in festive dress followed by the Brackettville fire truck complete with siren, and an assortment of cycles, wagons, autos, and young Buffalo Soldier reenactors in stiff blue wool uniforms. The Brackettville ambulance typically brings up the rear of the brief parade. Observers then scatter to the old school yard for the next event.

As we arrived at the school yard I thought of Miss Charles's story about selling chicken dinners to make money to buy this small parcel of land from the city of Brackettville. There, in the old one-room schoolhouse still standing, Miss Charles had taught before integration and it is there that the Black Seminoles traditionally meet on Seminole Days and Juneteenth. On this day, the grounds were haunted by the shadows of the children Miss Charles once taught and enlivened by the shrieks of their descendants playing.

The evocative smell of the smoked barbecue tended by Lilly Mae's husband, Louis Dimery, a Black Seminole descendant, filtered through the canopy of oaks as we arrived. The women would later apportion the chicken and brisket barbecue on plates heaped with Spanish rice and pinto beans to sell to eager customers, both Black Seminoles and Brackettville residents. The profits support activities of the Seminole Indian Scout Cemetery Association. But first the events needed to receive a blessing and include a formal introduction of attending dignitaries who waited in the audience under an awning. A minister stepped forward to the speaker's platform to say a prayer and Clarence Ward, a descendant of Teener and July Factor and the president of the association at the time, invited members of the audience to give testimonials and to introduce other guests. Miss Charles, although very feeble, stepped up to the speaker platform and greeted the assembled group and led it in a resounding hymn.

Alice, taking a breather from her food duties, stepped forward and stood next to Miss Charles at the platform. She wore a festive white straw hat and a flowered dress decorated with a Seminole button. "I thank the Lord to be here—I am from old Mexico," Alice began. She paused, caught up in the emotion of the moment. "First place I stop when I came over here. Thank the Lord, this is our freedom day from slavery. I still so proud. Lord giving us strength what the Creator has left for us."

The crowd dispersed after the ceremony. Alice and the other women retreated to their booths to begin the annual ritual of selling homemade food and visiting with relatives. Alice carefully unloaded her culinary treasures of fry bread and tamales on the table in her family booth, barking orders to lackadaisical grandchildren.

Later that night, fortified with food, refreshments, and beer, some commenced to dance to canned music reverberating under the tired old oaks. Alice, after abandoning her *sofkee* pot and other utensils left in her booth to Effie and her grandchildren to clear, watched the dancing, her cane in hand, smiling that luminous smile, thinking about the old days when she was known as a good dancer.

In earlier times, this celebration of the emancipation in Texas was held across the border in Nacimiento. Beth Dillingham in the 1960s reported that the Juneteenth commemoration was next to Christmas in importance. "Relatives come from Brackettville, and sons and fathers return from working in the States or on neighboring ranches," she noted. "Food is accumulated ahead of time, sheds are erected on the riverbank, and fires built for roasting meat. The day is spent preparing food, eating and gossiping, and drinking, and ends with a dance that lasts way into the night."[4]

Alice Fay recalled the Juneteenth celebration of years past in Nacimiento, wrapped in the warmth of a generation of women cooking their specialties. Her dark eyes a lens of memories of her mother and grandmother, she recalled, "I sure remember all of that, 'cause I had to help my grandmama, Amelia, and my mama, Nellie Fay. My children help me to . . . make the fry bread . . . and the *tettapoon* for afterwards."

The Christmas season was also a celebratory occasion in Nacimiento, when all matrifocal households became bustling centers of activity centered on food. Older women came to life with the increased responsibility and importance of their seniority, bolstered by the respect given to them. "At Christmas, they was just a few women cooking the food—the Sisters," Alice told me. Well-worn pots bubbled with traditional foods, the recipes of which traveled with the women from Florida. Outside the kitchen could be heard the pestle hitting the wooden mortar to crush the corn kernels for *sofkee*.

This ancient stage on which women played out their gender and status continued outside the premises of the matrifocal household and kitchen. Women also used space and positioning in the serving and display of food to act out their gender and status responsibilities as Sisters. There were rules and priorities as to seating arrangements and when one ate according to gender and age, a scripted sequence of events in which men were the audience. Alice informed me, "The men and women separated to cook and eat. The women, they eat by their selves. . . . The men would go and drink and have fights."

These habitual diversions seem to have been the primary job of the men. Curious about this division of labor at the feast table, I asked

Alice and her old friend, Gertrude Vázquez, for further clarification. "Did the men and women ever eat together?"

Gertrude folded her arms and looked at me sternly with her piercing black eyes. "*No*, ma'am!" she said. "The *Sisters* first. When the Sisters got through, then we called everyone."

Gertrude proceeded to describe the counterclockwise movement of people encircling the church at Easter that also occurred at Christmas. "On Easter, like when the fast was broken, we take the basket the Lord's Dish [supper] to the church house—hog bone, rice, *tettapoon*—we go around the church and bless the food."

Alice nodded in agreement: "We women eat first when we fast. . . . The men and the women ate separately. . . . Like during Christmas on the 23rd we start out cooking for the 25th. The Sisters did it all. After the New Year's, *then* we would have fun."

Wanting to record some of these cooking events in the early days of my research, I had made plans to return to Nacimiento in the spring of 1997 with Alice and a university video crew. Alice and I would talk about traditional Black Seminole foods and demonstrate how they were prepared. Before departing for Nacimiento on that occasion, I took Alice to the grocery store to choose vegetables and fruits for the demonstration. Finally, with groceries in tow, we set out for Mexico. We made a brief stop at a feed store in Hondo to purchase some deer corn, which is similar to the corn Alice's people traditionally use to make *sofkee* in Nacimiento and Las Moras.

We crossed the border and arrived in Múzquiz late that afternoon. Early the next morning we left for Nacimiento. As we drove up to Gertrude's compound, she and a bevy of relatives and friends were gathered under the canopy of old salt pines outside her adobe in anticipation. Gertrude's fat old hog, tied to a tree, waddled in the mud, patiently waiting to be become an actor in this video event.

Alice, relishing her role as instructor, carefully placed her purchases on a large, wooden table to begin her demonstration. Gertrude brought out her well-worn wooden mortar and pestle to demonstrate how she pounds the *sofkee*. It is back-straining work for an old woman. With a very serious demeanor, she began to crush the hard corn kernels with a vertical motion of the pestle. It made a sonorous sound—thud . . . thud—keeping a steady beat, evoking the rhythms of her Gullah and Indian heritage and the ancestors who preceded her. In short, clipped sentences, the serious Gertrude looked at the camera and explained:

> *Sofkee* is like a big hominy gruel. . . . *Sofkee* comes from the corn. We beat it. They [outsiders] say "big hominy" and we say *sofkee*. We beat in the mortar. Put in the water last. Sometimes we put in pumpkin or meat and other things. . . . Anytime we serve it, we make *tettapoon*. Mix up, put aside for day or so, and make fry bread. We kill the hog and cook the meat. We make crackling. We make Spanish sausage—*chorizo*—cut up the meat; grind *comino*, oregano, garlic and mix it for sauce. We have a good time. We tell everyone we are killing my hog. Then they all come to help.

Alice added, "You know we also go up into the hills to find foods like *nopales* [cactus pads], persimmons, wild apples. We got water-cress in the Sabinas and cook it with chilies."

The audience gathered under the salt pines listened to the steady beat of Gertrude's pestle hitting the mortar. The wooden mortar and pestle were not merely food-processing tools, but crucial props in the performance, a prelude for Alice's demonstration that followed.

I had seen Alice's wooden mortar and pestle, larger than Gertrude's and bearing a patina from use, on one of my previous visits to her ranch, and she had demonstrated its use briefly. I recalled my surprise the day I discovered it resting against an old mesquite tree next to her brother Henry's house in Nacimiento. When I asked her about it, Alice had proudly told me, "You know my mama Nellie gave me that old mortar." She boasted, "I know how to make a mortar—get a big wood and start a fire in the top—cool it and dig it out. There you are, ma'am. Today, lots of the women, they use a metate. You know, I have my old metate [stone] at Effie's house."[5]

Alice, looking festive in her bright pink dress, took charge of this food demonstration session. She began to speak to the camera as if she were Julia Child, fussing around the table and looking around for my reaction. "Now I'm gonna show you how to make the *tettapoon*. . . . You know that the *tettapoon* was made from the sweet potato."

Gertrude, not missing a beat, as if a Sister in church, provided the requisite shout response characteristic of her ancestors: "Yes, ma'am."

Alice continued her cooking demonstration: "See here, Shirley, this is a grater—you know—to grate the sweet potato [for *tettapoon*]. . . . Then you mix with vanilla, cane sugar, and eggs like this, and then you put it in the oven. Just like that." I had eaten her delicious *tettapoon*, like a sweet potato or yam pie, at Seminole Days, a food that the Black Seminoles adopted from the Seminole Indians.

After the *tettapoon* demonstration was over, Alice assessed the attention of her audience, and then introduced another Black Seminole (and Seminole Indian) specialty—coontie, a bread-like food made from flour processed from the *Sabal palmetto*, or cabbage palm.[6] Hernando de Soto in 1539, in his trek through Florida and accompanied by Indian guides, had incorporated corn and coontie into their diets. As the conflicts in the southeast had increased in Florida, the *Sabal palmetto* plant became more important as a staple for both maroons and Indians because it grew wild and, unlike corn, required little attention if cultivated. The U.S. military coming on the Black Seminole camps reported mounds of coontie flour that had been left by the maroons in their hurry to escape capture. Plantation blacks ate coontie in times of food scarcity and even poor whites would have perished from hunger without it. Slaves would eat coontie, so as to save their food allowances for special occasions.[7]

"We made the coontie too," Alice informed her audience. "The womens, they went up into those mountains to get the *palma* to make the coontie—all those old people."

Alice pointed up to the mountains behind her for dramatic effect. "You know where it is, Shirley," she said. "We ride the mule up there. . . . We bring it down and cut it up and let it soak in water. That made the flour we used for things like fry bread."

"You know, we didn't have the wheat flour, the *harina*, when my people came over here to Mexico," she continued. "We use the palm to make flour for the coontie and the fry bread. . . . Now we use white flour. I always make it for Seminole Days but now I can't do it."

Gertrude stopped pounding corn for *sofkee* to affirm Alice's account. "Coontie is our dish," she said. "We used to go get the palm off the mountain—chop it, beat it in the mortar, cook, pour water off to strain. We used to go up on donkeys and bring lots back. That was the coontie."

I recalled my horseback trip up to the mountains behind Guadalupe, guided by Alice's brother, Henry Fay, the *Sabal palmetto* trees rising unexpectedly out of the rugged hills and dense carpet of scrub pines, like soldiers on the horizon. Alice had been nervous about me making the trip and I realized why during the climb when Henry informed me, "You know up here we tracked deer, cougars, and bears." My memory of the trip includes the sighting of fresh bear tracks on the trail. Henry also warned me that if I saw any marijuana plants to ignore them: "You know those old guys plant it under those trees and those guys may be around, and they're real mean and can shoot a person."

Alice gathered up the rest of the vegetables we had purchased and proceeded to talk about growing them on the farm: onions, carrots, squash. She reported in an aside to me that they grew sugarcane to make syrup, plus tobacco and rice. "We used to have fruit trees, orange, peach, figs." She sighed, "They're all gone now." After her comments, I recalled the dried-out fields of corn that we had observed on our trip to her ranch.

The little girls attending the event with their mothers were growing tired. One of the little girls was crying continuously. Alice inquired solicitously of the mother of the screaming child, "Do you want to sing to the baby?" A young woman, Lucy, sitting next to Gertrude, talked to us. She is not Black Seminole but is married to the son of Gertrude's daughter, Frances. With a luminous smile, Lucy nestled her little baby boy against her breasts while she chatted. Gertrude hugged Lucy's other child, a beautiful little girl and her favorite grandchild, Panchy.

Lucy shyly told me that she wanted to continue the traditions of her husband—that they were special to her. "*Los tradiciones son especiales.*"

The morning cooking lesson orchestrated by Alice and accompanied by Gertrude around the old salt pines finally ended as the sun took over the area and the women and children dispersed. Gertrude, proud of her performance, heaved a sigh of regret at its termination.

Alice smiled at the video cameras as she gathered up the vegetables to distribute to the women as they left, concerned that each participant had a share.

As the years have passed, Alice has lost her enthusiasm for cooking traditional Black Seminole dishes and for sowing and tending the plants that were the basis for her traditional Mascogo dishes years ago in Nacimiento. In Mexico she was an avid farmer, bringing to life a garden of melons, peanuts, and pumpkins on the rich terrace soils of the Sabinas River. More recently, she has tried to nurture a few withered pepper plants in Effie's front yard, but they soon succumbed to predatory weeds. Sometimes she pickles peppers or chilies that Effie brings home from the grocery store. During one visit when she was in a feisty mood Alice told me that she was too young to cook. "If I get up and try to cook and dance I'll show you!" she said with fervor.

Alice's family members tell me that Granita was always cooking cakes and pies on her wood-burning stove in her little concrete block house in Mexico next to the burned-down adobe. Sometimes she traded these delicacies with the nearby Kickapoos for meat or moccasins. Recently, Effie reported that she was surprised when she got home from work one day. "My mama had made empanadas, and the smell was so sweet," she said. "But other days she doesn't want to cook."

As Alice understands, cooking is a ritual best done in the community of Sisters who share the spirit of the occasion, the smell of fresh cut corn ears roasting on coals and of baking *tettapoon*, the *sofkee* in bubbling pots. These olfactory occasions conjure up memories of female ancestors. Auntie Sara is remembered for her fry bread and Nellie Fay is remembered for her lemon cream pies by Alice's children. In the *cocina*, they talked about their dreams and discussed the meaning from their own bible of interpretations passed down in stories.

Preparing and sharing food is a social act that extends the bond of kinship among the female participants on occasions such as this that require planning, labor organization and allocation, and resource sharing.[8] Alice chuckled, "When we cook, we women get together and we tell stories and talk about the men. We sure do."

During a 2003 visit to Mexico, Alice's mortar and pestle, varnished by years of use, still leaned against Henry's house. I was surprised to discover that some of the older women in the village were walking up the gravel road to borrow the wooden tools to make *sofkee*. The Black Seminole foods and recipes are artifacts that, like the rhythm of Gertrude's mortar and pestle, reflect the steady beat of Black Seminole culture even today in Mexico. The stateside women no longer make *sofkee*, but as a symbol of womanhood and identity it is embedded in social memory, especially when one is fortunate to have the opportunity to eat some.

Since Black Seminole culture has been an oral culture for the most part, social memory has been transmitted by women in a number of other ways and other places than the *cocina*. Black Seminole women had a diverse set of social practices that extended the spirit of the *cocina* beyond the hearth to other celebrations and locations that also provided occasions to reiterate and celebrate their womanhood and evangelical beliefs. One of these was the "pray's house," or church, where they revealed their dreams after fasting and shouted and danced to the Lord and in a celebration of their ancestors.

CHAPTER FOURTEEN

Shouting to the Lord in the "Pray's House"

> She missed dancing, and whenever she heard the big drum beating and the accordion wailing she felt sad, but shouting at prayer-meeting was pleasure and old hymns and spirituals were beautiful. When the people all sang . . . she joined in and felt so holy that cold chills ran up and down her spine.
>
> Julia Peterkin, 2000

The Evangelical Baptist churches in Nacimiento, Las Moras, and later Brackettville provided another stage of female solidarity where the Sisters prayed to the Lord, buoyed by a vibrant background of oratory, song, shout-response dance, and fasting to obtain visions. As with other blacks (African Americans) of the nineteenth to early twentieth century, at the heart of the Black Seminoles' religious beliefs was Evangelical Baptist Christianity, to which some members of the community were exposed on southern plantations in "pray's houses" or in Indian Territory. Like the Black Seminoles, other practitioners of the religion lived isolated, on the margins of society, and practiced greater freedom in doctrine in contrast to what was permissible in other denominations.[1]

During their diasporas, Alice Fay's ancestors also were exposed to other cultures and religious traditions, and like artists they painted these new ideas on their own syncretic canvas of many colors and textures. Sometimes it is not clear why certain elements were chosen from one religion and how they were fashioned into the Black Seminoles' brand of evangelical Christianity. African-derived Gullah religion, Indian influences, and, for some, Catholicism in Mexico and Florida were merged into their worldview of spiritual redemption. They adopted and transformed elements from other belief systems that often paralleled their own practices and yet they fashioned them into their own unique brand of spiritualism. Among the Black Seminoles these inheritances were adapted, passed down, or transformed with no particular understanding of their origin.[2]

H. Conger Jones's observations in the 1930s in Brackettville support the Black Seminoles' eclectic worldview: "The religion of these people is a queer combination of Christianity and pagan rites, consisting of mixtures of Negro voodoo and Indian spirit worship."[3] Mary Louise Thompson, another observer in the early 1920s, witnessed a service in one Brackettville Baptist church and reported that the congregation blended traditions of Roman Catholics and old-fashioned fundamental Baptists.[4] One unusual characteristic of the Nacimiento, Fort Clark, and Brackettville communities was the presence of more than one Evangelical Baptist church, each differing in small details. Foster reported three Baptist churches in Brackettville in the 1930s, one of which Porter noted had disappeared by his visit in the 1940s.[5] Churches' existences and pastors were transient, the women's stories indicated to me. A new church would spring up when there was a disagreement or someone had a vision, and it could be replaced by another new visionary. The churches sometimes were named after the people who started them, just as towns in Florida such as Abraham's Town were traditionally named for their founders.

When I asked Alice why there were different churches, she explained, "Well, the Lord told them to have a church and they did it. If somebody came along better, the church was theirs." Each church, in a sense then, was owned by the person who had a prophetic vision that led to its creation.

Alice mentioned that when she lived in Brackettville with her grandmother, Rosa Dixon Fay, there was Uncle Tony's and the more progressive July church or St. John's, with a regular ordained minister. The determined Rebecca July Wilson, following the mission of education and change preached by her progressive father, Sampson July, spearheaded the construction of the church and chose the pastor. Her daughter, Miss Charles, recalled, "Before, we went to one church on the reservation [Las Moras] and the little church on the east side [of Brackettville]. I think it is just a Seminole characteristic. Some wanted to stay with the old ways. St. John's was a new church with tithing. My mother, Rebecca, wanted a minister."[6] St. John's Church, a little white structure with a bell tower facing Fort Clark, still exists today. When I last visited Brackettville I found out that with the death of Miss Charles, the church is now headed by a new, white pastor.

Alice also told me that Theresa (Cressy) Bruner and one of the Wilson sisters started another church. One of the Wilson sisters had also headed up a small church on Las Moras in 1902. Mary Warrior, grandmother of Dub Warrior, headed up the "Mother of Holiness church."

Porter correspondent Lilith Haynes commented on Brackettville churches in the mid–late twentieth century. A linguist, she visited the town for three weeks in December 1972 and January 1975 to interview the Black Seminoles about their language, and reported that she was welcomed into the community and had the opportunity to visit two of the churches. One probably was Mt. Gilead, established in the 1870s, the church that legend says was moved from Las Moras after 1914. Haynes observes that "prayer was essentially in English, albeit spontaneous, while shouting (i.e., group singing) tended to reflect Seminole phonology." She attended another church, probably St. John's, and observed that traditional Baptist hymnals and English were used. Haynes was asked to play the piano in this church. "It was interesting to me that people attending the latter church also attended the former, although the reverse did not seem to be true," she noted.[7]

Black Seminoles like Alice Fay and Rebecca July held no allegiance to a particular church, but felt free to choose between options, depending on the pastor's sermons or rituals, and they sometimes attended more than one church. Alice Fay even looked surprised that I would ask if she attended other churches, saying, "Why, sure we did, Shirley." Many of the women in Brackettville and Mexico, in attending more than one church, extended the spirit of reciprocity so characteristic of the Black Seminoles beyond one church to a flexible spiritual world of redemption, in which all churches were equal.

Porter reported that one of the most conservative and traditional churches he visited in the 1940s in Brackettville was a chink house or jacal structure. There was no sermon, only traditional singing, prayers, and "testimonials." He mentions that, along with a number of older women, only two men were present at the time. One of them was Warren (Juan/Wan) Perryman, the son of Lipán Apache Teresita, and the other was scout James Perryman, Cornelia's son.[8] Miss Charles informed me that Uncle Warren, as he was called, had taken over the church from Uncle Tony after he passed away.

Jones described another church in the 1930s that was one of the oldest, a church of adobe, stone, cedar, and thatched roof with six small windows and a small door. The church was twenty feet long and eighteen feet wide—old chairs, boxes, and logs used for pews were pushed aside for the shout-and-response and ring-shout dance.[9] This church may have been headed up by Miss Penny (Wilson) Factor, sister of Molly Perryman, a noted dream reader and religious woman born in 1874 in Mexico. Aunt Penny, whose name perhaps derived from the Gullah *Peni* or *Pene*, held spiritual reign over the Brackettville group in the mid-twentieth century. She lived a long life—she died in 1970 at 110. Some of her children preceded her in death. A photo taken of her at this age depicts a frail woman wearing a simple cotton dress and the typical Black Seminole head covering of a kerchief.

Alice Fay recalled, "We went to Aunt Penny's hard-shell Baptist church in Brackett. . . . Miss Penny's church had no windows, only shutters. . . . Everybody went to that old church. . . . Aunt Penny used to get happy singing and dancing. We sang and shouted and got happy at her church and then went around the building. We had to wear kerchiefs or little bonnets. Aunt Penny's church burned down. I remember the fire. All those old ladies fasted and read dreams there."

Alice Daniels Barnett, the great-great-granddaughter of Florida-born Cornelia Perryman, had similar remembrances. "My mama

Fig. 27. This was one of the Evangelical Baptist churches in Brackettville. Ethel Warrior recalled, "We used to shout around this church. They read dreams and fasted there. They were very dedicated women. They had faith." She explained that the tall chimney-like attachment adjacent to the door was a bell tower. "We rang the bell when someone in the community died," she said. Prints and Photographs Division, Library of Congress, LC-USZ62-125340, ppmsc 01229.

Eliza [Payne] Daniels went to Aunt Penny's little church. They were like Pentecostal, you know—holy rollers—fasting and making miracles," she said.[10]

The spry Genevieve Payne also attended the church and added her own recollections during one of Alice and my visits. "I remember that little old shack—adobe church—at Christmas," she said. "We would sing, shout, and pray. I remember Aunt Penny—when she told me something that's true. . . . You know, we had to carry Aunt Penny to church when she got old and couldn't walk."[11]

Miss Charles Wilson also recalled Penny fondly: "She was an old lady that used to work at the fort that lived to be very old. She was very religious. She said that one day people could fly."[12] Porter describes Penny as "a keen vigorous woman, full of hospitality, once serving me a Sunday lunch of ham and eggs which must have used up her [wartime] meat-ration for a week and insisting on doing my laundry without compensation—courtesies which, however, I was able to reciprocate by means of my own sugar and coffee rations." Aunt Penny told Porter, "The old people in those days was so loving with one another. . . . That's why things went that way in the fighting—none killed and few wounded. The old people were doing some powerful praying."[13]

Miss Penny and other spiritual mothers or older religious women—the Sisters—were instrumental in establishing rules for Black Seminole women, the appropriate way to present their gender and identity through certain standards of deportment and modes of dress.

On a Saturday during Seminole Days in 1999, the older women gathered with me at the old school grounds to reminisce about the Sisters, as elderly devout women are called, and their religious practices. The women sat in their metal chairs under the ancient oaks, their dresses reflecting the colors of the rainbow.[14]

Alice, as usual, began the conversation: "You know Aunt Penny took the hard line. You had to dress very careful at that time—long skirts and sleeves, not cross your legs. You know we couldn't show our arms either. . . . My grandmama, Rosa Fay, wore those cloths [kerchiefs] on her head." She paused in a distant memory. "You know those old women was real hard." Always the actress, Alice stretched out her arms in demonstration as if for Aunt Penny's inspection.

The women all laughed at this childhood memory. Miss Charles chimed in, "Those older people had very strict rules. The members always tied their heads and wore long dresses down to here." She shook her finger at the group: "No talking in church! The women had to cover their heads or they would be considered very sacrilegious."

Ethel Warrior enthusiastically added, "If you went to *that* church [Aunt Penny's] you had to take your hat off and put that kerchief on! Even Auntie Rebecca [Wilson] would take off her hat and put it on when she went to Aunt Penny's church!"

Beth Dillingham describes this head covering, still being worn as late as the 1960s. It was a scarf that the women wrapped low over the forehead and tied at the back of the neck. Dillingham observed that the "Negroes" considered it to be a Seminole habit that they had brought from Florida.[15] Albert Raboteau, a noted scholar on African American religion, reports that females in the Sea Islands, when seeking a spiritual experience in conversion or mourning, wore the same head scarf. Thus, its use may have been handed down from African and Gullah forbears as a potent symbol for propriety and identity among Black Seminole woman.[16]

Porter writes that another church he visited was a large, barn-like structure, certainly the Mt. Gilead church that overlooked Brackettville for many years from a hill guarded by tall junipers. Porter reported hearing a conventional sermon delivered by a young soldier from Fort Clark. Later, he was invited to deliver a speech himself, and he exhorted the listeners to recall their heroes Wild Cat and John Horse and to treasure their history.[17]

Jones described sermons in the 1930s that recounted scriptural accounts of the visions of the patriots of Israel: "The story of Daniel's reading the handwriting on the wall is a favorite selection. The participants were transformed through singing, dancing or dreaming into Biblical heroes by merging their being with that of a Christian God."[18]

Of particular interest in the singing done in Black Seminole worship is Porter's observation that the old Seminoles distinguished between "gospel hymns," like those by noted Protestants Charles Wesley and Isaac Watts, which one would get out of a book, and "dream songs," which were revealed in dreams and differed from context to context.[19] Porter's observations are interesting because they reveal that practices such as revealed dream songs typical of the old, conservative, Gullah-derived rituals traditionally headed up by women merged over time with new forms of formal Protestantism involving more male participation.

Thompson observed some of the other eclectic religious practices of the early twentieth century at the old Mt. Zion Baptist Church. Thompson relates:

> They call themselves "Mount Zion Baptists" and practice baptism by immersion, yet they keep Lent from the last Friday in November till the 25th of December commemorating the advent of Christ and they pray for the dead continually; every Friday is a fast day with them, and they meet at the church for prayer service, religiously, three times during

> the week, and twice on Sundays. . . . One strange custom followed even today is the closing of the church during Lent and about thirty days before Christmas. All members are excluded from the church, the doors are locked and only the preacher is permitted to enter during the period. In effect, the entire congregation is excommunicated in order that the righteous may purge the organization of all undesirables. A period of fasting takes place and dreams are closely watched. Certain "deacons," both men and women, are appointed to hear dreams related by those desiring to prove that they are worthy to again enter the house of God.[20]

Foster provides additional observations of a Brackettville church, probably Mt. Gilead, in the 1930s:

> When a "sinner" desires to become a Christian, he must first confess his sins and then ask the church members to pray for him. He then comes to the "mourner's bench," which is usually a front seat in the church, and there the members pray for him. The candidate must then go and pray for a long period—perhaps two months. If the candidate is to be accepted as having found the Lord, he must be able to relate his having seen the stars dash across the sky, or a "high" white man with wings, or something else unusual.[21]

Jones reports a similar focus on fasting and reading dreams: "Before Easter the fast closes with a feast on Good Friday night, followed by the opening of the church and a celebration of the Holy Communion, in which only those who have successfully 'Come Through' are admitted."[22]

Coming through, as explained in the next chapter, is a term applied to those churchgoers who have had an appropriate revelation or dream, indicating that they have had contact with the Lord or their ancestors. Central to all the churches, regardless of size or pastor, was the practice of fasting, during which the churchgoer went out to have dreams or revelations. Once the parishioner "came through," he or she returned to have the dream or revelation approved by the elders, usually the Sisters.

I asked Alice about fasting, and how and when the Black Seminoles practiced it. She looked at me in that way she has, when surprised that I would ask such a naïve question, and said:

> Shirley, well I tell you it was our way . . . the fasting. . . . It was the way the dark people have. We womens did it in Christmas and New Year and Easter. . . . You fast all day and then, like you have a piece of bread and tea, and the next day the same. Church people after they get used to it, it wasn't bothering them. . . . Yeah, we do it in the church—only the women. The reason why they was doing it is because that was the vision Christ had for the people who wanted to be in the church and that's what they had to do. They fasted and waited for a vision from God, and then they took it to the old "Sisters" [to analyze]. . . . You know we didn't eat red meat any of those times. Only during any fasts they could eat starches such as corn gruel [*atole*], fried bread, or *camote*, sweet potatoes. We drank tea from the *poleto* plant.

On a visit with Genevieve Payne, we discussed religious practices she experienced as a child in Nacimiento and later Brackettville. She shared similar recollections about the importance of fasting and the shout-response before Christmas and New Year's celebrations and fasting. She said:

> Christmas was the big time. On the day before Christmas they stayed in the church all night, fast into the night and sit around a fire until sun comes up. . . . All night all the women and the children and sing and shout until the end of the fast. . . . The next morning on Christmas Day, the fast was broken, and we all got together, and we'd go around the church singing and chanting. Same thing happened on New Year's. They'd break bread after the fast. . . . On New Year's, all the men and children would be in the church and the men were outside around the fire drinking.

Genevieve also revealed a concern with pollution that had been revealed in other conversations. She pretended to sweep. "We'd go around three times [counterclockwise]. Even the men would join in then. Then circle around each house in the village. . . . We'd go around the house and sweep. Get our brooms and make sure the dirt was gone." She chuckled. "You know we drank mescal, too."[23]

Alice shared similar memories of her experience in Nacimiento and the importance of the ring shout. "We celebrate New Year's in a big way," she said. "We sing, pray, and go out of the church and shout [sing] around the church till daylight. . . . Then we go round the houses and keep dancing and shouting after we broke the fast about seven o'clock."

The ring shout and response central to the celebrations among the Black Seminoles as described by Genevieve and Alice and other descendants is very similar to the practice reported among the Gullah in the Sea Islands. The two women described it as a group of people moving counterclockwise in a circle in a church or outside during a funeral. A chosen leader established a dance rhythm that the congregation followed with verbal responses, foot tapping, or swaying motions. At times their hands were held out. Sometimes the continued movement caused the attendees to be possessed by the Spirit or, as Alice told me, to see an ancestor. The similarity suggests that some of the Black Seminole women in Florida brought these practices into their eclectic mix; they may have been former slaves who had experienced the practices on plantations.

Raboteau and Hall determine that the evangelical Protestant revival and the call-and-response dance among blacks also presented an equivalent to the rituals held in Africa. Raboteau contends that the ring shout became widespread, necessary for calling up the Holy Spirit.[24] Hall discusses the survival of African religious practices in the Americas such as spirit possession and dancing. He determines that slaves merged African-style dancing with evangelical Protestantism.[25] These transformative events were sometimes informed by the Bible, as Theophus H. Smith argues, yet they followed west African prayer styles that used strong rhythm and chanted delivery.[26] Among slaves such events were new forms of religious practices that could be hidden from masters.

Parallels between enslaved blacks' services and those of the Black Seminoles in Texas and Mexico also are apparent in eyewitness accounts and recollections of the older women. Similarities in the Black Seminole events also were observed by Porter in the 1940s at church services he attended. One service he attended in the 1940s was held in Nacimiento, now the Yglesia Evanjélica church pastored by Zulema Vázquez. It featured elements of song, shout, and dance usually led by women: "I attended services one morning . . . the meeting consisted of singing spirituals, prayers, and a concluding 'ring shout' or circular dance. All those present—eight or nine—were women. The service was similar to, although on a smaller scale than the service I had attended in the most conservative of the three Baptist churches in Brackettville, although more emphasis was given to testimonies."[27] Porter also observed eight or nine of the older Black Seminole women singing spirituals and praying during a New Year's celebration in one Brackettville church, concluding the event with a ring shout or circular dance. Haynes, on her 1973 and 1975 visits, was fortunate to visit two churches and observe some of the practices over the Christmas season and New Year's. She reports that shouting took place in the oldest church, and that this service was filled with intense emotion as the older members of the community recalled their ancestors who had carried down the ring shout ceremony.[28]

Some of the older women I interviewed had referred to the ring shout as a stomp dance. I recall being surprised when Miss Charles Wilson exclaimed to me, "On New Year's we would be doing the stomp dance!" Curious about her statement, because the stomp dance was characteristic of the southeastern Indians, I also asked Alice about the tradition. She reaffirmed the continuation of these practices the Black Seminoles called the stomp, shrugging her shoulders impatiently and rolling her eyes in exasperation: "Shirley, you see me and Gertrude at the cemetery. That's *how* I do it. . . . Well, we go in a circle around and we move our feet, wave our hands, and sing and shout. We get the spirit. When somebody dies we do the dance too. My people shout and stomp. . . . There is a feeling that comes over you. You feel so happy. My people did it—the stomp."

I remember being at the Nacimiento cemetery when the two old friends sang hymns in front of the grave of Alice's mother, Nellie

Fay. Vibrant in their print dresses, their raised hands held out like crosses, they weaved side to side, following the swaying movement typical of the ring shout. They sang their version of a spiritual known as "Sing to Me Mother Lord, Sing to Me."

I was curious as to why the Gullah-derived shout-and-response dance or ring shout was called "the stomp" among Alice Fay's ancestors, but then her people were always surprising me with some new tidbit of information. I wondered if this term was some holdover from their days in Indian Territory or Florida and reflected their attachment to Indian practices or characteristics. In contrast to the slower shuffle of the Gullah-derived circle dance the Black Seminoles practiced, in which the feet do not leave the floor, the "stomp" dance of the southeastern Indians usually required lifting the feet.

To confuse things even more, I received conflicting descriptions of the dance from the older descendants I interviewed. When I asked Dub Warrior, he told me that he did not know why the old people called it the stomp but provided another explanation. He told me that the dance around the church was very energetic. "They only did the slower shuffle dance at funerals," he said.

This makes sense, for Raboteau also noticed different versions of the ring shout among slaves that ranged "from the exciting tempo and rhythms of the shout and the slow drawn out 'sorrow songs' which usually came to mind when the spirituals are mentioned."[29]

The eclectic history of the Black Seminoles thus demonstrates that they were not immune to new ideas, but incorporated them as they had occasions to observe other rituals among plantation blacks and dances among the Seminoles in Florida and Indian Territory. Interwoven with their Evangelical Baptist practices, the Black Seminoles may have adopted some Indian practices from both Florida and Indian Territory in connection to the busk (from the Creek word *poskita,* "to fast"), or the seasonal ripening of the corn known as the "green corn ceremony" and its related rituals.[30] Alice related they attended Kickapoo dances in Mexico. Her daughter Effie reported, "The Kickapoo had rain dances that were religious. Sometimes they'd let us join in." Robert Ritzenthaler and Frederick Peterson noted that the nearby Kickapoo in Nacimiento shuffled around the fire in a counterclockwise direction with little body movement. The Kickapoos also celebrated the green corn dance in January when the first corn crop ripened and older Seminole women report having attending their dances.[31]

Although these seasonal ritual events differed in details and timing and included more male participation among the Indians, they all included fasting, dream reading, confessions, and sleep deprivation. These events are very similar to the "coming through" ceremonies of the Black Seminoles that Alice Fay and her friends described in which dreams were revealed after fasting. William Bartram, an early observer of southeastern Indians, reports that they had fast days in connection to the green corn ceremony, during which time they allowed themselves only a meager gruel and a medicine-like tea, often called the "black drink," brewed from the roots of various plants, a powerful cathartic that caused purging for purification.[32] Porter records conversations in which the older Black Seminole women discuss using teas as emetics and purgatives as part of their fasting sessions. He suggests that the "potions" are similar to the black drink of the Seminoles taken during the annual busk ceremonies. An elderly woman reminisced to Porter, "[People] used to drink tea to make them vomit—it sure scraped us both up and down!"[33]

During their diasporas, Alice's ancestors were exposed to other cultures and traditions, with various strands bearing different levels of importance. Likewise, Michael Wolfe observes that the Gullah Sea Islanders continued using African-derived dance movements, but over time they infused new meanings in these patterns.[34] Inscoe's reflections on the Gullah reflect the syncretism or borrowings so characteristic of Alice's ancestors: "African elements were significant in shaping the new culture that emerged, but they were only several of many contributing factors and by no means the most dominant. Nor was it a process of assimilation by which slaves were merely 'Americanized,' absorbing fully the culture to which they were exposed. Rather, it refers to a creative and flexible process by which slaves took the culture of their owners and made it their own. . . . Foreign elements were adopted, altered, supplemented, and even rejected by their black recipients."[35]

Howard, a cultural anthropologist who has studied Black Seminoles in the Bahamas, cites Melville Herskovits and states in a similar vein that Africans reinterpreted aspects of their religion that may have mimicked certain tenets of Christianity in the Americans but retained the underlying "deep structures" of their African religion. Often these practices paralleled their own Gullah traditions and were passed down with no understanding of their origin.[36]

These cultural overlaps in the Black Seminole traditions and religious practices with other cultures, such as those of the Indians, again illustrate the Black Seminoles' syncretic tendency to take disparate bits and pieces of other cultures and creatively weave them into their own identity. Certainly, the busk—with its connections to the new year, reaffirmation of the community, the harvest of corn, and fasting and rebirth—offered a powerful and protracted series of celebrations that appealed to Black Seminoles in Florida, Indian Territory, and later in Mexico.

The Black Seminoles also incorporated other religious practices into their syncretic repertoire. An unusual proscription, probably with a Protestant derivation, that was reported by early eyewitnesses in the mid-1900s was the Black Seminoles' ban against knives and forks on the feast table. Thompson records, "Their peculiar law governing the feast table is that there shall be no knives and forks laid thereon. Grace is said by the minister before the religionists are seated and then everyone begins to break bread at once. Bread is never cut at the Seminole 'Negroe's' feast table—it must be broken with the bare hand only."[37] The reason for this eluded me, so I asked Alice. She confirmed this taboo, at least as practiced in Nacimiento: "No, we couldn't have no knives on the table," she said. "We had to pull the bread. That's the way they did it. . . . Also for a whole week you couldn't ride a horse, a donkey, nothing like that. You had to walk."

Other Black Seminole religious prohibitions drew more obviously from the Bible. Both the Old and New Testaments describe days of fasting, abstinence, and dietary proscriptions. Proscriptions among the Black Seminoles such as a ban on pork during fasts that Alice discussed may have originated in the Old Testament. The book of Leviticus, chapter 11, forbids the eating of any beast that is cloven-footed or chews a cud.

Early eyewitnesses of Black Seminoles such as Thompson, Jones, and Porter have commented about the presence of Catholic traditions wrapped into the people's Baptist Evangelicalism. At some point in the 1840s there was a priest and a Catholic church in Nacimiento, as observed by Maud McKellar, that Rosa Dixon Fay also attended. Rosa's daughter Sally explained they did not have idols—meaning saints—displayed, only a cross that the parishioners dressed. The priest left the church when Rosa Fay refused to punish her daughter Clary for having visions. Recalling this, I asked Alice and her friend Gertrude Vázquez if there was a Catholic church in Nacimiento that they attended when they were growing up.

Alice replied, "They didn't have no Catholic church in Nacimiento when I was there—just the one [Baptist] then. . . . You know I was baptized Catholic in Mexico, pretty old, but I came up as Evangelical [Baptist]."

Thus, when I visited Nacimiento with Alice Fay, I made it a point to visit the small, pastel Catholic church sitting on the main road. Maggie (Margarita) Factor is the dedicated caretaker of the freshly plastered church. Its congregation consists of around twenty-five females. On the day we visited she had just set out a colorful array of flowers on the simple altar and was happy to see us. Maggie explained that the priest did not reside in Nacimiento but made a visit every month on his rounds. Couples who desire a Catholic wedding must wait until he arrives or go to Múzquiz to wed. Maggie sighed in resignation as she described the difficulties in getting people—especially men—to attend the relatively new Catholic church. In response to Maggie's comment about male participation, Alice repeated her similar refrain: "Shirley, you know the women did it. Not the men."

On the same Sunday that Alice and I visited the Catholic church in Nacimiento, we also attended a service at the Yglesia Evanjélica that Alice attended as a young woman. It sits on a barren piece of land, a rickety fence separating it from the huisache and cactus clumps nearby. The church is pastored by the aforementioned Zulema Vázquez, a passionate and energetic forty-eight-year-old whom I met on my first visit to Nacimiento in 1994. On that occasion, she had graciously invited me into her home and introduced me to the hospitality food *sofkee*.

Alice proudly pointed to the church, newly remodeled: "You know we all help to build that church, everybody like my mama Nellie. . . . She made tamales and pies to sell to the Kickapoo. I sent my mama some money from my work to build that little church. . . . The pastor was Kellie [or Kelly] Dimery. Sometimes we went but we had to walk all the way from the ranch to town a long way [about six miles]."

Zulema, very intense, told me the story of how God called her to be a pastor in a revelation:

> I left Nacimiento for twenty years. My husband and I lived on a ranch. We didn't have food. There was no rain. I have been here five or six years. . . . I was sick and had to die and be reborn to get well. The Lord has done a lot for me. I went to the *curandero* and he said I only have eight days to live. All they want is money and then they say you will get well. . . .
>
> I am content with my church here because more people keep coming . . . they believe in God, not in me. We fast and pray. Not too many of the elder people come, though. I am the oldest. The young women today don't know about their history. They don't see what the elders did. The lady who raised me says that the women only got to go to church if the men brought them but the men didn't go into the church. The women were only allowed in the church, and they would be there all day and all night. Men gathered outside. If he did not stand outside then all the other men would talk about him and make fun. The Catholics ask me, "Why do the children go to your church?" The priest gets upset and jealous and says we're crazy. We don't get along very well.[38]

Zulema Vázquez's passionate recollections of her people's heightened but less formal forms of spirituality in days past reflect the interwoven filaments of Black Seminole culture, at the core of which are the group's profound African-derived religious beliefs. On their diasporic journeys, Rose Kelly's people rewove these strands to create their own understanding of the world. As Zulema recounted to us:

> They would sing the song you call "Happy New Year" or "Hop-e-way" inside this place. They would build a fire in the center of the dirt floor and eat, and sing, and dance in a daze until the dawn hours—both men and women. Now we get together here, but we do not eat here. We have a wooden floor now, but we don't dance here. But we do sing and fill ourselves with joy, sometimes we cry and we do some kind of body movement when the brothers bring instruments. We don't dance around a fire. I believe that is the only difference. I believe that they did believe in God, because there were idols, what you call saints, in this place.

Zulema paused, her eyes tearful.

> In the past there was more harmony, more love, more respect in the adult's faith. Today you tell a child if you believe in God, you will be with God, but if you are rebellious you're going someplace else. Nowadays the kids will question your intelligence and will tell you what place are they are going to—like if they are more experienced. The past Seminoles were simple people.[39]

As time passed, men assumed more prominent positions in the evangelical churches in Texas. Some of the males were deacons who generally had been formally ordained and were non-Seminoles. Women though, played a large role in choosing the male deacons and keeping them. Henry Wilson, chosen by Rebecca Wilson, was one of the new preachers who was ordained to the ministry by the Negro Baptist convention. He married into the group and was accepted as a member. Jones reported, "He is doing much to enlighten the Seminoles and rid their religion of many of the superstitious beliefs that have been handed down from the past."[40] By introducing new forms of more formal Evangelicalism, these male preachers created profound changes. Many of the old traditions and practices were replaced with more formal church doctrine.

The echoes of the lives of the Black Seminole women who fasted and danced and shouted around the fire, who passed down these cherished traditions to their daughters and granddaughters, are only a faint whisper now. On their diasporic journeys, Rose Kelly's people rewove these threads of inheritance to create their own understanding of the world. These strands linger in the minds of those like Alice Fay, Zulema Vázquez, and Genevieve Payne. Like gauzy clouds, they gradually drift away, taking with them the dreams of women who held a culture together—a culture created from dreams drawn from an African homeland, merged with evangelical Christianity, Catholicism, and other Indian cultures in a religious pluralism characteristic of Black Seminole identity.

CHAPTER FIFTEEN

DREAMING WITH THE ANCESTORS

> In the version I know the woman is the daughter of slaves, black, American, and lives alone in a small house outside of town. Her reputation for wisdom is without peer and without question. Among her people she is both the law and its transgression. The honor she is paid and the awe in which she is held reach beyond her neighborhood to places far away. . . .
>
> One day the woman is visited by some young people who seem to be bent on disproving her clairvoyance and showing her up for the fraud they believe she is. Their plan is simple: they enter her house and ask the one question the answer to which rides solely on her difference from them, a difference they regard as a profound disability: her blindness. They stand before her, and one of them says, "Old woman, I hold in my hand a bird. Tell me whether it is living or dead."
>
> Toni Morrison

Alice Fay always catches me with new snippets of information when I least expect it. On our visits they filter in like brief beams of light from her attic of memories. The revelation can occur in a casual phone call or, as on one occasion, on a trip together through Mexico when the car engine drowned out her voice on the tape recorder and I resorted to scribbling notes while driving. One visit to her daughter Carmen's home in Kerrville stands out in my mind for Alice casually revealed a crucial aspect of Black Seminole women's role in the spiritual and cultural life of their community. That role was the cultivation and analysis of dreams, in which the women had contact with the ancestors or the Lord either as part of church ceremonies, dreams during sleep, or visions due to fasting, often in isolation.

It was bitter cold that day, and when I arrived at Carmen's home, Alice's arthritis was bothering her. She sat next to a space heater in a blue warm-up suit and knitted cap. Pointing to her knees, she said sadly, "You see what happens when you get old?" Then we exchanged our usual greetings and updates regarding my mother's health. My mother, Louise, and Alice are the same age.

She was not in a talkative mood that day, and I was always careful in my approach to asking her questions, especially when she was not feeling well. On such occasions I would begin the conversation with humor—"Well, you have to be ready to kick up like you always tell me you can still do"—which would bring a smile to her face. Sometimes I would relay a question through her daughter Effie, knowing that it might receive more favor.

Rosa Dixon Fay, Alice's paternal grandmother, was such a vibrant person in her memories, and that day I asked Alice to reminisce about her. "Alice, will you tell me more stories about your grandmother Rosa Fay in Mexico?" She pondered over my question as usual, her dark eyes a mirror of childhood memories. I was unprepared for her response to my question:

> Well, Shirley, you know my grandmama Rosa Fay she read the dreams. The people they all called her Mother Mary. . . . One morning she gets up and has a dream. Rosa was a church leader, was telling them they had to go up into the mountains to dream, to fast, and sing—to tell dreams or the world would end. . . . Lots of the women went up to the mountains in Nacimiento. They made a little pen of brush in a cave.

Alice, moving her arms, pretended to gather up brush.

> They fast, had church and read the dreams. You know, behind my house on the ranch. . . . It surprises everybody. They pray until they had the right dreams. Then they come down and read the dreams for the people—what was gonna happen—how the crops were gonna be or the water dried up . . . a flood or something like that—and they all was

gonna die. You know I went up there to the mountains—would get up early and take that little trail. I liked to go.

Alice continued in her distant reverie, her story revealing more about the eclectic nature of her ancestors' religion mapped on their syncretic landscape of beliefs and traditions, of other religions they encountered in their diasporas. "We had *santos* [saints] and burned candles up there in the mountains, you know on the side of the ranch, and pray to Saint Martin [a saint of African descent] too for rain," she said. "I'd think about those old Sisters. Right up there. I think it's washed out now."

Alice's brother Henry Fay, on one of my later visits to Nacimiento, echoed her story. "My grandmama, they called her [Rosa] Mother Mary," he said. "She went up in the Canyon de Los Negros. The people called the place Mt. Zion church."

Rosa Dixon Fay's spiritual actions reflect the Mascogo women's creation of new traditions as well as the curating of those drawn from their past to deal with events such as incessant droughts and crop losses that plagued their lives in Mexico. They practiced their faith from improvised churches in the mountains to their "pray's houses" in Nacimiento, where they dreamed to contact a benevolent God and their ancestors. The remote caves they climbed to in Mexico became shrines where Catholicism and Protestantism merged with age-old traditions perpetuated from their African and Gullah roots.

Rosa Fay, like many of the older women Alice refers to, was a Sister, the honorary appellation representing the collective idea of a respected religious leader who interceded on behalf of her community. When Rosa led the women up into the remote caves in the foothills of the eastern Sierra Madre Oriental, together they created a liminal or remote space outside their community where they prayed and fasted to foretell the future. Fasting, or eating only small amounts of food for a period of time, caused visions, what the women called "coming through." This pilgrimage reflected the seriousness of their mission for, as Alice said, they wanted to know "what was gonna happen" or "how the crops were gonna be." After long hours praying, fasting, and "weighing" the dreams there to "get through," the women came down and shared their portent for the future with the community. This experience was similar to the Gullah belief system in which the search for a vision or dream was like a spiritual journey that the traveler took to a remote place in the bush.[1] The dream experience was different from the spirit or trance possession, or "getting happy," encountered in the ring shout.

"Were the men involved in the fasting and dreaming events?" I asked Alice on another occasion. I predicted her response to my question since the women from Nacimiento repeatedly told me that the men did nothing but "drink and gossip" and that they "never went in church." However, Jones reported in the 1930s on deacons who also participated in the interpretations of dreams of those seeking entry to a particular church in Brackettville.[2] Porter also reports that Joe Bruner, a member of the evangelical church, had dream songs.[3] Perhaps the male participation was more obvious in Brackettville. In responding to my question, Alice had that familiar look of chastisement on her face and emphasized, "Shirley, I *tell* you just the women fasted to read the dreams. . . . Just the women did it. I tell you the women did all the work. They took out the crops . . . like in Nacimiento. They cooked the food like the *sofkee* and the coontie. They went to church. Those old Sisters . . . they prayed and read the dreams. They was real strong."

I persisted, posing the same question on different occasions to the other older women to get different opinions or to make certain the men were not getting shortchanged. When Alice and her old friend Gertrude Vázquez were visiting together in Nacimiento, I asked Gertrude about the men's role in the spiritual well-being of the community. Gertrude wrinkled her brow and looked at me as if I were a heretic, saying, "Why, no ma'am, only the womens they do it—the *Sisters*." Alice then followed up with the familiar litany: "Well, the men didn't like it! Women do all the [spiritual] work. Men work in the fields."

Alice and her brother Henry's remembrances of Rosa Fay brought up a new flurry of insightful conversations I had with the women on my later visits to Brackettville. I repeated the story of Rosa Fay to the women with the intention of comparing the dream-reading practice with Alice's recollections. During one of the many Seminole Days festivities I attended, the ever gracious Ethel Warrior gathered some of the older women to discuss reading the dreams on the old Carver school grounds. The women included Miss Charles Wilson, the two sisters Ophelia Benson and Nancy Williams, all in their late eighties or early nineties; and Nancy's daughter Gracie Lasky and Alice Fay, who were in their early eighties.

Ultimately, the women's conversations at this time and others would reveal five characteristics of the dream-reading practice. Dreams were predictive, first of all. Second, the gift of clairvoyance could be inherited as in the case of Rosa Fay and her daughter Clary, who as a child on the McKellar ranch had prognostic visions, which her little sisters believed came from eating mulberries. A third characteristic is that the ability to interpret dreams also could be taught by a respected Sister, usually a mainline female or close descendant. As Alice had told me, "Others of the women . . . they learned to do it from the Sisters."

Fourth, a book of invisible "passwords" or typologies—like the presence of a certain bird or hooting of an owl—guided the dreaming process and interpretation, and could have different portents. As Alice had explained in her conversations, dreams of portent could be acquired in regular sleep, in fasting, at a remote location, or in a prescribed ritual setting such as a church. Finally, and significantly, as the women would reveal, dreams and their interpretations were a means of social control, for to join the church, the spiritual "traveler" had to be in good standing and reveal a dream accepted by the Sisters. The dream practices thus also acted as a form of female jurisprudence system.

On the day I met with the older women during the Seminole Days festivities, Ethel Warrior was the first one to bring up the dreams. "Dreams come true," she said, her expressive face lighting up when she talked. Like the other women, Ethel considered the dreams read by the Sisters to be prognostic. As she said,

> You had to go out to have a dream and it would take a while. Then you would bring the dream back to church where dream readers would interpret them. The dream was very real. It was like you were asleep but yet not—sort of like a trance or daydream. When you went to speak, the

reader [Sister] would pop out with an answer. Sometimes they wouldn't answer you right away.

Still curious about the women's definition of a dream and how it was achieved, I asked the group of women, "What kind of dreams were considered of merit? Did you do something in particular to acquire the dream? Where did you have to go to have the dream?"

Alice Fay took the lead in answering the question, drawing from her complex knowledge and understanding of her own experience. Her definition followed Ethel Warrior's comment that the dreaming also occurred in sleep and played a role in telling the future. Alice, though, had another, different take on the process, equating dreams with contacting the ancestors. She related, "Well, when you go to sleep, you go and have a dream and then talk to the older people [ancestors], and they talk to you. Then you'd pray, and they would tell you what's gonna happen."

In the women's conversations I detected some overlapping boundaries and ambiguities in how they differentiated between a dream quest and a daydream or nighttime dream—ambiguities etched in their minds that I could never hope to understand. However, some of the practices clearly were particular to specific times of the year—such as the twenty-five days preceding Christmas (Advent), or Easter—celebrated in the churches or "pray's houses," and also were derived from Catholic practices.

Ophelia, shaded by her lavender straw hat, continued the conversation but expanded the role of fasting during these seasons. In her lilting voice, she explained, "The Black Seminole women read dreams that were caused by them fasting at certain times of the year [Easter and Christmas]." She added an important perspective: "Dreams helped keep the people together. Part of our spirituality was the reading of dreams. They brought this from Florida, you know."

Ophelia's insightful comment about keeping the people together brings to light an adaptive feature of the dreams mentioned earlier and echoes interpretations offered by the other women. Aberrant behavior by a person could disrupt an insular community that had survived diasporas and traumas from wars in Florida to slave hunters in Indian Territory and revolutions and devastating Indian attacks in Mexico. Generations of women who had departed with their families on the steamships leaving from Florida to Indian Territory—women like Cornelia Perryman; Rose Kelly and her mother, Tina; Teener Factor; Wannah, John Horse's sister; Rosa Fay's mother Clara Dixon, and others—brought the practice along with other spiritual gifts they tenaciously carried on their arduous journeys. They read dreams to foretell the outcomes of conflicts or wars, predict success in hunting expeditions, heal the sick, or determine whether their diasporas and relocations would lead them to freedom and land they could call their own.

The women who gathered at the school grounds that day considered Ophelia's sister Nancy Williams to be an exceptionally good reader of dreams. She had been born in Mexico, but her family moved to Eagle Pass to seek a better life. There her father had died and her mother Mary Bowlegs had moved to Brackettville. In her dementia at the time of our conversation, Nancy's dark eyes were blank until an ancient suspended memory traveled through her mind. She related in her gravelly voice,

> I want to make everybody happy. God has been good to me. My mama Mary Bowlegs had seven children. My daddy died, and she moved and married a Wilson. . . . My mama read the dreams. They'd get all of us together to read—just the ladies like Rose Kelly, Rosa Fay, Auntie Molly Perryman, Penny Factor, Fanny and Eva Griner. They believed it.

Gracie, Nancy's daughter and the youngest member of the group, added that the ability was related to age:

> They were all big churchgoers. My grandmother Mary Bowlegs would call us together, and we would fast and go to church. . . . If you had a dream you would go to the older people and they would read it. Tell what was gonna happen. . . . Children was not allowed to hear the dreams. . . . Sometimes they [the Sisters] never would get it. It'd be real hard. . . . The woman was always dreaming.

The Sisters' decision as to the success of a dream determined whether a person could join the church. As Ophelia explained, "My grandmother said that one lady had a dream but she kept turning her away [she could not join the church or be baptized]. She never got nothing out of that dream. My grandmother said it was hard. The lady never did get the meaning."[4]

Ophelia's recollection speaks to the power of the Sisters to determine church membership and suggests that the dream tested the applicants' ability to access a positive outcome in their spiritual journey. When the women went up into the mountains, or another solitary place, to fast, pray, and dream, they were waiting for certain dreams before returning to the community. Still trying to clarify which Sisters read the dreams, I asked the group of women gathered in Brackettville that morning under the canopy of oaks another question.

"Who judged whether the dreams were right?" I asked.

"Well, the Sisters was the ones who said that the dreams were good," Alice responded quickly, repeating what Gertrude had said. "The others [usually younger women or outsiders] went to the 'farm' [a remote place]. The oldest ones, the Sisters was the ones that was telling you the dreams—probably was hundred years old or something like that. . . . After having the right dream the person could come back from the farm. . . . You ask me what is the farm? Well, it was the place they roamed around till they had the right dream."

It took me a while to understand what Alice meant, for this place was not an actual farm but a place of isolation where the person could dream and receive spiritual guidance.

Ophelia, with her dramatic flair, illustrated an instance when women sought the right dream:

> The Sisters like Auntie Penny would get together and fast and pray and weigh the dreams. Something would happen, and there was confusion [or uncertainty in the community]. They brought this from the other Sisters who came before. The dream had to take [the meaning had to be acceptable], though. . . . One time—it is hard to remember—we were undecided about our pastor. We had to know whether to get another. The Bible says if you seek and pray, the Lord will send you an answer. If you are troubled and can go to bed and think about it, it'll just come—what to do. The fasting and praying give you a guide. We found a new pastor.

The Sisters wove traditions and external experiences into a communally accepted interpretation of dreams memorized by years of practice. The dream interpretations were a maze of complex typologies based on a projection of their world into categories, prohibitions, and taboos that resonate with other aspects of Black Seminole culture. This "handbook" or "bible" of standardized dream interpretations reflected organizational rules for the interpretation of a dream that included either a match of similar qualities (e.g., white-pure) or a reversal (white-death).

Ethel Warrior elaborated on these rules in this "handbook" in the discussion of dream reading. "Sometimes it was the opposite of what you dreamed. That's how you read it." Or other times it was not, she said. "You might dream about a beautiful, clean house. It might mean that you were purified."

Jones reports that some of the dreams that were "weighed" included revelatory signs: "the sight of a naked man is interpreted to mean freedom, or if the man is hiding, shame and unatoned sin. Muddy water is a sign of a coming visitation of evil, and crossing a stream of flowing water, provided the water is clear, is considered as an evidence of worthiness and is spoken of as 'Coming Through.'"[5]

The women continued the lively discussion about dreams, based on their own experiences. Ophelia warned, "Never talk about a dream after breakfast or it would come true. To dream white meant death and snakes meant money."

Nancy interrupted her younger sister: "Snakes also meant an enemy."

Ophelia nodded, "That's right—money and an enemy."

Again Nancy interjected in her barely audible voice: "Muddy water meant trouble for the group. Clear water meant good for the church."

The old women all nodded in agreement. "Amen. Miss Nancy, she was the best."

"I had a dream that my sister got married and her husband left," Alice said. "I tell my mama. I was really worried."

"Amen," Ophelia said.

"If you hear a gunshot in your sleep, what would this be telling you?" Ethel asked the women.

Miss Charles pondered the question and shook her head. "Not very good," she said.

Nancy, the acclaimed dream reader, revealed her expertise in this complicated process. "It could be good or bad," she said. "It depends on what caused the shot—the story behind the shot. If two men were running by after the shot."

"What about if someone is getting married in white?" Ethel asked.

"Well, it's opposite—means death, someone dying—wouldn't be happy," Nancy replied. "Amen." With a sideways glance at Ophelia, she continued, as if chastising a member of the group. "You don't understand it? Well, if you pray, the Lord will bring it back to you."

"Yes, Lord," Ophelia said.

"What if you see a river of muddy water? Clear water? Crossing a bridge? What if you drop a rock in the water?" Ethel queried.

Nancy nodded gravely. "Well, you would have to speak on that to see what it means. . . . Amen."

The old women all nodded their heads again in agreement with Nancy.

"If you dreamed about being naked, then someone was going to die," Alice interjected.

Ophelia exclaimed, "Oh, if somebody dies in the dream, it means somebody getting married."

Listening to their conversation, it occurred to me that, all together, the imagery and action in the dream stories were like a well-thumbed scrapbook—each page providing a moral compass from the ancestors. In oral societies such as the Black Seminoles', this record keeping was crucial because it also was tied into genealogical recall, their maroon history, their identity, and spiritual dogma of the "pray's house." However, the cultivation and reading of dreams among the women also occurred in more pragmatic situations as indicated in a conversation I had with Alice Barnett in San Antonio about her mother, Eliza Payne Daniels, granddaughter of Cornelia Perryman. Alice Barnett revealed that dreams still had significance beyond the church, for she did not depend on the Sisters to interpret them. I had many conversations with Alice Barnett, a handsome woman with snow-white hair who had been born in Mexico and was knowledgeable about her family history:

> My mama Eliza was born in Mexico. She was well, profound. She didn't know much about church like her sister Molly [Payne Perryman]. She was raised by her grandmother, Cornelia, 'cause her mama Phebe Payne died in 1898. Both women were born in Florida. My mama was taught to pray to gods and about fasting and praying and reading the dreams. . . . She would have these dreams and she would tell them to me and my sisters in great detail. She said that Black Seminole women were like the Indians. They fasted, too, you know. . . . My mama also believed in the evil eye. . . . She's buried in Nacimiento, you know.[6]

Ethel Warrior also considered the influence of the Seminole Indians on her people's perspective on dreams. "You know Indians used to tell the dreams—sometimes they were very strong," she said.

Chosen Indians among the Seminoles, males or females, also had the ability to interpret dreams sought in sleep or fasting so as to prognosticate the outcome of planting crops, hunting, and warfare. The dream quest was often accompanied by fasting as with the Black Seminoles, but also the taking of medicines such as the black brew, a strong emetic and a version of which the early Black Seminoles reported drinking before a battle.[7] Other similarities included the focus on fasting, vision quests, and dreams acquired in solitary visits to a remote place like the "farm," the term Alice Fay used. The nearby Kickapoos in Nacimiento also watched and read dreams obtained through fasting or sleeping to prognosticate. However, unlike Alice's ancestors, dreams were read by both males and females.[8]

These differences highlight the uniqueness of the Black Seminole practice of dreaming and the role of women in it, for the roots of the practice hark back to the women's Gullah influences rooted in Africa. Like the Black Seminoles, Sea Islanders of South Carolina and Georgia who lived on remote rice plantations retained many aspects of African religious practices due to their insularity. Janie Gilliard Moore, a Gullah scholar, reports that signs and prognostications played a significant role in the Sea Island cultures.[9] Pollitzer and other Gullah scholars also note a similar retention of the fasting and dreaming complex among Sea Islanders. Pollitzer reports that a person would wait for a vision in the woods, which had to be told to an elder. Then the individual was prepared for baptism.[10]

On a different occasion in Nacimiento, I discussed the reading of dreams again with Gertrude Vázquez. Her conversation also emphasized the importance of the Sisters in Nacimiento. Gertrude explained in her Afro-Seminole–tinged language,

> When we grow up, we find out those old people were doing that. They go to the older ones—Sisters—she tell them what it was. Just the women from the church—like my mama and my great-grandmama—get together and go to church and tell the dreams. They get the dreams when they sleep. What the dreams mean. The old people fast and pray.

Responding to my question "Do you believe in dreams now?" Gertrude reflected, "*Sure*, I believe in dreams because my mama and old parents believe in dreams. Lots of parents wouldn't let you [children] be around when they talk about the dreams. It was secret. . . . If they had let us stay around, it would be better for us. When they talk to you, better mind. Yes, *mama*."

Another similarity to the Gullah Sea Islanders was the ability of older women through positions of authority to control community behavior through dream reading that also reflected a legacy of African roots. These Sisters who deemed the dreams to be worthy in many respects are like the older women among the Sea Island Gullah who are called "Mother." This honorific also may go back to the "altar parent" of Africa, a spiritual leader who would guide the initiate into church membership.[11]

Cheryl Townsend Gilkes discusses the role of community mothers in the modern-day African American church. The mothers wield considerable authority, and their followers owe their own power and authority to the sponsorship of such women.[12] These characteristics resonate with similarities to the importance of the Sisters in Black Seminole religious practices, in part due to their mainline status in the community as descendants from the first families from Florida. Older women like Penny Factor and Rosa Dixon Fay revealed leadership and control of social and spiritual mores and guided younger women in learning to read dreams.

The "Mother" instructed the one attempting to have the dream in appropriate conduct and how to pray with the expectation of having the right dream, usually focused on some community problem to solve. The spiritual mother then interpreted the vision or dream of the person, and if she did not deem the dream as acceptable or helpful to the community, she sent the person back to contemplate or fast and try again—just as Ophelia's grandmother, Mary Bowlegs, had turned back the poor woman with the dreams that didn't take. A vision derived from dreams, if accepted by the "Mother," was similarly said to "take," like an inoculation. Such "inoculation" also was a crucial element in the dream interpretations of Black Seminole women as explained by Ophelia.

I reflected on an impassioned speech by Zulema Vázquez, the pastor of the Yglesia Evanjélica church in Nacimiento, describing services and dream-reading practices:

> The old people who believed in dreams are gone. When something goes wrong, they got together to read the dreams. They had superstitions. They did not talk about the Bible but they had faith. There were rules. They couldn't take a bath during Holy Week. In the past they [Seminoles] had a belief, because every year they would prepare meals. They would come and eat here during Christmas and New Year's. They came together to go pray and exchange gifts for the kids. Only the women would go there. . . . They would gather around the fire in the center of the room and warm up their food on the fire, and they would talk about their dreams. They believed in dreams. If a bird sang, that meant something like someone was going to die. If something was broken, it would signify something to them. This was their belief.[13]

In the past, typically, among the Black Seminoles in the Christian evangelical church, as the women explained to me, one had to be baptized to formally become a member of the church. One could attend church but was not considered a member. Excluded were people who had committed a crime or who were disruptive to society. When a Sister had determined the person had a successful dream and that person was ready to be formally presented to the church, the next step was baptism. This acceptance came with a certain amount of prestige to the successful inductee. A noted characteristic of the baptism was total immersion in water, usually a river or creek. Baptisms among the Black Seminoles on Fort Clark or in Brackettville were joyous celebrations on the banks of the turquoise Las Moras Creek, shaded by canopies of ancient oaks. The women made specialties like *sofkee*, and there was gospel music and singing, again reflecting their exposure to evangelical traditions with African roots.

Alice recalled her experience with participating in baptisms:

> Well, I remember when they have a baptism at the river. Maybe you cook rice or chicken or something like that and make different bread and you take it down to the river where the people are. The members of the church they make white bread, no brown bread, and when they get ready to baptize they give them a piece of bread and shout and sing and pray. . . . Then they put them in the river . . . you know the Sabinas in Nacimiento. The women dressed in white, if they had a white dress to wear. Then the preacher put you under water three times. Then the people would sing and pray.

Ethel Warrior remembered laughingly that the girls would modestly tie their long dresses together at the ankles when they were immersed in the water during baptisms in Brackettville.

As the women gathered on the school grounds and I drew our discussion to a close, Ophelia or Gracie would correct Nancy about facts as her mind wandered. Alice and I attended Nancy's funeral in Del Rio in 2001. She was ninety years old when she passed away. One year later Ophelia joined her in peace. I think fondly of the last time I saw Ophelia alive. Despite her infirmities, she was attending the funeral of Tony Warrior, Ethel and Dub's son, in 2001, wearing her red wig and a wispy straw hat.

Dream reading in its many syncretic dimensions was a survival tool that the Black Seminole women carried with them and nurtured on their diasporas as a mode of accessing a creative, energizing power. Leaving their earthly possessions, their bountiful farms and homes in Florida, then Indian Territory, and even as they moved between Texas and Mexico, they traveled only with their memories as relics of the past—the names of and stories about their ancestors, the "broken" language, their foods, and religious beliefs. Living on the edge, enduring the threat of slave hunters, incessant conflicts, Indian attacks, devastating droughts, and profound discrimination, this small community feared that aberrant or nonconforming behavior would create an imbalance and could bring down misfortune. Black Seminole women's dream typologies and interpretations, like little Clary's taboos about burying her hair so harm would not come to her and a concern with dirt pollution during funerals, were carried down like passages from the Bible—montages of meanings, ideas, and rituals that were assembled and reassembled in new ways as part of their cultural ethos. They were a map for negotiating their lives. Like the blue, calm waters of Las Moras Creek that wind around the ruins of the Black Seminoles' abandoned village, Las Moras, today these typologies and interpretations continue to course through their identity as Black Seminoles.

CHAPTER SIXTEEN

THE JOYS OF PARADISE

> I visit with old Peazant every day since the day he died. It's up to the living to keep in touch with the dead. . . . Man's power doesn't end with death. We just move on to a new place, a place where we watch over our living family. . . . Respect your elders! Respect your family! Respect your ancestors!
>
> Nana Peazant in *Daughters of the Dust*

Funeral practices are the clearest signs of the unique worldview of maroon people such as the Black Seminoles. The values and behaviors associated with death can survive social crises and diasporas because—like religion, language, and naming patterns—they also resonate one aspect of the collective Black Seminole ethnic identity, an ongoing relation with the ancestors. Patricia Guthrie, a scholar of African American culture, reflects that historically, celebrations associated with memories of the dead provided slaves with "mooring posts." Mortuary rituals were referred to as "catching sense" by slaves in that the shared memories as well as obligations and privileges of belonging to the community were reiterated in the ritual.[1] Among the earlier Black Seminoles of Alice Fay's generation, fellowship with the dead reflected a profound respect for the elders. Indeed, the power of the older women was related to their genealogical knowledge linking them to the ancestors, and indirectly in that connection lay the ability to proscribe the correct mode of behavior as Black Seminole. This "beyond the grave" authority is attributed to African influence by scholars such as Igor Kopytoff as ancestors continue to retain a functional role in the world of their living descendants.[2]

Death posed a threat to the Black Seminole community in Nacimiento and Brackettville in the early days as it did in slave communities without written traditions, for it compromised the passing down of the accumulated knowledge of elders to the rest of the group, a close-knit community that had managed to survive through diasporas and wars. The community surrounded the dying person to sing and pray and offer support, believing that the dead continued to linger in their midst and could provide protection to the living if not offended. After death, it was believed a person could return to earth to punish the living if he or she had not been treated properly. One old Black Seminole who lived in Brackettville recalled, "Some Seminoles [Black Seminoles] won't live in the house for two or three weeks after one of their family dies. They say they is still there."

If the community believed that witchcraft or sorcery was involved in a person's death, the wish was for the dead spirit to reconcile with those still living. These beliefs translated into respect on the part of the younger members of the group for the elders who could come back after death to haunt the living if rituals were not properly performed.[3] Alice's ancestors also spoke complimentarily of the departed. "We want those old people to be happy," Alice emphasized. "If a dead person was unhappy then we would hear about it." Typically, any unexplained happening was attributed to spirits—bad luck was explained as the departed retaliating for some injustice or wrong. Thus, there was no chasm between those experiencing life and death. Jones reports in his observations of the Brackettville community in the 1930s:

> It is the belief of the old Seminole that the departed will linger in a state of waiting until the end of the world, when Gabriel will call forth all the elect to enter heaven together, where a great feast will mark the beginning of a blissful life of eternity. Many of the older Seminoles pray the lord will hasten the day when the "Doors of Heaven shall be opened."[4]

The shout-and-response dance or circle dance, like other aspects of the Black Seminoles' religious practices, blended seamlessly into the rituals of mourning. In the old days their shuffling continued until they were exhausted and in a trancelike state. As Miss Charles related to me, "We stay up all night—sometimes done in church—drink coffee and get a little strange [reach a trancelike state]."

Jones reports, "Fair weather from the date of death till the day of burial is considered a great blessing, for then a rousing wake of singing, crying, and coffee drinking can be carried on with impunity at the home of the dead."[5] As Genevieve Payne told me, "They did Indian dance around [the] body and around in a circle—all night. . . . We clapped and went real slow. . . . One lady, she jump like a cheerleader. . . . We children sat there quiet—no giggling."[6]

Dub Warrior also related that they did the shuffle at wakes. Unlike some of the other dances, he commented, the mode of dance was a more serious shuffle of feet as they moved in a circle in the church or around the house of the departed. He demonstrated the slow movement of the feet to me. "They would go around in a circle for hours and hours way into the night. The other dances at Christmas and New Year were different . . . they shuffled and called out the names of the people who passed. They would get happy and cry. Sometimes the occasion included the drinking of liquor." Gertrude Vázquez described the funeral wake among the old people in Nacimiento: "It was a good dance—a good funeral. We see the old peoples."

The key role of singing and dancing as an ingredient in the funeral proceedings was echoed by the spry Genevieve Payne. "We sing all night long and hang around the fire, laughing and singing," she said. "Anyone could start a song. Had a church bonfire outside where there was all kinds of drinking and smoking. Tradition was that everybody would be there to support the family, bring the body in, and always be there with the family or when someone got sick."

In more modern times, "It is somewhat cheerful," Ethel Warrior related. "Night vigils, singing, and praying are intended to strengthen the dying."

Fasting as part of seeking and reading dreams and its role in the praise house rituals was also an integral part of the funeral ceremony. Alice recalled from her childhood in Nacimiento, "We did the fast and our people danced around the grave so the spirit can pass

Fig. 28. Tina Payne Jefferson, third from left, appears in this photograph with her husband, far left, at a freedman funeral service in Seminole, Oklahoma. Institute of Texan Cultures, University of Texas at San Antonio. Courtesy of Alice Daniels Barnett.

[on]. . . . Some would cry but most of us would rejoice because they [the deceased] were no longer with the problems of the world. We [women] would comfort the brothers." Gertrude Vázquez said of the departed, "They are released from this sinful world!"

All these African-derived elements—the night vigils, singing, praying, and particularly dancing and even dreaming—unite in Thompson's description of a Brackettville funeral in the 1920s:

> Pulsating, quivering, almost becoming silent, growing slow, increasing in tempo as the Seminoles, a race of mixed Indian and Negro blood, shuffled around the coffin which held all that was mortal of one of them. The house of the deceased had been placed in order, the rough wooden burial box rested on a table in the yard before the door, the neighbors

> and friends had arrived and were marching around and around the corpse with a queer shuffling stride, chanting and mumbling prayers.
>
> Nearby, also in the yard, was another table loaded with an abundance of good things to eat, prepared only as a Seminole cook can, composed of various donations from helpful hands and free to all mourners. Chanting, marching with dragging feet, eating, the demonstration continues all night until the first rays of the sun heralds the approaching day. From time to time during the night . . . marchers drop out of the procession and snatch a few moments or an hour's sleep on the ground, to awake refreshed and assume the endless round.
>
> Before the corpse is removed to the cemetery for burial, as the last act of love and respect all the friends and relatives line up and march around the corpse, singing, and sometimes dancing. A strong belief of the Seminole Negro is that prayer should be made for the dead without ceasing, and that one should not depend so much on personal religious experience, but rather on dreams, for in dreams the Seminole's God reveals itself.[7]

In addition to the shout and response and other special preparations for burial, the Black Seminoles also carefully prepared the physical body for interment. Doug Sivad, a Black Seminole historian, reports that in the past Black Seminoles embalmed the body with lime and placed a saucer of salt on the navel to keep evil spirits away. If male, the body was dressed in Indian regalia. The casket was constructed of woven tree limbs chinked with mud and then covered. Sivad reported that the coffin was carried in a procession and placed in a grave with flowers and a flame set at the head of the dead.[8]

The related females of the departed played a key role in the funeral process or wake. "Sisters" were focused on the preparation of bodies and rituals surrounding the funeral. Miss Charles recalled, "The body is brought home and dressed by the women." The women also were involved in the preparation of traditional foods like *sofkee* and the appropriate display and distribution of food to the grieving group as occurred on other ritual occasions. Older women oversaw the appropriate deportment surrounding the burial rituals. The women, by following the correct burial protocol, as in other rituals, reaffirmed their identity and status, and provided an enduring ceremony to mitigate the ambivalences of death.

Alice provided a personal look at this process and the involvement of women in it: "When my Amelia died, the womens dressed the body," she said. "We made a coffin out of sticks—put them together, like the stick house—and put her in and then wrapped it with blue material. She looked so little. I never did get a picture. I wanted one."

Alice also described the body's travels, from house to grave: "In Nacimiento the body stayed in the house," she said. "We kept for twenty-four hours and the men they go out to dig the grave. We would carry the body in a wagon pulled by a horse to the cemetery singing all the way. . . . When they take the dead to cemetery only the womens would sing. . . . All the women walk behind till they get to cemetery. The men put the dirt on the grave. They all threw dirt on the grave."

Henry Fay also recalls his people throwing handfuls of dirt on the grave in Nacimiento. "After the wake the body would lie under a tarp for two days until they took it out," he said. "Those old people didn't sweep away anything until they moved the body. If an old parent was unhappy or couldn't rest in peace, the good Lord couldn't find them a resting place."

Again the Black Seminoles' concern with purity and pollution was expressed in their burial rites and internment. Dirt, whether tossed into the grave or found around it, represented inherent disorder and pollution that could interfere with and threaten a community on the fragile edge of survival. These beliefs that focused on the polluted state of the departed hark back to the Black Seminoles' multifaceted past. For instance, Gutman reports that the taboo on touching graveyard dirt has origins in west Africa and also is found in South Carolina. Those handling the body had to be purged and other mourners had to be careful not to step on the new dirt around the grave, for it could bring sickness and bad luck.[9]

Digging these graves, as Alice mentioned, was the work of men. The graves of Black Seminoles were dug east to west, with the person's head placed to the west. Alice said of the departed, "Your head goes sundown, and your feet go sunrise." This placement of the deceased is consistent with African burial practices. One descendant,

Jo Emily Williams, a great-granddaughter of Penny Factor, discussed the men's work in an amusing story about a funeral in Brackettville:

> They sing and dance all night . . . they made coffee and Indian sweet-bread. . . . They eat, and then the men would dig the graves, you know. . . . They didn't pay anybody, they did their own grave digging and everything and I remember Jonell [Daniels] married a man from down this way, east Texas, I guess, and they went out there, his first time out there [Brackettville]. So they asked him to go along with them to dig the grave. And so he went, he didn't know much about them, you know, when he went and he said these Seminole men were around the grave and they had their bottle of tequila or mescal or whatever they got in Mexico. . . . Whiskey, you know. . . . And he said they'd dig a little bit, and they'd pass the bottle around . . . and they'd dig some more.
>
> And he [Jonell's husband] said they would pass the bottle to him and he was being polite, you know. He said, "No, thank you, I don't care for any." And he said they'd pass the bottle around to him again and he says, "No thank you, I don't care for any." And he said the next time they passed it around, they put the bottle in front of him and said, "Drink!" So he took the bottle and he took a drink and said, "Oh, when he took a drink of that whiskey he saw Seminoles raising all up in that cemetery everywhere." . . . He would say that and then, after they'd dug the grave, and they'd come back and they have the sermon at the church. And they cry and they sing and they pray—all of this, then they go to the cemetery and they have it all again, before they bury the body![10]

Curious about the cemetery in Nacimiento on one of my visits there, I asked Alice, Gertrude, and Henry if they would take me to see it. I followed them down a winding gravel path through a maze of graves. Next to the trail, I noticed a gaping hole, where someone had obviously dug up a coffin.

"Grave robbers?" I inquired.

"No" shrugged Henry. "That was Blas Gutery, a bad guy. He was killed by Clata Payne for stealing. He was buried here, but his kinfolk didn't like him being buried with the blacks, so they took him out."

The resting place of the Black Seminoles' ancestors in Nacimiento, unlike the cemetery in Brackettville, lay in ruins on my last visit. The tombstones, toppled and strangled by dense vines, were surrounded by tall, predatory weeds. One of the crumbling graves sported a statue of a white Jesus, looking much like a Spanish conqueror. Some graves had surrendered any pretense of decorum, their pristine white stucco now stained with gray mildew. Rough-hewn wooden crosses bleached by the sun leaned against some of the markers. I felt pangs of disappointment, for some of these crumbling tombs had no markers. I wondered if the ancestors lying in them were in my story. Was Tina Payne lying there? Rose Kelly?

On this visit Alice paused at her mother Nellie's grave, saying:

> This is my mama lying right here under this pile of rocks. I am standing by the old lady. My mama's name is Nellie Valdez Fay. She passed on December 15th. We had the wake at the ranch. We sing and shout all night and bring her here. While the men dig the grave, we sing and pray. We get through. They sing Nellie to heaven. Nellie was 103 when she died. Pretty old. Tina, Rose, and Amelia buried in Mexico, too. Amelia, you know, she was 100 years, and Rose dies when 115.

The unrelenting sun threw a shadow on Gertrude's little granddaughter who had accompanied us, wearing an improvised paper hat. Gertrude pointed to her mother's grave. "This is my old mama, Mary [Jesuita] Payne Vázquez, and my daddy, Sam Santiago Vázquez," she said. "When the good Lord remember me in Nacimiento—me, I have two old sisters right over there—lay down my body with my mama and my daddy."

She pointed to a wooden cross. "My daddy was over there. I want to be right here with parents, my grandmama and granddaddy. This is where they walked for the land—hard time getting all here—interest to me to be here where they are at. They traveled over a year—day and night. My grand-people came from Florida."

Gertrude paused to reflect, her voice full of emotion. "Womens sat down and pray—praise—we sing, and if we don't sing stand up, we sit down. If we feel too happy, we get something like religion [a trance-like state]. We sing and walk around the body. Got a happy funeral. . . . Jesus. Yes, ma'am. We sing and give thanks to Lord that they are in resting place or home, and not suffering in this *sinful* world!"

Fig. 29. Alice Fay and her old friend Gertrude Vázquez visit the graves of their ancestors at the cemetery in Nacimiento. Photo by Shirley Boteler Mock. Author's collection.

Gertrude and Alice held hands and began to sing, swaying from side to side. The song of the two old childhood friends had a cadence to it that harked back to their African ancestors:

Oh the day is a breaking.
Master Jesus is gone.
The day is a breaking, Sister.
Oh, Glory up to heaven. Glory in the Lord.
Went to heaven, Sisters.
When all day lonely, walk with me.
Yes, mama!

In the cemetery, an ancient stage of shared memories, Alice and Gertrude walked with the Sisters who had gone before them and who they hoped to join in the kingdom of heaven one day. Their female ancestors, resting around them, had fasted, read dreams, and danced to the Lord amid profound sacrifices and tribulations, even death. But more than just survival, their story is both one of creation and transformation chronicled in their diasporic journeys to freedom. Their stories are treasures of the spirit.

CHAPTER SEVENTEEN

TREASURES OF THE SPIRIT

> There were so many happy moments but there is one much greater now, to be able to see my family again that preceded me. So I say to all who are here, "Be Strong!" and continue to love one another for me. "I'm just away to visit for a while and I'll wait for you, so I'll see you again."
>
> Mary Hall Williamson

> We's cullud people. I don't say we don't has no Indian blood, cause we has. But we ain't no Indians. We's cullud people.
>
> Rosa Fay

I still visit Alice in Del Rio, but lately she and Effie have been driving up to San Antonio, since Effie's daughter, Merry, a volleyball coach at a local high school in Hondo, has moved to San Antonio with her two children. Effie phoned me not long ago, saying, "We're coming to town on Saturday. My mama's not in a good mood so maybe it will help if you talk to her." She added, "You've spoiled my mother."

Alice Fay, although she was ninety-three years old in 2009, still travels with her family to Seminole Days and Juneteenth every year despite the fact that she recently broke her hip and is using a walker. "I'm still kicking up," she told me on one of my recent visits to her home in Del Rio. I know her movements are more limited, though, and that, combined with her arthritis, she is sometimes in pain.

When I saw Alice at the 2009 Seminole Days, she was in her booth as usual, selling her delicious tamales and greeting visitors with her luminous smile. The usual testimonials had been completed that morning and the crowd had scattered. Dub Warrior, dressed in western attire, was holding court with visitors as usual and some of the descendants. His vivacious wife, Ethel, and his sister Izola were wearing bright-colored Seminole patchwork dresses typical of those worn by the Indians in Florida today. The Buffalo Soldier group that attends every year was sharing stories under the oaks and trying to survive the heat in their stiff wool uniforms.

Descendants from all over the world continue to come to Brackettville to pay their respects to the ancestors lying in the Seminole Indian Scouts Cemetery on Seminole Days. Some travelers on Highway 90 will see the sign and stop to visit it. The cemetery serves as a landscape of remembrance where ancestors and descendants come together. Like other places in the landscape that play key roles in particular narratives, it helps to memorialize the stories that are associated with the ancestors. As Christopher Tilley observes, "Places, like persons, have biographies in as much as they are formed, used and transformed in relation to practice."[1] The cemetery, much less one of its graves, has mythic value in its historical relevance. As a link between the ancestors and the living, this burial ground continues as a landscape for communal action among members of the group.

During Seminole Days in 2007, I visited Dub and Ethel Warrior on the screened porch of what they call their "camp," an old Fort Clark building that family members purchased. Dub had told me he wanted to talk about the cemetery and the graves. He brought up a concern that we had discussed previously: ancestors are buried out there, but some graves have no markers while others have rudimentary markers with no name. He asked me as an archaeologist if I could determine the location of graves. Some of the Black Seminoles also are concerned that the cemetery is running out of room and that the ground left is solid limestone. Dub wiped his brow in frustration. "You know the land is real rocky and it's hard to dig," he emphasized. "That's why we've started moving people to the front of the cemetery. We need to buy some more land."

Many of Alice Fay's ancestors who rest there were sent to the heavens from the old clapboard Mt. Gilead church that legend says was moved from Las Moras in 1914. The church was another tangible part of their landscape of remembrance. As I drove by the church on my many trips from Brackettville to Del Rio I could hear the fervent old Sisters singing and praising the Lord, their Afro-Seminole–tinged voices echoing down the hill to Fort Clark below. I could see squirmy children in white, starched frocks filing out of the red doors, happy to be set free from the Sisters and the Aunties. Here was the stage where the departed were sung to the heavens to join their ancestors. This was the stage where the old Sisters pondered over the dreams of the community to foretell the future and prayed for harmony—where they shouted and danced to the Lord.

By 2007 the shingle roof of the old church had finally fallen in, and the brick steeple lay toppled over on its side. By 2008 the church was a pile of rubble. Trailer homes and chain-link fences now surround and eclipse the remains of the old church, relegating it to obscurity on its rocky hill. The junipers still stand forlornly around the ruins, faithfully guarding their fallen comrade.

Dub and Ethel Warrior recently drove me around Brackettville, pointing out the lots where there had been homes occupied by Black Seminoles after they were forced to leave Fort Clark. Many of the lots are now vacant, choked by weeds, scrub, or shrouded with mounds of rubble dotted with pieces of broken glass or crockery that await to tell a story. Occasionally a former residence is indicated by a remnant brick fireplace or a weathered picket fence. The home of the vivacious Molly Perryman is now gone, but I think of the many lively conversations that she and Sara Daniels, Rose Kelly's first daughter who lived nearby, had on their front porches. Nearby was the devout Aunt Penny's little testimonial church, also gone, now a bulldozed lot.

I vividly recall the last two occasions on which Alice and I saw Gertrude Vázquez. One occasion followed the National Park Service's visit to Brackettville on April 11, 2000, when the group was entertained with a barbecue. Alice and Miss Charles provided the entertainment with songs at the cemetery. On the following day,

Alice and I traveled with the National Park Service coordinators to Múzquiz. After arriving there, we met with representatives from the Casa de Cultura and Mexico's National Institute of Anthropology and History (INAH), local government-funded organizations, and historians to discuss documentation of the Mascogos' history in Coahuila. The Múzquiz mayor's young wife and the Nacimiento women had greeted us, the Mascogos all dressed in typical long, Black Seminole–style calico dresses, wearing the familiar headscarves, and holding up embroidery they had done. The purpose, initiated by Casa de Cultura, was to encourage some craft among the women that would bring money into the desperately poor village. Sitting in the forefront, Gertrude was beaming with pride and thrilled to see her old friend.

The last time Alice and I saw Gertrude Vázquez was during a sweltering heat wave in Brackettville in June 2001. It was five years after Alice and I had made our first road trip to Gertrude's Nacimiento home, following the route of their ancestors to Mexico mapped onto the landscape more than a century and a half before. Alice had ridden up from Del Rio with her daughter Effie to see her old friend, who had crossed the border with other members of the Nacimiento community. It was a special occasion because the National Park Service and U.S. Citizenship and Immigration Services had arranged for some descendants to cross the border for the Juneteenth celebration in Brackettville.

I recall the group gathered around a picnic table in the backyard of the Brackettville host. Hanging baskets of verdant green ferns decorated the branches of oaks overhead. Alice and Gertrude sat on metal chairs in the center of the group with their canes posed before them like staffs of authority. Gertrude's eyes shone bright in her crinkled face at seeing her childhood friend and the prospect of celebrating Juneteenth in Brackettville.

Besides Gertrude, other residents of Nacimiento at the gathering included one of the schoolteachers, accompanied by her husband, a tall, lean cowboy. Also present were Zulema Vázquez, pastor of the Yglesia Evanjélica church, and her son, Jesus, and Maggie Factor, caretaker of the small Catholic church in Nacimiento. Gathered around the table laden with a steaming pot of *caldo de gallina,* barbecued chicken, *cabrito*, and corn bread, they were chatting about Juneteenth and sharing stories of troubles in crossing the border.

The same group from Mexico crossed the border again for Seminole Days in Brackettville on the third weekend in September. That day of celebration was different, though, for it followed the September 11, 2001, terrorist attacks in New York City. American flags were flying half-mast, and those among the Black Seminoles associated with the military had pulled out their insignias and placed patriotic stickers and flags on their cars. The tragedy held the center of attention, and the descendants forgot their minor internal squabbles as they bonded together in grief.

Not long after, Gertrude Vázquez passed away in Nacimiento in 2003. The death of her old friend was a severe blow to Alice Fay, and she became silent in contemplation on my visits as she usually does on the death of a relative. I recently made the mistake of remarking to Alice, "Now that Gertrude is gone, it seems like all the old Mascogos are dying out." She looked at me in surprise and scowled, "What you mean? Lucia [Gertrude's sister] is still there and the others. We call ourselves Mascogos. Our old parents are Indian and black. We're still here!" It is a comment one has to remember as passing years find fewer and fewer of Alice's contemporaries left to share their stories.

Carmen, Alice's oldest daughter, who still returns to Nacimiento occasionally, informed me that conditions in Nacimiento have deteriorated in recent years:

> The gravel road to the ranch is all grown over, and you can only get to it by horseback now. All the people is fighting over water and land. Only two wells. Nobody can farm 'cause it's just too dry. They had telephone, electricity, and running water but everything is falling down and the people don't care anymore. All the old people are gone. Others from the outside are coming in and taking over. . . . When the older people were living, things were different in Nacimiento. They're dying out. They used to clean the place up. We didn't have running water or telephones. Now they have brick houses, and they don't even try to make the place look nice. When I was young, people would go over there. Now they're not too friendly.

Zulema Vázquez also sees a bleak future for the people in Nacimiento as the young people leave and the old ones pass on. "We didn't used to have fights, no marijuana," she said. "We had a school, hospital, jail, and theater. Now there's no respect. They fight over land now."

Recently, Alice confided in me that she would like to go back to Nacimiento one more time before she dies to see her mother Nellie Fay's grave. Her dark eyes mirrored ancient memories as she told me of her vision of the afterworld, of life after death with her ancestors. She said the future "was like the first time that the men and the women get together. The old people, like my great-grandmama, Rose Kelly, rise up, and they are doing lots of work, like taking care of the beasts." She imagines the Sisters doing chores and planting the fields—a seemingly idyllic vision for Alice, despite the hard life she led on her mother Nellie's ranch in Mexico. This biblical worldview is woven with threads stretching from Africa to Florida and Texas. Steeped in evangelical Christianity, it is a prism through which her people viewed their world and that provided a blueprint for their lives.

Similarly, the dreams recalled by the old Sisters are like fleeting clouds of memories that waft through her mind. Alice Fay, among other older Black Seminole women, still sees portent in her dreams. One morning when I met her at her daughter Carmen's house in San Antonio, she was visibly upset. Her nephew's son had been killed in a random drive-by shooting in San Antonio. She said a dream had foretold his death:

> A week before he was killed I had a dream. I was at the ranch. Lots of people come. I say to myself, why are all the people here? I was naked. My brother Henry, he was looking for me. I say to myself that I need to put on some clothes. I put on a slip and tried to work. A lady says they are waiting for me to get dressed and get married. Then I was going down to another place, down a creek, but I couldn't get across. I try to cross the creek to get married but there was too much water. I tell Carmen that I didn't like the dream because something bad was gonna happen to somebody . . . like my mama and my grandmama. Well, it did, you know.

Alice is one of the last old Sisters who still fasts and reads dreams, while the bones of her ancestors Tina and Carolina, and little Rose Kelly, who boarded steamboats for Indian Territory in 1838, rest in their rocky graves nestled in the arms of the eastern Sierra Madre Oriental mountains. Her paternal grandmother, Rosa Dixon Fay, lies under a faded white cross at the Seminole Indian Scouts Cemetery. Effie and Alice talk about fixing up the worn marker some day.

After all these years of shared trips and conversations, Alice still manages to catch me off guard with tidbits of information that reflect the depths of her religious beliefs. On one of my visits to Del Rio, Effie reminded Alice of her upcoming fast the next week. Surprised, I asked Alice, "Which fast is this?" Her response revealed the syncretic mixing, characteristic of her maroon ancestors, of Catholic, Baptist, and African-derived religious traditions. Alice scowled at me, surprised that I would not remember: "Why, my fast before Easter, Shirley—five weeks then I fast. I take water—that's all on Friday. We don't eat no meat, but I can eat fish. I do it at Christmas, too. I told you that. . . . Fasting came from the Baptist. I went to the Catholic church to visit, but not too much."

Alice still confides in me her intent to go back to Mexico and live, but her determination is tempered by the realities of life and her frailty. On one visit she confided sadly, "Well, I think I'll be gone by the next year. . . . I'm ready to go." Effie told me recently that she had made funeral plans for her mother, out of concern that she would not be able to do it when the occasion arrives. With tears in her eyes, she said, "I had to do it myself, because none of the other family wanted to do it."

Having given up on her idyllic dreams of a garden of tasseled corn and thriving pepper plants in Mexico, Alice has begun to feed the pigeons in her front yard in Del Rio. She sits in her striped glider and calls them to attention every morning. Every pigeon in the area gathers in formation to descend like a dark cloud, swooping down over her yard and squabbling over grains of corn. Alice brings out her bag of kernels and talks to them like babies. She calls them her birds and smiles as she feeds them, just as she did when feeding her goats in Mexico many years ago.

The old sisters, Ophelia and Nancy, and Nancy's daughter Gracie, who grace the pages of this book with their insightful comments, have passed on to be with their ancestors, but I have met many of their descendants and shared in their conversations. I miss the wise words of the deep-voiced Nancy, the good-natured humor of Gracie. I miss Ophelia's lovely voice, burnished with the grace of God.

In 2006 Miss Charles Wilson also joined her remarkable mother Rebecca July Wilson and her sister Dorothy in the arms of heaven. When I visit Miss Charles's grave in the Seminole Indian Scouts Cemetery, I often recall her poignant words: "We have given our loyalty and our skill to our country, and we have contributed to its history. I can rest now, knowing that this has been recognized at last and that future schoolchildren, both American and Seminole, will learn the part we have played in the growth of our great nation."[2]

During one of the Seminole Day celebrations, a discussion with the women about their history came up that has remained in my mind. "How do you feel today about all your ancestors?" I asked. "How do you identify yourselves today?"

I brought up the subject with the forthright Gracie. She laughed. "I think of myself as a black American," she said. "I raise my granddaughter who is nineteen. I tell her I'm going home. I'm gonna sit in a tree and eat goat meat. They don't have goats where I live now."

Wearing a striking indigo-blue dress and tie-dyed turban, Izola (Choach) Warrior Raspberry, Dub's sister who was born in 1924, pointed over to the old schoolhouse where Miss Charles had taught:

> I went to school here and graduated in the building you see over there. I met my husband Will Raspberry here in Brackettville in 1942. He was a Buffalo Soldier. We had nine children. We live in Missouri now, but we come here every year because we want our children to know about the old people. . . . We had three cars come here for Juneteenth—all my family.

She wiped her forehead under the hot September sun, the strong features of her face resembling those of her brother and reflecting their Indian genes.

> The Mexican side is still with us—the chilies and tamales. I've never been to Nacimiento. I want to see it because I was always told where the people started. . . . I just want to walk on the ground—just walk on the ground. I get so sad. . . . You ask me, "Why do we celebrate on this day?"

Izola's face flooded with emotion as she explained.

> You see Seminoles was already free. For the black people that were freed—we celebrate. It has been a tradition all these years. . . . How do I feel? What happens here? It's so sad and proud feeling. I get over there and look at the headstones—all the Warriors—Bill Warrior, my great-grandfather, John Jefferson and Curly Jefferson, Mary Warrior, my grandmother—she was very industrious. Mary Warrior's mother delivered me. . . . She could read and write—sent to school. John Ward was my great uncle. My granddaddy was the Seminole scout Kalina [Carolina] Warrior.

She paused and turned away with tears in her eyes, but continued, her comment reflecting some of the Black Seminoles' reluctance to talk about the past: "Some here don't like to talk about it."

Alice's daughter Effie, much younger than the other women, reflected on my question about how she felt about the past. She said, "You know, I have mixed emotions. You come and all the older people are gone. You go to Brackett and you see vacant lots—there were houses, there were Seminoles who lived there."

I asked the same question of Steven Warrior, who had traveled from Arizona with his family to participate in Seminole Days. Steven was in his early twenties at the time and had just graduated from the Air Force Academy. He provided an insightful perspective on how his heritage was misunderstood by outsiders. "You know, people used to tease me when I attended the Air Force Academy about being Seminole," he said. "That was fine, because I could deal with it, but I found one thing different—that black people could not be part Indian but other people could." I recall my own experience when discussing the Black Seminoles with a visitor to my museum. She exclaimed in surprise, "Why I didn't know there were black Indians—and even in Texas!"

As I came to know the Black Seminoles, I began to understand that—just as with the African American community in San Antonio I wrote about years before—they are not a homogeneous group. They reveal a range of different interests, intentions, and agendas according to age, gender, socioeconomic group, or geographic location. Their own understanding of their ethnicity also may differ when speaking to reporters, writers, tourists, or even among themselves. "Black Seminole" is a consciousness reinforced by a long duration of learned and shared cultural practice. However, this people's ethnicity also has been shaped and transformed by exposure to other cultures, religions, and environments. The past continues to provide raw material for contemporary struggles with leadership among members of the present-day group in Texas. Other schisms occurred in the Black Seminole church in Brackettville in the old days between the traditionalists and the progressive groups. But when faced with diversity, all Black Seminoles come together, bonded with those ancestral ties and shared identity.

Black Seminole identity as a maroon community that fought for freedom is a strong ethos today among many descendants and separates them from other African Americans who were emancipated. Their birth from the ashes of conflict in Florida historically resonates with the stories told in the voices of Black Seminole women, for theirs is a culture of remembrance. Stored in their archives of memory are interwoven strands of cultural influences mapped on a landscape of diasporic journeys. As guardians of culture, the women's stewardship is embodied in a complex genealogical system of names and naming practices inherited from Africa, a religion embroidered with syncretic threads of Protestant Evangelicism fashioned from Gullah and African roots and blended with Catholicism from Spain and Mexico. Their mourning rituals bore strong African and Gullah roots. They nurtured an Afro-Seminole language adapted from Gullah, an African-derived creole language they called Seminole. They fashioned their own eclectic culinary inheritance from the Seminole Indians, colored with African roots. Black Seminole women fasted and read dreams to keep their community together and prognosticate the future, like other women before them on plantations in the Carolinas and Georgia. Together, these practices and traditions are seamlessly synchronized into their identity as Black Seminoles, or—when they speak or joke with each other—as "Seminoles."

With Alice Fay guiding me I have striven to record the voices of Black Seminole women through the orchestration of histories, archival records, eyewitness accounts, military and federal documents, and descendant interviews. In a partnership with their allies, the Seminole Indians, and in the shadows of wars and slavery, Alice Fay's ancestors raised generations of families in their maroon communities sheltered by chiefs Micanopy, Payne, and Billy Bowlegs and elite Seminole women such as Harriet Bowlegs and Nelly Factor. These multigenerational families surrendered together and boarded steamships from Florida for Indian Territory in 1838: Alice's great-grandmother Rose Kelly, a five-year-old girl traveling with her parents; the young warrior Carolina Payne, his siblings, and his wife, Tina; the dashing John Kibbetts, with whom Rose Kelly had a relationship later in Texas; Clara, a small child owned by Micanopy and the future mother of Rosa Dixon Fay; John Horse's wife Susan and his sister Wannah, who later lost children in Indian Territory; Teener Factor, wife of the warrior July, and her large extended family, many members of which would later become well-known leaders at Fort Clark, Texas; July's brothers August, Dembo, and Thomas, and his aged parents, Sandy and Lucy, who were born in 1773 and 1783 during the British occupation of Florida and the ethnogenesis of the Black Seminoles as a cultural group; Cornelia Perryman, a twenty-eight-year-old widow, and her sons who later headed up an extended household on Fort Clark in 1900; and the Bowlegs family—Davis, Rabbit, and Jack and his wife Nancy, who was killed during Indian raids in Mexico. These families, bound in complex kinship ties, made the decision to follow their chief, John Horse, and embark on a desperate journey across the plains of Texas to freedom in Mexico. In 1870, some made the decision to cross the border again for new lives in Texas. There are others whose stories remain in the shadows of time.

I still gaze at the sepia-colored photos of their descendants, Alice Fay's ancestors, wishing that they could speak to me—the brave Mirtes Payne, raising a large family alone in the throes of the Mexican Revolution, captured by Pancho Villa. I can hear Rosa Fay's little daughter Clary whispering her prophesies and her mother's musings as she pondered over dreams to foretell the future. I picture Nellie Fay tending her rose garden on the red soils of her ranch, Guadalupe, in Mexico. I hear Gertrude Vázquez's fervent voice exclaiming, "Church makes me feel good—talk about the *work* of God. Yes, *mama*." And I think of Miss Charles, the female warrior, whose spirit lingers on to remind Black Seminoles and all Americans of her people's role in our nation's history.

Finally, I think of Alice Fay, who listened to her great-grandmother Rose Kelly's stories as a young girl on her ranch, Guadalupe, and who remembers them. It is important that the stories of these Black Seminole women are told, for they encompass the stories of many women who linger unknown in the shrouds of American history. The favorite hymn Miss Charles and Alice Fay often sang during Seminole Days at the cemetery reflects their worldview, vested in courage and the ethos of their people.

By and by
When all morning come
We will tell the story
How we overcame
And we'll understand it better by and by.

Notes

INTRODUCTION: BLACK SEMINOLE WOMEN

Epigraph 1. Emma Tenayuca, interview by Jerry Poyo, 21 February 1987, University of Texas at San Antonio's Institute of Texan Cultures.

Epigraph 2. Turner and Ehlers, *Sugar's Life in the Hood,* 21.

1. Blacks in Texas, and parts of Louisiana, Arkansas, and Oklahoma adopted June 19 as the official date of their independence. In 1980, the Texas legislature designated June 19 or Juneteenth as a state holiday.

2. Rosa Fay was born around 1856, Porter surmises; see Kenneth Wiggins Porter, "The Seminole in Mexico, 1850–1861," *Hispanic Historical Review* XXXI, no. 1 (February 1951), 13–35. John Jefferson describes Rosa Fay in a letter to Kenneth Porter; see Jefferson to Porter, 20 August 1950, Porter Papers, Archives Division, Schomburg Center for Research in Black Culture, New York (this archive is hereafter cited as "Schomburg Center for Research in Black Culture").

3. Another Rebecca July namesake, the daughter of Rena and Charles July (Rebecca's brother), is listed in the 1900 census.

4. By "a full year," Miss Charles means the Black Seminoles arrived in Mexico a full year after they left Indian Territory.

5. Wright, *Creeks and Seminoles,* 42.

6. The term "maroon" (marronage) is often substituted for Black Seminole, but "Seminole" is the term used by Black Seminoles to describe themselves in Brackettville, Texas. The term "Mascogo" is interchanged with Black Seminole in this book because Alice's people lived both temporarily and permanently on both sides of the United States–Mexico border ("Mascogo" is used in Mexico to refer to Black Seminole people).

7. Mock, "San Antonio, Texas. 1990–1940: A Period of Mutual Aid," in *Archaeology at the Alamo Dome,* 1:84–113.

8. Lorenzo Turner recorded African-derived names like Dub's in his seminal 1949 book *Africanisms in the Gullah Dialect*. Based on his interviews of Gullah peoples living in coastal South Carolina and Georgia, he asserted that many African words were present in their vocabularies. See page 78 in Turner for the Gullah personal name "Duba." Possible African-derived names taken from Turner not used as given or surnames are presented in italics in *Dreaming with the Ancestors*.

9. Billy July was one of Rebecca July's seven brothers.

10. Jeff Guinn, "Seminole Negro Heritage Fading in Border Town," *San Antonio Express News*, 18 September 1994, 1D.

11. See Kenneth Wiggins Porter, "A Farewell to John Horse: An Episode of Seminole Negro Folk History," *Phylon Quarterly* 8, no. 3 (Third Quarter, 1947), 265–73; see also Porter, *The Black Seminoles*, 37, 99–100, 106 for description; see Porter to Jefferson, 30 April 1953, Porter Papers, Schomburg Center for Research in Black Culture. Bertha Daniels, Elijah Daniels's daughter-in-law, described John as looking like an "American-Race Negro" because he was so intelligent-looking and could write.

12. See Michael Davis's field notes and photos from the 1993 CRM excavations by Macaw Consulting, Austin, Texas, in Mock and Davis, "Black Seminole Culture on the Texas Frontier," *Cultural Resource Management* 20, no. 2 (1997), 8–10.

13. For additional history, see Cloyd L. Brown, *Black Warrior Chiefs*; Sivad, *The Black Seminole Indians of Texas*; Katz, *Black Indians: A Hidden Heritage*, 31–38. Katz's 1997 book, *History's Missing Chapter: Black Indians. American Legacy*, provides an overview of black Indians and their contributions to western history; also see Edwin L. Williams, "Negro Slavery in Florida," *Florida Historical Quarterly* XXVIII (October 1949), 93–110 and Willis, "Anthropology and Negroes on the Southern Colonial Frontier," in *The Black Experience in America*, 47–48.

14. See Long, "Perspectives for a Study of African-American Religion," in *African-American Religion*, 32–33; see Meisenhelder, "Conflict and Resistance, in Zora Neale Hurston's 'Mules and Men,'" *Journal of American Folklore* 109, no. 433 (Summer 1996), 267–88. She explores the subversive aspect of these tales as presented by Zora Neale Hurston in *Mules and Men*.

15. Porter, *The Black Seminoles*, 120, notes that in the official correspondence Juana's name appears as Warner or Wannah, a Gullah-derived name; Turner, *Africanisms in the Gullah Dialect*, 177; also see page 101 for the Gullah *Ju'ana*. Similarly, Juan is spelled and pronounced as *Wan*. Porter, *The Black Seminoles*, 100, 106, provides details about Susan and their marriage.

16. See Paula Ebron, "Enchanted Memories of Regional Differences in African American Culture," *American Anthropologist* 100, no. 1 (March 1998), 97, 100.

17. Shirley Boteler Mock and Alice Fay Lozano, "The Dream Readers: Black Seminole Women in Texas and Mexico," paper on file at the Institute of Texan Cultures, University of Texas at San Antonio, 1998. I do not provide an endnote citation for many of my conversations with the Black Seminole women that occurred over a period of twelve years. The informal conversations were numerous, and additional

endnotes would be distracting to the reader. The formal interviews and some informal interviews are listed in the bibliography.

18. Price, *Maroon Societies,* 1–30; Mulroy, *Freedom on the Border,* 1; see Rebecca Bateman, "Naming Patterns in Black Seminole Ethnogenesis," *Ethnohistory* 49, no. 2 (Spring 2002), 227–57. Both she and Mulroy, *Freedom on the Border,* discuss the cultural autonomy of the Black Seminole communities. They argue that maroon communities share commonalities with a category of similar communities that exist in areas such as the Caribbean and South America; also see Nichols, "Linguistic Options and Choices for Black Women in Rural Areas," in *Language, Gender and Society*; refer to Forbes, *Africans and Native Americans.*

19. Littlefield records the lists of deportees on file at the Library of Congress in the appendix of *Africans and Seminoles.* See also List E, National Archives Record Group 75, Records of the Bureau of Indian Affairs, Misc. Muster Rolls, 1832–1846: "Seminole"; List G, National Archives Record Group 75, Records of the Bureau of Indian Affairs, Misc. Muster Rolls, 1832–1846: "Seminole"; List I, National Archives Record Group 75, Records of the Bureau of Indian Affairs, Misc. Muster Rolls, 1832–1846: "Seminole"; "Seminole Claims to Certain Negroes, 1841–1849." See National Archives Microfilm Publications, Microcopy M574, roll 13, Special File 96.

20. Josephine A. Beoku-Betts, "When Black Is Not Enough: Doing Field Research Among Gullah Women," *NWSA National Women's Studies Association Journal* 6, no. 3 (Fall 1994), 413–33.

21. Littlefield, *Africans and Seminoles,* 4, 7, 10, provides a thorough discussion of the Manifest Destiny policies of President Andrew Jackson; also see Wright, *Creeks and Seminoles,* 130–31, 191, 206, 209, 232; Landers, "African and African American Women and Their Pursuit of Rights"; Landers also discusses black women's absence in the historical literature.

22. Linda W. Reese, "Cherokee Freedwoman in Indian Territory, 1863–1890," *Western Historical Quarterly* 33, no. 3 (Autumn 2002), 273.

CHAPTER ONE. THE BIRTH OF THE BLACK SEMINOLES

Epigraph 1. "Song of Sinnugee" from an interview with Elsie Edwards, 17 September 1937, as recorded in Saunt, *Black, White, and Indian,* 11, 14. A part Spanish, Mesoamerican, and African woman, Sinnugee took refuge among and was adopted by the Muscogees (Creeks) in the late 1700s.

Epigraph 2. This interaction occurred as Col. Ethan Allen Hitchcock met an Indian woman he was transporting by boat to Indian Territory in 1842. The passage is cited by Foreman, *Traveler in Indian Territory,* 383n33.

1. See Landers, "Traditions of African-American Freedom and Community in Spanish Colonial Florida," in *The African American Heritage of Florida,* 1–17, for a broad history; Rout, Jr., *The African Experience in Spanish America.* Porter, "Negroes and the Seminole War, 1835–1842," *Journal of Southern History* 30, no. 4 (Novem-

ber 1964), 427–50, discusses "Fort Mosé" and notes that the Spaniards were slave owners as of 1725; both Porter, *The Black Seminoles,* 1–3, and Mulroy, *Freedom on the Border,* 9–10, provide general discussion of Spanish attempts to defeat the British. For a detailed account of the history of Fort Mose, refer to Deagan and MacMahon, *Fort Mose: Colonial America's Black Fortress;* Mulroy describes maroon communities in *The Seminole Freedmen,* 12–15.

2. Landers, in her paper, "Slave Resistance on the Southeastern Frontier: Fugitives, Maroons, and Bands in the Age of Revolutions," *El Escribiano* 32 (1995), 28, provides rare glimpses of free black women's activities from a variety of documents; see also Landers, "A Nation Divided," in *Coastal Encounters* 102, 107, and Landers, "African and African American Women and Their Pursuit of Rights," 56–76.

3. Most of the Indians were members of the so-called Creek Confederacy or nation, a loosely organized association of Upper Creeks living in Indian towns who moved into northwest Florida and Lower Creeks or Red Sticks living in eastern Indian towns in Georgia who eventually moved on the Alachua plain. For discussion, see Fairbanks, "Creek and Pre-Creek," in *Archaeology of Eastern United States,* 285–375; Sturtevant, "Creek into Seminole," in *North American Indians in Historical Perspective,* 92–128; Milanich, *Florida's Indians from Ancient Times.* Names in parentheses in this paragraph are the Seminole names. However, in the rest of the book English names will be used because of their familiarity with the reader and the Black Seminoles.

4. See Mahon, *History of the Second Seminole War,* 7; Wright, *The Only Land They Knew,* 262; Littlefield, *Africans and Seminoles,* 3; Mulroy, *Freedom on the Border,* 20–21; also see Simmons, *Notices of East Florida,* for descriptions of Seminoles and blacks in the southeast. Theresa Singleton provides archaeological information pertinent to slave life in Florida in her 1995 paper, "The Archaeology of Slavery in North America," *Annual Review of Anthropology* 24 (October 1995), 119–40, and her 1998 paper, "Cultural Interaction and African American Identity," in *Studies in Culture Contact,* 172–88; see also Klos, "Blacks and the Seminole Removal Debate 1821–1835," in *The African American Heritage of Florida,* 59; Twyman, *Black Seminole Legacy.* Note that the names and spellings of the names of the chiefs or mikkos provided in this paragraph differ in many accounts.

5. Porter, *Negro on the American Frontier,* 302–303 and *The Black Seminoles,* 5–6; Foreman, *Five Civilized Tribes,* 99; Foreman, *Traveler in Indian Territory,* 325–26 cites Thompson to Cass, 27 April 1833, 533. See Littlefield, *Africans and Creeks,* 27. Mulroy, *Freedom on the Border,* 17–23 discusses the flexible rules of inclusion in the Seminole community. In *The Seminole Freedmen,* 6–7, Mulroy provides an explanation of the deep roots of this economic arrangement; see also Melinda Micco, "Seminole Freedmen and the Forging of the Seminole Nation" (PhD diss., University of California, 1995), 55. Among other scholars she observes that treatment of slaves differed among the southeastern Indian groups such as the Creeks, Cherokees, and Seminoles. For discussion of homes, see Terrance Weik, "The Role of Ethnogenesis

and Organization in the Development of African–Native American Settlements," *International Journal of Historical Archaeology* 13, no. 2 (June 2009), 225–26.

6. Information on other black Indian women's economic contributions provides examples of similar activities by Black Seminole women; see Zellar, *African Creeks,* 16, 38, which reports that Creek women benefited from Black Creek knowledge of horticultural techniques; Foreman, *Five Civilized Tribes,* 325–26; Kathryn E. Holland Braund, "The Creek Indians, Blacks, and Slavery," *Journal of Southern History* 57, no. 4 (November 1991), 611–13, 615, 622–23. Foreman, *Five Civilized Tribes,* 205 observes that the women were skilled in weaving; John R. Swanton, "The Indians of the Southeastern United States," *Bureau of American Ethnology Bulletin* 137, 443–44 discusses the tanning of animal skins and other activities among the Indian women. See also Opala, "Seminole-African Relations on the Florida Frontier," *Papers in Anthropology* 22, no. 1 (University of Oklahoma, 1981), 1–52. Weik, "The Role of Ethnogenesis and Organization," 225–26 also provides accounts of gifts given to Seminoles and Black Seminoles and other examples of women's probable activities at Pilaklikaha.

7. Wright, *Creeks and Seminoles,* 98, discusses the role of black women as linguists.

8. Klos, "Blacks and the Seminole Removal Debate," 128–56, reports that Abraham married Bowlegs's half-black widow and had three or four children; see Porter, "The Negro Abraham," *Florida Historical Quarterly* 25, no. 1 (July 1946), 11, for a discussion of the identification of Abraham's wife; for other instances of the intermarriage of Indians and blacks see Giddings, *Exiles of Florida,* 315, 324; Littlefield, *Africans and Seminoles,* 42, 53, 63n42; Patrick Minges, "Beneath the Underdog: Race, Religion and the 'Trail of Tears,'" *American Indian Quarterly* 25, no. 3 (2001), 472; Forbes, *Africans and Native Americans,* 18. Wright, *Creeks and Seminoles,* 63, 148–50, 255, argues that some blacks were adopted into Indian households and became part of the matrilineal clan system, and over time with their progeny became more and more Indian. He also contends that intermarriage over time resulted in the development of a Black Seminole identity; Mulroy, *Freedom on the Border,* 186, disagrees with Wright's argument for extensive intermarriage of blacks with Indians.

9. The emancipation of Rose and her children was witnessed by the Creek Indian Milly Thompson; Wright, *Creeks and Seminoles,* 304; James H. Johnston, "Documentary Evidence of the Relations," *Journal of Negro History* 14, no. 1 (January 1929), 21–43, cites a letter written by Daniel Boyd in the Office of Internal Audit (OIA), Florida File Letters, received 15 July 1838; Littlefield, *Africans and Seminoles,* 30, 53–55, provides a complete account of Rose Sena Factor's experiences and claims by owners.

10. Littlefield, *Africans and Seminoles,* 15–16, 21–22, 27–30, discusses Andrew Jackson's relations with the Black Seminoles; for Jackson's campaigns and criticism of his removal policy by slave owners, officials, and the military, see pages 20, 25, 31, 83. Also see Porter, *The Black Seminoles,* 31–35, 71–78, and *Negro on the American Frontier* for details of the removal act to the West; Wright, *Creeks and Seminoles,* 281–98.

Indian Territory at the time of their arrival included parts of Kansas, Missouri, and Arkansas. The territory included Oklahoma prior to the granting of statehood.

11. The most notorious incident of increased retributive guerilla attacks against Americans was the Dade Massacre, described by Mulroy in *Freedom on the Border,* 28. It ignited the long and protracted Second Seminole War (1835–42); see Mahon, *History of the Second Seminole War,* 106. Hudson, *Southeastern Indians,* 465, reports that realizing defeat, the Seminoles and blacks initially tried to compromise with the U.S. Army authorities but they were assigned undesirable swampland in Florida where they could not even grow crops and had to survive by stealing cattle. Giddings, a prominent abolitionist, presents information in *Exiles of Florida,* 279, 315, as to the role of the U.S. government in perpetuating destruction of black and Indian communities in Florida.

12. Wright, *Creeks and Seminoles,* 262.

13. James F. Sunderman, "Army Surgeon Reports on Lower East Coast," *Tequesta* X (1950), 25–34.

14. Foreman, *Traveler in Indian Territory.*

15. Mullin, *Africa in America,* 51–52, 54; Porter, "Negroes on the Southern Frontier, 1670–1763," *Journal of Negro History* 33 (January 1948), 53–78.

16. See National Archives Microfilm Publications, Microcopy 234, roll 291, frames 430–31, which details the African Americans such as Rose Sena Factor who departed on June 1, 1841, for Indian Territory. "Microcopy" in National Archives Microfilm Publications and the bibliography is hereafter abbreviated as "M."

17. For discussion of the matrilineal kinship system, see Braund, "Creek Indians, Blacks, and Slavery," 625; Hudson, *Southeastern Indians,* 184–200. Littlefield, *Africans and Seminoles,* 42, discusses the legal entanglements in the overlap of practices relating to the inheritance of human property; see also Wright, *Creeks and Seminoles,* 99. Micco, "Seminole Freedmen and the Forging," 56, discusses the pervasive Seminole clan system; Swanton, "Early History of the Creek Indians and Their Neighbors," *Bureau of American Ethnology Bulletin 73,* 1922, describes descent groups; see also Rebecca Bateman, "Africans and Indians: A Comparative Study of the Black Carib and Black Seminole," *Ethnohistory* 37, no. 1 (Winter 1990), 1–24. A similar pattern among the descendants of freedmen in Oklahoma today points to the remnants of this matrilineal practice. Art Gallagher, "A Survey of the Seminole Freedmen," master's thesis (University of Oklahoma, 1951), 99, reports that the freedmen descendants are represented in two bands out of the fourteen bands in the Seminole Nation today. Membership in the band is determined matrilineally among both freedman descendants and Indians. Beth Dillingham, in her 1976 paper "Integration of the Seminole Negroes of Northern Mexico," on file in the Schomburg Center for Research in Black Culture archives, reports a matrilineal bias in the Black Seminole community.

18. Jesup determined that he was not engaged in an Indian war but a "Negro" war; for example, see Porter, "Negroes and the Seminole War," 30, and *Negro on the American Frontier,* 238, 258–59, in which he cites Major Childs's diary in *Historical*

Magazine 34th ser. III, 280–82, which discusses conditions for removal. Other discussions of removal are provided by Littlefield, *Africans and Seminoles,* 16, and Mulroy, *Freedom on the Border,* 10–11. Giddings, *Exiles of Florida,* 140–41, determines that Jesup in speaking of the conditions of capitulation is speaking not of the Seminoles' black allies but of the "bona fide property" or slaves who would accompany them west; see National Archives Microfilm Publications, M234, roll 227, frame 579, 12 January 1847, "Letter from the Creek agency to Com. Indian Affs." The writer complains of the great numbers of African Americans claiming to be free in the Creek Nation.

19. Littlefield, *Africans and Seminoles;* see also U.S. Congress, House, *Indians: Creek and Seminole,* 33rd Cong., 2nd sess., 1854, H. Doc. 701 for numbers of Black Seminoles traveling to Indian Territory.

20. Saunt, *Black, White, and Indian,* 39–41; Porter, *The Black Seminoles,* 79, 95 reports various witnesses' descriptions. See Foreman, *Indian Removal.*

21. Weik, "The Role of Ethnogenesis and Organization," 206–38 discusses the Pilaklikaha settlement. See Landers, "A Nation Divided," in *Coastal Encounters,* 99–116. She provides discussion of Pilaklikaha as an autonomous town. See also Canter Brown, Jr., "Race Relations in Territorial Florida, 1821–1845," *The Florida Historical Quarterly* 73, no. 3 (January 1995), 428; Giddings, *Exiles of Florida,* 317; Porter, *The Black Seminoles,* 112.

22. See Porter, *The Black Seminoles,* 71, for this passage; the passage also is found in Major Childs's diary. See "Maj. Childs' correspondence," *Historical Magazine,* 3rd ser., III (1844), 280–82.

23. Milanich, *Florida Indians and the Invasion,* describes the De Soto expedition of 1538 and De Soto's ambitious attempt to conquer La Florida.

24. Littlefield, in *Africans and Seminoles* and *Africans and Creeks,* presents information about the complex problems and legal entanglements of removal. On pages 36–61, 84, and 167 in *Africans and Seminoles* he discusses the unjust or fraudulent claims of former slave owners and legal entanglements. Many of the blacks would never reach the West: Foreman, *Traveler in Indian Territory,* 349, reports a "Twenty Dollar reward" for the capture of thirty-five slaves. The other blacks who were confined at Fort Pike in New Orleans while waiting to depart to Indian Territory were sold to the United States for eight thousand dollars; see Jesup to Searle, 9 September 1837, "Seminole Emigration," OIA, File J 153; National Archives Microfilm Publications, M234, roll 290, frames 179–80. See also Porter, "Notes Supplementary to Relations between Negroes and Indians," *The Journal of Negro History* 18, no. 3 (July 1933), 282–321; U.S. Congress, House, *Negroes Captured from Indians in Florida,* 25th Cong., 3rd sess., 1839, H. Doc. 225, which describes blacks captured from the Indians in Florida.

25. Indians and black Indians were detained for different lengths of time before departure at Fort Jupiter or Tampa or left on different vessels. Time of departure to Indian Territory depended on when they were captured or the circumstances of surrender or capture; see Littlefield, *Africans and Seminoles,* 9–10, 12, 16, 27–28, 31,

49–55, 71–78. For additional accounts of removal, see Mahon, *History of the Second Seminole War*; Wright, *Creeks and Seminoles*, 281–98; Porter, *The Black Seminoles*, 31–35, 52, 71–78; Porter, "Negroes and the Seminole War," 427–50. Some of the blacks were captured by other Indians while others surrendered. Bounties also were offered to capture blacks; see Foreman, *Five Civilized Tribes*, 224–25, 228, 248, 251, and Foreman, *Traveler in Indian Territory*, 348, citing *Army and Navy Chronicle* III, 217, 281, 326; Mahon, *History of the Second Seminole War*, 193; Ronnie C. Tyler, "Fugitive Slaves in Mexico," *Journal of Negro History* 57, no. 1 (January 1972), 1–12. See also U.S. Congress, House, *Indians: Creek and Seminole*, 33rd Cong., 2nd sess., 1854, H. Doc. 701, for reports about Creek/Seminole conflicts and the activities of black Indian chiefs and Wild Cat on their removal.

26. See Porter, "Relations between Negroes and Indians within the Present Limits of the United States," *Journal of Negro History* 17, no. 3 (July 1932), 287–367; also see Zellar, *African Creeks*, 89, who opines race consciousness among southeastern Indians came later. Other scholars provide similar opinions on a lack of concept of race among southeastern Indians: Littlefield, *Africans and Seminoles*, 6, similarly argues that racial prejudice did not exist; Braund, "Creek Indians, Blacks, and Slavery," 602, 608, argues that the Creeks did not equate slavery with race. It was in the late 1730s that Creeks began to assimilate the view of blacks as imperfect; William C. Sturtevant, "Seminole Myths of the Origins of Races," *Ethnohistory* 10, no. 1 (Winter 1963), 80–86, provides a similar interpretation for racial categories to emerge as a result of acculturation among the Seminoles. For other general discussion of Indians' interpretation of race see Minges, "Beneath the Underdog," 453–79.

27. Weisman, in *Like Beads on a String*, 299–318, and "Archaeological Perspectives on Florida Seminole's Ethnogenesis," in *Indians of the Greater Southeast*, 299–320, attributes stress initiated by the Second Seminole War as a major factor in the formation of Black Seminole identity in Florida. He contends that the group members did not consider themselves Black Seminoles until they met and resisted the historic onslaught of white settlers and the advance of the U.S. Army; also see Sattler, "Remnants, Renegades, and Runaways: Seminole Ethnogenesis Reconsidered," in *History, Power, and Identity*, 36–590. Littlefield, *Africans and Seminoles*, 4–6, discusses the Muskogee use of the name "Estelusti" as applied to blacks upon removal; the Creek term Estelusti is still a preferred term among many black Indians today in Oklahoma. Other scholars who discuss Black Seminoles as a distinct cultural group include Howard, *Black Seminoles in the Bahamas*, and Mulroy, *Freedom on the Border*, 17–22, 26–27, 43. In Mexico the Black Seminoles call themselves Indios Mascogos, a term used interchangeably with Black Seminoles in this book. In Texas the group members refer to themselves as Black Seminoles or Seminoles.

28. See Hancock, *The Texas Seminoles and Their Language*; Weik, "The Role of Ethnogenesis and Organization," 206–38, provides a detailed discussion of diverse groups of African origin in Florida. He provides an alternate term for maroons or African–Native Americans.

CHAPTER TWO. A COMMUNITY OF BRETHREN

Epigraph. "Speech by Honorable Margaret Mead, fourth Plenary Session," doc. 62, in *The Spirit of Houston: The First National Women's Conference,* National Commission on the Observance of International Women's Year (Washington D.C.: U.S. Government Printing Office, 1978), 230–31.

1. See National Archives Microfilm Publications, M234, roll 290: frames 164–68, "Registry of Negro Prisoners captured by the Troops commanded by Major General Thomas S. Jesup in 1836 and 1837, and owned by the Indians, or who claim to be free"; frames 358–61, "List of Seminole Indians captured at Fort Jupiter E. F. by the Troops, from 22d Feb 1838 to 29th March 1838"; and frame 364, "List of Seminole Indians and Negroes sent from Fort Jupiter to Tampa for emigration to the West." See M234, roll 239: frames 333–35, "Muster Roll of Emigrant Creek Indians who have emigrated west of the Mississippi River and arrived upon their lands West." See M234, roll 291: frames 430–31, "Creek and Seminole Slaves Immigration West 1841, Record 25, Aug. 1842." See M234, roll 290, frame 506, for lists of Seminole Indians and blacks sent from Fort Jupiter to Tampa Bay for emigration to the West.

2. Mulroy, *The Seminole Freedmen* and Weik, "The Role of Ethnogenesis and Organization," 206–38, provide a history of the maroon settlements in Florida. See Littlefield, *Africans and Seminoles,* 151–52, for accounts of Billy and his slaves, and Porter, "Billy Bowlegs (Holata Micco) in the Seminole Wars," *Florida Historical Quarterly* 45, 219–42. "Bowlegs" was derived from the English "Bowles," the name of a prominent abolitionist in eighteenth-century Florida. Descendants of runaways from southern plantations to Andros Island in the Bahamas carry the Bowleg surname today as discussed by Howard, "The Promised Land: Reconstructing History and Identity among the Black Seminoles of Andros Island" (PhD diss., University of Florida, 1991) and *Black Seminoles in the Bahamas;* other Black Seminole descendants in Oklahoma are discussed by Bateman, "Naming Patterns," 227–57. Graves in the Seminole Indian Scouts Cemetery bear the Bowlegs surname, including a namesake, Billy Bowlegs. Seminoles characteristically carried many names, but with the advent of western influences, chiefs began to take on additional English surnames, such as Payne, as a sign of prestige and status. See also Gutman, *Black Family in Slavery and Freedom,* 186.

3. For accounts of the Dade attack, see Mulroy, *Freedom on the Border,* 149; Littlefield, *Africans and Seminoles,* 11, 28, 43; and Porter, *Black Seminoles,* 40–46. For accounts of the wars, see Porter, *Negro on the American Frontier,* 182–357.

4. National Archives Microfilm Publications, M234, roll 290, frame 508, provides a list of Carolina's siblings.

5. I use the given name Tina (Bowlegs) in this book to avoid confusion with other women, such as Teener Factor, who went by different versions of that name.

6. Misc. Muster Roll, 1832–1846: "Seminole," Records of the Bureau of Indian Affairs, Record Group 75, National Archives. Record Group 75 lists Black Seminoles received at Tampa Bay; Records of the Bureau of Indian Affairs, Misc. Muster Roll, 1832–1846: "Seminole" reports blacks turned over to the military on 9 April 1838.

7. Mulroy, *Freedom on the Border,* 26, 31, 71, provides accounts of July in Florida. The Factor surname is probably derived from the factoring or trading system of the British during their occupation of Florida; see Porter, *The Black Seminoles,* 100, 106, and 28 August 1952 and 30 April 1953 letters to Mrs. D. S. McKellar, Latorre Collection, Benson Latin American Collection, University of Texas, Austin (this collection is hereafter cited as "Latorre Collection, Benson Latin American Collection"). In these sources, Porter discusses the Factors' preference for Gullah names. For discussion of Teener Factor and her family, see National Archives Microfilm Publications, M234, roll 290, frame 508; U.S. Congress, House, 25th Cong., 3rd sess., Executive Document 225, 74–78, 115; and General Jesup's Papers, Records of the Office of the Adjutant General, Record Group 94, National Archives.

8. See Porter, *The Black Seminoles,* 100, for an account of Susan Factor.

9. Sampson, a son of July and Teener, carried a popular name, for there are three Sampsons included on the list of Black Seminoles who left for Indian Territory.

10. For an account of attempts to capture Dembo Factor in Indian Territory, see Mulroy, *Freedom on the Border,* 38, and Littlefield, *Africans and Seminoles,* 85, 103, 145.

11. See Misc. Muster Rolls, 1832–1846: "Seminole," Records of the Bureau of Indian Affairs, Record Group 75, National Archives; see also National Archives Microfilm Publications, M574, Roll 13, Special File 96, for names of departing Black Seminoles. Isaac and Pompey are listed as privates in the Seminole Negro Indian Scouts at Fort Clark. However, they are recorded as being born in Arkansas in Swanson's *Enlistment Records of Indian Scouts*. It is probable, though, that they were Cornelia's sons born in Florida, not Mexico, since they are listed on manifests with her.

12. John Kibbetts was known as Snake Warrior or *Siteetastonachy* among the Seminoles. Or, the name may have been derived from the Gullah *kuba*; see Turner, *Africanisms in the Gullah Dialect,* 116. Like John Horse, Kibbetts had probably been adopted as a member of the Seminole Indian tribe. The 1880 U.S. census reports his wife Nancy Kibbetts as born in Florida, not a refugee from Louisiana as descendant stories relate. Like Kibbetts, she belonged to Micanopy.

13. Mulroy discusses Davis Bowlegs's attempts to move to Indian Territory in *Freedom on the Border,* on pages 95, 108, 116, 153–54, 156, 158, and 114. The Seminole tribal leadership in Indian Territory tried to evict them since they were there illegally. They were sheltered by fellow blacks but never received a land allotment. See Mulroy, *Freedom on the Border,* 107, for discussion of Jack and Friday Bowlegs. Porter details the story in *The Black Seminoles,* 209–11.

14. For accounts of John Horse's trips as interpreter for the U.S. military, see Porter, *The Black Seminoles,* 96–97,100, 103, 105, 120–21, and "A Farewell to John Horse," 265–73; Littlefield in *Africans and Seminoles,*108, and *Africans and Creeks,* 46, reports

that the blacks living among the Indians adopted such articles of dress as turbans and moccasins.

15. For accounts of Wannah and her family's departure, see Box 15, General Jesup's Papers, Records of the Office of the Adjutant General, Record Group 94, National Archives. Littlefield, *Africans and Seminoles,* 108, and Porter, *The Black Seminoles,* 87–88, provide an account of her departure. Wannah is described in Porter's notes archived at the Schomburg Center for Research in Black Culture.

16. Littlefield, *Africans and Creeks,* 42.

17. See Littlefield, *Africans and Seminoles,* 36–43 for accounts of Black Seminole departures from New Orleans and claims by former owners; also see Mulroy, *Freedom on the Border*, 3; Foreman, *Indian Removal,* 33–34, 42–43, 52, 156–58; also see letters of 15 August 1850, National Archives Microfilm Publications, M640, roll 7, frames 614–16.

18. Littlefield, *Africans and Seminoles,* reports on the departure of the 249 blacks from New Orleans; also see National Archives Microfilm Publications, M234, roll 290, frame 503B, for a letter from Lt. John G. Reynolds detailing the emigrating party that required boat transportation. He commanded the *South Alabama*; see Amanda L. Paige, Fuller L. Bumpers, and Daniel F. Littlefield, "Historical Documentation of Indian Removal through the North Little Rock Site," The North Little Rock Site on the Trail of Tears National Historic Trail: Historical Contexts Report, Part IV, 2003.

19. According to the terms of the 1832 Treaty of Payne's Landing and the 1833 Treaty of Fort Gibson, the Seminoles were not given a separation reservation and were expected to rejoin the Creeks; Mulroy, *The Seminole Freedmen,* 53–54, notes that while some Seminoles were hostile to the Creeks, other Seminoles assimilated with no difficulty.

20. Foreman, *Five Civilized Tribes,* 230–35, provides a broad discussion of the various Cherokee complaints about Seminoles and blacks in Indian Territory. He also cites the impressions of a traveler in Cherokee country in Foreman, *Traveler in Indian Territory.*

21. See Porter, *Black Seminoles,* 112, for a visitor's account of Black Seminoles who chose to live on the Deep Fork in Creek territory under Micanopy rather than on Cherokee land. Saunt, *Black, White, and Indian,* 77, reports on the problems that ensued when the Creeks permitted Seminoles to settle on their lands in 1845. See Littlefield, *Africans and Seminoles,* 70. See Mulroy, *Freedom on the Border,* 37–39, 42, 48–49.

22. Littlefield, *Africans and Seminoles,* 80; Foreman, *Five Civilized Tribes,* 52, and *Indian Removal* reports the provisioning of Indians departing Florida for Indian Territory. See National Archives Microfilm Publications, M234, roll 291, frames 430–31. M234, roll 236, frame 671 lists agricultural implements for western Creeks; see also A. P. Chouteau's proposals for furnishing agricultural implements for the western Creeks, M234, roll 291, 1231–33.

23. Saunt, *Black, White, and Indian,* 54, reports these desperate accounts; also see Porter, *Black Seminoles,* 113.

24. It is unclear why Susan did not depart with her mother Teener in 1838 but remained in Florida since her name is on the removal rolls; see Porter, *The Black Seminoles,* 11.

25. See Porter, *The Black Seminoles*, 101–102.

26. Porter, *The Black Seminoles,* 111–18 describes John Horse's trips.

27. See Porter, *The Black Seminoles,* 119 for discussion of Creek complaints and claims on Black Seminoles; also see Giddings, *Exiles of Florida,* 324–25, and Foreman, *Five Civilized Tribes,* 226–30, 234, 236–37, 242, for discussion of continued Seminole opposition to union with the Creeks in Indian Territory; Porter in *The Black Seminoles,* 113–15, provides an account of assassination attempts on John Horse. Gen. Thomas Jesup arrived at Fort Gibson in 1845 and the Black Seminoles approached him about his promises of freedom and land after their surrender in Florida. But his promises fell on barren ground in the stormy, anti-black political climate of the times, and he could do nothing to assure their safety; for additional accounts of worsening conditions in Indian Territory and kidnapping attempts, see Littlefield, *Africans and Seminoles,* 106–107, and Porter, *The Black Seminoles,* 112–13, 116–18, 187–88. The situation worsened and a second attempt was made on John Horse's life in which he was wounded and his horse was killed.

28. For accounts of John Horse's attempts to rescue his family at Deep Fork and bring them to Fort Gibson, see Porter, *The Black Seminoles,* 114–15.

29. John Horse had met Loomis, a major at the time, in Florida around 1840, during John Horse's attempts to negotiate surrender and migration to Indian Territory for remaining Seminole Indians.

30. Porter, *The Black Seminoles,* 120–21, details Wannah's difficulties. Wannah had surrendered in Florida with the other Black Seminoles, determined to leave her Seminole Indian mistress, but her mistress died and the woman's half-blood Indian son, Jim, claimed Wannah, her five children, and even her freedman husband Sam Mills; see Littlefield, *Africans and Seminoles,* 108–10, and Mulroy, *Freedom on the Border,* 42.

31. After arriving in Indian Territory, Carolina's brother Plenty Payne was killed in a raid. His wife Rose was threatened but survived and joined the group on the trip to Mexico.

32. See Littlefield, *Africans and Seminoles,* 129. He discusses John Horse's realization in 1848 that not only was his future uncertain but his people would be turned over to their former owners; Littlefield, *Africans and Seminoles,* 113–14, reports on Clary's attempted kidnapping. Porter, "The Seminole in Mexico," 3, attributes some of the kidnappings as a decisive factor in the Black Seminoles' decision to escape to Mexico.

33. Littlefield, *Africans and Seminoles,* 42.

34. Littlefield, *Africans and Seminoles,*111 discusses Harriet's reactions to the loss of her slaves. Mulroy, *The Seminole Freedmen,* 104, also provides details about Harriet's change of mind toward her slaves.

35. Porter also remarks that Rose Kelly was literate. See Porter notes at Schomburg Center for Research in Black Culture.

36. For accounts of Bemo and Loomis, see Foreman, *Five Civilized Tribes,* 239–40, and Littlefield, *Africans and Seminoles,* 112. Porter, *The Black Seminoles,* 118–19, provides details of Loomis's intercession on behalf of the blacks at Fort Gibson. Littlefield, *Africans and Seminoles,* 106–15, and Foreman, *Five Civilized Tribes,* 259, provide an account of the Black Seminoles' refuge at Fort Gibson.

37. Littlefield, *Africans and Seminoles,* 127–28, details of the return of the blacks to their owners; see also Mulroy, *The Seminole Freedmen,* 70–71.

38. Nelly Factor had claimed Teener Factor's family, including Susan and her children, and John Horse attempted to purchase them in 1848; see Mulroy, *The Seminole Freedmen,* 68; delivery of the blacks occurred the same year (May 31, 1848) that the Cherokees made complaints about blacks to authorities and requested that they be removed and returned to their rightful owners. Littlefield, *Africans and Seminoles,* 123–27, discusses the problems in returning the blacks to their former Seminole owners and the unraveling of the alliance; Mulroy, *Freedom on the Border,* 44–45, discusses the reversal of Jesup's emancipation proclamation.

39. Porter, *Black Seminoles,* 124–26, provides a broad description of the Black Seminoles' delivery to their owners and ensuing problems; for additional details see Foreman, *Five Civilized Tribes,* 260–63; Littlefield, *Africans and Seminoles,* 98. Foreman, *Five Civilized Tribes,* 258–59, discusses the Black Seminoles' removal to Wewoka in 1849 and John Horse's fears about being kidnapped. On page 263, Foreman also suggests that other blacks had planned to escape with Wild Cat and John Horse but were detained in order to prevent their escape. For additional information, see Mulroy, *Freedom on the Border,* 49–50, 158, 179.

40. Wild Cat, greatly admired by the blacks, had been a fellow comrade-in-arms with John Horse in the Seminole Wars in Florida; see Foreman, *Five Civilized Tribes,* 244–45, 260. Porter, in *Black Seminoles,* 127, and "The Seminole in Mexico," 3, reports three trips to Mexico by Wild Cat in 1846 to meet with the Kickapoo, Lipán Apache, Tonkawa, Comanche, Waco, and Kichai Indians; also see Foreman, *Five Civilized Tribes,* 244–45, for accounts of Wild Cat's attempts to leave for Mexico. Mulroy, *Freedom on the Border,* 46–47, similarly discusses Wild Cat's exploration of the Southwest and the renewed alliance with John Horse that led to the emigration to Mexico. See Schwartz, "Negroes: Mexico as an Alternative for United States Blacks (1825–1860)," (master's thesis, California State University–San Diego, 1974), 6, 37. Foreman, *Five Civilized Tribes,* 260–61, notes a trip taken in 1846 to winter hunting grounds on the Colorado River.

CHAPTER THREE. THE BIG TRIP: ESCAPE TO MEXICO

Epigraph. Parsons's address to the founding convention of Industrial Workers of the World, Chicago, 1905, reprinted from William Loren Katz, "Lucy Gonzales Parsons," *The Black World Today,* June 29, 2005.

1. See Porter, *The Black Seminoles,* 128, for account; Rebecca Wilson tells Miss Charles, "White people were about to seize them all and sell them as slaves."

According to Bill Wilson, Florida-born Jack Bowlegs, who showed up many years later at Fort Clark, also had to leave his family; Mulroy, *Freedom on the Border,* 54, also discusses the departure for Texas.

2. Miles, *Ties that Bind.*

3. It is argued that the men's absences reinforced the matrilineal tendencies of the Creeks and Seminoles; see Wright, *Creeks and Seminoles,* 63, and Susan Allison Miller, "Wild Cat's Bones: Seminole Leadership in a Seminole Cosmos" (PhD diss., University of Nebraska, 1997; microfilm edition, 973462), 175.

4. Parker, *Notes Taken during the Expedition Commanded by Capt. R. B. Marcy,* in *Handbook of Texas Online,* www.tshaonline.org/handbook/online/articles/MMfma43.html (accessed April 23, 2008). Also available from Philadelphia: Hayes and Zell, 1856.

5. The proposed number of Seminoles and blacks leaving for Mexico varies among sources: Porter, *Black Seminoles,* 128, proposes the number to be thirty men and families; other blacks fled to Texas later the same year; Mulroy, *Freedom on the Border,* 54–55, reports a total of two hundred people on the trip.

6. See Joseph B. Thoburn, "The Naming of the Canadian River," *Chronicles of Oklahoma* 6, no. 2 (June 1928).

7. Porter Papers, Schomburg Center for Research in Black Culture.

8. Giddings, *Exiles of Florida,* 333, reports that the Creeks came upon them in three days.

9. Porter, *The Black Seminoles,* 128, and Mulroy, *Freedom on the Border,* 54, discuss the two parties separating; also see Porter notes on file at the Schomburg Center for Research in Black Culture.

10. Porter, "My Mama Came with Wild Cat and Picayune John," in "Freedom over Me," Porter Papers, Schomburg Center for Research in Black Culture. Kitty Johnson married three times: Benjamin Shields (daughter Julia), Florida-born David Bowlegs, and Ben Wilson (daughter Penny Factor).

11. See Porter notes on file at the Schomburg Center for Research in Black Culture. Porter, *The Black Seminoles,* features a photograph of Molly Perryman with her husband at that time, John July, and daughter, Annie, who appears in figure 13 in this work. John died in 1900, and Molly, a twenty-five-year-old widow, remarried Ignacio Perryman. She would have been around seventy-six years old when Porter interviewed her in Brackettville. Stories relate that she was raised by John Horse.

12. Porter, *The Black Seminoles,* 128. Many of the descriptions in this chapter are based on other travelers' accounts. For example, see Dewees, *Letters from an Early Settler.*

13. Porter, *The Black Seminoles,* 123, 128, also suggests that Wild Cat was returning to Indian Territory to recruit more runaways and discusses their arrival at Cow Bayou.

14. C. C. Cox, "From Texas to California in 1849: Biographical Memoir of Cornelius C. Cox," ed. Mabelle Eppard Martin, *Southwestern Historical Quarterly* 29, no. 1, 1–12.

15. Mulroy, *Freedom on the Border,* 55.

16. Jim Bowlegs, the leader of the Black Seminoles in Indian Territory in John Horse's absence, also led a group of about 180 runaways to Mexico. The runaways may have included fifty-six Black Seminoles owned by Billy Bowlegs, who remained in Florida. Members of his party were pursued and apprehended by Creek militia. Jim escaped and later became an advisor to John Horse in Mexico; see Mulroy, *Freedom on the Border,* 62–64; see "Report relative to the seizure of certain Negroes in the Seminole Nation by Creeks and others," by F. T. Dent, Fort Gibson, 15 July 1850, National Archives Microfilm Publications, M640, roll 4, frames 610–12. Other ill-fated attempts to flee Indian Territory are recorded in Porter, *The Black Seminoles,* 133; also see Mulroy, *Freedom on the Border,* 62; Littlefield and Underhill, "Slave 'Revolt' in the Cherokee Nation," 121–31. Other stories passed down by descendants about narrow escapes are recorded by Kenneth Porter in his papers, Schomburg Center for Research in Black Culture; Foreman, *Five Civilized Tribes,* 264–65, describes another attempt by Wild Cat to set out for Mexico with runaway Indians and blacks.

17. Frost Woodhull interviewed one of the old-timers, and the account is provided in "The Seminole Indian Scouts on the Border," *Frontier Times* 15, no. 3 (1937), 118–17; also see Porter Papers, Schomburg Center for Research in Black Culture.

18. Porter, "A Farewell to John Horse," 265–73, provides an account of John Horse's departure; see Mullin, *Africa in America,* 73, who cites records pertinent to time reckoning among Africans: "The Africans . . . reckoned time as 'before the Potatoes were all taken' or 'the time of digging potatoes,' or 'when the corn was about three feet high.'"

19. See Puckett, *Folk Beliefs of the Southern Negro,* for information on folk medicine among blacks; see "folk medicine" entry in the *Handbook of Texas Online,* www.tsha.utexas.edu/handbook/online/articles/FF/sdf1.html (accessed September 12, 2006).

20. See Porter, *The Black Seminoles,* 130nn14–15.

21. See McGraw, Clark, Jr., and Robbins, *A Texas Legacy,* for description of the road.

22. See Porter, *The Black Seminoles,* 129–30.

23. There are differences reported in terms of where the fleeing group was located and when it was seen. See, for example, Mulroy, *Freedom on the Border,* 55.

24. Mulroy, *Freedom on the Border,* 55, reports that Wild Cat explored the area and visited with nearby Indians to generate interest in his plans to settle a new colony in Mexico. He was able to convince only a band of Kickapoos to join him; Foreman, *Five Civilized Tribes,* 262, provides reports of seven or eight hundred Indians encamped on the Llano with Wild Cat; also see Cox, "From Texas to California in 1849," 1–12, and Gibson, *The Kickapoos,* 182.

25. German immigrants had settled in small communities such as New Braunfels, Castroville, and Fredericksburg in this area between the Llano and Guadalupe rivers near San Antonio.

26. Porter, *The Black Seminoles,* 129, notes that the trip to the fort was unsuccessful because Wild Cat could not see the general; also see Mulroy, *Freedom on the Border,* 55.

27. For an account of what happened in Fredericksburg as told by Penny Wilson Factor, Molly Perryman's sister, see Porter, *The Black Seminoles,* 130. Years later in the 1940s, the black Seminole women regaled Kenneth Porter with different versions of this story on his visit to Brackettville. Some women argue that Wild Cat was serious at the time while others, like the outspoken Rosa Fay, insist that he was just kidding.

28. Bandelier, ed., *The Journey of Alvar Nuñez Cabeza de Vaca.*

29. Pingenot, *Paso de Aguila.*

30. John T. Sprague was the officer in charge; see Mulroy, *Freedom on the Border,* 57; Porter, *The Black Seminoles,* 130–31. According to legend, Sprague invited the chiefs into his camp and gave them supplies for their people and, of course, whiskey. John Horse, losing his traditional composure and thinking the group was safe, reportedly got drunk with Wild Cat. Another version of the story relates that the officer gave Wild Cat and the group a pass to travel to Eagle Pass, their destination.

31. See Porter notes archived at the Schomburg Center for Research in Black Culture.

32. Porter interview with Rosa Fay. See Porter Papers, Schomburg Center for Research in Black Culture; see also Porter, *The Black Seminoles,* 131.

33. The small settlement, located on the California Road, a main artery for aspiring miners to the gold fields, was established in 1848, the same year the Mexican War ended. Later, Fort Duncan to the north would receive infamy as a wild place where the notorious John "King" Fisher came in with a dozen men and shot up the town.

34. See Montgomery, *Eagle Pass;* William T. Kerrigan, "Race, Expansion, and Slavery in Eagle Pass, 1852," *Southwestern Historical Quarterly* 101, no. 3 (January 1998), 282–83. Kerrigan provides a good overview of the political situation in Eagle Pass. Porter writes of Cora Montgomery's unscrupulous activities in a 23 March 1947 letter to Mrs. D. S. McKellar (Latorre Collection, Benson Latin American Collection); Montgomery was expressly anti-peonage as practiced in Mexico at the time and charged in a newspaper article that the Mexicans had been kidnapping Texas residents. She described her copious impressions in a diary that she kept about her new life in the West. Her ambivalence about her new home is expressed in her acknowledgment of the dangers but glowing description of the landscape as "one wide-rolling, ever-varying ocean of verdure, 'romantic hill slopes'. . . and an endless succession of orchards." The opinionated Cazneau may have been the first one to suggest that Wild Cat's group might serve as effective border deterrents if hired by the U.S. Army. Although she admired Wild Cat, like the other residents of Eagle Pass, she dismissed John Horse as an impudent escaped slave who flaunted his freedom.

CHAPTER FOUR. EL RIO GRANDE, RIO BRAVO, AND RIO BRAVO DEL NORTE

Epigraph. Hurston, *Their Eyes Were Watching God,* 1.

1. Littlefield and Underhill, "Slave 'Revolt' in the Cherokee Nation," 121–31.

2. Olmsted, in *Journey through Texas,* 314, provides a description of what the Black Seminoles may have faced in crossing into Mexico.

3. The future Gen. Ethan Allen Hitchcock was sent to spy on the Mexicans by U.S. Army Gen. Winfield Scott. Prior to that, in the 1840s, Hitchcock had been involved in Indian removal efforts in Florida, despite his sympathies toward the Indians. He had publicly opposed Gen. Andrew Jackson's oppressive policies toward the Seminoles and Black Seminoles in Florida.

4. Becky's description of the trip is first detailed in Foster, "Negro-Indian Relationships in the Southeast" (PhD diss., University of Pennsylvania, 1978 [1935]), 42–43; see also Mulroy, *Freedom on the Border,* 58. Becky (also spelled Beckey), a free, two-year-old female, was probably one of five children of Polly and Tony Barnett (also spelled Barnet). She is listed on a manifest of Black Seminoles leaving Florida with her five sisters; see the National Archives Microfilm Publications, M234, roll 290, frames 164–68, which provides a registry of "Negro prisoners captured by the troops commanded by Maj. Gen. Thomas S. Jesup in 1836 and 1837, and owned by the Indians, or who claim to be free"; see M234, roll 227, frames 119–20, and Littlefield, *Africans and Seminoles,* 84, for correspondence pertaining to Tony Barnett's freedom. He emigrated to Indian Territory in 1839 with Abraham (age fifty), the Black Seminole advisor and his son Washington (age eleven), owned by Micanopy; they settled at Deep Fork like John Horse; see also list provided by Littlefield, *Africans and Seminoles,* appendix A; however, later he and his family fled to Fort Gibson like John Horse. Tony returned to Florida in 1840 and 1843, presumably as an interpreter. His name is on a muster roll of fifty-nine Seminoles and three blacks about to emigrate from New Orleans to Fort Gibson in February 1843. When interviewed by Foster between 1929 and 1930, Becky would have been around ninety years old; George Simmons, a runaway from Mississippi and possible relation to Becky, joined the Seminole Negro Indian Scouts at the age of forty-four. See "Muster Roll of Emigrant Creek Indians who have emigrated West of the Mississippi River and arrived upon their lands West," M234, roll 239, frames 333–35; also see Army service records, "Army Service: Seminole, Creek, Cherokee, Tonkaway and Apache Indians," Fort Clark, Texas, at http://www.coax.net/people/lwf/SEM _ASIS.HTM.

5. Interview with Rosa Fay, Porter Papers, Schomburg Center for Research in Black Culture; also see Porter, *The Black Seminoles,* 131.

6. See Roger Di Silvestro and Shirley Boteler Mock, "Freedom Train to Mexico," *Americas* 52, no. 6 (November 1, 2000), 22 and Schwartz, *Across the Rio to Freedom,* 44; Forbes, *Africans and Native Americans,* 186–87, provides some background on the mulatto populations in Mexico; Tyler, "Fugitive Slaves in Mexico," 1–12 and Tyler and Murphy, *The Slave Narratives of Texas,* 69, provide the most thorough discussion of Texas slave owners' concerns about runaways to Mexico; Sean Kelley, "Mexico in His Head: Slavery and the Texas-Mexico Border, 1810–1860," *Journal of Social History* 37, no. 3 (Spring 2004), 709–23, also provides an account of blacks in Mexico; Schwartz, "Negroes: Mexico as an Alternative," 39, offers a detailed view of runaway blacks and Mexico as an alternative for settlement from 1825 to 1860; Porter,

"The Seminole in Mexico," 13–35, reports an estimated number of three thousand blacks living in Mexico in the 1850s.

7. See archives at Schomburg Center for Research in Black Culture; Mulroy, *Freedom on the Border*, 64–65, remarks that Pink Hawkins had moved to Texas in the 1830s. Porter to John Jefferson, 26 March 1949, and Porter to Amos, 16 July 1977, discuss the Black Creeks. Porter in "The Hawkins' Negroes Go to Mexico," *Chronicles of Oklahoma* XXIV, no. 1, 56, bases his interpretations on interviews of Black Creek descendants Rena and Dolly July. Another family joining the Mascogos was the Graysons, descendants of the Creek Grierson or Grayson family in Indian Territory related to the Hawkins family; see Saunt, *Black, White, and Indian*, 69, for an account of the Grierson family. Among families discussed in Mulroy, *Freedom on the Border*, 65, as present in Mexico is that of Laura (Nadra) Neco, one of two Biloxi Indian women (also see María) discussed in this book. Nadra was married to descendant Adam Wilson.

8. Mulroy, *Freedom on the Border*, 58.

9. Interview with Rosa Fay, Alice's paternal grandmother; see Porter Papers, Schomburg Center for Research in Black Culture.

10. John Horse signed an agreement with Antonio Maria Jauregui, inspector general of the eastern military colonies in San Fernando de Rosas, present-day Zaragoza. Porter provides a discussion of the relocations in "The Seminole in Mexico," 11, 16; see also Porter to Mrs. D. S. McKellar, 1 April 1947 (Latorre Collection, Benson Latin American Collection). Mulroy, *Freedom on the Border*, 67, also provides an account of early settlement.

11. Mulroy, *Freedom on the Border*, 58; Foster, "Negro-Indian Relationships in the Southeast," 43.

12. Mulroy, *Freedom on the Border*, 82, writes that John Horse's godfather was Juan Nepomuceno Vidaurri, from whom he acquired the name Capitán Juan de Dios Vidaurri or Capitán Juan Caballo. Vidaurri instructed the Black Seminoles in the Catholic faith and acted as an advisor to the group. He also involved them in his political aspirations; after John Horse complained that his people lacked the necessary resources to fight Indians, Vidaurri gave them ammunition and money but warned the Black Seminoles to stay away from the non-Mascogo blacks; see Porter, "The Seminole in Mexico," 13–35, in which he provides a discussion of the alliances of Vidaurri and the Mascogos; also see Porter, *The Black Seminoles*, 146–47, for discussion of other requirements of the Mexican government.

13. See Mischa B. Adams, "Naming Practices among the Black Seminole of the Texas-Mexico Border Region," *Journal of Big Bend Studies* 11 (1999), 219–44, for an in-depth discussion of the names given to the Mascogos in Mexico. The Spanish substitutions for the English names provided by descendants Alice Fay and Dub Warrior point to inconsistencies in their use; also see Porter, *Black Seminoles*, 146, for additional discussion of the names. However, in a 16 August 1946 letter to Mrs. D. S. McKellar, he contends they are aware of Spanish substitutions (Latorre Collection, Benson Latin American Collection).

14. See Porter, "The Seminole in Mexico," 14. See also Porter notes, Schomburg Center for Research in Black Culture.

15. Mulroy, *Freedom on the Border,* 73, reports on the treaty and allotment of land. Colonia Nacimiento was part of the Sanchez Navarro holdings, thirty miles northwest of the colonial *municipio* of Santa Rosa (Múzquiz); see Latorre and Latorre, *The Mexican Kickapoo Indians;* La Vere, *Life among the Texas Indians;* also see Ronald W. Ralph, "Seminole-Negro Colonia Nacimiento," 1969, paper on file at the Institute of Texan Cultures, University of Texas at San Antonio, and with the author. The term "hacienda" at that time referred to extensive plots of land with buildings and areas for raising livestock. For a comprehensive overview of the Mascogos' problems in acquiring land and trouble with marauding Indians see Porter, *The Black Seminoles,* 137–58, and Mulroy, *Freedom on the Border,* 78–82. The government also gave the Mascogos other land in Durango, Mexico, that the group never occupied. For more information on the Hacienda de Nacimiento and Mascogos, see Del Moral and Siller, *Recetario Mascogo de Coahuila,* 51.

16. Guinn, "Seminole Negro Heritage Fading in Border Town," 1D.

17. Mulroy, *The Black Seminoles,* 74.

18. Tanner, "Matrifocality in Indonesia and Africa and among Black Americans," in *Women, Culture, and Society,* 129–56, and Mintz and Price, *The Birth of African-American Culture,* 66–67, discuss the African-derived practice of matrifocality. This practice is another enduring characteristic of the Black Seminole community brought from Florida, and their former lives on plantations in the Carolinas and Georgia.

19. See Guinn, "Seminole Negro Heritage Fading in Border Town," for Dub Warrior's comments; the Seminole and Mascogo expeditions and the dangers Alice's people faced from slave hunting expeditions and Indian raids are covered by Mulroy, *Freedom on the Border,* 65–69, 73; also see Porter, *The Black Seminoles,* 140–41, and "The Seminole in Mexico," 21; one invasion of three hundred Texas Rangers with the intent to capture fugitive blacks was forced back by a coalition of Wild Cat's Seminoles, the Mascogos, and Mexican troops; see discussion of continued troubles in La Vere, *Life among the Texas Indians,* 17. Mulroy, *Freedom on the Border,* 61–75, details the continued efforts of slave hunting parties such as those instigated by the Creek Marcellus Duval in Indian Territory.

20. Porter to Sara (Mrs. D. S.) McKellar, 5 August 1950, discusses la Loma de Buena Vista and changes in location over time (Latorre Collection, Benson Latin American Collection). He was told the old people lived where the Kickapoos live now.

21. Mulroy, *Freedom on the Border,* 85–86, provides accounts of and complaints against other blacks in Mexico; Porter, *The Black Seminoles,* 150–51, 170, also discusses their presence and Mexican reaction. The Black Seminoles' acceptance of other blacks into the community is often ambiguous. Past records report that they separated themselves out from other blacks in Mexico and Brackettville, but oral accounts also testify that they welcomed runaway blacks or free blacks.

22. Dillingham, "Integration of the Seminole Negroes," 24, reports on Mascogo traditions in Mexico.

23. Foster, "Negro-Indian Relationships in the Southeast," 51.

24. Gutman, *The Black Family in Slavery and Freedom,* 282–83.

25. Foster, "Negro-Indian Relationships in the Southeast."

26. For discussion, see Porter to Mrs. D. S. McKellar, 14 May 1948; Porter to Mrs. D. S. McKellar, 20 May 1947; Porter to Mrs. D. S. McKellar, 16 August 1946. Also see Porter to Mrs. D. S. McKellar, 1 April 1947 (Latorre Collection, Benson Latin American Collection). By the mid-1800s Mexican officials had intentions to encourage more Black Seminoles and Seminole Indians to settle in Mexico as a deterrent to the relentless raiding of border Indians; Wild Cat continued to go back to Indian Territory to induce more Seminoles and blacks to flee to Mexico. His return to Indian Territory in the summer of 1852 was unexpected, and it unnerved the Creeks, who were concerned that their slaves would flee with him.

27. Mulroy, *Freedom on the Border,* 84, 87–88; by 1855, some disputes had begun to develop between the Mascogos and the Seminole Indians that would have portent for a disintegration of their relationship. In Mexico there were continued raids, and the promises made by Mexican officials to the Seminole Indians and Mascogos had not been realized. By 1861 most of the remaining Seminole Indians had left.

28. Parras is located in north-central Mexico, approximately three hundred miles south of the Rio Grande; see Ben F. Lemert, "Parras Basin, Southern Coahuila, Mexico," *Economic Geography* 25, no. 2 (April 1949), 94–112. Porter, *The Black Seminoles,* 160, describes the trip to Parras; also see Pingenot, *Paso de Aguila,* 15.

29. In 1891 Philip Fay was seventy years old, so presumably he was born in Florida and around seventeen when his people departed Florida for Indian Territory. Fay is a name of an eighteen-year-old male—son of Fanny and Possy, all owned by Sock-ah-wah-pee—leaving for the west. Within the Black Seminole Gullah-derived tradition of alternating given names and surnames, Fay became a surname. See M234, roll 290, frames 358–61, for a list of Black Seminoles captured by troops at Fort Jupiter in 1838.

30. Porter, *The Black Seminoles,* 156, 160, reports on the trip to Parras; the Mexican official Vidaurri gave orders to John Horse to separate his people from the *cuarterones* since they were stealing cattle. They were given separate wagons; see J. B. Bird, "The Largest Slave Rebellion in U.S. History," www.johnhorse.com/highlights/essays/largest.htm (retrieved Aug. 29, 2005). He discusses the difference between maroons and slaves. There is no way now, however, to ascertain clearly the roots of the community. Partly as a result, interesting and often contradictory legends and stories abound.

31. The stories of the Gordon brothers' escape from plantations vary as Porter, *The Black Seminoles,* 161–62, details; also see Porter to Mrs. D. S. McKellar, 16 August 1946 (Latorre Collection, Benson Latin American Collection). Genevieve Payne's mother, Mirtes, whose story is detailed later in this book, was the daughter of Isaac Gordon.

32. Mulroy, *Freedom on the Border,* 107.

33. Samuel Jerome Spindle, "Diary of Samuel Spindle's Travels through Mexico," on file with author. See also Box, *Adventures and Explorations,* 203–204, for an account of meeting with John Horse.

34. Ibid. Mulroy, *Freedom on the Border,* 81–86, writes that John Horse's godfather was Juan Vidaurri and he acquired the name Capitán Juan de Dios Vidaurri or Capitán Juan Cabello; see Porter, *The Black Seminoles,* 161, 155–56, 158, 163, 173, and Porter, "The Seminole in Mexico," 13–35, for discussion of the relationships between Vidaurri and the Mascogos.

35. Mulroy, *Freedom on the Border,* 107. See Jefferson to Porter, 12 July 1946 and Porter to Jefferson, 4 February 1950, Schomburg Center for Research in Black Culture. In a 20 May 1947 letter to Mrs. D. S. McKellar, Porter's account differs (Latorre Collection, Benson Latin American Collection). Julia Payne, in a 1944 interview (Schomburg Center for Research in Black Culture), recalled that the killings occurred as the Mascogos were attacked as a group. They counterattacked and defeated the Indians, rescuing the young Dick Grayson (Grierson), who later died as a result of his treatment during captivity.

36. Porter interviews with Amelia Kelly and Nellie Fay, Schomburg Center for Research in Black Culture.

37. See Mulroy, *Freedom on the Border,* 107–109, which describes power struggles during the French invasion, continued efforts to own land, and continued Indian raids.

38. See Porter, *The Black Seminoles,* 168, and Mulroy, *Freedom on the Border,* 107–109. By this time, the community was divided geographically. Some members of the group were situated at Hacienda de los Hornos while some chose to stay at Hacienda de San Marcos. The Julys also remained in the Laguna as late as 1875 according to Porter in a 1 April 1947 letter to Mrs. D. S. McKellar (Latorre Collection, Benson Latin American Collection). Their principal residence, though, was at Hacienda El Burro, where they still held out hope to obtain a permanent land grant.

39. See Porter, *The Black Seminoles,* 170–71, for an account of the Mascogos' return to Nacimiento, and interview with Julia Payne, 1944, Schomburg Center for Research in Black Culture. Julia was the daughter of John Kibbetts's stepdaughter.

40. Mulroy, *Freedom on the Border,* 109, reports that the Mascogos were concerned by the presence of the Kickapoo, who had received a grant for Nacimiento. John Horse and John Kibbetts's request for land equal to the Kickapoos' was granted by President Juárez in 1867 in a written document.

CHAPTER FIVE. ROSE KELLY MOVES TO TEXAS

Epigraph. Dyk, *Son of Old Hat: A Navajo Autobiography.*

1. See "Papers related to the Return of the Kickapoo and the Seminole (Negro) Indians from Mexico to the United States, 1870–1885," Letters Received by the Office of the Adjutant General {Main Series} 1861–1870, National Archives Microfilm Publications, M619, roll 799. The Black Seminoles considered the arrangement

between Kibbetts and the U.S. Army as an official "treaty," a written document that has never been found. The letters discuss permission to cross the Rio Grande to Fort Duncan, and to join the army as scouts until the group's request to move to the Seminole Nation was granted. Correspondence between army officials also discusses the expense of rations and moving the Black Seminoles to Indian Territory; see Porter, *The Black Seminoles,* 195. Kibbetts's request for rations and other support for a move to Indian Territory was still pending as late as 1872; John Horse traveled to Washington in 1873 to plead with the U. S. government to provide rations and land in Florida or Indian Territory. The army correspondents determined there were no funds for this relocation. The Davis (David) Bowlegs and other Black Seminole families later returned to settle in the Seminole Nation in 1882 despite an 1866 treaty that had declared they must have permission to do so from tribal authorities.

2. For descendant's account, see Porter notes, Schomburg Center for Research in Black Culture; also see Porter, *The Black Seminoles,* 176–77.

3. Porter, *The Black Seminoles,* 177–80, and Porter, "The Seminole Negro-Indian Scouts 1870–1881," *Southwestern Historical Quarterly* LV, no. 3 (January 1952), 359–76 provide accounts of the scouts at Fort Duncan; see also Britten, *Brief History of the Seminole-Negro Indian Scouts.* In 1871 the scouts were elevated to permanent military status and supplied with arms, ammunition, and rations, as well as the standard salary of privates in the regular army. Kibbetts served as company sergeant. By July of 1872, some of the scouts and their families were transferred to Fort Clark.

4. Porter, *The Black Seminoles,* 180, provides Julia Payne's account; John Horse in 1875 visited Fort Clark but never joined the scouts. He was out with scout Titus Payne when killed in an ambush.

5. See "Memoranda Relative to Seminole Negro Indians," List of Negroes at Fort Duncan, Texas, 9 May 1875, and U.S. census records, 1870; military correspondence indicates that the rations were not sufficient to support the infirm and the old, women, and children. For an account of Kibbetts's negotiations with the army and enlistments at Fort Duncan, see Mulroy, *Freedom on the Border,* 111–14; for an account of removal to Fort Clark, see Mulroy, *Freedom on the Border,* 115.

6. See Porter notes, Schomburg Center for Research in Black Culture; see also Porter to Mrs. D. S. McKellar, 8 August 1944 (Latorre Collection, Benson Latin American Collection).

7. See Porter, "Willie Kelley of the Lost Nigger Mine," *Western Folklore* XIII, no. 1 (January 1954), 13–26, and *Negro on the American Frontier,* 15–17; Porter refers to Amelia Kelly (Valdez) and Sara as the older half-sisters of Willie Kelly, presumably Rose Kelly's child by another man. Porter also discusses the Kelly story in a 30 April 1953 letter to Mrs. D. S. McKellar (Latorre Collection, Benson Latin American Collection); also see Dobie, *Coronado's Children,* and Porter, "A Farewell to John Horse," 269.

8. See Turner, *Africanisms in the Gullah Dialect,* 107. Chapter 12 covers these traditions.

9. Dobie, *Coronado's Children,* and Porter, "Willie Kelley of the Lost Nigger Mine," 13–26.

10. Porter doubts young Kibbetts belonged to John Kibbetts's son, Robert (Bob) Kibbetts, who was about seventeen years younger than Rose. Other than possibly supporting Rose Kelly's family, John Kibbetts also supported other relatives—Julia Payne and Molly Perryman—while living at Fort Duncan. The old warrior also had a son named Sam Washington by another woman, presumably a descendant of John Horse's sister Wannah.

11. See Johanna July interview with Florence Angermiller by American Memories Collection, Library of Congress, 1936–1940, August 1996, www.lcwseb.loc.gov. Also see Coffey, "Johanna July: A Horse-Breaking Woman," in *Black Cowboys of Texas*.

12. Jerry Daniels is the son of Rose Kelly's daughter, Sara Daniels, and Charles (Chalow) Daniels.

13. Lt. John L. Bullis was in command of the scouts for eight years, from May 1873 until June 1881. By 1888, realizing the futility of moving to Indian Territory, the Black Seminole leaders requested land on Fort Clark; see accounts in Porter, *The Black Seminoles*, 211.

14. For an account of inadequate rations, see Porter, *The Black Seminoles*, 184–85.

15. The arbor was also characteristic of slave houses in South Carolina; see Pollitzer, *The Gullah People and Their African Heritage*, 9. Mulroy, *Freedom on the Border*, 98, provides a photo of a typical household unit circa 1900; see Milanich, *Florida's Indians from Ancient Times*, 162–63, for an illustration of a clay daub house built by Florida Indians.

16. See Porter, "The Seminole Negro-Indian Scouts," 359–76, and "A Legend of the Biloxi," *Journal of American Folklore* 59, no. 232 (April–June 1946), 168–73; also see Porter interview with Penny Factor in Schomburg Center for Research in Black Culture.

17. See Porter, *The Black Seminoles*, 183; Woodhull, "Seminole Indian Scouts on the Border," 118–27.

18. See Mulroy, *Freedom on the Border*, 98, for a photo of Sampson and Mary July with their son Ben July. Their son Jim and his wife Rena had a son named Charles (*Cobo*) J. July, a scout, who accidently died in Kansas. There were two Charles Julys. The older Charles was Rebecca July's brother.

19. Major French's Diary, 1882, diskette provided by family; personal communication with Bill Haenn, 24 July 2008.

20. Haenn, *Images of America*; also see Porter notes, Schomburg Center for Research in Black Culture.

21. Porter notes, Schomburg Center for Research in Black Culture.

22. Rosa Fay interview, Schomburg Center for Research in Black Culture; see Porter to Mrs. D. S. McKellar, 1 April 1947 (Latorre Collection, Benson Latin American Collection).

23. Col. D. S. Stanley to Adjt. Gen., Dept. of Texas, 19 May 1882, AGO 1870, No. 2, National Archives; Swanson, *Enlistment Records*, Fort Clark.

24. Porter, "The Seminole in Mexico," 13–35; Porter, "A Farewell to John Horse," 271; also see Porter to Lilith Haynes, 10 May 1977.

25. The story of the Black Seminoles' removal from Nacimiento and John Horse's attempts to reclaim their land grant is recorded in Porter, *The Black Seminoles,* 222–23. He also discusses it in a 25 October 1944 letter to Mrs. D. S. McKellar (Latorre Collection, Benson Latin American Collection).

26. In 1906 it was determined that the Black Seminoles were not entitled to any benefits or lands. Efforts by prominent figures such as General Bullis, General Mackenzie, Col. Edward Hatch, and even Gen. Philip H. Sheridan did not succeed in securing the Las Moras land for the Black Seminoles; Mulroy, *Freedom on the Border,* provides more details on these correspondences; see Porter to Mrs. D. S. McKellar, 30 April 1948, in which he points out that many of the Black Seminoles were illiterate and could have misunderstood the treaty document (Latorre Collection, Benson Latin American Collection). See Woodhull, "Seminole Indian Scouts on the Border," 120, 126–27; Porter, *The Black Seminoles,* 214.

27. Guinn, "Seminole Negro Heritage Fading in Border Town," 1D. This memory of the scouts being disbanded and her people being forced off of the fort in 1914 was one of Miss Charles's favorite stories to tell over the years. It was perhaps told to her by Rebecca, her mother.

28. Nancy's (Nannie) mother was Mary (Mirah) Bowlegs (1887–1951), and her father was Ben Thompson, who was raised by Alice's paternal grandmother, Rosa Dixon Fay. Nancy's stepfather was John or Julio Bowlegs, one of the Mascogos who left the Laguna in 1870 and moved across the border to Brownsville. Her family had crossed from Mexico to Eagle Pass, Texas, but her father got sick and died. Then they moved to Brackettville.

29. Miss Else Sauer, written correspondence to Shirley Mock, 23 July 1995.

30. Mock interview with Miss Charles, 12 May 1995, Brackettville; see Porter, *The Black Seminoles,* 213, for further information on the disbandment of the Seminole Negro Indian Scout unit at Fort Clark in 1914.

31. See Porter, *The Black Seminoles,* 167–68; see Freeman, *A Communion of the Spirits,* 250, for more information on quilt making.

CHAPTER SIX. ANCESTORS IN THE HOUSE

Epigraph. Pollitzer, *The Gullah People and Their African Heritage,* 130.

1. Tanner, "Matrifocality in Indonesia and Africa," in *Women, Culture, and Society,* 129–56, discusses matrifocal societies in west Africa, the Caribbean, and Indonesia; also see Mintz and Price, *The Birth of African-American Culture,* 65–67, for a discussion of kinship. Audrey Lawson Brown, "Africanisms in the 'Old Ship of Zion': What Are Their Forms and Why Do They Persist?" (paper presented at "Places of Cultural Memory: African Reflections on the American Landscape" Conference, National Park Service, Atlanta, Ga., May 9–12, 2001) argues that this matrifocality is derived from west Africa. Mintz and Price, *The Birth of African-American Culture,* 65, provide a discussion of kinship and sex roles among maroons. Both he and Howard, *Black Seminoles in the Bahamas,* 87, argue that outsiders reify the west-

ern concept of family. Howard discusses the concept of family among the Black Seminoles. See also Foster, "African Patterns in Afro-American Family," *Journal of Black Studies* 14, no. 2 (December 1983), 208, 222–23. See Mullin, *Africa in America,* 209, for discussion of remoteness of the Gullah in contrast to mainland slaves as a factor in retention of African traditions.

2. Giddings, *Exiles of Florida,* 324, provides a discussion of the mixture of blacks and Indians and how they belonged to clans; Wright, *Creeks and Seminoles,* 278, argues that acculturated blacks belonged to clans and many "Indian-Negroes" were essentially Indians, not blacks; Mulroy, *Freedom on the Border,* 186 opines that there is no evidence that the Black Seminoles adopted the Indian's matrilineal clan system. Also see Mulroy, *The Seminole Freedmen,* 32, for a discussion of differences between Seminoles and maroons. On page 34 he discusses matrilineal descent and elite Seminole women who owned or served as guardians of blacks. Tanner, "Matrifocality in Indonesia and Africa," in *Women, Culture, and Society,* 129–56 discusses matrifocal societies in west Africa, the Caribbean, and Indonesia; also see Mintz and Price, *The Birth of African-American Culture,* 66–67. Beth Dillingham, "The Seminole Negroes of Nacimiento" (paper presented at the Central States Branch of the American Anthropological Association, 1967) suggests a matrilineal bias in the Black Seminole community. Porter to Dillingham, 5 August 1969 discusses the retention of maiden names.

3. Dillingham, "The Seminole Negroes of Nacimiento," 9, 13.

4. Gutman, *The Black Family in Slavery and Freedom,* 199, 204–205, 216–17, calls these collateral ties.

5. Landers, "African and African American Women and Their Pursuit of Rights," 57–76.

6. Braund, "Creek Indians, Blacks, and Slavery," 624; Landers, "African and African American Women and Their Pursuit of Rights," 57–76; see also interview with Lucinda Davis, *Slave Narratives,* 58. She tells the interviewer that her mother and father lived together even though they belonged to different plantations. Johnson Ajibade Adefila, "Slave Religion in the Antebellum South: A Study of the Role of Africanisms in the Black Response to Christianity" (PhD diss., Brandeis University, 1975), 2 reports that a number of slaves were given a free hand to choose their own spouses.

7. Gutman, *The Black Family in Slavery and Freedom,* 192–98, 215.

8. Audrey Lawson Brown, "Afro-Baptist Women's Church and Family Roles: Transmitting Afrocentric Cultural Values," *Anthropological Quarterly* 67, no. 4 (October 1994), 173–86.

9. Dillingham, "The Seminole Negroes of Nacimiento," 9.

10. Ophelia Benson interview with Mock, 21–22 September 1997, Brackettville.

11. Howard, *Black Seminoles in the Bahamas,* 88–89.

12. See Foster, "African Patterns in the Afro-American Family," 216. Robert J. Quinlan, "Gender and Risk in a Matrifocal Caribbean Community," *American Anthropologist* 108, no. 3 (September 2006), 465, reports that in other maroon communities the culture is matrifocal and reciprocity between family members is linked through women. Houses are identified with women.

13. Porter, *The Black Seminoles* provides an account of this on page 169.

14. Nancy Williams interview with Mock, 21–22 September 1997, Brackettville.

15. Howard, *Black Seminoles in the Bahamas,* 89, discusses the Gullah-derived practice of polygyny in the Bahamas; also see Mulroy, *The Seminole Freedmen,* 32, 274, for discussion of polygyny among the maroons and later in Indian Territory, and Mulroy, "Ethnogenesis and Ethnohistory of the Seminole Maroons," *Journal of World History* 4, no. 2 (Fall 1993), 287–305; Bateman, "Naming Patterns," 227–57. Perdue, *Cherokee Women,* 175 discusses polygyny among the Black Cherokee. Pollitzer, *The Gullah People and Their African Heritage,* 132–33, discusses the practice of polygyny in Africa as reflected among Gullah in the Sea Islands; also see Foster, "African Patterns in the Afro-American Family," 208.

16. Howard, *Black Seminoles in the Bahamas,* 87–89, and Pollitzer, *The Gullah People and Their African Heritage,* 13, among other scholars observe common-in-law relations are recognized by the community and illegitimacy has no social stigma. A child born out of such a union usually carries the mother's surname, as is true among the Black Seminoles; Porter, in a 1 April 1947 letter to Sara (Mrs. D. S.) McKellar, states that whoever raises a child is considered the parent (Latorre Collection, Benson Latin American Collection).

17. Conversation with Alice Daniels Barnett, 11 December 1998, San Antonio; Barnett interview with photos, 20 May 1999; Foster, "Negro-Indian Relationships in the Southeast," 18; see C. Vann Woodward, "History from Slave Sources," *The American Historical Review* 79 (April), 470–81; Porter to Lilith Haynes, 10 May 1977, Schomburg Center for Research in Black Culture.

18. Gutman, *The Black Family in Slavery and Freedom,* 215; Howard, *Black Seminoles in the Bahamas,* 88.

19. Foster, "African Patterns in the Afro-American Family," 208, discusses symbolic kinship.

20. Mintz and Price, *The Birth of African-American Culture,* 66. See also Brown, "Afro-Baptist Women's Church and Family Roles," 177–78, for a discussion of the practice.

21. See McClaurin, *Women of Belize: Gender and Change,* 141.

22. Foster, "African Patterns in the Afro-American Family," discusses symbolic kinship.

CHAPTER SEVEN. NANA ROSA FAY: LIFE ON A RANCH IN MEXICO

Epigraph. Allende, *The House of the Spirits,* 72.

1. Dub Warrior interview with Mock, 12 August 2008; Rosa Fay moved to Brackettville later and lived with Annie Cole, the daughter of John July (Rebecca July's brother).

2. Porter, "A Farewell to John Horse," 270, reports that Clara belonged to a Wilson family in Florida. Porter, *The Black Seminoles,* 130 remarks that Joe was Black

Creek, but Porter is referring to the Joe Dixon who was a scout at Fort Clark. This scout would have been too young to have been married to Clara, who in 1890 was probably around fifty-two years old; for general discussion, see Porter Papers, Schomburg Center for Research in Black Culture.

3. Adam is called Fay—his surname—by the McKellars; enlistments in the scouts were usually for short periods.

4. McKellar, *Life on a Mexican Ranch.*

5. At some point Amelia took on the surname Valdez by marriage, but also carried the Kelly of her mother, Rose; it is the Spanish equivalent of Payne or Wilson. See Dobie, *Coronado's Children*; Porter, "Willie Kelley of the Lost Nigger Mine," 17. In his notes Porter refers to Amelia Kelly as the older half-sister of Willie Kelley (he says the same of her sister Sara).

6. See McKellar, *Life on a Mexican Ranch,* 167–68, for quotations; see also Brady, "The Paynes of Texas: Black Seminole Cowboys of the Big Bend," in *Black Cowboys of Texas,* 248–55, for an account of descendants in Brownsville. See also McKellar, *Life on a Mexican Ranch,* 56. By 1870 both Monday and Friday are reported to have moved from the Laguna in Mexico to Brownsville, Texas, where they worked as farm laborers. Friday was eventually deemed to be employable as a scout at Fort Clark and he served in that capacity from 1872 to 1881. After that he showed up on the McKellar Ranch in 1891 as a hired hand. Monday, however, had deserted the scouts after four enlistments in 1875.

7. McKellar, *Life on a Mexican Ranch,* 54–55.

8. Ibid., 55. The 1880 U.S. census in Brackettville reveals that eight-year-old Sophy (Sophia) Washington is the youngest child of Florida-born Clara Dixon, who was then forty-five. Sophy and her sister's father was forty-eight-year-old Andrew Washington, Wannah's son. The practice of generational double naming is illustrated in this case for one of Clara's sons, Dixon Washington. He is named after her first husband, Dixon, whose name Clara continued to carry; see Records of the Office of the Adjutant General, Record Group 94, National Archives, or Littlefield, *Africans and Seminoles,* appendix list B, for Wannah and Andrew departing Florida.

9. McKellar, *Life on a Mexican Ranch,* 55.

10. Genevieve Payne and Alice Fay interview with Mock, 29 June 1998, Kerrville. During the Revolution, Pancho Villa took Clara prisoner with other women from Nacimiento like Mirtes Payne, Genevieve Payne's mother.

11. McKellar, *Life on a Mexican Ranch,* 54, 143.

12. Ibid., 147.

13. Ibid., 147–49.

14. Ibid., 55.

15. Ibid., 95.

16. Ibid., 94, 148.

17. Ibid., 94, referring to Clary's practices regarding her hair and "picture."

18. Drawn generally from McKellar, *Life on a Mexican Ranch,* 92–94.

19. McKellar, *Life on a Mexican Ranch,* 93.

20. Ibid., 92–93.
21. Ibid., 93
22. Ibid.
23. Ibid., 93.
24. Ibid., 92–93.
25. Ibid.
26. Ibid., 148.
27. Ibid., 94.
28. Ibid., 128.
29. Ibid., 174.
30. Ibid., 127.
31. Sara (Mrs. D. S.) McKellar reports on this marriage in an 8 August 1944 letter to Porter (Latorre Collection, Benson Latin American Collection). Sara's name also appears as "Sarah" in some contexts. Her maiden name was Scott.
32. Porter to Mrs. D. S. McKellar, 1 April 1947 (Latorre Collection, Benson Latin American Collection).

CHAPTER EIGHT. MISS CHARLES WILSON, FEMALE WARRIOR

Epigraph. Quotation appears in Copage, *Black Pearls: Daily Meditations, Affirmations, and Inspirations for African-Americans.*

1. "Beka" is a Gullah name meaning "a rope made of grass" according to Turner, *Africanisms in the Gullah Dialect,* 61; Porter to Lilith Haynes, 10 May 1977, 3, Schomburg Center for Research in Black Culture.
2. Since the Brackettville school did not go beyond the elementary level, Miss Charles and Dorothy also had to leave Brackettville to attend high school in another city.
3. Quotes from and information on Miss Charles in this chapter are compiled from several sources, including this Rodgers and Schott article, "My Mother Was a Mover: African American Seminole Women in Brackettville, Texas, 1914–1964," 587, which appears in *Writing the Range: Race, Class, and Culture in the Women's West* and Rodgers's 24–25 February 1992 interview with Miss Charles; also see Allison Pollan, "Ahead of Her Time," *Kerrville Daily Times* 4 (February 1989), 288. Miss Charles also discussed the topic of this chapter in Mock's interviews of 21–22 September 1996, Brackettville, Texas, as well as in many additional conversations with the author. Miss Charles's conversations often overlapped—she repeated herself—due to her encroaching dementia, and this is also apparent in newspaper interviews. For the author's conversations with Miss Charles when she repeated material found in multiple sources, no single-source-specific notes are provided. See also Miss Charles's quotes in Guinn, *Our Land before We Die.*
4. Pollan, "Ahead of Her Time," 288.

5. Rodgers and Schott, "My Mother Was a Mover," 592, mention that Miss Charles modified registration requirements so as to coordinate with the pecan season to increase attendance.

6. Foster, "Negro-Indian Relationships in the Southeast," 51; see Porter to Lilith Haynes, 10 May 1977, Schomburg Center for Research in Black Culture.

7. Foster, "Negro-Indian Relationships in the Southeast," 51.

8. Miss Charles interview with Rodgers, 24–25 February 1992.

9. Lillie Mae Dimery interview with Mock, 21–22 September 1997, Brackettville.

10. Miss Charles interview with Mock, 21–22 September 1996; Rodgers interview with Miss Charles, 24–25 February 1992.

11. Rodgers interview with Miss Charles, 24–25 February 1992.

12. Ibid.

13. Ibid.

14. Mock interview with Ethel and Dub Warrior, 19 September 2007; Porter reports these "relaxed racial attitudes" in a letter to Lilith Haynes, 10 May 1977, Schomburg Center for Research in Black Culture.

15. Rodgers interview with Miss Charles, 24–25 February 1992; Mock interview with Miss Charles, 21–22 September 1996.

16. Porter notes, Schomburg Center for Research in Black Culture; also see Rodgers interview with Miss Charles, 24–25 February 1992, and Mock interview with Miss Charles, 21–22 September 1996.

17. Rodgers interview with Miss Charles, 24–25 February 1992; Mock interview with Miss Charles, 21–22 September 1996.

18. Ibid.

CHAPTER NINE. THOSE OLD PEOPLE LIKED TO "KICK UP"

Epigraph. Excerpt from "Still I Rise," in Angelou, *And Still I Rise.*

1. Effie corresponds to *A'fi,* which means to salute a female born on Friday, or *A'fe,* meaning companion; Turner, *Africanisms in the Gullah Dialect,* 40.

2. Foster, "Negro-Indian Relationships in the Southeast"; Hancock, *The Texas Seminoles and Their Language,* 319, discusses Indian elements in their speech.

3. Alice's other siblings included Flora, George, Henry, and Roosevelt. George worked on a ranch in Sanderson, Texas, where Alice met her second husband, Tomás. George later returned to Mexico to run Guadalupe.

4. Gertrude Vázquez interview with Mock, 21–22 July 1997, Nacimiento.

5. Dillingham, "Integration of the Seminole Negroes."

6. Porter Papers, Schomburg Center for Research in Black Culture; Guinn, "Seminole Negro Heritage Fading in Border Town," 1D.

7. Gracie Lasky interview with Mock, 21–22 September 1996, Brackettville.

8. I later learned that the area was part of the Hacienda Los Hermanos, famed for its hot springs. Box, *Adventures and Explorations.*

9. The Mexican government awarded the Kickapoo tribe 78,000 acres of land near Zaragoza and Remolino. In 1852 the tribe traded this grant for 17,352 acres at El Nacimiento and an equal amount in Durango that the tribe never occupied. This El Nacimiento grant established a permanent home for the Kickapoos in Coahuila, and the settlement remains home to many Kickapoos. See *Handbook of Texas,* Texas State Historical Association.

10. In the *ejido* system, the government owns the land and banks finance the operation of the land and agriculture.

11. Turner, *Africanisms in the Gullah Dialect,* 137.

12. Foster, "Negro-Indian Relationships in the Southeast," 57.

13. Porter Papers, Schomburg Center for Research in Black Culture.

14. Dillingham, "Integration of the Seminole Negroes," 5–6, 10–11.

15. Dillingham, "Integration of the Seminole Negroes," notes that by 1965 goats had become the primary means of livelihood. The result was further deterioration of the land.

16. Cassandra Smith, "Warrior Still," *Capital Outlook* 23, no. 9 (February 26–March 4, 1998), 1, 14.

17. Here Gertrude means that she was not one of the older female spiritual leaders in the community.

18. See Porter Papers, Schomburg Center for Research in Black Culture.

19. See Los Vázquez genealogy, Archivo de Dr. José Guadalupe López, Colegio de Investigaciones Históricas de Múzquiz. Porter reports this practice in the event of a spouse's death; Porter Papers, Schomburg Center for Research in Black Culture. Both Dillingham, "Integration of the Seminole Negroes," and Foster, "Negro-Indian Relationships in the Southeast," report this practice. Porter reports that women reverted back to their maiden name after a spouse's death. See Porter to Dillingham, 5 August 1969.

20. See Porter Papers, Schomburg Center for Research in Black Culture.

21. Foster, "African Patterns in the Afro-American Family," 201–32.

22. See Gallagher, "A Survey of the Seminole Freedmen." He discusses the role of men rather than women in arbitration matters and as household heads and advisers in the freedmen community in Oklahoma; see Mulroy, *The Seminole Freedmen,* 209–10.

CHAPTER TEN. RETURN TO NACIMIENTO

Epigraph. Gerda Lerner, on "The Future of Our Past," interview by Catharine R. Stimpson, *Ms.*, 1 September 1981, 94–95.

1. Foster, "Negro-Indian Relationships in the Southeast"; Dillingham, "Integration of the Seminole Negroes," 24.

2. Dillingham, "Integration of the Seminole Negroes."

3. Foster, "Negro-Indian Relationships in the Southeast"; Porter notes, Schomburg Center for Black Research; Dillingham, "Integration of the Seminole Negroes."

CHAPTER ELEVEN. TWO OLD "SISTERS" TALK ABOUT THE OLD PEOPLE

Epigraph. Rachel Russell, *Letters,* ca. 1793.

1. The revolution was brought on by the people's discontent with the presidents of Mexico, in particular the dictatorship of President Porfirio Díaz. In office from 1876 to 1911 (the Porfiriato) except for a brief period, he opened the doors of Mexico to foreign investors and speculators. Upon return to office in 1884, Díaz protected the Mascogos' right to Nacimiento. Emilio Zapata became president of Mexico in 1911 after Díaz was sent into exile; in 1916, the year that Alice Fay was born, Pancho Villa sent his División del Norte to attack a town on the border in New Mexico. His act provoked a punitive expedition by U.S. Army general John J. Pershing. However, Villa left Texas and pushed into the northern frontier of Coahuila. Venustiano Carranza, a foe of Villa, took over the presidency of Mexico in 1917.

2. Porter discusses John Payne and his involvement in the conflicts in Mexico in an 8 August 1944 letter to Mrs. D. S. McKellar (Latorre Collection, Benson Latin American Collection).

3. In the 1890 census, Theresa (Cressy) Wilson is listed at Brackettville as a widow at age thirty. In 1902 she appeared on the Fort Clark survey as the head of a household.

4. Sophie was the daughter of Clara by Washington.

5. Sivad, *The Black Seminole Indians of Texas,* 31; Maggie Kelly, a descendant of Rose Kelly, was born in 1919 and died in 1994.

CHAPTER TWELVE. THE "BROKEN LANGUAGE" AND THOSE "BASKET" NAMES

Epigraph. Phoebe Gilbert, an Ibo descendant living on Sapelo Island off the Georgia coast, recalls the capture of her grandfather, Calina, by slavers in Africa in this excerpt from a Georgia Writers' Project Works Progress Administration (WPA) interview (*Drums and Shadows,* 157).

1. Hancock reports on Afro-Seminole in *The Texas Seminoles and Their Language,* 14, 20–21; "Texas Gullah: The Creole English of the Brackettville Afro-Seminoles," in *Perspectives on American English;* and "On the Classification of Afro-Seminole Creole," in *Language Variety in the South.* Porter did not recognize Afro-Seminole as a language, seeing it only as a dialect of English; see letter to Lilith Haynes, 10 May 1977. Lilith Haynes in "Candid Chimaera: Texas Seminole," in *Southwest Areal Linguistics Then and Now,* also discusses the language she encountered in 1974 and 1975 on two visits to Brackettville. She determines that they spoke English, border Spanish, and some Creek. Dub Warrior has some knowledge of Afro-Seminole; see Mulroy, *Freedom on the Border,* 22.

2. For discussion of baby talk, see Turner, *Africanisms in the Gullah Dialect,* 5; Mille and Montgomery in the introduction to *Africanisms in the Gullah Dialect* discuss Gullah. Pollitzer, *The Gullah People and Their African Heritage,* 129, emphasizes the dynamic aspects of Gullah as a language. Also see Rawick, *The American Slave.* Since Gullah was never intended to be written, there are no hard-and-fast rules governing its orthography or written recordings; many of the WPA interviews of former slaves done in the 1930s and 1940s were recorded by untrained people. Not schooled in the phonetic transcriptions of speech, the interviewers recorded the words as they heard them. They also were influenced by the baggage of preconceptions of black speech as written during those decades.

3. Foster, "Negro-Indian Relationships in the Southeast," 53; Porter to Lilith Haynes, 10 May 1977, Schomburg Center for Research in Black Culture; Spindle, "Diary of Samuel Spindle's Travels."

4. Porter, *The Black Seminoles,* 180; Adam Paine (Payne), even sported a Plains-style buffalo-horn headdress; see Porter to Amos, 31 March 1966, Schomburg Center for Research in Black Culture. Wannah was married to Sam Mills, the father of her children, upon departure from Florida. However, at some point her son Andrew took on the Washington surname. He continued to carry the Washington surname many years later as a scout at Fort Clark.

5. See Mrs. D. S. McKellar's interview with Julia Payne, La Mariposa, 1932, for account (Latorre Collection, Benson Latin American Collection). Sara McKellar was the wife of David Skene McKellar, who inherited the ranch from the original owner, David Harkness McKellar. For Miss Charles's quote, see Pollan, "Ahead of Her Time," 288.

6. Johanna July, interview with Florence Angermiller, *American Life Histories,* http://www.lcwseb.loc.gov.

7. Porter discusses Wannah in *The Black Seminoles,* 29. He provides a more detailed description of Wannah in his notes, Schomburg Center for Research in Black Culture.

8. Woodward, "History from Slave Sources," 479–80.

9. Foster, "Negro-Indian Relationships in the Southeast," 49.

10. Mock interview with Alice Barnett, 20 May 1999, San Antonio.

11. May, *African Americans and Native Americans,* 18 (cites George P. Rawick, *The American Slave: A Composite Autobiography*).

12. An example of this attachment to Indian qualities appears in an interview with former slave Sarah Ford, recorded in Tyler and Murphy, *Slave Narratives of Texas,* 65.

13. Miss Charles repeated this conversation in multiple interviews.

14. Sivad, *The Black Seminole Indians of Texas,* 29.

15. Porter to Mrs. D. S. McKellar, 21 July 1951 (Latorre Collection, Benson Latin American Collection). Also see 21 August 1952 letter from Mrs. D. S. McKellar to Porter for additional discussion (Latorre Collection, Benson Latin American Collection).

16. Turner, *Africanisms in the Gullah Dialect,* 218, writes: "The same variety of word order is quite common also in several west African languages"; see also Patricia Jones-Jackson, "Gullah: On the Question of Afro-American Language," *Anthropological Linguistics* 20, no. 9 (December 1978), 422–28 and "Contemporary Gullah Speech: Some Persistent Linguistic Features," *Journal of Black Studies* 13, vol. 3 (March 1983), 289–303; for insight into the Gullah language, also see Holloway, "Africanisms in Gullah Oral Tradition," *Western Journal of Black Studies* 13, no. 3 (Fall 1989), 115–24.

17. For these conversations of Rosa Dixon Fay's family, see McKellar, *Life on a Mexican Ranch,* 172.

18. See Turner, *Africanisms in the Gullah Dialect,* 218, and Foster, "Negro-Indian Relationships in the Southeast," 53. A Porter letter to Dillingham, 5 August 1969, Schomburg Center for Research in Black Culture, discusses the fact that Gullah is noted for parsimonious abbreviations and the use of one word to complete different thoughts. For additional explanation of these conventions, see Pollitzer, *The Gullah People and Their Gullah Heritage,* 115; Hancock, "Texas Gullah: The Creole English," 313–29; Jones-Jackson, "Gullah: On the Question of Afro-American Language," 422–28.

19. See McKellar, *Life on a Mexican Ranch,* 172.

20. Porter to Dillingham, 5 August 1969, and Porter to Lilith Haynes, 10 May 1977 (Schomburg Center for Research in Black Culture).

21. These conversations with the women about their experiences speaking Afro-Seminole were recorded in two sessions of group meetings.

22. Anita Daniels interview with Mock, 12 August 1999, San Antonio.

23. Pollitzer, *The Gullah People and Their African Heritage,* 129.

24. Bateman, "Naming Patterns," 227–57.

25. Adams, "Naming Practices among the Black Seminole," 219–44.

26. Porter notes, Schomburg Center for Research in Black Culture.

27. John C. Inscoe, "Carolina Slave Names: An Index to Acculturation," *Journal of Southern History* 49, no. 4 (November 1983), 529–30.

28. For general discussion of slave names, see Turner, *Africanisms in the Gullah Dialect*; Baird and Twining, "Names and Naming in the Sea Islands," in *The Crucible of Carolina;* Twining, "An Examination of African Retentions in the Folk Culture of the South Carolina and Georgia Sea Islands" (PhD diss., Indiana University, 1977); Joyner, *Down by the Riverside,* 220; Jerome S. Handler and JoAnn Jacoby, "Slave Names and Naming in Barbados: 1650–1830," *William and Mary Quarterly* 53, no. 4 (October 1996), 710; Wood, *Black Majority,* 181–82; Inscoe, "Carolina Slave Names," 536–37.

29. Hall, "African Religious Retentions in Florida," in *Africanisms in American Culture.*

30. Bateman, "Naming Patterns," 227–57; John Thornton, "Central African Names and African-American Naming," *Williams and Mary Quarterly* 50, no. 4 (October 1993), 727–28.

31. Turner, *Africanisms in the Gullah Dialect,* 41; see also Inscoe, "Carolina Slave Names," 537.

32. See 10 January 1949 letter from Porter to Mrs. D. S. McKellar (Latorre Collection, Benson Latin American Collection).

33. Inscoe, "Carolina Slave Names," 543; scholars such as Pollitzer, the author of *The Gullah People and Their African Heritage,* discuss these names; Baird and Twining, "Names and Naming in the Sea Islands," and Dillard, *Black English: Its History and Usage,* also have pointed to this coincidence.

34. For a discussion of Pompey, see Pollitzer, *The Gullah People and Their African Heritage,* 113.

35. Caesar Daniels was a scout at Fort Clark. Caesar in one case is written as Sneezar on the list of deportees from Florida; see National Archives Microfilm Publications, M234, roll 290, frame 358–61.

36. Turner, *Africanisms in the Gullah Dialect,* 163.

37. Handler and Jacoby, "Slave Names and Naming in Barbados," 700; see also Inscoe, "Carolina Slave Names," 535; Dillard, *Black English: Its History and Usage,* 123–25. Wood, *Black Majority,* 82–83, observes that the similarity of Gullah names to English names helped the survival of the names; also see Thornton, "Central African Names and African-American Naming," 727–42, for additional discussion of African-derived naming patterns.

38. See Inscoe, "Carolina Slave Names," 534; Pollitzer, *The Gullah and Their African Heritage,* 55. Hancock, in an August 15, 2002, correspondence with the author discusses the common use of the diminutive and "Englishfied" African names.

39. Thornton, "Central African Names and African-American Naming," 729–31 discusses Christian-derived names that were deep rooted in Africa before the slave trade.

40. Ibid., 741.

41. Chief Cowkeeper left Fa'i to one of his female descendants, and upon his death she was passed to Chief Bowlegs. On Bowlegs's death, she was passed to Harriet Bowlegs; refer to National Archives Microfilm Publications, M234, roll 290, frames 606–10, Tampa Bay, Florida, 11 July.

42. Bateman, "Naming Patterns," 239.

43. Ibid., 227–57; Thornton, "Central African Names and African-American Naming," 738, determines that the practice of alternating surnames and given names is taken from the Angolan system of double naming used to show descent.

44. Turner, *Africanisms in the Gullah Dialect,* 40; see also Twining, "An Examination of African Retentions"; Joyner, *Down by the Riverside,* 220; Handler and Jacoby, "Slave Names and Naming in Barbados," 710; Inscoe, "Carolina Slave Names," 536–37.

45. Hurston, *Mules and Men.*

46. Adefila, "Slave Religion in the Antebellum South."

CHAPTER THIRTEEN. THE "SISTERS" MAKE THE *SOFKEE: CASA DE LA COMIDA*

1. Josephine A. Beoku-Betts, "We Got Our Way of Cooking Things: Women, Food, and Preservation of Cultural Identity among the Gullah," *Gender and Society* 9, no. 5 (1995), 536; Sidney W. Mintz and Christine M. Du Bois, "Anthropology of Food and Eating," *Annual Review of Anthropology* 31, 99–119, discuss the role of food in creation of values and cultural memory.

2. See Swanton, "The Indians of the Southeastern United States," 285, 342–43, 360–61, 368–71, for general discussion of Indian cooking techniques. He also notes that Gullah rice farmers once used the mortar and pestle; also see Wright, *Creeks and Seminoles*, 98.

3. See discussion in Porter to Dillingham, 5 August 1969, Schomburg Center for Research in Black Culture.

4. Dillingham, "Integration of the Seminole Negroes," 25.

5. A stone metate and pestle were used by Mexican women to grind corn, and the Mascogos soon adopted it, too.

6. Coontie has many spellings, including "kunti."

7. See Swanton, "The Indians of the Southeastern United States," 332, 354; also see Adin Baber, "Food Plants of the DeSoto Expedition, 1539–1543," *Tequesta* II (1942), 34–40; Gifford, "Some Reflections on the South Florida of Long Ago," *Tequesta* VI (1946) for a detailed description of coontie processing and use.

8. Beoku-Betts discusses this social act in "'We Got Our Way of Cooking Things'," 536.

CHAPTER FOURTEEN. SHOUTING TO THE LORD IN THE "PRAY'S HOUSE"

Epigraph. Pulitzer Prize–winner Julia Peterkin, writing about a recently converted Gullah woman, cited in Wolfe, *The Abundant Life Prevails*, 43–44.

1. Raboteau, *Slave Religion*, 68, 70–71, and Creel, "Gullah Attitudes toward Life and Death," in *Africanisms in American Culture*, 93, note that the term "pray's house" was used, not "praise house." For a discussion of African retentions, see Hall, "African Religious Retentions in Florida," 57; Pollitzer, *The Gullah People and Their African Heritage*, 130; Timothy Baumann, "African American Ethnicity," *SAA Archaeological Record* 4, no. 4 (September 2004), 16–19; Raboteau, *Slave Religion*, 92–106; Campbell, *Empire for Slavery: The Peculiar Institution*. Pitts, *Old Ship of Zion*, 53, writes that blacks were overwhelmingly Baptist; Howard, "The Promised Land: Reconstructing History and Identity," discusses maroon retentions among Black Seminole descendants on Andros Island; Wolfe describes the interface of the African and Christian practices in *The Abundant Life Prevails*, 51.

2. Pollitzer, *African Religious Groups and Beliefs*, 130.

3. H. Conger Jones, "Seminole Scouts, Old Enemy of Indians, Still Thrive on Border," in *La Hacienda,* edited by Rosemary W. Jones (Del Rio, Texas).

4. Thompson, "The Black Watch of Texas," in *Kinney County, 1852–1977* (Kinney County Historical Commission, 1976–77), 23–24.

5. Foster, "Negro-Indian Relationships in the Southeast," 19.

6. Miss Charles Wilson interview with Mock, 12 May 1995, Brackettville.

7. Haynes, "Candid Chimaera," in *Southwest Areal Linguistics Then and Now,* 291.

8. Porter to Lilith Haynes, 10 May 1977, Schomburg Center for Research in Black Culture; Porter Papers, Schomburg Center for Research in Black Culture.

9. Jones, "Seminole Scouts, Old Enemy of Indians"; Turner, *Africanisms in the Gullah Dialect,* postures that the word "shout" is derived from the word *saut,* a term used by west African Muslims to describe dancing.

10. Alice Daniels Barnett interview with Mock, 11 December 1998, San Antonio.

11. Genevieve Payne and Alice Fay interview with Mock, 1 January 1999, Kerrville.

12. Miss Charles Wilson interview with Mock, 12 May 1995, Brackettville.

13. Porter Papers, Schomburg Center for Research in Black Culture.

14. In this case, the women were all recorded at the same time.

15. Dillingham, "Integration of the Seminole Negroes," 22. Seminole women in Indian Territory are pictured wearing an identical headscarf; see Library of Congress print 1900–1930, call number SSF-Indians of North America—Food, reproduction number LC-USZ62-113243. Raboteau, *Canaan Land: A Religious History,* 73, reports that cloth bands were worn by Sea Islanders seeking a spiritual experience in conversion or mourning.

16. Raboteau, *Slave Religion, 73.*

17. Porter to Lilith Haynes, 10 May 1977, Porter Papers, Schomburg Center for Research in Black Culture.

18. Jones, "Seminole Scouts, Old Enemy of Indians."

19. Porter to Lilith Haynes, 10 May 1977, 3, Schomburg Center for Research in Black Culture. Porter refers to Isaac Watts's 1707 book of *Hymns and Spiritual Songs.*

20. Thompson, "The Black Watch of Texas," 23–24.

21. Foster, "Negro-Indian Relationships in the Southeast," 53.

22. Jones, "Seminole Scouts, Old Enemy of Indians."

23. Genevieve Payne and Alice Fay interview with Mock, 9 January 1999, Kerrville.

24. Raboteau, *Slave Religion,* 36–37, 65–75, discusses spirit possession and dance and shout among Sea Islanders. He also notes that blacks substituted new forms of religious practices hidden from masters; see Creel, "Gullah Attitudes toward Life and Death," 80, for description of ring shout; Washington, *Black Sects and Cults,* 75, also provides a description of black religious ritual.

25. Hall, "African Religious Retentions in Florida," 55, 60, discusses the survival of African religious practices in the Americas such as spirit possession and dancing. He determines that slaves merged African-style dancing with evangelical Protestantism.

26. Smith, *Conjuring Culture: Biblical Formations of Black Culture,* 72.

27. Porter to Lilith Haynes, 10 May 1977, Schomburg Center for Research in Black Culture.

28. Haynes, "Candid Chimaera," in *Southwest Areal Linguistics Then and Now,* 291.

29. Raboteau, *Slave Religion.*

30. Wright, *Creeks and Seminoles,* 95, provides a discussion of black participation in busk rituals; also see Zellar, *African Creeks: Estelusti and the Creek Nation,* 36 for accounts of "bangas" among the Creeks. Lucinda Davis in Works Progress Administration: Oklahoma Writers Project, *Slave Narratives* (Washington, D.C.: U.S. Government Printing Office, 1932), 58, refers to the dances as "bangas"; also see Preston Kyle's in Works Progress Administration: Arkansas Writers Project, *Slave Narratives* (Washington, D.C.: U.S. Government Printing Office, 1932), 220. Archaeologists excavating Abraham's Black Seminole village, Pilaklikaha, in Florida have recovered evidence that they adopted some Seminole spiritual and cultural practices connected to the green corn ceremony such as the black drink and dance; see Milanich, *Florida's Indians from Ancient Times to the Present,* and Terrance Weik, "Florida Researchers Launch First Excavation of Black Seminole Town," http://news.ufl.edu/2001/06/14/black-seminole/. Mulroy, *Freedom on the Border,* 186n38, states that there is no evidence to suggest that the Black Seminoles ever participated in the busk on a large scale.

31. See Ritzenthaler and Peterson, *The Mexican Kickapoo Indians*; the Black Seminoles' belief system incorporated other Indian cultural practices such as salt taboos. The Black Seminoles consumed their main dish, the corn-based *sofkee,* with no salt during a fast, and Molly Perryman pointed out that there was "no salt at a hunting or war dance." Presumably salt was not good to take, for it would dehydrate the warriors. Among the Kickapoos living next to the Mascogos in Nacimiento today, it is crucial to make certain that one's home is not being salted by a person with harmful intent, for if salt is mixed with soil and "deposited near one's home it is bad luck." To counter ill effects of salting, one performs a smoking (*sahumerio*) or incense burning in the house.

32. Bartram, *Travels through North and South Carolina,* 203–204; Hudson, *The Southeastern Indians,* 336, 373–74.

33. Porter Papers, Schomburg Center for Research in Black Culture.

34. Wolfe, *The Abundant Life Prevails,* 41–43.

35. Inscoe, "Carolina Slave Names," 528.

36. Howard, "The Promised Land: Reconstructing History and Identity," 40.

37. Thompson, "The Black Watch of Texas," 23–24.

38. Zulema Vázquez interview with Mock, 21–22 July 1997, Nacimiento.

39. Ibid. Zulema's comment that the paritioners had saints ("idols") contradicts Sally's.

40. Jones, "Seminole Scouts, Old Enemy of Indians," 453.

CHAPTER FIFTEEN. DREAMING WITH THE ANCESTORS

Epigraph. Tony Morrison, Nobel Lecture, December 7, 1993.

1. Creel, "Gullah Attitudes toward Life and Death," 79–81.

2. Jones, "Seminole Scouts, Old Enemy of Indians," 452.

3. Porter notes, Schomburg Center for Research in Black Culture.

4. Wolfe, *The Abundant Life Prevails,* 48, notes a similar situation in which an elderly Gullah woman was always turned back or denied admission to the church, but finally got "through" (had the right dream) and was baptized.

5. Jones, "Seminole Scouts, Old Enemy of Indians," 452.

6. Alice Barnett is a cousin to Alice Fay, so in reality Alice also is a descendant of Florida-born Cornelia Perryman. Eliza's sister Tina was married to Curly Jefferson. The 1910 U.S. census lists Curly, Tina, and a son Roosevelt living in Texas, but soon after that Tina left Curly and moved to Oklahoma with Roosevelt.

7. Hudson, *The Southeastern Indians,* 226–29, 336–45, 372, discusses the black drink and its use. Hoxie, *Encyclopedia of North American Indians* reports the cultivation of dreams and visions among the southeastern Indians.

8. Latorre and Latorre, *The Mexican Kickapoo Indians,* 359, discuss Kickapoo religious practices.

9. Janie Gilliard Moore, "Africanisms among Blacks of the Sea Islands," *Journal of Black Studies* 10, no. 4 (June 1980), 477 discusses African-derived practices among the black Sea Islanders; see Twining and Baird, *Sea Island Roots,* 2.

10. Pollitzer, *The Gullah People and Their African Heritage,* citing Turner, *Africanisms in the Gullah Dialect,* 271–75. Wolfe, *The Abundant Life Prevails,* 41–48, explores this Gullah vision quest that was typical of the Black Seminole community; see Nelson, Yokley, and Nelson, *The Black Church in America*; Gilkes, "The Roles of Church and Community Mothers: Ambivalent American Sexism or Fragmented African Familyhood," in *African American Religion,* 368; and Raboteau, *Slave Religion,* 267, 272.

11. Creel, "Gullah Attitudes Toward Life and Death," 81.

12. Gilkes's interpretation in "The Roles of Church and Community Mothers," 368, 370, however, has a different twist. She argues that the role of community mothers reflects roots in African patrilocal and patriarchal societies, which were not characteristic of the Black Seminoles, who were matrifocal and had matrilineal tendencies, probably due in part to the men's frequent absences and insularity over the years; also see Brown, "Afro-Baptist Women's Church and Family Roles," 173–86.

13. Zulema Vázquez interview with Mock, 21–22 July 1997, Nacimiento, Mexico.

CHAPTER SIXTEEN. THE JOYS OF PARADISE

Epigraph. Julie Dash, *Daughters of the Dust,* 164.

1. Guthrie, *Catching Sense: African American Communities,* 6.

2. Kopytoff, a scholar of African religion, provides additional similarities between the Black Seminole funerary rituals and belief system in his article "Ancestors as Elders in Africa." See http://lucy.ukc.ac.uk/ERA/Ancestors/kopytoff.html.

3. Creel, "Gullah Attitudes toward Life and Death," 69–97, documents similar Gullah beliefs about death; Mullin, *Africa in America,* 63–66, describes the religious beliefs, customs, and traditions that survived despite enslavement in the Sea Islands. See also Creel, *A Peculiar People: Slave Religion,* 312; Guthrie, *Catching Sense: African American Communities,* 307–308.

4. Jones, "Seminole Scouts, Old Enemy of Indians," 454.

5. Ibid., 452.

6. Genevieve Payne, phone conversation with Mock, 1 June 2010, Kerrville, Texas.

7. Thompson, "The Black Watch of Texas," 22–24.

8. Sivad, *The Black Seminole Indians of Texas,* 26.

9. Gutman, *The Black Family in Slavery and Freedom,* 281; William Russell Bascom, "Acculturation among the Gullah Negroes," *American Anthropologist* 43, 43–50.

10. Jo Emily Williams interview, 2 November 1992, San Antonio, Institute of Texan Cultures, University of Texas at San Antonio. Mescal is distilled liquor made from the maguey plant.

CHAPTER SEVENTEEN. TREASURES OF THE SPIRIT

Epigraph 1. Quotation on funeral program for Nancy Williams, sister of Ophelia Benson, 20 September 1998. Nancy was the great-granddaughter of Renty Grayson, a Black Creek descendant and scout.

Epigraph 2. Rosa Fay, quoted in Porter, *Negro on the American Frontier,* 3.

1. Tilley, *A Phenomenology of Landscape,* 33.

2. Charles Emily Wilson, "Texas Seminole Scouts," in 1992 Festival of American Folklife program, ed. Peter Seitel, 80.

Note on Sources

Looking for the "Sisters"

It has been a challenge to excavate this story, given the lack of information about Black Seminole women. The process has been like perusing a scrapbook of memories with missing pages. In addition to my search through the lists of Black Seminole deportees in the National Archives, as discussed in the introduction, the research archived in other institutions and work of other scholars, eyewitnesses, and observers have been integral in unearthing the stories of Alice Fay's ancestors in the dark corners of history. The colorful folklorist, historian, and social activist Kenneth Wiggins Porter, born in 1905, played a prominent role in recording this little-known swath. He was born in Kansas, a state with a substantial black population. His mother related the oral version of *Uncle Tom's Cabin* and told him stories of the African American community. In 1942 and 1943, Porter interviewed Black Seminoles over brief periods in Brackettville, Del Rio, and Nacimiento, the results of which were blended into his many publications. They provide invaluable insight into black history in a time of racism and ignorance.

In the initial stages of my research I was hopeful that Porter's interviews would dovetail with my interviews with descendants. I planned a visit to the Schomburg Center for Research in Black Culture in Harlem, where his copious notes and field interviews are archived. I had never been to the center and was guided in my task by Alcione M. Amos and Thomas P. Senter, the co-editors of a compilation of Porter's notes in *Black Seminoles: History of a Freedom Seeking People* (1996). Porter's notes, provided on file cards, reveal that he blended together conversations from his informants in Mexico and Texas. He did this, as he admits, to enhance readability, though his subjects had differing interpretations of historical events. After interviewing his informants, many of them women, he wrote down the conversations he remembered, trying to provide a sense of the informants' personality and use of English. I soon determined that this method provides a particular bias to the interviews, a factor that I endeavored to keep in the back of my mind as I wrote this book.

Alice's great-grandmother Rose Kelly had passed away by the time of Porter's interviews, but Rose Kelly's daughter Amelia (Kelly) Valdez and Alice's paternal grandmother Rosa Dixon Fay were alive at the time of his visits in the 1940s, as well as other women present in this work. They reflect an ethos of warrior women, who vied for power and autonomy in a world of men. The women's weapons are words that reflect the resistance so entrenched in the identity of Black Seminoles as a maroon culture. To my disappointment, Porter did not invite the women to discuss their own lives. In an August 5, 1969, letter to Beth Dillingham, he states, "I was in Nacimiento to collect recollections of Seminole Negro history, and particularly the career of John Horse, rather than investigate their current way of life."

I patiently completed my perusal of Porter's files in the Schomburg Center, frustrated in my search for any additional pieces of information concerning Black Seminole women. Finally, there was one file left—one containing all of Porter's correspondence. One Porter correspondent was the aforementioned Beth Dillingham, an anthropology professor at Illinois University. She intended to do fieldwork in the Kickapoo village near Nacimiento, Mexico, with her husband, the sociologist Harry C. Dillingham. Her son Clay related that his parents, with four children in tow, drove through the Nacimiento village and were amazed to find black people there speaking English. Dillingham, her husband, and children lived among the Black Seminoles in Nacimiento for four summers in the 1960s. She provides insightful observations into their lives and culture in her letters and a 1976 paper (see Porter's August 5, 1969, letter to her).

I also discovered a letter from Porter to Lilith Haynes, a linguist who visited the community for three weeks in December 1974 and January 1975 and who published a paper about her experiences. She provided insightful comments about the religious practices and the language spoken.

Laurence Foster, a young black anthropology student working toward a doctorate at the University of Pennsylvania, spent a period off and on for four years in Nacimiento, Brackettville, and Oklahoma doing research for his 1929 dissertation on African American–Indian relationships (Foster, *Negro-Indian Relationships in the Southeast,* 1935). His objective was to record physical characteristics in the Brackettville population to determine the degree of interracial mixture compared to in southeastern Indian and black populations. His dissertation, published in 1935, reveals his avid interest in the elders' accounts of the community's traditions, rituals, and celebrations. He provides crucial information that enhanced my research endeavors and served as a valuable complement to Porter's interviews.

I found the letters of another Porter correspondent, Sara McKellar, while going through the Felipe and Delores Latorre files at the Benson Library at the University of Texas, Austin. A published writer herself, McKellar shared Porter's passion for the folklore and history of the Mascogos, who lived on the ranch property belonging to Sara's husband's family in Nacimiento in the 1940s to 1950s. She wrote many letters describing her conversations with the Mascogos. Interestingly, Porter's early letters to her reveal the evolution of his ideas for his many papers and book, and additional information on the group not published elsewhere. I also was fortunate to have had access to the published diary of Maud McKellar (*Life on a Mexican Ranch,* 1994). Maud is the daughter of David Harkness McKellar, who was the original owner of the ranch from 1893 to 1895 and who was murdered. In her diary, Maud recorded many conversations with the Mascogos from nearby Nacimiento. Her writings include, in particular, accounts of Alice Fay's grandmother Rosa Dixon Fay and her large extended family who worked on the ranch.

My volume of Kevin Mulroy's book, *Freedom on the Border* (1993)—now with dog-eared pages, written notes, stickums, and a worn-out cover—was also a constant companion while writing this book.

Daniel Littlefield's *Africans and Seminoles* was my lifeline in helping me understand the history of the Black Seminoles and the various individuals who showed up many years later in Texas. I could not have made those connections without his seminal work.

In order to comprehend the tenacious African roots and ethos of the Black Seminole community, I perused Works Progress Administration (WPA) interviews of former slaves (for a discussion of slave narratives, see Tyler and Murphy, *The Slave Narratives of Texas,* 1997 and Barr, *Black Texans: A History of African Americans in Texa*s, 1996). I also immersed myself in the complex, tumultuous politics of Mexico during the late nineteenth to early twentieth century, when that country's conflicts consumed and demoralized the Black Seminoles.

I also became an avid student of Jane Landers's works on colonial Spanish in Florida. Albert J. Raboteau, Timothy E. Furlop, William S. Pollitzer, Margaret Creel, Robert L. Hall, and Joseph E. Holloway enlightened me on Gullah religion. Ian Hancock, Rebecca Bateman, Keith E. Baird, Mary A. Twining, and, in particular, Lorenzo Dow Turner led me to understand the Gullah roots in the Black Seminole language and naming customs.

Other insightful recorders of Black Seminole culture could not know at the time that they too would embellish this story of women. Their observations, perhaps subjective in some cases, proved to be subtle but valuable sources of information. H. Conger Jones, a Brackettville resident and Episcopal priest, was an astute observer of religious practices in the Black Seminole community in the 1930s. His firsthand accounts provide invaluable information on the retention of African-derived practices such as the shout-and-response dance, fasting, the reading of dreams, and mortuary practices (Jones, "Seminole Scouts, Old Enemy of Indians," 1976). He records with remarkable insight the merging of two belief systems—one focused on dreams and revelations from the Black Seminoles' eclectic past, the other focused on the growing influence of the Christian Bible and formal evangelical religion with ordained ministers.

Mary Louise Thompson, another early observer of Black Seminoles in Brackettville, provided a spirited discussion of Black Seminole religious practices in a short paper, "The Black Watch of Texas, 1852–1977," which also was useful.

I also have tried to grasp the essence of Back Seminole women across a space-time continuum through an eclectic blending of ethnographic reflections, archival documents, diaries, memoirs, oral histories, and informal observations. As the anthropologist Michael Shanks suggests, the process is similar to the creative act of an artist cutting and reassembling fragments of photographs, images, objects, quotations, and other borrowings into a sort of archaeological montage (Shanks, *Photography and the Archaeological Image,* 1997).

The accounts and diaries of other observers and scholars I encountered over time provide occasional props for the stage on which this story plays out. I perused the historical accounts of early visitors to Florida, Indian Territory, Mexico, and Texas, taking into account the ethnocentrism that colors some of those sources. Olmsted, in his 1856 account *A Journey in the Seaboard Slave States,* discusses travels through North and South Carolina, and east and west Florida; Olmsted also offers a view of Texas on pages 324–25 in *A Journey Through Texas: Or, a Saddle-Trip on the Southwestern Frontier* (1978). Another source, Foreman, *Indian Removal* (1972) covers a broad swath of southeastern history. Foreman also edited the 1996 volume *A Traveler in Indian Territory,* which provides details of Ethan Allen Hitchcock's travels in Indian Territory and visits with the Cherokee, Creek, Chickasaw, and Cherokee tribes. Hitchcock filled nine notebooks, housed in the Library of Congress, with his impressions.

Another valuable source of information dovetailing with the departure lists of Black Seminoles from Florida to Indian Territory was unexpectedly provided by the U.S. Army. The U.S. Army records list the full names of men who joined the Seminole Negro Indian Scouts, along with their birthdates, enlistment periods, ages, and times of death. I was able to trace many of these men back to Florida. The military census provided additional information as to their presence with families on Fort Duncan or Fort Clark. The Seminole Indian Scouts Cemetery in Brackettville also has tombstones for some of the men and women with their dates of birth and death. These records and a perusal of the U.S. censuses from 1880 to 1910 for Fort Clark and Brackettville assisted me in making some sense of the genealogical trails and historical connections of some of Alice Fay's ancestors from Florida to Texas. However, I exercised caution with census data because dates and birthplaces are sometimes incorrect, and names are misspelled or have substitutions and are duplicated through generations. A 1902 plane table survey map of Fort Clark and households provided me with some of the households led by Black Seminoles.

While these sources, primary and secondary, were key in my research, intrinsic to the soul of this book are the Black Seminoles' tenacious African-derived cultural practices, which are entrenched in social memory. The voices of Alice Fay's female ancestors were enlivened through many conversations with descendants, both men and women, who graciously shared their stories with me—stories that are preserved in cultural memory and everyday practice. Their overarching story is not seamless—it is fraught with lingering ambiguities, contradictions, and differences of opinion. Historical recollection among the Black Seminoles has been influenced by published accounts. But to the Black Seminoles, these lingering and often paradoxical practices have provided a sort of moving force field in which they continue, even today, to negotiate their identity.

Bibliography

BOOKS, ARTICLES, THESES, AND DISSERTATIONS

Adams, Mischa B. "Naming Practices among the Black Seminole of the Texas-Mexico Border Region." *Journal of Big Bend Studies* 11 (1999): 219–44.

Adefila, Johnson Ajibade. "Slave Religion in the Antebellum South: A Study of the Role of Africanisms in the Black Response to Christianity." PhD diss., Brandeis University, 1975.

Allende, Isabel. *The House of the Spirits*. New York: Penguin, 1980.

Angelou, Maya. *And Still I Rise*. New York: Random House, 1978.

Baber, Adin. "Food Plants of the DeSoto Expedition, 1539–1543," *Tequesta* II (1942).

Baird, Keith E., and Mary A. Twining. "Names and Naming in the Sea Islands." In *The Crucible of Carolina: Essays in the Development of Gullah Language and Culture*, edited by Michael Montgomery, 23–37. Athens: University of Georgia Press, 1994.

Baird, Keith E., and O. Chuks-Orji, eds. *Names from Africa: Their Origin, Meaning, and Pronunciation*. Chicago: Johnson Publishing, 1972.

Baker, T. Lindsay, and Julie P. Baker, eds. *The WPA Oklahoma Slave Narratives*. Norman: University of Oklahoma Press, 1996.

Bandelier, Adolph Francis, ed. *The Journey of Alvar Nuñez Cabeza de Vaca and His Companions from Florida to the Pacific 1528–1536*. Translated by Fanny Bandelier. New York: A. S. Barnes & Co., 1922 (1905).

Banks, Dean. "Civil War Refugees from Indian Territory in the North." *Chronicles of Oklahoma* 4 (Autumn 1963): 286–89.

Barr, Alwyn. "African Americans in Texas: From Stereotypes to Diverse Roles." In *Texas through Time: Evolving Interpretations*, edited by Walter L. Buenger and Robert A. Calvert. College Station: Texas A&M University Press, 1991.

———. *Black Texans: A History of African Americans in Texas, 1528–1995*. 2nd ed. Norman: University of Oklahoma Press, 1996.

———. *The African Texans*. College Station: Texas A&M University Press, 2004.

Barrios, Joseph. "Eighty-three-year-old Helps Reveal History of Black Seminoles." *San Antonio Express News*, 22 April 1998.

Bartram, William. *Travels through North and South Carolina, Georgia, East and West Florida*. A facsimile of the 1792 London edition. Savannah, Ga.: Beehive Press, 1973.

Bascom, William Russell. "Acculturation among the Gullah Negroes." *American Anthropologist* 43 (1941): 43–50.

Bascom, William R., and Melville J. Herskovits, eds. *Continuity and Change in African Cultures*. Chicago: University of Chicago Press, 1959.

Bateman, Rebecca. "Africans and Indians: A Comparative Study of the Black Carib and Black Seminole." *Ethnohistory* 37, no. 1 (Winter 1990): 1–24.

———. "Naming Patterns in Black Seminole Ethnogenesis." *Ethnohistory* 49, no. 2 (Spring 2002): 227–57.

Baumann, Timothy. "African American Ethnicity." *SAA Archaeological Record* 4, no. 4 (September 2004): 16–19.

Beoku-Betts, Josephine A. "'We Got Our Way of Cooking Things': Women, Food, and Preservation of Cultural Identity Among the Gullah." *Gender and Society* 9, no. 5 (1995): 535–55.

———. "When Black Is Not Enough: Doing Field Research among Gullah Women." *NWSA National Women's Studies Association Journal* 6, no. 3 (Fall 1994): 413–33.

Bird, J. B. "Jesup's Proclamation." Rebellion: John Horse and the Black Seminoles, the First Black Rebels to Beat American Slavery, 2005. http://www.johnhorse.com/trail/02/d/25.htm (retrieved 29 August 2005).

———. "The Largest Slave Rebellion in U.S. History." Rebellion: John Horse and the Black Seminoles, the First Black Rebels to Beat American Slavery, 2005. http://www.johnhorse.com/highlights/essays/largest.htm (retrieved 29 August 2005).

Botume, Elizabeth Hyde. *First Days amongst the Contrabands*. Boston: Lee and Shephard, 1893.

Box, Capt. Michael James. *Adventures and Explorations in New and Old Mexico*. New York: James Miller, 1869.

Boyd, Mark F. "The Seminole War: Its Background and Onset 1835." *Florida Historical Quarterly* 30 (22 July 1951): 3–115.

Brady, Marilyn. "The Paynes of Texas: Black Seminole Cowboys of the Big Bend." In *Black Cowboys of Texas*, edited by Sara Massey, 248–55. College Station: Texas A&M Press, 2000.

Braund, Kathryn E. Holland. "Guardians of Tradition and Handmaidens to Change: Women's Roles in Creek Economic and Social Life during the Eighteenth Century." *American Indian Quarterly* 14, no. 3 (Summer 1990): 239–58.

———. "The Creek Indians, Blacks, and Slavery." *Journal of Southern History* 57, no. 4 (November 1991): 601–36.

Britten, Thomas. *A Brief History of the Seminole-Negro Indian Scouts*. Lewiston, N.Y.: Edwin Mellen Press, 1999.

Brown, Audrey Lawson. "Africanisms in the 'Old Ship of Zion': What Are Their Forms and Why Do They Persist?" Paper presented at "Places of Cultural Memory: African Reflections on the American Landscape" Conference, National Park Service, Atlanta, Ga., May 9–12, 2001. http://www.nps.gov/history/crdi/conferences/afr_acro5_p83-126.pdf#page=3

———. "Afro-Baptist Women's Church and Family Roles: Transmitting Afrocentric Cultural Values." *Anthropological Quarterly* 67, no. 4 (October 1994): 173–86.

Brown, Canter, Jr. "Race Relations in Territorial Florida, 1821–1845." *The Florida Historical Quarterly* 73, no. 3 (January 1995): 287–307.

Brown, Cloyd L. *Black Warrior Chiefs: A History of the Seminole Negro Indian Scouts: A True Story*. Fort Worth: C. I. Brown, 1999.

Bruhns, Karen Olsen, and Karen E. Stothert. *Women in Ancient America*. Norman: University of Oklahoma Press, 1999.

Buck, Pearl S. *What America Means to Me*. New York: John Day, 1943.

Campbell, Randolph B. *An Empire for Slavery: The Peculiar Institution in Texas, 1821–1865*. Baton Rouge: Louisiana State University Press, 1991.

Childs, Major. "Maj. Childs' correspondence." *Historical Magazine* 3rd ser., III (1844): 280–82.

Chuks-orji, Oganna. *Names from Africa. Their Origin, Meaning and Pronunciation*. Edited by Keith E. Baird, with commentary. Chicago: Johnson Publishing, 1972.

Coe, C. "Koontie and the Seminole Bread Root." *Scientific American* (1989): 19–29.

Coffey, Jim. "Johanna July: A Horse-Breaking Woman." In *Black Cowboys of Texas*, edited by Sara R. Massey. College Station: Texas A&M University Press, 2000.

Colburn, David R., and Jane L. Landers. *The African-American Heritage of Florida*. Gainesville: University Press of Florida, 1995.

Copage Eric V. *Black Pearls: Daily Meditations, Affirmations, and Inspirations for African-Americans*. New York: Harper Collins, 1993.

Courlander, Harold. *A Treasury of Afro-American Folklore*. New York: Marlowe and Co., 1996 (1976).

Covington, James W. *The Seminoles of Florida*. Gainesville: University Press of Florida, 1993.

Cox, C. C. "From Texas to California in 1849: Biographical Memoir of Cornelius C. Cox," edited by Mabelle Eppard Martin. *Southwestern Historical Quarterly* 29, no. 1: 1–12.

Crawford, Anne F., and Crystal Sasse Ragsdale. *Texas Women: Frontier to Future*. Austin, Texas: State House Press, 1998.

Creel, Margaret. *A Peculiar People: Slave Religion and Community Culture among the Gullahs*. New York: New York University Press, 1988.

———. "Gullah Attitudes toward Life and Death." In *Africanisms in American Culture*, edited by Joseph E. Holloway, 69–97. Bloomington: Indiana University Press, 1989.

Cuney-Hare, Maud. *Norris Wright Cuney: A Tribute to the Black People*. Facsimile reproduction of the 1913 first ed. Austin, Texas: Steck-Vaughn Co., 1986.

Dash, Julie. *Daughters of the Dust.* New York: Penguin Group, 1997.

Davis, Lucinda. "Slave Narratives." In *Works Progress Administration: Oklahoma Writer's Project*. Washington, D.C.: U.S. Government Printing Office, 142.

Davis, Michael. "Field Notes and Photos." In 1993 CRM Excavations by Macaw Consulting report. Austin, Texas.

Deagan, Kathleen. "Colonial Transformation: Euro-American Cultural Genesis in the Early Spanish-American Colonies." *Journal of Anthropological Research* 52, no. 2 (Summer 1996): 154.

Deagan, Kathleen, and Darcie MacMahon. *Fort Mose: Colonial America's Black Fortress of Freedom.* Gainesville: University of Florida Press, 1995.

Del Moral, Paulina, and Alicia Siller V. *Recetario Mascogo de Coahuila: Colección Cocina.* Cocina Indigena y Popular series, vol. 51. México City: Conaculta, 2000.

Del Rio Times Herald. "Penny Factor Recalls Scouts of Old Ft. Clark." September 10, 1967.

Dewees, William B. *Letters from an Early Settler of Texas*. Compiled by C. Cardelle. Louisville, Ky.: New Albany Tribune Print, 1858.

Di Silvestro, Roger, and Shirley Boteler Mock. "Freedom Train to Mexico." *Americas* 52, no. 6 (November 1, 2000): 22.

Dillard, Joe L. *Black English: Its History and Usage in the United States*. New York: Random House, 1972.

Dillingham, Beth. "The Seminole Negroes of Nacimiento." Paper presented at the Central States Branch of the American Anthropological Association, 1967.

Dobie, J. Frank. *Coronado's Children: Tales of Lost Mines and Buried Treasures of the Southwest*. Austin: University of Texas Press, 1978 (1930).

Douglas, Mary. *Purity and Pollution: An Analysis of Concepts of Pollution and Taboo.* New York: Routledge Classics, 1966.

Dyk, Walter. *Son of Old Hat: A Navajo Autobiography*. Recordation by Walter Dyk with a foreword by Edward Sapir. Lincoln: University of Nebraska Press, 1938.

Ebron, Paula. "Enchanted Memories of Regional Differences in African American Culture." *American Anthropologist* 100, no. 1 (March 1998): 94–105.

Fairbanks, Charles H. "Creek and Pre-Creek." In *Archaeology of Eastern United States,* edited by James B. Griffin, 285–375. Chicago: University of Chicago Press, 1952.

Ferguson, Leland. *Common Ground: Archaeology and Early African America, 1650–1800*. Washington, D.C.: Smithsonian, 1992.

Forbes, Jack D. *Africans and Native Americans: The Language of Race and the Evolution of Red-black Peoples*. Urbana: University of Illinois Press, 1993.

Foreman, Carolyn Thomas. "Journal of a Tour in the Indian Territory by N. Sayer Harris in the Spring of 1844." *Chronicles of Oklahoma* X, no. 2 (June 1932): 219.

Foreman, Grant, ed. *A Traveler in Indian Territory: The Journal of Ethan Allen Hitchcock: Late Major-General in the United States Army*. Foreword by Michael D. Green. Norman: University of Oklahoma Press, 1996.

———. *Indian Removal: The Immigration of the Five Civilized Tribes*. Norman: University of Oklahoma, 1972 (1953).

———. *The Five Civilized Tribes*. Norman: University of Oklahoma Press, 1934 (1968).

Fortes, Meyer. *Religion, Morality and the Person: Essays on Tallensi Religion*. Introduction by Jack Goody. Cambridge: Cambridge University Press, 1987.

Foster, Herbert J. "African Patterns in the Afro-American Family." *Journal of Black Studies* 14, no. 2 (December 1983): 201–32.

Foster, Laurence. "Negro-Indian Relationships in the Southeast." PhD diss., University of Pennsylvania, 1978 (1935).

Freeman, Ronald L. *A Communion of the Spirits: African American Quilters, Preservers, and Their Stories*. Nashville: Rutledge Hill Press, 1996.

French, Major. "Diary." 1882. Diskette provided to author by family.

Fulop, Timothy E., and Albert J. Raboteau. *African-American Religion: Interpretive Essays in History and Culture*. New York: Routledge, 1997.

Gallagher, Art. "A Survey of the Seminole Freemen." Master's thesis, University of Oklahoma, 1951.

Georgia Writers' Project. *Drums and Shadows: Survival Studies among the Georgia Coastal Negroes*. Athens: University of Georgia Press, 1940.

———. "Sapelo Island." In *Drums and Shadows: Survival Studies among the Georgia Coastal Negroes*. Available online at Internet Sacred Text Archive. http://www.sacred-texts.com/afr/das/das23.htm.

Gibson, Arrell Morgan. *The Kickapoos: Lords of the Middle Border*. Norman: University of Oklahoma Press, 1975.

Giddings, Joshua R. *The Exiles of Florida*. New York: Arno Press, 1969 (1858).

Gifford, John C. "Some Reflections on the South Florida of Long Ago." *Tequesta* VI (1946).

Gilkes, Cheryl Townsend. "The Roles of Church and Community Mothers: Ambivalent American Sexism or Fragmented African Familyhood." In *African American Religion: Interpretative Essays in History and Culture,* edited by Timothy E. Fulop and Albert J. Raboteau, 365–88. New York: Routledge, 1997.

Goggin, John M. "The Seminole Negroes of Andros Island, Bahamas." *Florida Historical Quarterly* 24, no. 3 (January 1946): 201–206.

Gonzales, Ambrose E. *The Black Border: Gullah Stories of the Carolina Coast*. South Carolina: State Printing Co., 1964 (1922).

Goody, Jack, ed. *Religion, Morality, and the Person: Essays on Tallensi Religion*. Cambridge: Cambridge University Press, 1997.

Granger, Mary. *Drums and Shadows: Survival Studies among the Georgia Coastal Negroes*. Athens: University of Georgia Press, 1940.

Guinn, Jeff. *Our Land before We Die: The Proud Story of the Seminole Negro*. New York: J. P. Tarcher/Putnam, 2002.

———. "Seminole Negro Heritage Fading in Border Town." *San Antonio Express News*. 18 September 1994, 1D.

Guthrie, Patricia. *Catching Sense: African American Communities on a South Carolina Sea Island.* Westport, Conn.: Bergin and Garvey, 1996.

Gutierrez-Mier, John. "Freedom to the South." *San Antonio Express News,* 18 June 2000, 5b.

Gutman, Herbert G. *The Black Family in Slavery and Freedom, 1750–1925.* New York: Vintage Books, 1976.

Haenn, William F. *Images of America, Fort Clark and Brackettville: Land of Heroes.* Chicago: Arcadia Publishing, 2002.

Hall, Robert L. "African Religious Retentions in Florida." In *Africanisms in American Culture,* edited by Joseph E. Holloway, 224–48. Bloomington: Indiana University Press, 1990.

———. "African Religious Retentions in Florida." In *The African American Heritage of Florida,* edited by David. R. Colburn and Jane L. Landers. Gainesville: University Press of Florida, 1995.

Halliburton, R., Jr. "Black Slave Control in the Cherokee Nation." *Journal of Ethnic Studies* 3 (Summer 1975): 23–35.

Hancock, Ian. "On the Classification of Afro-Seminole Creole." In *Language Variety in the South: Perspectives in Black and White,* edited by Michael Montgomery and Guy Bailey, 85–101. Montgomery: University of Alabama Press, 1986.

———."Texas Gullah: The Creole English of the Brackettville Afro-Seminoles." In *Perspectives on American English,* edited by Joseph L. Dillard, 305–33. Mouton: The Hague, 1980.

———. *The Texas Seminoles and Their Language.* Austin: University of Texas African and Afro-american Studies and Research Center, 1980.

Handbook of Texas Online, 2006., s.v. "Biloxi Indians." http://www.tsha.utexas.edu/handbook/online/articles/BB/bmb8.html.

Handler, Jerome S., and JoAnn Jacoby. "Slave Names and Naming in Barbados, 1650–1830." *William and Mary Quarterly* 53, no. 4 (October 1996): 685–728.

Hart, Edward Brantley, Jr. "Gullah Spirituals in Prayer Meetings on John's Island, South Carolina." D.M.A. diss., University of South Carolina, 1992.

Hawkins, Benjamin. *Letters of Benjamin Hawkins, 1796–1806.* Spartenburg, S.C.: The Reprint Co., 1947.

Haynes, Lillith. "Candid Chimaera: Texas Seminole." In *Southwest Areal Linguistics Then and Now: Proceedings of the Fifth Southwest Areal Language and Linguistic Workshop,* edited by Bates L. Hoffer and Betty Lou Dubois, 280–300. San Antonio, Texas: Trinity University, 1976.

Hazzard-Gordon, Katrina. *Jookin': The Rise of Social Dance Formations in African-American Culture.* Philadelphia: Temple University Press, 1990.

Helms, Mary W. "Matrilocality and the Maintenance of Ethnic Identity: The Moskito of Eastern Nicaragua and Honduras." *International Congress of Americanists* 38 (1968): 459–64.

Hernandez, Lolita. "Quiet Battles." In *Abandon Automobiles: Detroit City Poetry 2001*, edited by Melba Joyce Boyd and M. L. Liebler. Detroit: Wayne State University Press, 2001.

Herskovits, Melville J. *The Myth of the Negro Past*. New York: Beacon Press, 1958 (1941).

———. "The Negro in the New World: The Statement of a Problem." *American Anthropologist* 32, no. 1 (January–March 1930): 145–55.

Hillman, Eugene. *Polygamy Reconsidered: African Plural Marriage and the Christian Churches*. New York: Orbis Books, 1975.

Hitchcock, Ethan Allen. *A Traveler in Indian Territory: The Journal of Ethan Allen Hitchcock*. Edited by Grant Foreman. Norman: University of Oklahoma Press, 1996 (1930).

———. *Fifty Years in Camp and Field: Diary of Major-General Ethan Hitchcock*. Edited by William A. Croffut. New York: Putnam, 1909.

Holloway, Joseph E. "Africanisms in Gullah Oral Tradition." *Western Journal of Black Studies* 13, no. 3 (Fall 1989): 115–24.

———. "The Origins of African-American Culture." In *Africanisms in American Culture*, edited by Joseph E. Holloway, 1–18. Bloomington: Indiana University Press, 1990.

———. "The Sacred World of the Gullahs." In *Africanisms in American Culture*, edited by Joseph E. Holloway, 187–223. Bloomington: Indiana University Press, 1990.

Howard, James H. *Oklahoma Seminoles: Medicines, Magic, and Religion*. In collaboration with Willie Lena. Norman: University of Oklahoma Press, 1984.

Howard, James H., and Victoria Lindsay Levine. *Choctaw Music and Dance*. Forward by Bruno Nettle. Norman: University of Oklahoma Press, 1990.

Howard, Rosalyn. *Black Seminoles in the Bahamas*. Gainesville: University of Florida Press, 2002.

———. "The Promised Land: Reconstructing History and Identity among the Black Seminoles of Andros Island." PhD diss., University of Florida, 1991.

———. "The 'Wild Indians' of Andros Island: Black Seminole Legacy in the Bahamas." *Journal of Black Studies* 37, no. 2 (2006): 278–79.

Hoxie, Frederick E., ed. *Encyclopedia of North American Indians: Native American History, Culture, and Life from Paleo-Indians to the Present*. New York: Houghton Mifflin, 1996.

Hudson, Arthur P. "Some Curious Negro Names." *Southern Folklore Quarterly* 2 (December 1938): 179–93.

Hudson, Charles. *The Southeastern Indians*. Knoxville: University of Tennessee Press, 1976.

Hurston, Zora Neale. *Mules and Men*. New York: Harper Collins, 1935.

———. *The Complete Stories*. New York: Harper Perennial, 1995.

———. *Their Eyes Were Watching God*. New York: Harper Collins, 1999 (1937).

Inscoe, John C. "Carolina Slave Names: An Index to Acculturation." *Journal of Southern History* 49, no. 4 (November 1983): 527–54.

Jacoway, Elizabeth. *Yankeee Missionaries in the South: The Penn School Experiment*. Baton Rouge: Louisiana State University Press, 1980.

Johnston, James H. "Documentary Evidence of the Relations of Negroes and Indians." *Journal of Negro History* 14, no. 1 (January 1929): 21–43.

Jones, H. Conger. "Seminole Scouts, Old Enemy of Indians, Still Thrive on Border." In *La Hacienda*, edited by Rosemary W. Jones. Del Rio, Texas.

Jones-Jackson, Patricia. "Contemporary Gullah Speech: Some Persistent Linguistic Features." *Journal of Black Studies* 13, no. 3 (March 1983): 289–203.

———. "Gullah: On the Question of Afro-American Language."*Anthropological Linguistics* 20, no. 9 (December 1978): 422–28.

———. "Let the Church Say 'Amen': The Language of Religious Rituals in Coastal Carolina." In *The Crucible of Carolina*, edited by Michael Montgomery, 115–32. Athens: University of Georgia Press, 1994.

———. "On Decreolization and Language Death in Gullah." *Language in Society* 13, no. 3 (September 1984): 351–62.

Jordan, Barbara, and Shelby Hearon. *Barbara Jordan: A Self-Portrait*. Garden City: Doubleday, 1979.

Joyce, Rosemary. *Gender and Power in Mesoamerica*. Austin: University of Texas Press, 2000.

Joyner, Charles. *Down by the Riverside: A South Carolina Slave Community*. Urbana: University of Illinois Press, 1986.

———. "Introduction." In *Drums and Shadows: Survival Studies among the Georgia Coastal Negroes*. Georgia Writers' Project, WPA. Athens: University of Georgia Press, 1984.

Kashif, Annette I. "Africanisms upon the Land: A Study of African Influenced Place Names in the USA." Paper presented at "Places of Cultural Memory: African Reflections on the American Landscape" Conference, National Park Service, Atlanta, Ga., May 9–12, 2001. http://www.nps.gov/history/crdi/conferences/AFR_15-34_Kashif.pdf.

Katz, William Loren. *Black Indians: A Hidden Heritage*. New York: Athenaeum, 1986.

———. *History's Missing Chapter: Black Indians. American Legacy*. New York: Peabody Museum, 1997.

———. "Lucy Gonzales Parsons." Lucy Parson's address to founding convention of Industrial Workers of the World, Chicago, 1905. Reprinted in *The Black World Today*, June 29, 2005.

Kelley, Sean. "Mexico in His Head: Slavery and the Texas-Mexico Border, 1810–1860." *Journal of Social History* 37, no. 3 (Spring 2004): 709–23.

Kerrigan, William T. "Race, Expansion, and Slavery in Eagle Pass, 1852." *Southwestern Historical Quarterly* 101, no. 3 (January 1998): 275–301.

Kinsall, Al. "Catholic Religion: Coahuila and Catholicism." The Cherokee Nation of Mexico, 2000. http://www.cherokeediscovery.com/rel_catholic.html.

Klein, Laura E., and Lillian A. Ackerman. *Women and Power in Native North America.* Norman: University of Oklahoma Press, 1995.

Klos, George. "Blacks and the Seminole Removal Debate, 1821–1835." In *The African American Heritage of Florida,* edited by David R. Colburn and Jane L. Landers, 128–56. Gainesville: University Press of Florida, 1995.

Kopytoff, Igor. "Ancestors as Elders in Africa." Available online from The Centre for Social Anthropology and Computing, University of Kent at Canterbury. http://lucy.ukc.ac.uk/ERA/Ancestors/kopytoff.html.

La Barre, Weston. *The Peyote Cult.* Norman: University of Oklahoma Press, 1989.

Landers, Jane L. "African and African American Women and Their Pursuit of Rights through Eighteenth-Century Spanish Texts." In *Haunted Bodies: Gender and Southern Texts,* edited by Anne Goodwyn Jones and Susan V. Donaldson, 56–76. Charlottesville: University of Virginia Press, 1998.

———. "A Nation Divided: Free Blacks and Indians on the Florida Frontier." In *Coastal Encounters: Confrontations, Accommodations, and Transformations in the Eighteenth-Century Gulf South,* edited by Richmond E. Brown, 99–116. Omaha: University of Nebraska Press, 2007.

———. Black Community and Culture in the Southeastern Borderlands. *Journal of the Early Republic* 18, no. 1 (Spring 1998): 117–34.

———. *Black Society in Spanish Florida.* Urbana: University of Illinois Press, 1999.

———. "Slave Resistance on the Southeastern Frontier: Fugitives, Maroons, and Bands in the Age of Revolutions." *El Escribiano* 32 (1995): 12–49.

———. "Traditions of African-American Freedom and Community in Spanish Colonial Florida." In *The African American Heritage of Florida,* edited by David R. Colburn and Jane L. Landers. Gainesville: University Press of Florida, 1995.

Landers, Jane M., and Kathleen A. Deagan. "Black Society in Spanish Florida. Fort Mose: Earliest Free African-American Town in the United States." In *I Too, Am America: Archaeological Studies of African-American Life,* edited by Theresa A. Singleton, 261–82. Charlottesville: University of Virginia Press, 1999.

Latorre, Dolores L. *Cooking and Curing with Mexican Herbs.* Austin: Encino Press, 1977.

Latorre, Felipe A., and Dolores L. Latorre. *The Mexican Kickapoo Indians.* Texas Pan American Series. Austin: University of Texas Press, 1976.

La Vere, David. *Life among the Texas Indians: The WPA Narratives.* College Station: Texas A&M Press, 1998.

Lawton, Samuel. "Religious Life of Coastal and Sea Island Negroes." PhD diss., George Peabody College for Teachers, 1938.

Lemert, Ben F. "Parras Basin, Southern Coahuila, Mexico." *Economic Geography* 25, no. 2 (April 1949): 94–112.

Lerner, Gerda. "The Future of Our Past." Interview by Catherine R. Stimpson. *Ms.* 1 September 1981: 94–95.

Lévi-Strauss, Claude. *The Savage Mind.* Chicago: University of Chicago Press, 1966.

Lincecum, Jerry Bryan, and Edward Hake Phillips. *Adventures of a Frontier Naturalist: The Life and Times of Dr. Gideon Lincecum.* College Station: Texas A&M University Press, 1994.

Littlefield, Daniel F. *Africans and Creeks: From the Colonial Period to the Civil War.* Westport, Conn.: Greenwood Press, 1979.

———. *Africans and Seminoles: From Removal to Emancipation.* Westport, Conn.: Greenwood Press, 1977.

Littlefield, Daniel F., and Lonnie E. Underhill. "Slave 'Revolt' in the Cherokee Nation, 1842." *American Indian Quarterly* 3, no. 2 (Summer 1977): 121–31.

Long, Charles H. "Perspectives for a Study of African-American Religion." In *African-American Religion,* edited by Timothy E. Fulop and Albert J. Raboteau, 21–36. New York: Routledge, 1995.

"Los Vázquez genealogy." In Archivo de Dr. José Guadalupe López. Colegio de Investigaciones Históricas de Múzquiz.

MacCauley, Clay. "The Seminole Indians of Florida." *Fifth Annual Report of the Bureau of Ethnology, Smithsonian,* 475–93. Washington, D.C.: Government Printing Office, 1887.

Mahon, John K. *History of the Second Seminole War, 1835–1842.* Gainesville: University of Florida Press, 1967.

Marks, Morton. "You Can't Sing Unless You're Saved: Reliving the Call in Gospel Music." In *African Religious Groups and Beliefs: Papers in Honor of William R. Bascom,* edited by Simon Ottenberg. Berkeley: The Folklore Institute, 1982.

Mason, Julian. "The Etymology of 'Buckaroo'." *American Speech* 35, no. 1 (February 1960): 51–55.

May, Katja. *African Americans and Native Americans in the Creek and Cherokee Nations, 1830s to 1920s: Collision and Collusion.* New York: Garland Publishing, 1996.

McCall, George. *Letters from the Frontiers.* Philadelphia: J. B. Lippincott & Co., 1868.

McClaurin, Irma. *Women of Belize: Gender and Change in Central America.* New Jersey: Rutgers University Press, 2000.

McGraw, A. Joachim, John W. Clark, Jr., and Elizabeth A. Robbins, eds. *A Texas Legacy: The Old San Antonio Road and the Caminos Reales.* Austin: Texas State Department of Highways and Public Transportation, 1991.

McKellar, Margaret (Maud). *Life on a Mexican Ranch.* Edited by Dolores Latorre. Bethlehem, Penn.: Lehigh University Press, 1994.

McLoughlin, William G. *Cherokees and Missionaries 1789–1839.* Norman: University of Oklahoma Press, 1995 (1984).

———. "Red Indians, Black Slavery, and White Racism: America's Slaveholding Indians." *American Quarterly* 26, no. 4 (October 1974): 367–85.

McReynolds, Edwin C. *The Seminoles.* Norman: University of Oklahoma Press, 1957.

Meisenhelder, Susan. "Conflict and Resistance in Zora Neale Hurston's 'Mules and Men.'" *Journal of American Folklore* 109, no. 433 (Summer 1996): 267–88.

Micco, Melinda. "Seminole Freedmen and the Forging of the Seminole Nation." PhD diss., University of California, 1995.

Miethaner, Ulrich. "Orthographic Transcriptions of Non-Standard Varieties: The Case of Earlier African-American English." *Journal of Sociolinguistics* 44, no. 4 (November 2000): 534–60.

Milanich, Jerald. *Florida Indians and the Invasion from Europe*. Gainesville: University Press of Florida, 1995.

———. *Florida's Indians from Ancient Times to the Present*. Gainesville: University Press of Florida, 1998.

———. *Laboring in the Fields of the Lord: Spanish Missions and the Southeastern Indians*. Gainesville: University Press of Florida, 2006.

Milanich, Jerald T., and Charles H. Fairbanks. *Florida Archaeology*. Orlando, Fla.: Academic Press, 1980.

Miles, Tiya. *Ties That Bind: The Story of an Afro-Cherokee Family in Slavery and Freedom*. American Crossroads Series. Berkeley: University of California Press, 2005.

Mille, Katherine, and Michael Montgomery. "Introduction." In *Africanisms in the Gullah Dialect*, by Lorenzo Dow Turner, xix. Columbia: University of South Carolina Press, 2002.

Miller, Susan Allison. *Coacoochee's Bones: A Seminole Saga*. Lawrence: University Press of Kansas, 2003.

———. "Seminoles and Africans under Seminole Law: Sources and Discourses of Tribal Sovereignty and 'Black Indian' Entitlement." *Wicazo Sa Review* 20, no. 1 (Spring 2005): 23–47.

———. "Wild Cat's Bones: Seminole Leadership in a Seminole Cosmos." PhD diss., University of Nebraska, 1997. Microfilm edition, 973462.

Minges, Patrick. "All my Slaves, whether Negroes, Indians, Mustees, or Molattoes: Towards a Thick Description of 'Slave Religion.'" *The American Religious Experience*, 1999, 1–16. http://are.as.wvu.edu/minges.htm.

———. "Beneath the Underdog: Race, Religion and the 'Trail of Tears.'" *American Indian Quarterly* 25, no. 3 (2001): 453–79.

Mintz, Sidney W., and Christine M. Du Bois. "The Anthropology of Food and Eating." *Annual Review of Anthropology* 31 (2002): 99–119.

Mintz, Sidney W., and Richard Price. *The Birth of African-American Culture: An Anthropological Perspective*. Boston: Beacon Press, 1992.

———. "The Birth of African-American Culture." In *African American Religion*, edited by Timothy E. Fulop and Albert Raboteau, 37–56. New York: Routledge, 1997.

Mock, Shirley Boteler. "San Antonio, Texas. 1990–1940: A Period of Mutual Aid." In *Archaeology at the Alamo Dome: Investigations of a San Antonio Neighborhood in Transition*, edited by Anne A. Fox, Marcie Renner, and Robert J. Hard, 1:84–113. San Antonio, Texas: Center for Archaeological Research, the University of Texas at San Antonio Archaeological Survey Report 236.

———. "Singing to the Ancestors: Revitalization Attempts among the Black Seminoles in Mexico and Southern Texas." Paper on file at Institute of Texan Cultures, University of Texas at San Antonio, 1992.

Mock, Shirley Boteler, and Alice Fay Lozano. "The Dream Readers: A Ritual Complex." Paper on file at Institute of Texan Cultures, University of Texas at San Antonio, 1996.

———. "The Dream Readers: Black Seminole Women in Texas and Mexico." Paper on file at the Institute of Texan Cultures, University of Texas at San Antonio, 1998.

Mock, Shirley Boteler, and Michael Davis. "Black Seminole Culture on the Texas Frontier." *Cultural Resource Management* 20, no. 2 (1997): 8–10.

Montgomery, Cora. *Eagle Pass; or, Life on the Border*. New York: Putnam's Semi Monthly Library for Travelers and the Fireside, 1852.

Montgomery, Michael, ed. *The Crucible of Carolina: Essays in the Development of Gullah Language and Culture*. Athens: University of Georgia Press, 1994.

Moore, Janie Gilliard. "Africanisms among Blacks of the Sea Islands." *Journal of Black Studies* 10, no. 4 (June 1980): 467–80.

Morrison, Toni. "Nobel Lecture," December 7, 1993. In *Nobel Lectures, Literature 1991–1995*, edited by Sture Allén. Singapore: World Scientific Publishing Co., 1997.

Mullin, Michael. *Africa in America: Slave Acculturation and Resistance in the American South and the British Caribbean, 1736–1831*. Urbana: University of Illinois Press, 1992.

Mulroy, Kevin. "Ethnogenesis and Ethnohistory of the Seminole Maroons." *Journal of World History* 4, no. 2 (Fall 1993): 287–305.

———. *Freedom on the Border: The Seminole Maroons in Florida, the Indian Territory, Coahuila and Texas*. Lubbock: Texas Tech University Press, 1993.

———. "Seminole Maroons." In *Handbook of North American Indians Southeast*, 465–77. Washington, D.C.: Smithsonian Press, 2004.

———. *The Seminole Freedmen: A History*. Norman: University of Oklahoma Press, 2007.

Nash, Roy. "Survey of the Seminole Indians of Florida." In *A Seminole Source Book*, edited by William C. Sturtevant, 3–49. New York: Garland Publishing, 1987 (1931).

National Commission on the Observance of International Women's Year. "Speech by Honorable Margaret Mead, fourth Plenary Session," in *The Spirit of Houston: The First National Women's Conference*, doc. 62. Washington, D.C.: U.S. Government Printing Office, 1978.

Needham, Rodney. "Polythetic Classification: Convergence and Consequences." *Man*, New Series 10, no. 3 (1975): 349–69.

Nelson, Hart M., Raytha L. Yokley, and Anne K. Nelson. *The Black Church in America*. New York: Basic Books, Inc., 1971.

Neumann, Thomas W. "A Biocultural Approach to Salt Taboos." *Current Anthropology* 18, no. 2 (June 1977): 289–308.

Nichols, Patricia. "Linguistic Options and Choices for Black Women in Rural Areas." In *Language, Gender and Society*, edited by Barrie Thorne, Chris Kramarae, and Nancy Henley. Cambridge, Mass.: Newberry House, 1983.

Olmsted, Frederick Law. *A Journey in the Seaboard Slave States*. New York: Burt Franklin, 1969 (1856).

———. *Journey through Texas: Saddle-Trip on the Southwestern Frontier with a Statistical Appendix*. Austin: University of Texas Press, 1978.

Opala, Joseph A. *A Brief History of the Seminole Freedmen*. Austin: University of Texas African and Afro-American Studies and Research Center, 1980.

———. "Seminole-African Relations on the Florida Frontier." *Papers in Anthropology* 22, no. 1 (University of Oklahoma, 1981): 11–52.

———. *The Gullah: Rice, Slavery, and the Sierra Leone-American Connection*. Freetown, Sierra Leone: United States Information Service, 1986.

Ottenberg, Simon, ed. *African Religious Groups and Beliefs: Papers in Honor of William R. Bascom*. Berkeley: The Folklore Institute, 1982.

Paige, Amanda L., Fuller L. Bumpers, and Daniel F. Littlefield. "Historical Documentation of Indian Removal through the North Little Rock Site." The North Little Rock Site on the Trail of Tears National Historic Trail: Historical Contexts Report, Part IV, 2003. http://www.anpa.ualr.edu/trail_of_tears/indian_removal_project/site_reports/north_little_rock/northlittlerock_report.htm.

Parker, Susan. "The Cattle Trade in East Florida, 1784–1821." In *Colonial Plantations and Economy in Florida*, edited by Jane Landers, 119–209. Gainesville: University Press of Florida, 2003.

Parker, W. B. *Letters from an Early Settler of Texas; Notes Taken During the Expedition Commanded by Capt. R. B. Marcy, U.S.A., through Unexplored Texas, in the Summer and Fall of 1854*. Philadelphia: Hayes and Zell, 1856.

———. *Notes Taken During the Expedition: Thirty Years of Army Life on the Border*. Philadelphia: Hayes and Zell, 1984 (1856).

Parsons, Lucy. Address to founding convention of Industrial Workers of the World, Chicago, 1905. Reprinted in William Loren Katz, "Lucy Gonzales Parsons," *Black World Today*, June 29, 2005.

Pearson, Elizabeth W. *Letters from Port Royal, 1862–1868*. New York: Arno Press, 1969 (1906).

Perdue, Theda. *Cherokee Women: Gender and Culture Change, 1700–1835*. Lincoln: University of Nebraska Press, 1998.

———. *Slavery and the Evolution of Cherokee Society 1540–1866*. Knoxville: University of Tennessee Press, 1979.

Pingenot, Ben E. *Paso de Aguila: A Chronicle of Frontier Days on the Texas Border as Recorded in the Memoires of Jesse Sumpter*. Austin, Texas: Encino Press, 1969.

Pinn, Anthony B. *The African-American Religious Experience in America*. Westport, Conn.: Greenwood Press, 2005.

Pitts, Walter F. *Old Ship of Zion: The Afro-Baptist Ritual in the African Diaspora*. New York: Oxford University Press, 1996.

Pollan, Allison. "Ahead of Her Time." *Kerrville Daily Times* 4 (February 1989): 288.

Pollitzer, William S. *The Gullah People and Their African Heritage*. Athens: University of Georgia Press, 1999.

Porter, Kenneth Wiggins. "A Farewell to John Horse: An Episode of Seminole Negro Folk History." *Phylon Quarterly* 8, no. 3 (Third Quarter, 1947): 265–73.

———. "A Legend of the Biloxi." *Journal of American Folklore* 59, no. 232 (April–June 1946): 168–73.

———. "Billy Bowlegs (Holata Micco) in the Seminole Wars." *Florida Historical Quarterly* 45: 210–43.

———. *Negroes and Indians within the Present United States.* Washington, D.C.: The Association for Negro Life and History, 1931.

———. "Negroes and the Seminole War, 1835–1842." *Journal of Southern History* 30, no. 4 (November 1964): 427–50.

———. "Negroes on the Southern Frontier, 1670–1763." *Journal of Negro History* 33, no. 1 (January 1948): 53–78.

———. "Notes Supplementary to Relations between Negroes and Indians." *The Journal of Negro History* 18, no. 3 (July 1933): 282–321.

———. "Relations between Negroes and Indians within the Present Limits of the United States." *Journal of Negro History* 17, no. 3 (July 1932): 287–367.

———. *The Black Seminoles: History of a Freedom Seeking People.* Edited by Alcione M. Amos and Thomas P. Senter. Gainesville: University Press of Florida, 1996.

———. "The Episode of Osceola's Wife: Fact or Fiction?" *Florida Historical Quarterly* 26, no. 1 (July 1947): 92–98.

———. "The Hawkins' Negroes Go to Mexico." *Chronicles of Oklahoma* XXIV, no. 1: 55–58.

———. "The Negro Abraham." *Florida Historical Quarterly* 25, no. 1 (July 1946): 1–43.

———. *The Negro on the American Frontier*. New York: Arno Press, 1971.

———. "The Seminole in Mexico, 1850–1861." *Hispanic Historical Review* XXXI, no. 1 (February 1951): 13–35.

———. "The Seminole Negro-Indian Scouts 1870–1881." *Southwestern Historical Quarterly* LV, no. 3 (January 1952): 359–76.

———. "Willie Kelley of the Lost Nigger Mine." *Western Folklore* XIII, no. 1 (January 1954): 13–26.

Price, Richard. *Maroon Societies: Rebel Slave Communities in the Americas.* Baltimore: Johns Hopkins University Press, 1996 (1979).

Puckett, Niles N. *Folk Beliefs of the Southern Negro.* Chapel Hill: University of North Carolina Press, 1926.

Quinlan, Robert J. "Gender and Risk in a Matrifocal Caribbean Community." *American Anthropologist* 108, no. 3 (September 2006): 464–79.

Raboteau, Albert J. *Canaan Land: A Religious History of African Americans.* New York: Oxford University Press, 2001.

———. *Slave Religion, the Invisible Institution in the Antebellum South.* Westport, Conn.: Greenwood Press, 1978.

———. "The Black Experience in African-American Religion." In *African American Religion: Interpretive Essays in History and Culture,* edited by Timothy E. Fulop and Albert Raboteau, 89–106. London: Routledge, 1997.

Ralph, Ronald W. "Seminole-Negro Colonia Nacimiento," 1969. Paper on file at the Institute of Texan Cultures, University of Texas at San Antonio.

Rawick, George P. *From Sundown to Sunup: The Making of the Black Community*. Westport, Conn.: Greenwood Press, 1972.

———, ed. *The American Slave: A Composite Autobiography*. Westport, Conn.: Greenwood, 1969.

Reese, Linda W. "Cherokee Freedwomen in Indian Territory, 1863–1890." *Western Historical Quarterly* 33, no. 3 (Autumn 2002): 273–96.

———. *Women of Oklahoma, 1890–1920*. Norman: University of Oklahoma Press, 1997.

Rippy, J. Fred. "Border Troubles along the Rio Grande 1848–1860." *Southwestern Historical Quarterly* 23, no. 2 (1919): 91–111.

Ritzenthaler, Robert E., and Frederick A. Peterson. *The Mexican Kickapoo Indians*. Milwaukee, Wis.: North American Press and Alltone Photo-engravers, 1956.

Rivers, Larry Eugene. *Slavery in Florida*. Gainesville: University Press of Florida, 2000.

Rodgers, B. Ann, and Linda Schott. "My Mother was a Mover: African American Seminole Women in Brackettville, Texas, 1914–1964." In *Writing the Range: Race, Class, and Culture in the Women's West*, edited by Elizabeth Jameson and Susan Armitage, 585–600. Norman: University of Oklahoma Press, 1997.

Rout, Leslie B., Jr. *The African Experience in Spanish America*. Cambridge: Cambridge University Press, 1976.

Russell, Rachel. *Letters*, ca. 1793.

Sattler, Richard A. "Remnants, Renegades, and Runaways: Seminole Ethnogenesis Reconsidered." In *History, Power, and Identity: Ethnogenesis in the Americas, 1492–1992*, edited by Jonathan D. Hill. Iowa City: University of Iowa Press, 1996.

Saunt, Claudio. *Black, White, and Indian: Race and the Unmaking of an American Family*. New York: Oxford University Press, 2005.

Schwartz, Rosalie. *Across the Rio to Freedom: U.S. Negroes in Mexico*. El Paso: Texas Western Press, 1975.

———. "Negroes: Mexico as an Alternative for United States Blacks (1825–1860)." Master's thesis, on file at California State University–San Diego, 1974.

Shanks, Michael. *Photography and the Archaeological Image. The Culture of Images: Representation in Archaeology*. Edited by B. Molyneaux. London: Routledge, 1997.

Sharp, Henry S. "Women and Men among the Chipewyan." In *Women and Power in Native North America*, edited by Laura E. Klein and Lillian A. Ackerman, 46–74. Norman: University of Oklahoma Press, 1995.

Simmons, William H. *Notices of East Florida: With an Account of the Seminole Nation of Indians*. Introduction by George E. Buker. Gainesville: University Press of Florida, 1973 (1822).

Singleton, Theresa. "Cultural Interaction and African American Identity in Plantation Archaeology." In *Studies in Culture Contact: Interaction, Culture Change, and Archaeology*, edited by J. Cusick, 172–88. Carbondale, Ill.: Center for Archaeological Investigations, 1998.

———. "The Archaeology of Slavery in North America." *Annual Review of Anthropology* 24 (October 1995): 119–40.

Sivad, Doug. *The Black Seminole Indians of Texas*. Austin, Texas: Publisher's Marketing House, 1986.

Skiles, Jack. *Judge Roy Bean Country*. Lubbock: Texas Tech University Press, 2007.

Small, John K. "Seminole Bread—The Coonti." *Journal of the New York Botanical Garden* 22 (1921): 121–37.

Smith, Cassandra. "Warrior Still." *Capital Outlook* 23, no. 9 (February 26–March 4, 1998): 1–14.

Smith, Hale. "The Ethnological and Archeological Significance of Zamia." *American Anthropologist* 53, no. 2 (April–June 1951): 238.

Smith, Theophus H. *Conjuring Culture: Biblical Formations of Black Culture*. New York: Oxford University Press, 1994.

Southhall, Eugene P. "Negroes in Florida Prior to the Civil War." *Journal of Negro History* XIX, no. 1 (January 1934): 78–79.

Sprague, John T. *The Origin, Progress, and Conclusion of the Florida War*. New York: D. Appleton, 1848.

Spindle, Samuel Jerome. "Diary of Samuel Spindle's travels through Mexico," 1861. Diary in private collection and on file with author.

Sterling, Stuckey. *Slave Culture*. New York: Oxford University Press, 1987.

Sturtevant, William C. *A Seminole Source Book*. Edited with an introduction by William C. Sturtevant. New York: Garland, 1987.

———. "Creek into Seminole." In *North American Indians in Historical Perspective*, edited by Eleanor B. Leacock and Nancy O. Lurie, 92–128. New York: Random House, 1971.

———. "Seminole Myths of the Origins of Races." *Ethnohistory* 10, no. 1 (Winter 1963): 80–86.

Sunderman, James F. "Army Surgeon Reports on Lower East Coast, 1838." *Tequesta* X (1950): 25–34.

Swanson, Don A. *Enlistment Records of Indian Scouts Who Served in One of the Scout Detachments at Fort Clark, Texas*. Bronte, Texas: Ames-American Printing, 1985.

———. "Fort Clark, Texas. A Bootstrap on the Nueces Strip to Headquarters of the Military District Nueces." Unpublished manuscript, on file at the Fort Clark Museum, 1985.

Swanton, John R. *Creek Religion and Medicine*. Introduction by James T. Carson. Lincoln: University of Nebraska Press, 2000 (1928).

———. "Early History of the Creek Indians and Their Neighbors." *Bureau of American Ethnology Bulletin 73*. Washington D.C.: Government Printing Office, 1922.

———. "The Indians of the Southeastern United States." *Bureau of American Ethnology Bulletin 137*. Washington, D.C.: Government Printing Office, 1979 (1946).

Tanner, Nancy. "Matrifocality in Indonesia and Africa and among Black Americans." In *Women, Culture, and Society*, edited by M. A. Rosaldo and L. Lamphere, 129–56. Palo Alto, Calif.: Stanford University Press, 1974.

Taube, Karl. "The Teotihuacan Spider Woman." *Journal of Latin American Lore* 9, no. 2: 107–89.

Thoburn, Joseph B. "The Naming of the Canadian River." *Chronicles of Oklahoma* 6, no. 2 (June 1928).

Thompson, Mary Louise. "The Black Watch of Texas." In *Kinney County, 1852–1977,* 22–24. Kinney County Historical Commission, 1976–77.

Thompson, Robert Farris. *Flash of the Spirit: African and Afro American Art and Philosophy.* New York: Random House, 1983 (1965).

Thornton, John. "Central African Names and African-American Naming Patterns." *Williams and Mary Quarterly* 50, no. 4 (October 1993): 727–42.

Thybony, Scott. "Against All Odds, Black Seminoles Won Their Freedom." *Smithsonian* 22, no. 5: 90–101.

Tilley, Christopher. *A Phenomenology of Landscape: Places, Paths and Monuments.* Oxford: Berg, 1994.

Towne, Laura M. "Pioneer Work on the Sea Islands." *Southern Workman* 30 (July 1901): 137–50.

Turner, Edith. "Preface," in *Images and Pilgrimage in Christian Culture,* paperback edition. New York: Columbia University Press, 1992 (1978).

Turner, Lorenzo D. *Africanisms in the Gullah Dialect.* Ann Arbor: University of Michigan Press, 1973 (1949).

Turner, Sugar, and Tracy Bachrach Ehlers. *Sugar's Life in the Hood.* Austin: University of Texas Press, 2000.

Turner, Victor, and Edith Turner. *Images and Pilgrimage in Christian Culture.* New York: Columbia University Press, 1992.

Twining, Mary A. "An Examination of African Retentions in the Folk Culture of the South Carolina and Georgia Sea Islands." PhD diss., Indiana University, 1977.

Twining, Mary A., and Keith E. Baird. *Sea Island Roots: African Presence in the Carolinas and Georgia.* Trenton, N.J.: African World Press, 1991.

Twyman, Bruce Edward. *The Black Seminole Legacy and North American Politics 1693–1845.* Washington, D.C.: Howard University Press, 1999.

Tyler, Ronnie C. "Fugitive Slaves in Mexico." *Journal of Negro History* 57, no. 1 (January 1972): 1–12.

Tyler, Ronnie C., and Lawrence R. Murphy. *The Slave Narratives of Texas.* Austin, Texas: State House Press, 1997.

Urrea, José. "Diary of the Military Operations of the Division which under the Command of General José Urrea Campaigned in Texas February to March 1836." Translated by Carlos E. Castañeda. In *The Mexican Side of the Texas Revolution, by the Chief Mexican Participants.* Dallas: P. L. Turner Co., 1928 (1838).

Vann, Lucinda. "Cherokee Freedwoman." In *The WPA Oklahoma Slave Narratives,* edited by T. Lindsay Baker and Julie P. Baker. Norman: University of Oklahoma Press, 2005 (1996).

Vlach, John Michael. *The Afro-American Tradition in Decorative Arts.* Athens: University of Georgia Press, 1978.

Walker, Alice. "The Unglamorous but Worthwhile Duties of the Black Revolutionary Artist, or of the Black Writer Who Simply Works and Writes." In *In Search of Our Mothers' Gardens: Womanist Prose,* 130. New York: Harcourt Brace, 1988.

Ware, Elizabeth, ed. *Letters from Port Royal Written at the Time of the Civil War 1862–1868*. New York: Arno Press, 1906.

Warrior, William. "Warren Perryman." http://www.coax.net/people/lwf/sem_wp.htm (March 14, 2000).

Washington, Joseph R. *Black Sects and Cults*. Garden City, N.Y.: Doubleday, 1972.

Watkins, June. "Strategies of Social Control in an Isolated Community: The Case of the Gullah of South Carolina's St. Helena Island." PhD diss., University of Pennsylvania, 1993.

Weik, Terrance. "Archaeology of the African Diaspora in Latin America." In "Transcending Boundaries, Transforming the Discipline: African Diaspora Archaeologies in the New Millennium," edited by Maria Franklin and Larry McKee. Special issue, *Historical Archaeology* 38(1) (2004): 32–49.

———. "Florida Researchers Launch First Excavation of Black Seminole Town." University of Florida News. 14 June 2001. Available online at http://news.ufl.edu/2001/06/14/black-seminole/.

———. "The Role of Ethnogenesis and Organization in the Development of African-Native American Settlements." *International Journal of Historical Archaeology* 13, no. 2 (June 2009): 206–38.

Weisman, Brent R. "Archaeological Perspectives on Florida Seminole's Ethnogenesis." In *Indians of the Greater Southeast, Historical Archaeology and Ethnohistory,* edited by Bonnie McEwan, 299–320. Gainesville: University Press of Florida, 2001.

———. *Like Beads on a String. A Culture History of the Seminole Indians in North Peninsular Florida*. Tuscaloosa: University of Alabama Press, 1989.

———. "The Plantation System of the Florida Seminole Indians and the Black Seminoles during the Colonial Era." In *Colonial Plantations & Economy,* edited by Jane Landers, 134–47. Gainesville: University Press of Florida, 2000.

———. *Unconquered People: Florida's Seminole and Miccosukee Indians*. Gainesville: University of Florida Press, 1999.

Willett, John. *Document Regarding Hacienda Nacimiento*. 17 June 1895, San Antonio, Texas.

Williams, Edwin L., Jr. "Negro Slavery in Florida." *Florida Historical Quarterly* XXVIII (October 1949): 93–110.

Williamson, Mary Hall. "Farewell!" In funeral program for Nancy Williams, sister of Ophelia Benson. 20 September 1998.

Willis, William. "Anthropology and Negroes on the Southern Colonial Frontier." In *The Black Experience in America,* edited by James C. Curtis and Lewis L. Gould, 47–48. Austin: University of Texas Press, 1970.

Wilson, Charles Emily. "Texas Seminole Scouts." In 1992 Festival of American Folklife program, edited by Peter Seitel, 80.

Wolfe, Michael. *The Abundant Life Prevails: Religious Traditions of Saint Helena Island.* Waco, Texas: Baylor University Press, 2000.

Wood, Peter H. *Black Majority: Negroes in Colonial South Carolina from 1670 through the Stono Rebellion.* New York: W.W. Norton and Co., 1996 (1974).

Woodhull, Frost. "The Seminole Indian Scouts on the Border." *Frontier Times* 15, no. 3 (1937): 118–27.

Woodward, C. Vann. "History from Slave Sources." *The American Historical Review* 79 (April 1974): 470–81.

Works Progress Administration: "Arkansas Writers' Project." *Slave Narratives.* Washington, D.C.: U.S. Government Printing Office, 1932.

Works Progress Administration: "Oklahoma Writers' Project." *Slave Narratives.* Washington, D.C.: U.S. Government Printing Office, 1932.

Wright, James Leitch, Jr. *Creeks and Seminoles: The Destruction and Regeneration of the Muscogulge People.* Lincoln: University of Nebraska Press, 1986.

———. *The Only Land They Knew: The Tragic Story of the American Indian in the Old South.* New York: Free Press, 1981.

Zellar, Gary. *African Creeks: Estelvste and the Creek Nation.* Norman: University of Oklahoma Press, 2007.

MANUSCRIPT COLLECTIONS AND MISCELLANEOUS ARCHIVAL SOURCES

"Army Service: Seminole, Creek, Cherokee, Tonkaway and Apache Indians." Army Service: Indian Scouts. Fort Clark, Texas. http://www.coax.net/people/lwf/SEM_ASIS.HTM.

Dillingham, Beth. "Integration of the Seminole Negroes of Northern Mexico," 1976. Archives Division, Schomburg Center for Research in Black Culture, New York.

Handbook of Texas Online. http://www.tshaonline.org/handbook/online. Texas State Historical Association, 1999.

July, Johanna. Interview with Florence Angermiller. In American Memories Collection, 1996. Library of Congress, 1936–1940. Available online at http://www.lcwseb.loc.gov. Works Progress Administration, 1932.

Latorre Collection. Benson Latin American Collection, University of Texas, Austin.

Museum collections. Institute of Texan Cultures, University of Texas at San Antonio.

Payne, Julie. Interview with Mrs. D. S. McKellar. La Mariposa, 1932. Latorre Collection, Benson Latin American Collection, University of Texas, Austin.

Porter, Kenneth. "My Mama Came with Wild Cat and Picayune John," in "Freedom over Me." Porter Papers. Archives Division, Schomburg Center for Research in Black Culture, New York.

———. "Notes on the Payne Family of the Seminole Nation in Florida, the Indian Territory, Mexico, Texas, and Oklahoma," 1–14. Porter Papers. Archives Division, Schomburg Center for Research in Black Culture, New York.

———. Papers, 1950. Archives Division, Schomburg Center for Research in Black Culture, New York.

———. "Papers on the Payne family of the Seminole Nation in Florida, Indian Territory, Mexico, Texas, and Oklahoma," 1950. Porter Papers. Archives Division, Schomburg Center for Black Culture, New York.

GOVERNMENT DOCUMENTS

General National Archives Materials

National Archives. Records of the Bureau of Indian Affairs. Miscellaneous Indian Removal Muster Rolls, 1832–1846: Seminole, "List of Negroes turned over to Lieut. Terrett, 9th April 1838." Record Group 75.

National Archives. Records of the Office of Adjutant General, 1780s–1917. "Negroes brought in by August and Latty at Fort Jupiter." General Jesup's Papers, Box 15. Record Group 94.

National Archives. War Department, Military Division of the Missouri. "Memoranda Relative to Seminole Negro Indians." List of Negroes at Fort Duncan, Texas. 9 May 1875.

National Archives Microfilm Publications Microcopy (M)

M234, roll 227, frames 119–20. "Letters pertaining to Tony Barnett's freedom."

M234, roll 227, frame 579, 12 January 1847. "Letter from the Creek agency to Com. Indian Affs."

M234, roll 227, frames 854–55. "Abstract of Claims by the McIntosh (followers) for property taken and destroyed."

M234, roll 232, frames 259–69. "Creek and Seminole Slaves. Immigration West."

M234, roll 236, frame 671. "Agricultural Implements for Western Creeks, March 18, 1836."

M234, roll 238, frame 401. Jesup to J. R. Poinsett. 11 April 1837. Removal of Creeks to Mobile Point, Ala.

M234, roll 239, frames 333–35. "Muster Roll of Emigrant Creek Indians who have emigrated west of the Mississippi River and arrived upon their lands West."

M234, roll 290, frames 164–68. "Registry of Negro Prisoners captured by the Troops commanded by Major General Thomas S. Jesup in 1836 and 1837, and owned by the Indians, or who claim to be free."

M234, roll 290, frames 179–80. Discussion of dispossession of blacks belonging to Seminoles, 1837.

M234, roll 290, frames 358–61, page 1. "List of Seminole Indians captured at Fort Jupiter E. F. by the Troops, from 22d Feb 1838 to 29th March 1838."

M234, roll 290, frame 364. "List of Seminole Indians and Negroes sent from Fort Jupiter to Tampa for emigration to the West."

M234, roll 290, frame 503B. "Letter from Lt. Reynolds detailing the emigrating party that requires boat transportation."

M234, roll 290, frame 506. "Lists of Seminole Indians and blacks sent from Fort Jupiter to Tampa Bay for emigration to the West."

M234, roll 290, frame 508. Letter from 1st Lieut. Reynolds, May 26, 1838, presenting Muster Rolls of passengers on the two steamers, *Renown* and *South Alabama.*

M234, roll 290, frames 606–10. "Tampa Bay, Florida, 11 July."

M234, roll 291, frames 140–46. Muster Roll of a Company of Seminole Indians about to emigrate west of the Mississippi River.

M234, roll 291, frames 430–31. "Creek and Seminole Slaves Immigration West 1841. Record 25, Aug. 1842."

M234, roll 291, 1231–33. "A. P. Chouteau's proposals for furnishing Agricultural Implements for the Western Creeks."

M574, roll 13, frames 143–55, Special File 96: "Seminole Claims to Certain Negroes, 1841–1849."

M619, roll 800, frames 627–29, 631, 639–40, 625–26, 638. Letters Received by the Office of the Adjutant General (Main Series) 1861–1870: "Papers related to the Return of the Kickapoo and the Seminole (Negro) Indians from Mexico to the United States, 1870–1885."

M640, roll 4, frames 610–12. "Report relative to the seizure of certain Negroes in the Seminole Nation by Creeks & Others, by F. T. Dent, Fort Gibson, July 15, 1850."

Miscellaneous Government Documents

Jesup, General, Volusia, Florida, to Governor Wm. Scheley, Milledgeville, Georgia. 9 December 1836. Box 50, folder 15, doc. 3. Hargrett Rare Book and Manuscript Library, The University of Georgia Libraries. Available online at http://dlg.galileo.usg.edu/meta/html/dlg/zlna/meta_dlg_zlna_tcc600.html?Welcome.

Jesup to Searle. 9 September 1837. "Seminole Emigration." OIA, file J 153.

Stanley, Col. D. S., Fort Clark, to Adjt. Gen., Dept. of Texas. 19 May 1882. National Archives, AGO, 1870, No. 2.

U.S. Bureau of the Census. United States Census Records, 1870, 1880, 1885, 1890.

U.S. Congress. House. *Executive Document 225*, 74–78. 25th Cong., 3rd sess.

———. House. *Indians: Creek and Seminole*. 33rd Cong., 2nd sess., 1854. H. Doc. 701.

———. House. *Information in relation to the destruction of the Negro fort in East Florida.* 25th Cong., 2nd sess., 1819. H. Doc. 122.

———. House. *Negroes Captured from Indians in Florida*. 25th Cong., 3rd sess., 1839. H. Doc. 225.

———. Senate. *Message from the President of the United States transmitting a report from Major General Jesup of his operations whilst commanding the army in Florida, in compliance with a resolution of the Senate of the 6th instant.* 25th Cong., 2nd sess., 1838. S. Doc. 507.

INTERVIEWS, INFORMAL INTERVIEWS, AND ELECTRONIC COMMUNICATION

Interviews

Barnett, Alice Daniels. Interviews with Mock. 11 December 1998, San Antonio, Texas; 11 April 1998; 14 October 1998, San Antonio, Texas.

Benson, Ophelia. Interview with Mock. 21–22 September 1996, Brackettville, Texas. Institute of Texan Cultures, University of Texas at San Antonio.

Brown, Effie. Interview with Mock. 12 October 2001, Del Rio, Texas; series of interviews, 1997–2007, San Antonio, Texas; Del Rio, Texas; Kerrville, Texas; Brackettville, Texas.

Daniels, Anita. Interview with Mock. 12 August 1999, San Antonio, Texas. Series of interviews, 2000–2006, San Antonio, Texas.

Daniels, Jonelle. Interview. April 1986, San Antonio. Institute of Texan Cultures, University of Texas at San Antonio.

Dimery, Lillie Mae. Interview with Mock. 21–22 September 1997, Brackettville, Texas.

Fay, Alice. Interviews with Mock. Interview, 21–22 July 1997, Nacimiento, Mexico, Institute of Texan Cultures, University of Texas at San Antonio; series of interviews 1997–2009, Nacimiento, Mexico; Kerrville, Brackettville, and Del Rio, Texas.

Fay, Alice, and Gertrude Vázquez. Interview with Mock. 21–22 July 1997, Nacimiento, Mexico. Institute of Texan Cultures, University of Texas at San Antonio.

Fay, Alice, and Tommy Brown. Interview with Mock. 23 May 2008, Kerrville, Texas.

Fay, Henry. Interview with Mock. 21–22 July 1997, Nacimiento, Mexico. Institute of Texan Cultures, University of Texas at San Antonio.

Fay, Henry, and Alice Fay. Interview with Mock. 12 June 1998. Nacimiento, Mexico.

July, Johanna. Interview with Florence Angermiller. In American Memories Collection, 1996. Library of Congress, 1936–1940. Available online at http://www.lcwseb.loc.gov. Works Progress Administration, 1932.

Lasky, Gracie. Interview with Mock. 21–22 September 1996, Brackettville, Texas. Institute of Texan Cultures, University of Texas at San Antonio.

Payne, Genevieve, and Alice Fay. Interview with Mock. 29 June 1998, Kerrville, Texas; 1 January 1999, Kerrville, Texas.

Raspberry, Izola. Interview with Mock. 21–22 September 1996, Brackettville, Texas. Institute of Texan Cultures, University of Texas at San Antonio.

Spankey, Yvonne. Interview with Mock. 21–22 September 1996, Brackettville, Texas.

Tenayuca, Emma. Interview by Jerry Poyo. 21 February 1987, San Antonio, Texas. Institute of Texan Cultures, University of Texas at San Antonio.

Vázquez, Carmen. Interview with Mock. 10 July 1997, 25 January 1998, San Antonio, Texas.

Vázquez, Carmen, and Alice Fay. Interview with Mock. 9 April 2000. Kerrville, Texas.

Vázquez, Gertrude. Interview with Mock. 21–22 July 1997, Nacimiento, Mexico. Institute of Texan Cultures, University of Texas at San Antonio.

Vázquez, Rogelia Palao, Maira Irasema Hidalgo Gonzalez, and Feria Vsenia Cervantez Gonzalez. Interview with Mock. 21–22 July 1997, Nacimiento, Mexico. Institute of Texan Cultures, University of Texas at San Antonio.

Vázquez, Zulema. Interview with Mock. 21–22 July 1997, Nacimiento, Mexico. Institute of Texan Cultures, University of Texas at San Antonio.

Warrior, Ethel July. Interviews with Mock. 21–22 September 1996, Brackettville, Texas; 20 September 2007; 12 August 2008, Del Rio, Texas; series of interviews, 1995–2009.

Warrior, Steve. Interview with Mock. 19 September 1990, 21–22 September 1996, Brackettville, Texas. Institute of Texan Cultures, University of Texas at San Antonio.

Warrior, William (Dub). Interviews with Mock. 15 April 1994, 12 August 2008, Brackettville, Texas; series of interviews, 1995–2009.

Williams, Jo Emily. Interview. 2 November 1992, San Antonio, Texas. Institute of Texan Cultures, University of Texas at San Antonio.

Williams, Nancy. Interview with Mock. 21–22 September 1996. Brackettville, Texas. Institute of Texan Cultures, University of Texas at San Antonio.

Wilson, Miss Charles. Interview with Ann Rodgers. 24–25 February 1992, Brackettville, Texas.

———. Interviews with Mock. 14 March 1994, 12 May 1995, 21–22 September 1996, 15 June 1997, Brackettville, Texas.

Informal Interviews, Letters to, or Conversations with Author

Barnett, Alice. Conversations with Mock. 11 April 1998, 14 October 1998, 11 December 1998, 20 May 1999, San Antonio, Texas.

Brown, Lewis. Conversation with Mock. 18 June 2007, Del Rio, Texas.

Dillingham, Clay. Phone conversation with Mock. 22 April 2007.

Flowers, Charlesetta. Conversation with Mock and Alice Fay. 15 June 2000, Del Rio, Texas.

Haenn, Bill. Conversation with Mock. 13 April 2008, Brackettville, Texas.

Longoria, Alex. Conversation with Mock. 19 June 1999, Brackettville, Texas.

Payne, Albert. Conversation with Mock. 19 June 1999, Brackettville, Texas.

Payne, Genevieve. Conversation with Mock. 1 June 2010, Kerrville, Texas.

Payne, John. Conversation with Mock. 19 July 2004, Del Rio, Texas; 20 September 2009, Brackettville, Texas.

Payne, Lorraine. Conversation with Mock. 19 July 2004, Del Rio, Texas.

Pingenot, Ben. Conversation with Mock. 28 July 1995, Fort Clark, Texas.

Sauer, Else. Letter to Mock, about land given to Seminoles. 23 July 1995.

Warrior, Clarence. Conversation with Mock. 19 June 2000, Brackettville, Texas.

Warrior, William, and Ethel Warrior. Conversation with Mock. 19 September 2007, Brackettville, Texas.

Electronic Communication

Amos, Alcione. Electronic communication with Mock. 18 October 2007.

Hancock, Ian. Electronic communication with Mock. 15 August 2002; 22 February 2005.

Landers, Jane. Electronic communication with Mock. 18 December 2007.

Weik, Terrance. Electronic communication with Mock. 22 July 2006.

CORRESPONDENCE IN ARCHIVES

Amos, Alcione to Kenneth Porter, 27 February 1977. Porter Papers, Archives Division, Schomburg Center for Research in Black Culture, New York.

Dillingham, Beth to Kenneth Porter, 23 September 1969. Porter Papers, Archives Division, Schomburg Center for Research in Black Culture, New York.

Factor, Penny to Mrs. William H. Halcomb, 23 July 1952. Institute of Texan Cultures, University of Texas at San Antonio.

Jefferson, John to Mrs. William S. Halcomb, 31 July 1952. Institute of Texan Cultures, University of Texas at San Antonio.

Jefferson, John to Kenneth Porter, 12 July 1946. Porter Papers, Archives Division, Schomburg Center for Research in Black Culture, New York.

Jefferson, John to Kenneth Porter, 6 June 1947. Porter Papers, Archives Division, Schomburg Center for Research in Black Culture, New York.

Jefferson, John to Kenneth Porter, 5 August 1947. Porter Papers, Archives Division, Schomburg Center for Research in Black Culture, New York.

Jefferson, John to Kenneth Porter, 20 August 1950. Porter Papers, Archives Division, Schomburg Center for Research in Black Culture, New York.

Kirkham, Lt. R. W. to General Jesup, concerning "Wan-nah" and Jim's claim to her. Schomburg Center for Research in Black Culture, New York.

McKellar, Mrs. D. S. to Kenneth Porter, 8 August 1944. Latorre Collection, Benson Latin American Collection, University of Texas, Austin.

McKellar, Mrs. D. S. to Kenneth Porter, 21 August 1952. Porter Papers, Archives Division, Schomburg Center for Research in Black Culture, New York.

Porter, Kenneth to Alcione Amos, 31 March 1966. Porter Papers, Archives Division, Schomburg Center for Research in Black Culture, New York.

Porter, Kenneth to Alcione Amos, 16 July 1977. Porter Papers, Archives Division, Schomburg Center for Research in Black Culture, New York.

Porter, Kenneth to Beth Dillingham, 5 August 1969. Porter Papers, Archives Division, Schomburg Center for Research in Black Culture, New York.

Porter, Kenneth to John Jefferson, 26 March 1949. Porter Papers, Archives Division, Schomburg Center for Research in Black Culture, New York.

Porter, Kenneth to John Jefferson, 22 May 1949. Porter Papers, Archives Division, Schomburg Center for Research in Black Culture, New York.

Porter, Kenneth to John Jefferson, 11 July 1949. Porter Papers, Archives Division, Schomburg Center for Research in Black Culture, New York.

Porter, Kenneth to John Jefferson, 4 February 1950. Porter Papers, Archives Division, Schomburg Center for Research in Black Culture, New York.

Porter, Kenneth to John Jefferson, 26 April 1950. Porter Papers, Archives Division, Schomburg Center for Research in Black Culture, New York.

Porter, Kenneth to John Jefferson, 30 April 1953. Porter Papers, Archives Division, Schomburg Center for Research in Black Culture, New York.

Porter, Kenneth to Lilith Haynes, 10 May 1977. Porter Papers, Archives Division, Schomburg Center for Research in Black Culture, New York.

Porter, Kenneth to Mrs. D. S. McKellar, 8 August 1944. Latorre Collection, Benson Latin American Collection, University of Texas, Austin.

Porter, Kenneth to Mrs. D. S. McKellar, 25 October 1944. Latorre Collection, Benson Latin American Collection, University of Texas, Austin.

Porter, Kenneth to Mrs. D. S. McKellar, 16 August 1946. Latorre Collection, Benson Latin American Collection, University of Texas, Austin.

Porter, Kenneth to Mrs. D. S. McKellar, 23 March 1947. Latorre Collection, Benson Latin American Collection, University of Texas, Austin.

Porter, Kenneth to Mrs. D. S. McKellar, 1 April 1947. Latorre Collection, Benson Latin American Collection, University of Texas, Austin.

Porter, Kenneth to Mrs. D. S. McKellar, May 1947. Latorre Collection, Benson Latin American Collection, University of Texas, Austin.

Porter, Kenneth to Mrs. D. S. McKellar, 20 May 1947. Latorre Collection, Benson Latin American Collection, University of Texas, Austin.

Porter, Kenneth to Mrs. D. S. McKellar, 30 April 1948. Latorre Collection, Benson Latin American Collection, University of Texas, Austin.

Porter, Kenneth to Mrs. D. S. McKellar, 14 May 1948. Latorre Collection, Benson Latin American Collection, University of Texas, Austin.

Porter, Kenneth to Mrs. D. S. McKellar, 10 January 1949. Latorre Collection, Benson Latin American Collection, University of Texas, Austin.

Porter, Kenneth to Mrs. D. S. McKellar, 5 August 1950. Latorre Collection, Benson Latin American Collection, University of Texas, Austin.

Porter, Kenneth to Mrs. D. S. McKellar, 21 July 1951. Latorre Collection, Benson Latin American Collection, University of Texas, Austin

Porter, Kenneth to Mrs. D. S. McKellar, 28 August 1952. Latorre Collection, Benson Latin American Collection, University of Texas, Austin.

Porter, Kenneth to Mrs. D. S. McKellar, 30 April 1953. Latorre Collection, Benson Latin American Collection, University of Texas, Austin.

Index

References to illustrations are in italic type.